# New German Architecture
A Reflexive Modernism

Edited by Ullrich Schwarz

## NGA
NEW GERMAN ARCHITECTURE

Initiative Architektur und Baukultur

Hatje Cantz Publishers

# Contents

# Greetings

Social change—increasing individualization, demographic shifts, and economic development—poses new challenges to architects. Modern technologies and materials are needed to meet new needs and requirements.

As science and technology expand the range of possibilities for modern forms of building, the responsibility incumbent upon architects and clients to create a humane architectural environment grows accordingly—a mandate that must reflect the voice of the people if it is to be accepted by the public.

Germany has a sophisticated architectural infrastructure and high planning standards. Some 215,000 buildings were erected in our country in the year 2001 alone. More than half of all investments in tangible fixed assets goes to construction measures. We are the leaders in building activity in Europe. One out of every thirteen employees in Germany is involved in construction. We place a high premium on planning and construction quality, on building culture, and social innovation.

German architecture is a hallmark of value. The works presented at this exhibition are among its most outstanding achievements. The twenty-five examples of contemporary architecture selected by the German and international juries cover a spectrum that encompasses the Biosphere Hall of the National Garden Show in Potsdam, schools, a children's day-care center, a church and a synagogue, an experimental house, and an automobile-free housing development, to mention only several. The cooperative housing development in Weimar bears particularly striking witness to the importance attached to ecological architecture in Germany today.

The exhibition is presented in conjunction with the Federal Government's "Architecture and Building Culture" initiative. Our goal is to promote discussion of architectural issues in political circles and the public forum. The Federal Government recognizes the unique responsibility of building clients, as the new federal buildings in Berlin clearly demonstrate.

The opening of the exhibition coincides almost exactly with the gathering of participants from all over the world at the XXI World Architecture Conference in Berlin. Here in Berlin, where the boundaries between different philosophies of architecture have been overcome after more than a decade of Germany unity, the face of new German architecture is more clearly recognizable than anywhere else. I am convinced that the works of architecture featured at this exhibition and the abundance of newly erected and reconstructed buildings in our nation's capital will serve to enrich the public discussion devoted to a modern culture of building that meets the needs of our people.

Gerhard Schröder
Chancellor of the Federal Republic of Germany

An exhibition like this one does not simply take shape of its own accord, and certainly not overnight. It has taken considerable time to pave the way for its realization, and a number of obstacles had to be overcome in the process. The existence of this exhibition is not something to be taken simply for granted. Nor can we overlook the fact—as we organizers should point out with all due modesty—that it has been conceived and realized by the Hamburgische Architektenkammer, a relatively small institution. Yet this very fact sheds some light on a weakness in German architectural policy: in this country there is as yet no central, well-equipped institute of architecture comparable to, say, the Nederlands Architectuurinstituut (NAI) in Rotterdam. Unwilling to wait until the day when Germany finally has an NAI of its own, we have taken the initiative ourselves—with the approval of the Bundesarchitektenkammer—convinced as we are that the world deserves at long last to learn something about some of the most interesting achievements of contemporary German architecture.

Perhaps it is no coincidence that this exhibition was neither created in Berlin nor does it focus on Berlin as a theme. Berlin architects are presented, of course—how could it be otherwise—as are buildings erected in Berlin, but they are presented within the larger context of new German architecture. After the fall of the Berlin Wall, the architectural design of the nation's capital in Berlin was the dominant theme in the German architecture discussion. Countless publications and exhibitions have been devoted to aspects of urban development as they relate to the merger of East and West Berlin and to the new government buildings in the city. In a symbolic sense, this "Berlin Decade" came to a close with the opening of the Federal Chancellor's Office in the year 2001—although much remains to be done in Berlin. Thus it is appropriate to say that this date marked the end of the postwar era in Germany. A new, though surely difficult period of normalcy has begun, and Germany faces new perspectives. And the time has come for a new German architecture.

There are many people to thank for making this exhibition project a reality. Federal Chancellor Gerhard Schröder spontaneously agreed to serve as patron for the exhibition. Michael Naumann, the first German Minister of Culture, so to speak, and his successor Julian Nida-Rümelin have provided generous support, and in this context we wish to thank not only them, but also Knut Nevermann and Peter Conradi for their help. The Kulturstiftung der Länder put this support into practice. We thank Karin von Welck as the representative of the Kulturstiftung for her outstanding cooperation. Ursula Zeller of the Institut für Auslandsbeziehungen included the project in her exhibition program early on and has supported it with extraordinary commitment. Our heartfelt thanks are due to her as well. This project could not have been realized with assistance from sponsors, and we wish to thank all private sponsors and supporters for their help. The Deutsche Bank deserves special mention in this context.

Konstantin Kleffel
President of the Hamburgische Architektenkammer

The Institut für Auslandsbeziehungen is dedicated to the goal of promoting cultural exchange between Germany and the nations and peoples of the world. Activities in pursuit of that objective include the presentation of regionally and internationally significant cultural phenomena from Germany to both experts and lay people abroad in the form of exhibitions. Like sculptors, architects often find it difficult to present their designs and works to a wider public audience. Many do not realize building projects of their own until they have entered their fourth decade of life. This handicap to public exposure in their own homeland poses an even greater obstacle to international recognition. Thus the younger generation of architects in particular needs a forum that offers access to international attention and dialogue. The exhibition *New German Architecture: A Reflexive Modernism* offers just such an opportunity. There has been no project of this kind in Germany—or of this magnitude at the international level—for quite some time. And that in itself is reason enough for the Institut für Auslandsbeziehungen to incorporate this exhibition into its program and to provide an international platform for younger German architects by presenting it abroad.

Architects develop the visual qualities of their designs in the field of tension between intellectual involvement in contemporary reality and conceptual confrontation with architectural tradition. And that is why our exhibition embeds the work of the twenty-five young architects' firms in the context of established "classics" of German architecture; for new developments stand out much more clearly in juxtaposition with the old. Comparison clarifies the relationships of interaction and influence between the generations and helps identify the criteria of change.

The architects selected for the exhibition have shaped the architecture of the nineties in Germany with their pioneering building projects. Our project is devoted to highlighting the unique qualities of the work of this generation of architects born during the postwar years. And in doing so, it illuminates one of the most exciting periods of recent history—the nineties, a decade of revolutionary political, social, and cultural change.

New German architecture? Is it still possible in an era of global architectural dialogue, international training, worldwide architectural competitions, multinational partnerships, and architects' firms operating across national boundaries to take such a narrow view of a definition of architecture? The organizers of this exhibition believe so. Although the work of these younger architects is by no means restricted in a geographic sense, their architectural concepts bear the indelible imprint of the cultural and artistic environment in which they live and work. Thus we recognize affinities of both ideas and interest among architects of the younger generation. Despite their individuality and a wide range of outside influences, we find evidence of a shared attitude, which the curator describes as "reflexive, critical Modernism." The exhibition offers this observation for discussion. It is perhaps best examined in the light of international comparison.

Together with his team, Ullrich Schwarz, Managing Director of the Hamburgische Architektenkammer, has approached this project with great commitment, conviction, and professionalism. I wish to thank him as well as the participating architects' firms, who took up the theme of the exhibition with great interest. This project could not have been realized without their enthusiasm and cooperation. The appealing form of the exhibition is the achievement of Andreas Heller. I wish to thank him along with the authors for their interesting and instructive catalogue essays.

Ursula Zeller
Institut für Auslandsbeziehungen

"Architecture as a Resource" is the slogan chosen by the Union Internationale des Architects (UIA) for its 2002 World Architects' Conference in Berlin. One of the German contributions to the conference is the exhibition entitled *New German Architecture*, featuring outstanding examples of contemporary architecture in Germany. The exhibition is also an integral part of the "Architecture and Building Culture" initiative launched by the German Federal Government. The goal is to heighten public awareness of the importance of the architectural environment and the significance of contemporary architecture, following the lead of other countries in which architecture enjoys a greater degree of public attention than is the case in Germany.

Germany has some catching up to do in this respect. Like Helsinki, Stockholm, Copenhagen, Rotterdam, Vienna, and Paris, Berlin should have an architecture center, a German academy of architecture at which architecture is presented, studied, and discussed. And just as parliaments in other countries have deliberated on architectural issues and enacted architectural policies, the German Bundestag should also give its attention to the government's Status Report on Building Culture and draw the appropriate consequences from it.

The years of debate on building in Berlin's center have shown how necessary public discourse on architecture is in Germany. This process exposed a degree of ignorance of and disrespect for German architecture that would be inconceivable in other European capitals. In Paris or Vienna, the challenge posed by such an undertaking would be met with confidence in the future and in the creative power of our time. In Germany, the product of faint-heartedness, fear of the future, intellectual poverty, and a dearth of creativity was an appeal for reconstruction of a Baroque palace!

Our exhibition of *New German Architecture* demonstrates what German architects are capable of. We are proud of that, as we are proud of many of the other products of our country. After the UIA conference in Berlin, the exhibition will go on tour in Germany and abroad to demonstrate the creativity and productivity of German architects.

The Hamburgische Architektenkammer has invested considerable commitment and effort into planning and preparing for this exhibition. The choice of projects for exhibition was not determined by the Chamber. Projects were selected by a German panel of critics and then by an international jury. I wish to thank the members of both juries and to congratulate the architects whose projects were selected for exhibition. The state chambers of architects represented in the Bundesarchitektenkammer express their thanks to the Hamburgische Architektenkammer for planning and preparing for this exhibition—the achievement of its President, Konstantin Kleffel, and its Managing Director, Ullrich Schwarz. We are also grateful to the Commissioners for Cultural and Media Affairs, Michael Naumann and Julian Nida-Rümelin, for the funding assistance provided to the exhibition by the Federal Government and to the Institut für Auslandsbeziehungen, which will support the exhibition on its journey through other countries.

We are very pleased that German Chancellor Gerhard Schröder has assumed the role of patron for the exhibition. With its "Architecture and Building Culture" initiative, the Federal Government clearly shows that it recognizes the importance of this theme. It is now time for deeds to follow words: principles of a German architecture policy, for example, and first steps toward the establishment of a German academy of architecture in Berlin.

I wish the exhibition *New German Architecture* many interested visitors and all the best on its upcoming tour!

Peter Conradi
President of the National Chamber of Architects

New German Architecture
A Reflexive Modernism

New German Architecture
A Reflexive Modernism

# New German Architecture—An Exhibition

Ullrich Schwarz

For

Kristin Feireiss—on her birthday

Wolfgang Pehnt—with thanks for his cooperation and support

Dagmar, Friederike, Harriet, and Carl-Christian—for more than just their patience

The whole world knows that Germans build good cars. Anyone who drives a German automobile in the United States is automatically recognized as a connoisseur of technical perfection and style. And a German car is like a badge of social distinction, a sign that says the driver is in the Big Leagues.

Has German architecture achieved as much in the world? Mies van der Rohe, of course, is something like our Mercedes of architecture: hot-dip galvanized and guaranteed rust-free for the next three eternities. But what about his successors? This question usually ties the tongues of our foreign friends. Perhaps they can recite a handful of names, but as a rule they have no grasp of the larger picture, particularly with respect to the current situation. They simply do not have enough information for a discerning appraisal.

People have been lamenting this situation for decades, but the situation itself has not changed—at least not very much. Today, Germany architects are building in Moscow, in China, and who knows where else. And they are proving wherever they work that German architecture is of high quality.

But is anyone aware of that? The fact is that the world's most influential architecture magazines are not exactly bursting at the seams with lengthy articles about current projects by German architects. Germans are rarely in attendance at the important international conferences and meetings of the architectural jet set. Indeed—to cite just one example—not a single German architect was a featured speaker at even one of the ANY conferences organized by Peter Eisenman during the nineties. Nor has a single German voice succeeded in making itself heard in international discourse on architectural theory.

In his article for the catalogue, Dietmar Steiner identifies several aspects that have influenced the international response to German architecture—a response that has not always been particularly flattering. Many of the shapers of opinion in the international architecture scene find German architecture simply uninteresting and unexciting. It is important to be aware of this international assessment. As a rule, such catastrophic judgments are based on an extremely spotty knowledge of German architecture. More importantly, the standards of evaluation that underlie such disastrous appraisals have gathered quite a bit of dust and have long since been overtaken by reality. There is considerable evidence to suggest that the architectural currents that have dominated international architectural discourse during the past ten years have exhausted themselves over the course of increasingly short cycles, despite their remarkable market presence, and have suffered from a dramatic loss of intellectual substance in spite of their eager devotion to self-repetition. Yet apart from this, of course, we recognize a specific quality of German architecture—despite globalization—that must be examined in the context of 20th-century German history.

But let us begin with a few plain facts. It did not dawn on us in Germany that architecture is a product which needs to be positioned in a market (an international one, at that) until the eighties. This requires communication and marketing activities which must be pursued not only by individual architects but by the government as well. The deficit in this area is critical. We in Germany failed to establish strong and, above all, internationally effective architectural policy-making institutions at the national level. Institutions comparable to the Nederlands Architectuurinstituut (NAI) or the Institut français d'architecture (IFA), which promote their national architectures on a massive scale, are non-existent in Germany.

A second important reason for the insufficient recognition of contemporary German architecture is to be found in German architecture itself, however—not in its quality, I would hasten to point out, but in its visual impact. Its visual language does not make use of the media criteria that hold sway in the international architecture circus. "Where is your Koolhaas, your Gehry, your Zaha Hadid?" the Germans are asked over and over again. The global economy of attention demands the spectacular; it wants events and stars—and always the same ones, wherever possible, because of their high recognition value.

If the Bilbao effect is truly the measure of all things in architecture, then, one is forced to admit, those who look for it in German architecture are likely to search in vain. Indeed, the "superficial media bang" (Ernst Hubeli) is not a quality to which current German architecture aspires. Thus it becomes interesting at a moment in which the spectacle of the singular object as a model for architectural production has undermined itself through inflationary use and must be regarded as "outmoded thinking" today.

German architecture appears different: more restrained, more subdued, quieter. It does not tend toward extremes or show effects, and it does not aim for the heroic gesture. It makes no false promises and avoids empty innovation and progressive posing; it strives for substance and sometimes for depth. It is not content with the technical and functional perfection one automatically expects of it. It goes beyond that. German architecture does not take Modernism for granted as program but practices it in a modified form filtered by critical appraisal. This critical self-discipline is not to be confused with the aesthetic pathos of formal reduction. It is a social attitude.

What looks at first glance like specifically national quality—and in some respects surely is—actually has a much more fundamental significance, one that has been totally overlooked by most observers to date. Recognizable in the new German architecture are the basic characteristics of a contemporary architectural formation at the dawn of the 21st century, fundamental traits of Modernism in the most striking form it has ever assumed. This Modernism is enlightened—with respect to itself as well. It is demystified—stripped even of its own mystique. It is free of illusions—even about its own program. It recognizes no utopias and knows that the supply of reliable and self-evident solutions is nearly depleted. Its knowledge of the world is a source of concern, and its knowledge of that knowledge enlarges its ignorance. Yet it refuses to succumb to cynicism or discouragement. It remains practical and constructive in a situation in which openness poses the greatest challenge. It explores possibilities in an indeterminate context. It knows that there can be no more simple solutions, and it knows that its only source of help lies within itself. The new Modernism is reflexive.

Postmodernism treated the end of the "great narratives" (François Lyotard) as if it represented liberation from an oppressive burden. Today, the abandonment of the all-encompassing systems that have traditionally given meaning to life—God, nature, and history—is seen more clearly as a loss, although no substitute is in sight. And thus unavoidable philosophical restraint and self-imposed restriction to the obvious are joined by a growing sense of "mourning."[1]

Reflexive Modernism is a child of Postmodernism that no longer accepts the joyful hedonism of its parents as a truly convincing program for life and now, having emerged from the confusing trials of puberty somewhat disillusioned but not paralyzed, seeks its own way of coping with the world. Its rejection of utopian and, in fact, all programmatic thinking goes hand in hand with the renunciation of fundamental criticism, be it political or philosophical. In its understanding that the process of modernization is inherently self-destructive, the attitude of Reflexive Modernism shares only a superficial similarity to Max Horkheimer's or Theodor W. Adorno's analyses of the dialectic of enlightenment. A radical critique of reason and rationality in the tradition of Nietzsche–Heidegger–Adorno plays little or no role for Reflexive Modernism. The idea of questioning capitalist market logic is regarded as obsolete.

A vague concept of globalization conceals the void in political and social analysis. Reflexive Modernism is not only without a utopia, it also refuses to rely in any emphatic way on politics and theory. Yet it is not affirmative. It has no illusions, and it is highly sensitive to the ambiguities, risks, and uncertainties of the present. Aware of no convincing alternatives, it also places no trust in the course of events. Its interventions are the products of a thoughtful contemporaneity and culminate in a reflexive micro-policy that breathes a spirit that is very different from that of the classical social-democratic reform program of piecemeal engineering. One can simply no longer be certain in our day that everything truly is going to get better, step by step. The child's dream of "anything goes" has given way to a new sense of responsibility and the understanding that it must set its own standards over and over again.

The significance and the consequences of this new situation for architecture have not been sufficiently analyzed. Thus the presentation of examples of new German architecture and the sketchy development of a theory of Reflexive Modern Architecture are inseparably bound together. The exhibition and the catalogue undertake precisely this two-pronged attempt.

The signature of contemporary German architecture cannot be explained on the basis of developments in German architecture alone. The specific characteristics of present-day German architecture must be understood as the expression and the product of German postwar history, of the end of the East-West ideological conflict, of German reunification and the intellectual climate it has produced in the so-called Berlin Republic. When we examine German architecture of today, it is not "architecture" itself we are dealing with, but a social and cultural phenomenon.

The deeply rooted sense of German guilt that is still evident everywhere today and which even the postwar generation cannot escape, despite all its glib protestations, is the product of fascism and its aftermath. As the debates about the Holocaust Memorial in Berlin clearly show, this subject is still very much alive in the minds of the German public. Its permanent and explicit presence in German political discourse is only one aspect, however. Of much greater importance to the German condition is the estrangement of the German people from themselves, which is also a consequence of fascism. "Good Germans identify themselves today by their efforts to show that they are not really German," writes the literary scholar Heinz Schlaffer.[2] Yet even fifty years after the end of the Second World War, such mild self-irony itself can still lead to misunderstanding.

A more far-reaching consequence of so-called efforts to come to grips with the past in the postwar era is a philosophical retreat which—as a way of getting rid of the past—is intended to protect against all forms of ideological involvement. And thus the German people—relieved of this heavy burden—devoted itself with pleasure in the fifties and sixties to building an affluent society purged of conflicts on the firm foundations of the welfare state.

Viewed in retrospect, it is clear that the wild era of non-parliamentary opposition in the sixties and seventies did not represent an earth-shaking disruption of pragmatic progress toward success in the Federal Republic. Though its end left many of those actively involved with a sense of grave disillusionment, it also led substantial segments of the former protest generation—now more realistic and willing to compromise—to join the political system they once so vigorously criticized as pillars of the state.

The successful step-by-step political integration of the former left-wing non-parliamentary opposition movement explains German society's rejection of all emphatic visions of the future in the eighties and the disillusioned yet eagerly consumption-oriented leveling of the political horizon to the practical plane of the here and now. The collapse of the communist system in 1989 and the fall of the Wall marked the end of global competition between rival systems. It now appeared that there was and would be no alternative to western capitalism. World history, as Hegel pointed out, is the world's judge. Yet this did not make the social situation any clearer that it had been. The idea of a "new obscurity" (Jürgen Habermas) began to take hold. The pragmatism that developed into a government philosophy in the eighties merely dared to express openly the non-secret secret of this new German mood.

Sociologist Heinz Bude put it this way: "The lesson of 1989 is that no further uprisings are needed to fulfill the promise of the great bourgeois revolution. Thus, for all intents and purposes, the project of Modernism can be put to rest. All alternatives to a capitalist, parliamentary, individualistic, consensualistic form of Modernism have fallen by the wayside."[3]

But these triumphant-sounding words fail to mention the other side of the coin of this "end of the story"—the looming threat of a paralyzing absence of perspective or—as Habermas describes it—a creeping "entropy of the scarce resource of meaning."[4]

Western society at the dawn of the 21st century exhibits a highly advanced form of Modernism that can no longer imagine any alternatives to itself. But this places it in the grips of a difficult dilemma. "It can neither surpass itself nor truly imagine its own future," as philosopher Peter Sloterdijk contends.[5]

But can we conceive of a Modernism that does not evade its own future? It must not deny the risks and dangers it has created for itself. What is more, it must recognize its limitations. Then, perhaps, damage can be controlled, and proposals for therapy might be forthcoming. But Modernism must first learn to practice self-critical reflection.

The goal of the exhibition and the catalogue is to place current German architecture in just such a social context—in the context of a Reflexive Modernism. It is an attempt to establish a diagnosis, of course, and not to postulate or invent a new programmatic concept.

The catalogue presentation begins with an outline of developments in German architecture from 1945 to the present (see the articles by Wolfgang Pehnt und Andreas Ruby). This discussion is accented by brief portraits of ten exemplary architects or architects' firms, each of whom or which has left a characteristic imprint upon German architecture since the sixties and continues to do so today.

The articles by Wilfried Dechau, Hanno Rauterberg, and Wolfgang Kil are devoted to themes that have—in both a social and a political sense—shaped and influenced the development of German architecture and German architectural discourse in very specific ways since 1990 (in the case of ecological architecture, since 1970). Kil shows quite clearly that architects from eastern Germany have been given little opportunity to develop independent positions of their own in the course of the process known as "rebuilding the East."

In his article, Werner Sewing describes the convictions, moods, and mentalities that characterize the generation of younger German architects—broadly defined as those aged thirty-five to fifty-five—and the conclusions these findings suggest with respect to new German architecture.

The essays by Ullrich Schwarz and Ernst Hubeli are devoted to an attempt to establish a preliminary definition of the position of a Reflexive Modernism from the perspectives of architectural theory and criticism.

The oldest of the twenty-five individual works of architecture that comprise the heart of this exhibition was completed in 1996. This most recent phase of German architectural history—and this presumably applies to other countries as well—cannot be given a single label in formal terms. More importantly, it defies obvious stylistic classification. There are many reasons to believe that the era of dominant epoch-making styles has finally come to a close in architecture as well. After all, the most recent "epochs" have spanned only a very few years.

The examples of new German architecture presented in the exhibition can be understood only if we perceive them as moments in an ongoing process of self-enlightenment in an advanced form of Modernism.

We have known since the nineties, if not even longer, that an approach through style no longer contributes to an understanding of contemporary architecture. Not only do widely differing stylistic forms coexist, they overlap, intermingle, and combine to form a broad range of hybrid forms. The crucial point is this: despite all of the clamorous battling for position among the different architectural factions, it is now absolutely impossible to determine on the basis of form or style alone whether a building is "progressive" or "regressive," more modern or less modern.

At present, architectural modernity can no longer be defined in terms of stylistic, formal, or intrinsically architectural criteria. Today, architecture must be modern in a social sense—or it is not modern at all.

For this reason, and not in the interest balance or parity, a number of very different architectural languages and divergent strategic approaches to the contemporary situation are represented in the exhibition *New German Architecture.*

Although Postmodernism was still concerned with asserting the principle of simultaneous diversity, pluralism can no longer be celebrated as a new discovery. By now, the existence and legitimacy of pluralism, radicalized as individualism, must be taken for granted.

Our objective today must be to identify a fundamental common ground beneath the shimmering surface of diversity. This common ground does not yet exist at the level of the architects themselves. New group identities have emerged under the umbrella of Reflexive Modernism.

Thus the contention that new German architecture, represented by twenty-five exemplary structures, stands for a Reflexive Modernism, does not presuppose an explicit program but seeks instead, applying standards derived from contemporary social-science and philosophical theory, to describe the social and cultural status of current German architecture. As a theoretical approach, Reflexive Modernism has not established itself on a broad basis in architecture, although architecture operates in a real world that conforms very closely to this theory (Ernst Hubeli).

The essential elements of the social status of new German architecture would appear to include the following: distance from, indeed a lack of interest in, philosophical and political doctrines and "visions" of every kind; extreme sensitivity to the ambiguities, inconsistencies, and even risks of social developments; architectural responses that involve conscious, "reflexive" application of this sensitivity—not in blind pursuit of paths already chosen but in a critical, therapeutic, compensatory approach. The architectural answers vary and each responds to specific aspects. Four fields of focus appear to play a particularly important role:

Heightened awareness of the global threat to our natural environment gives rise to concepts of engineering and design oriented toward environmental concerns—transcending traditional concepts of "ecological architecture" and characterized by reliance on highly sophisticated technologies.

A skeptical view of the promises of the new leads on the one hand to an altered concept of normalcy and the ordinary and on the other—in view of the looming threat of the loss of historical roots—to a critical review of approaches to tradition and the past.

The rejection of the mandate to express the present in architectural images—be they positive or negative—at all costs, a distanced attitude toward grand gestures, and the tendency toward simplicity in the face of excessive social complexity give rise to an attitude of formal restraint.

The understanding that, although advanced Modernism continuously generates new consumable knowledge, that process is opposed by a increasingly alarming lack of the kind of knowledge that provides orientation—in other words, by the depletion of the "resource of meaning" (Jürgen Habermas)—clearly fosters a tendency to create spaces of stillness, concentration, and intense experience, spaces of self-encounter and reflection on what we are, what we want, and what we do not want. Yet this also strongly implies a conscious concern with perceptual qualities, sensory aspects, and material characteristics.

In many ways, this kind of architecture has outgrown the "first," heroic Modernism of bygone days. Its unspectacular reflexiveness is the source of its strength.

The exhibition features twenty-five buildings which, with only two exceptions, were completed between 1996 and 2002. In addition, ten architecture firms are presented along with characteristic examples of their work—ten architecture firms which, like others, have exerted a formative influence on architecture in the Federal Republic of Germany since about 1960. We sincerely regret that it was not possible to include Frei Otto in this part of the exhibition.

The twenty-five buildings and ten architecture firms were chosen by two independent juries, one German, the other international, which were comprised of the following members: Wolfgang Bachmann, Ursula Baus, Gert Kähler, Wolfgang Kil, Peter Rumpf, Olaf Winkler, and Günther Uhlig (German jury); Jean Louis Cohen, Marco De Michelis, Kristin Feireiss, Ernst Hubeli, Marja-Riitta Norri, Dietmar Steiner, and John Zukowsky (internationale jury). I wish to thank all jury members and all of the authors of texts for the catalogue for their commitment, co-operation, advice, and support.

This project could not have been realized without the tireless dedication of Stephan Feige and Claas Gefroi and the many discussions in which they were involved. I wish to thank them as well.

The Studio Andreas Heller is responsible for exhibition architecture and design. Catalogue design was entrusted to the capable hands of the Grafikbüro Qart. We are indebted to both for their creative commitment and close cooperation.

The idea for this exhibition is the child of countless discussions with Daniel Gössler. And the project could hardly have been realized without the steadfast determination of Konstantin Kleffel, Jürgen Böge, and Henning Bieger. They all deserve my very special thanks.

# Reflexive Modernism

Perspectives of Architecture at the Beginning of the 21st Century

Ullrich Schwarz

The transnationalization of place is regarded as one of the most important by-products of the process generally referred to as globalization. Local culture is no longer taken for granted or regarded as the unquestioned world order. No longer a "natural" phenomenon, it becomes a responsibility, an object of thought and action. We see this distancing as a process of tradition becoming reflexive. Contents of tradition and previously implicit cultural background systems become explicit and subject to discourse. In this way, they emerge from a timeless limbo and become historical. This brings about a fundamental change in their status: from now on, they are no longer valid per se but require factual support and argumentative justification. They can be shaped and altered; they assume their place in a practical societal program but are not fixed within an eternal order of existence or supported by cosmological or ontological structures. They lose their social guarantee of perpetuity. "The increasing mediatization of the experiences from which we construct our image of the world and ourselves does not put an end to all tradition but simply exposes it to reflection."[1] Yet what is referred to today as globalization is only a radical, accelerated form of a social process that Karl Marx and Friedrich Engels described in the mid-19th century: "Constant revolutionizing of production, uninterrupted disturbance of all social conditions, everlasting uncertainty and agitation distinguish the bourgeois epoch from all earlier ones. All fixed, rigidly defined relationships, with their train of ancient and venerable prejudices and opinions, are swept away, all new-formed ones become antiquated before they can ossify. All that is solid melts into air, all that is holy is profaned, and man is at last compelled to face with sober senses his real condition of life and his relations with his kind."[2] When social norms and cultural contents are transposed into a state of metaphysical homelessness, the resulting sense of endangerment can lead to emphatic and, in extreme cases, potentially violent defensive responses. And thus globalization is accompanied by opposing tendencies toward a revival of traditions and the defense and renewal of national, regional, and local traditions, including even fundamentalist movements of an ethnic or religious character. Compensation theory, as formulated by Hermann Lübbe, for example, showed some time ago the extent to which the prevailing tendency to "museumize" the past is nothing other than a therapeutic treatment of losses incurred through modernization. The loss of the familiar is only one side of this problem. The other is the invasion of the alien, the different.

The search for identity becomes a central cultural problem. Who am I? Where am I? To whom do I belong? On what can I rely? What is right, and what is wrong? What is good, and what is evil?[3] This quest for identity is pursued within the field of tension between universalism and particularism, between globalism and regionalism, between the "space of flows" and the longing for permanence and continuity, between the neutralization and the defense of place. Whether architecture can play a role in such processes of identity-building, and if so, what that role could be, is not really clear. Its dilemma is self-evident. Traditionally, it was regarded as the embodiment of the dominant culture. But what should it embody today? Rem Koolhaas posed the question of whether contemporary architecture is more concerned with stability and instability than with the tension between globalism and regionalism. But what can that mean for architecture? Should it create structures of order, permanence, and stability or vehicles of constant change, fragmentation, and uncertainty? Vittorio Magnago Lampugnani, for one, voices a plea for a modernity in permanence, arguing that "One of the most important tasks of architecture is to create places that are stable, places one can recognize and where one feels at home."[4]

Urban theorist Manuel Castells, on the other hand, sees tendencies toward a global architectural language of retreat—retreat to a zero line, so to speak, that has nothing more to say and has no characteristics of its own—an architecture for a global society that may not be approaching the end of its history but could be near the end of its specific histories. Rem Koolhaas is also known as an advocate of the theory that the city has entered a state of disenfranchisement in the age of globalization. Yet his diagnosis should not be misunderstood as a culture critic's lamentation. In fact, Koolhaas considers it naive and illusory to believe that tendencies toward globalization and disenfranchisement can be confronted or even resisted by architectural form. Koolhaas uses the term "bigness" in articulating his answer to the globalization and museumization of the historical inner city: large, multifunctional units he provocatively calls "containers," which accommodate every conceivable form of utilization—as parking garages, department stores, movie theaters, restaurants, offices, railway stations, and perhaps even airports—but whose architectural form is really no longer important. These containers are shapeless—"shapeless architecture"—but does that truly mean the end of architecture? Would architecture's answer to globalization be self-denial? But perhaps what we see here only appears to be self-sacrifice and is, in fact, a radical purge of function resulting in a functional transformation that opens up new programmatic perspectives.

In architecture, in particular, the globalization debate is anything but the result of the most recent developments. It reached a first milestone during the sixties at the height of concern with Classical Modernism and the International Style, which was not merely a theoretical program but actually existed. The debate is documented in books published during the sixties by such authors as Jane Jacobs, Robert Venturi, Aldo Rossi, and—in Germany—Alexander Mitscherlich. This reassessment of Modernism, which was generally regarded as internationalist and anti-historical, helped Heinrich Klotz achieve a last breakthrough in the discussion pursued in the German press. Although his diagnosis was overstated for polemical effect, it described a critical attitude toward the International Style that had been widely accepted for quite some time. The world of our cities, Klotz argued, had begun to turn barren. Our cities had become accumulations of smooth boxes, oceans of monotony. As Klotz wrote in 1984, "After seventy years, the architectural forms that gave Modernism a basis for argumentation, the 'pure forms in light' (Le Corbusier), had not only lost their power of aesthetic persuasion but had also begun to contribute to severe environmental destruction."[5] One of the most important outcomes of this reassessment of Modernism was the rediscovery of history and place. The past and the local were once again seen as legitimate sources of inspiration for architecture. But they would not remain the only ones. In the following discussion, I would like to sketch out four paradigms through which architecture seeks to justify its existence and affirm its identity in a globalized world—as ideal concepts and with no claim to exhaustiveness.

The Old

Evidently, the maelstrom of randomness engenders a strong desire to have safe, solid ground under one's feet. This need seems to be satisfied in part by a body of reliable rules whose legitimacy is not based solely on a thousand years of verification by virtue of "having always been" but to an even greater extent by its aura of unshakeable correctness, if not indeed truth. I am talking about Vitruvianism, the non-relativist architectural aesthetic that prevailed until the late 18th century and is now a glaring anachronism upon which some continue to rely in our day.

The debates waged during the early phase of Modernist consciousness over Classicist attempts to formulate fixed and even absolute laws of beauty have paradigmatic significance. In the course of this struggle between the *anciens* and the *modernes*, which began at the French academy of architecture but soon spilled over into all fields of culture, the epoch-making fundamental structures of Modernist thinking took shape. Viewed from the perspective of the end of that conflict, Classicism appears as the first and last attempt to mount a defense against the impending onslaught of cultural relativism. Although Classicism remained dominant in practice until the end of the 18th century, it had already begun its intellectual retreat in the person of its first academic apologist, François Blondel. And to

the extent that contemporary science played a role at all at the time, it contributed with ontological dedication and dependability to undermining the possibilities for defining absolute beauty. Those who sought fixed laws of beauty and a clearly defined formal order could no longer rely on science at the dawn of the 19th century.

Jürgen Habermas has written on this issue: "Since the late 18th century, a new sense of time has emerged in Western culture. History is understood as a world-encompassing, problem-generating process. Within that process, time is regarded as a scarce resource to be used in finding future-oriented solutions to problems left to us by the past. Exemplary past histories from which the present could safely take guidance have faded into obscurity. The modern age can no longer rely on the models of earlier eras to provide its standards of orientation. The modern age is left entirely to its own devices—it must create its norms from within itself."[6]

Nor could nature continue to serve as a source of norms and standards. The bone of contention in the dispute between Claude Perrault and François Blondel was the importance of proportion to the beauty of an architectural work. Blondel argued that proportions originated in nature as unalterable mathematical relationships without which there could be no beauty.[7] Perrault contended that the perception of certain proportions as beautiful was not a matter of natural relationships but of customs and conventions. Perrault was not intent upon negating proportion but sought to establish their relative character. Whereas Blondel insisted that proportions were dictated by the laws of nature, Perrault analyzed the Pythagorean-Platonic tradition in psychological terms, denying its ontological legitimacy altogether.

The outcome of the dispute between the *anciens* and the *modernes*, in which belief in the exemplary character of antiquity stood opposed to the idea of progress, was an emerging awareness of the historical distinctiveness of different eras and of the historical nature of beauty. At the pan-European level, the result of the process of enlightenment born of this dispute was the historification of antiquity and beauty. Realist art history began with Johann Joachim Winckelmann, and Johann Gottfried Herder founded the historicist movement.

Stripped of the power to establish norms, world history became a museum of past cultures and was aestheticized in the process. Historical works of art were no longer perceived as manifest forms of timeless beauty but as variables in the continuum of history.

Temporalization replaced classification based on the spatial character of geometric configuration as the epoch-making paradigm of Modernism. The dynamization of all aspects of life against the backdrop of the emerging capitalist industrial society put an end to the imitation theories of Classicism. Nature and history are in flux. Nature is no longer that which never changes, as Alberti still believed; and in history, the progressive power of the present and especially the future overtrumps every earlier model. Based upon this concept of imitation, yet, as we have seen, socially determined, the Classicist science of beauty became obsolete. Reviewing the sentimental bourgeois aesthetic of the 18th century, Immanuel Kant finally legitimized the subjective spirit as opposed to Classicist aesthetic laws and mathematical-geometric methods in the production of art, categorically declaring the truth embraced as self-evident by the enlightened modern age—that a science of beauty does not, and cannot exist.[8]

In architecture, the evolution of cultural beliefs outlined here manifested itself as the decline of Vitruvianism.[9] The historification of antiquity, Modernist philosophy grounded in the concept of progress, and a legitimization of subjectivity, based primarily on the aesthetics of effect and response, eventually stripped the traditional concept of beauty of its function in architecture. "Character, expression, poetry—these are the new values that depose 'beauty,' the predominant value of the elder Classicists."[10] Marc-Antoine Laugier gave dignity to the interesting and the irregular. In lieu of Baroque geometry, he even recommended "reforestation" of the city. Étienne-Louis Boullée applied Edmund Burke's concept of the sublime to architecture. Though the anti-Classicist movement effectively reached its end in the theories of Jean-Nicolas-Louis Durand, his rejection of superfluous adornment and his appeal for functionality and frugality clearly suggest that this was not a case of one architectural style replacing another, of one scientific orientation giving way to the next, but that, in fact, a whole new social reference system was replacing the old one: bourgeois rationalism as opposed to the representational ideals of feudal class society.

The historical analysis of Classicism has paradigmatic significance. It reveals a broad-based attempt to establish a normative architectural aesthetic justified by science—and it exposes the failure of that attempt. This concept, which is deeply entangled in pre-modern traditions, failed because it could not withstand the enlightened reflection of Modernism. The dispute between the *anciens* and the *modernes* gave substance to fundamental structures of modern thought which could no longer be evaded. These include the self-reflective character of traditions, the equal availability of pasts and cultures and their simultaneous loss of relevance (which applies as well to all styles and forms of expression in art), and the tension-ridden estrangement of art and science.

Heritage – What Is Ours

Heritage and the old are closely related. According to one branch of conventional architectural wisdom, heritage is generally interpreted as the old per se—as old heritage. Heritage is derived from the past, and thus the idea of a new heritage obviously seems to offer little promise. Yet the old and heritage differ in a methodological sense. The old, in my interpretation of the term, has a number of universal characteristics as a body of rules that transcends boundaries of time and space, while heritage is understood in this context as the rediscovery of history in the plural, rather than the singular. At issue here is the history and the unique quality of a specific place, a specific region, a specific locale.

The theories of *genius loci* and regionalism seek to establish architecture within the tradition of orientation to place as opposed to the destructive abstraction of non-site-specific building. They favor continuity, coherence, and convention, though not merely or primarily as regionalistic visual policy. Instead they pursue a social objective as well. The actual goal of the most ambitious versions of regionalism and rediscovery of place is to counteract a process of socio-cultural displacement and alienation—in which globalization also plays a part through architecture, although not through architecture alone. Thus an attempt is actually made, as Jan Assmann has expressed it, "to give time-resistant form to traditional currents"[11] as a means of preserving a collective memory that "builds community."[12] The concept of collective memory is discussed explicitly in Aldo Rossi's *L'Architettura della città*, published in 1966. Rossi anchors the city's identity in its history; he isolated typologies and structures which, in his view, make them sustainable or, as he says, ensure its permanence. Contemporary architecture must relate to these truly archetypal foundations. Nothing needs to be invented, as everything is always there already.

Rossi's book must be read as a radical critique of Modernism, and in particular of the *tabula rasa* approach to the existing premodern city. The heroic Modernist concept of the future has disappeared from view. History is not remade; it can only be preserved or rescued. And thus Peter Eisenman explains in his foreword to the American edition of Rossi's book that Rossi replaces history with memory.[13] Yet it is precisely at this point that the real problem involved in such a concept appears. It would seem highly questionable whether architectural forms, regardless of how precisely they are derived typologically from the past, are capable in themselves of preserving, much less reviving, the social and cultural contents with which they are historically intertwined. And thus Manfredo Tafuri goes a step further than Eisenman in his criticism of Rossi. Rossi, he argues, has retreated from real history into the universe of signs, of empty signs that can no longer be filled with real life by any collective memory.[14] This, he reasons, explains the fundamental melancholy undercurrent of Rossi's work.

The Norwegian author Christian Norberg-Schulz published a significant book with the programmatic title *Genius loci* in 1979. His starting point, as is Rossi's, is the failure of Modernism. Norberg-Schulz write that "The general symptoms point to a loss of place. Lost is the settlement as a place in nature, lost are the urban centers as settings for community life, lost is the work of architecture as a meaningful subordinate place in which people can experience both individuality and a sense of belonging. Lost as well is the relationship to the earth and the sky. Most modern buildings exist in a 'nowhere land.'"[15] This loss of place is not viewed as a crisis of architecture and urban planning but, in a much more fundamental sense, as a crisis of humanity.[16] In his discussion of cultural structures, Norberg-Schulz comes close to Rossi, whose theory of the city he believes cannot be properly understood as a concept of architecture.

The point of departure for both authors is the exclusion of the individual from supra-individual contexts and allegiances, the loneliness and uprootedness of the individual, which merges in Norberg-Schulz's discussion with the image of the modern nomad. In this context, Norberg-Schulz quotes the Old Testament, which declares this erratic nomadic life a fundamental human condition: "A fugitive and a vagabond shalt thou be in the earth." The crisis of humanity can be overcome only if the "lost place is found again."[17] Architecture can make an important contribution if it is consistently understood as the restoration of place. Yet it can achieve that objective only if it relates place and architecture oriented toward place to the cosmic order which, though Norberg-Schulz defines it in atheological terms, is viewed as a meaningful overall context that is much larger than mankind but includes it as well. His primary basis is the phenomenology of the natural place in the field of tension between heaven and earth. To Norberg-Schulz, the landscape-related and climatic characteristics of a place are not only aspects of topography but also determinants of system of meaning that informs not only the place itself but also the people who live there. It is precisely this higher system of meaning that was lost in Modernism, whereas it was an absolute determinant of life in pre-modern societies. Norberg-Schulz presumes that the original sin of Modernism can be absolved, in principle, and that concretization of the natural context at a place is possible in our time as well. Accordingly, he is concerned with incorporating the potential that is always inherent in a place into the work of architecture or, in other words, with hearing the "call" of the place. Thus restored, place counteracts the rootlessness of contemporary humanity and gives people the sense of being an integral part of their environment. The restored place communicates a feeling of belonging to a larger whole, but one which draws its substance not from social relationships but from sources beyond the reach of mankind. Norberg-Schulz refers to this larger context as a cosmological one. In his view, the existential support and emotional security provided by such a place integrated within the cosmological order cater to fundamental human needs. Expressed differently, people need to experience their environment as a meaningful order. The crucial aspect of Norberg-Schulz's approach is precisely the fact that he refuses to accept that this order can be the work of mankind alone, a product of political, economic, and technical planning and organization. The human being, he believes, cannot create substantial meaning from within himself.

Since Norberg-Schulz makes no attempt in his book to analyze historical developments or the structural forces that drive them, the social causes of the crisis of Modernism he diagnoses must be as incomprehensible to him as the possibility or impossibility of overcoming them. He thus describes Modernism as a phase of "oblivion of being"—although he does not use Heidegger's term *(Seinsvergessenheit)*—that enveloped us, but without causing the loss of potential for rediscovery of the lost place. That potential, he argues, has merely submerged into latency and is waiting to be "recovered." Norberg-Schulz does not say how this can be done, however, as he is unwilling to allow his theory of *genius loci* to sink to the level of the planner doctrine of a harmless regionalistic contextualism. That it has nothing to do with such a doctrine or with the inflationary use of the term *genius loci* is what gives his concept such great aporetic power.

Kenneth Frampton explicitly advocates a program of critical regionalism. He expounded his concept in the early eighties in several publications that have now become classic standard texts within the context of the contemporary discussion. Frampton makes it clear from the outset that critical regionalism pursues no project devoted to a return to pure vernacularism—the illusory embrace of a self-enclosed place that rejects all outside influences in order to retain its purity and authenticity. Frampton flatly rejects the nostalgic reproduction of local architectural forms. The critical regionalism he propagates distances itself in equal measure from the myth of progress of Classical Modernism and from a return "to the architectural forms of a pre-industrial past."[18] Thus it comes as no surprise that Frampton ultimately attributes only secondary importance to the peculiarities of place—be they cultural, topographic, or climatic. His thoughts about an architecture of resistance against global modernization revolve instead around the concept of the tectonic, which he also interprets in a unique way. In Frampton's view, the basic principle of an architecture of resistance is a "structural poetry,"[19] which not only comprehends a work of architecture in scenographic, and thus visual, terms but also presents its various different component parts and materials in their respective objective character and consequently fosters more comprehensive sensory perception of architecture.

Frampton sees the concept of the resistant quality of the material entity as an effective means of opposing the total availability of architecture, its total subjection to and appropriation by society, its boundless consumption and thus its cultural annihilation. Like Rossi and Norberg-Schulz, he no longer expects architecture to embody an idealized future. He speaks of the decline of utopia. Yet in contrast to Rossi and Norberg-Schulz, Frampton places no trust in the past, and thus the term "regionalism," which he himself employed in the eighties, is actually misleading.

Astonishingly enough, we realize at the end of this brief review of three prominent positions on heritage that they by no means base their ideas about architecture on direct heritage or specific region. Instead, they seek to establish a connection with the non-individual—in Frampton's case, in fact, with the inaccessibility of the objective material world. Yet what links and sets all three of these positions apart is their tendency to downplay the value of the new, if not actually to reject it. In the architectural debates of the nineties, however, the new experienced a kind of revival, though not necessarily as a utopian social project.

The New

As we know, the new is not readily available as a quality of social life, especially if we associate the new with the utopian from the perspective of a theory of progress. This also applies to the assessment of technological innovations. Technical progress is no longer blithely taken for granted as social progress. The basic principle underlying a critique of the model of progress and utopias founded on historical philosophy is familiar to most readers and need not be recapitulated here. It is worth calling to mind, however, when we encounter models of the new in architectural discourse.

Alienation, de-automatization, and the disruption of perceptual habits—these are the basic operations used by artists of the avant-garde. They go hand in hand with the implicit or explicit expectation that they will bring something new to light. We still encounter this attitude in contemporary architecture from time to time. In response to complaints by the curators of the Wexner Center for the Visual Arts that it was

virtually impossible to exhibit paintings in the exhibition spaces he had designed because of the many glass walls, architect Peter Eisenman replied that he thought that was just fine and that the artists should come up with a different kind of art. Eisenman's early repertoire of architectural disruptions of the customary included such things as unclimbable stairs and slots in a bedroom floor that made it impossible to put up large beds. When the architects of Seaside, Florida, a small town modeled on a time-worn American nostalgia style, said that their intent was to create architectural order, it was Eisenman who suggested that the point should be to create precisely the opposite—disorder. Yet such a late, indeed overly delayed adaptation of a provocative avant-garde style inevitably runs the risk of running into a dead end. One reason for this is that society is flexible enough to appreciate such challenges while resisting change at the same time. More important, however, is the inherent conceptual weakness of such an approach. The concept of de-automatization that emerged from Russian Formalism is a prerequisite for the practical function of this artistic operation—making it possible to see reality in a new way. The purpose of art, argues Viktor Sklovsky, "is to restore a sense of life, to feel things, to make the stone a stone."[20] It should be evident that the socially relevant function of this aesthetic process is not to leave the de-automatized in the no-man's land of a normative denial of applicability or semantic annihilation but to organize the formation of a new non-aesthetic meaning: a new way of seeing. Unless the dual character of de-automatization and the new way of seeing is reflected in society, the alienating gesture of irritation remains empty and merely rhetorical. In art and especially in architecture, however, this avant-garde attitude is regarded as an anachronism today. Whereas the indeterminacy and indeterminability of the new can still be seen as a conceptual weakness in this context, it is decidedly programmatic in the current versions of the new based on theories of event, emergence, or virtuality. Bernhard Tschumi, for example, designs an architecture of event spaces derived from deliberate functional ambiguities and undefined phenomena. In the tradition of the Situationists, he views the event character of his architecture as social rather than formal. The Situationists had demanded architecture that produced exciting situations rather than exciting forms. In this sense, it is the social actors themselves who create and become the event. We occasionally find similar ideas in Koolhaas's work. In considering these aspects, however, the question arises as to whether they really require the concept of the event and its somewhat pompous connotations. For when we speak of "events" in plural, the concept appears relatively trivial and ultimately superfluous. Yet when we speak of "the event" in the singular, we evoke the idea of something spectacular, something entirely unusual, something that changes everything. While Tschumi still defines the event as the result of social interaction, it is stylized in other contexts into a kind of *deus ex machina*, an abrupt breakthrough of the new and different. What we have here is the synthetic creation of social progress without a social project. For a dialectician—albeit a negative one—like Theodor W. Adorno, the concept of the new was inconceivable without reference to utopia. The new could not be a voluntaristic vision but needed a correlative in the objective potentials of the social process. In this context, Adorno wrote, "The model for the relationship to the new is the child trying to play a chord it has never heard or fingered on the piano. But the chord has always been there. The range of possible combinations is limited. They are all contained within the claviature."[21]

Adorno's piano keys stand for the emancipatory potential of the productive forces of society. The idea of "always having been there" was injected without any historical excess baggage whatsoever into the architecture discussion of the nineties with the aid of a concept of the virtual interpreted by Henri Bergson and Gilles Deleuze: the new in the age of unlimited, random generatability.[22] The potentiality that endlessly transcends the existent—according to Bergson and Deleuze—need not even be conceived but merely brought to light, since, as we have seen, it is "always there already." Thus the real appears to be embedded in a dimension of the virtual that can never be fully explored, one that is no less real than the manifestations of any concrete reality. This the earth-bound validity of the existent is abandoned. Everything could be altogether different at any given time. All that matters is setting the dynamics of the virtual in motion. This is a new theory of being or, expressed differently, a theory of "being new," which heralds something like ontological transcendence, a transcendence of the immanence of being, but without dialectic—that is, without any thought whatsoever of negation or conflict. The available reserve of difference is never exhausted. Beneath every reality is an ocean of virtualities. Nothing remains undone; this world is always in a state of liberation. The unspoken theology implicit in this line of thinking leads to the conclusion that we are always beyond the point of the actual Here and Now—without a God but also without either critical potential or social project of any kind: a philosophy of affirmation that derives the false aura of the critical from the conceptual virtualization of every factual reality.

In another version, the synthetic generation of the new in architecture is based on the so-called new sciences. In contrast to traditional physics, they paint a picture of an essentially dynamic, self-organizing, and unpredictable nature. Chaos and order are no longer understood as opposites. Indeterminate and irregular states and processes are identified in terms of

their creative, structure-generating potential. Nature is creative because it brings forth the unpredictable and the singular. This genesis of new system characteristics is referred to as emergence.

In contemporary American architecture, in particular, we recognize a tendency to apply the theorems of the new sciences and the new geometry both to the genesis of architectural form and to the process of architectural. Sanford Kwinter and Greg Lynn published theoretical discussions of this principle of a "new architecture"[23] that was to replace Deconstructivism. The outcome is a new theory of the development of architectural form that relies on movement rather than fixed points, on dynamic processes rather than isolated elements.

The American architect Peter Eisenman was also inspired by theorems of the new sciences and non-Euclidian mathematics. In his view, they represent models which can be used as tools in design. He attributes no philosophical character to them. Eisenman uses non-linear processes to achieve unpredictable results that cannot be traced to an origin, an intention, or an author.

Thus what Eisenman does has no connection with architectural design in the traditional sense at all. Eisenman does not design architecture, as he explains in his dialogue with Derrida,[24] he writes it. Whereas design and composition impose an order on the object from the outside, writing attempts to liberate the object from this state of standstill and to allow it to develop in accordance with its own inherent, self-organized dynamics. Eisenman sees this as an act of excess, an act of transgression. What is transgressed is the territory of linear order, clear identity, and preconceived meaning.

The affixation through the singular leads to an experience that Eisenman defines, with reference to Walter Benjamin, as aura. In a letter to Jacques Derrida, Eisenman writes, "Aura is the presence of absence, the possibility of something else becoming present. My architecture aims to expose this other to experience."[25] Which brings us to the last paradigm: the other.

The Other

Eisenman is concerned with a very different, radical objectification of experiences which allows objects to retain their objective quality, their opacity, their alien character, and their illegibility. Illegibility means that the conventional correlation between object and meaning does not hold. The object is without meaning, a semantic orphan, so to speak, that manifests itself as raw being.

Wherever pre-interpretation and preconceived notions of the perceived object no longer apply, the observer must leave the conventional framework in order to perceive anything at all. He must, if only momentarily, abandon his established position of certainty. He must step out of himself, go beyond himself in order to risk encounter with more than himself and what he has made, if only for a brief moment of vulnerability. Eisenman speaks in Jean-Paul Sartre's sense of the reciprocating gaze of the other. We recognize a decisive aspect here. Eisenman is fundamentally interested in the process of interaction between a different architecture and a perceiving subject. He is not content to examine the architectural object alone but constructs/deconstructs/reconstructs that object as a place of experience. Eisenman calls for an architecture that is not only effective, in that it meets defined technical expectations and other requirements, but affective as well, in that it mobilizes qualities of resistance and uninterpretability in the object. Eisenman uses the concept of singularity to denote this restoration of the object of experience as a resistant reality.

His actual architectural designs show that this approach confronts him with the dilemma of creating an equally singular architectural object as a prerequisite for a singular experience. Whether willingly or not, he is thus drawn into the current of the conventional avant-garde architecture program of the 20th century, which seeks to break through horizons of expectation in order to open itself to the new.

Quite apart from the absolute indeterminacy of the new and the problematic contention that the new is preferable to everything else, it is impossible to overlook the fact that, in the real world, the new easily degenerates into the opposite of what Eisenman regards as critical strategy. Were architecture to dedicate itself to the continual creation and presentation of the new, it would affirm precisely the logic of global capital utilization and commodity production it seeks perhaps to overcome through "innovation." And thus the new, as Benjamin once expressed it, may be nothing other than a "deceptive transfiguration of the world of goods," a kind of merchandising aesthetics of the international real estate business.

In the meantime, the strategy of the singular architecture objects has actually rendered itself ineffective through inflationary devaluation. The architectural economy of maximum attention works just like every other market. Gehry's museum in Bilbao represented both the zenith and the end of this development. Now, every ambitious mayor and board chairman wants to have "something like that" as well. Accordingly, brand architecture copies itself with great success but with rapidly dwindling architectural fringe benefits. Nothing is more conventional than the strained new, nothing more taste-oriented than the unprecedented.

Even an architect like Eisenman senses the fundamental character of this break, which impacts upon the heart of his concept of critical architecture. He, too, must realize that it is no longer singular form that permits and engenders the experience of singularity. Yet the architectural exploration of the affective and non-identical need not be abandoned entirely. It must simply distance itself from the phantasm of unique and irreproducible form, a concept that has proven to be a dead end.

Distrust of the extravagant now gives way in architecture to an embrace of neutrality, of the absence of expression. For in light of the sufficiently analyzed confusion of problems in historical philosophy, the primary objective can no longer be to understand architecture as the embodiment or even the representation of social structures and developments, be they old, new, or "contemporary," and this does not make matters any easier. The unbearable burden of the need to be meaningful and to demonstrate firm roots in social tendencies is now being cast off as a matter of principle today. Through the silence of material and form, architecture rejects the unreasonable demand that it must mean something. The Swiss architects Peter Zumthor and Herzog & de Meuron offer good examples. Yet this certainly does not make architecture an "empty medium,"[26] as it is regarded in Holland today by followers of Koolhaas.

In fact, it was primarily Dutch architectural marketing strategies of the nineties that propagated the thesis that any given building—*cum grano salis*—could stand at any place in the world today.[27] This neo-liberal alternative solution for the presumed wavelike movements of the international market and the vociferous declaration of servitude to the economic requirements of globalization do not lead to emancipation from form, however, but to the de facto revival of a style, a new international style.[28] With regard to fifties Modernism and datascape projects alike, Andreas Ruby speaks quite rightly of "compromising stylistic uniformity."[29]

Current perspectives for a Reflexive Modernism in architecture may be found in efforts to overcome the concept of exquisite form that is so firmly anchored in the heart of European architecture. Modernism would not become "formless" but instead, as Ernst Hubeli argues, an *Überform*[30] by abandoning the one-dimensionality of the pretentious "perfect" form and accepting the indeterminate and the incomplete within itself. The *Überform* no longer seeks—as the Deutscher Werkbund and the Bauhaus propagated—to improve everyday life from the outside, so to speak, through unique form and "good design." Instead, it retreats and tends to be inconspicuous, even ordinary. But in doing so, it liberates this everyday normality, enabling it to achieve its own inherent multidimensionality and potential. In this sense, an architecture of the *Überform* would be both post-formal and post-functional.

But how can we abandon the messianic faith in the singularity of form without suffocating in the mere affirmation of the factual? We may draw a clue from a very German tradition—early German Romanticism and the history of its influence to the present day. In advance of the discussion, let it be established that Romanticism serves as a model of reflection which—*mutatis mutandis*—offers fertile insights applicable to what we call Reflexive Modernism today.[31]

Modernizing Modernism: The Impulse of Romanticism

"What is romanticism?" asked Charles Baudelaire in 1846, answering that "To say romanticism is to say modern art."[32] For Baudelaire, regarded as the founder of modern lyrical poetry, Romanticism has nothing to do with looking into the past or with choice of object. Baudelaire's Romanticism does not recognize a category of "outstanding" Romantic objects or themes. A similar attitude formulated solely from a defensive historical position can be found at about the same time in the writings of Friedrich Theodor Vischer and his theory of the "green spots" that represent the last remaining refuges of poetry in the midst of the prose of the bourgeois world—but only as long as that world exists. These "spots" openly display their own expiration date, the temporal index of their demise. A programmatic theory of art that claims to find the poetic—or let us say the Romantic—only in places and objects that have not yet been subjugated historically by the bourgeois world and developing capitalist industrial society would have been more than aporetic—a declaration of bankruptcy—even as early as 1850. Thus Baudelaire clearly distinguished Romanticism from the choice of objects, particularly from a choice of objects restricted to the representation of pre-modern realities, and in so doing established a modern Romanticism.

Baudelaire proceeds from the fundamental definition of the Romantic art form provided by Hegel in his lectures on aesthetics. In the Romantic art form, Hegel contends, "the entire content of the outside world"[33] can be the object. The "perfect randomness and superficiality of the material"[34] is taken under consideration, including, and in particular, its "unappealing and prosaic aspects."[35] "Therefore, the romantic inner content can exhibit itself in all circumstances, in thousands upon thousands of positions, states, deviations and confusions, conflicts and resolutions, for what is sought and what matters is only its subjective articulation of itself, the expression and the mode of perception of the spirit, and not an objective content that is valid in and of itself. Thus there is room for everything in the works of Romantic art, for all spheres of life and all of their manifestations, the great and the small, the highest and the lowest, morality, immorality, and evil. And art, the more worldly it becomes, makes itself more and more at home in the finite things of the world, turning its attention to them, fully accept-

ing their validity, and the artist, when he represents them, is within them as they are."[36] The concept involves a poeticization of the prosaic that makes the ordinary and the insignificant the relevant field of aesthetic reflection.

Philosophically speaking, one of the most important aspects of early Romantic aesthetics is its emphasis on the undeniable reflectivity of Modernism, which is incapable of accepting anything in the world as plain, unquestionable fact, whether in relation to the world of things, to the historical power of tradition and origin, or to the subject's relationship to itself.

Reflexivity could be understood as the awakening of the spirit, which then liberates itself from all external influences and restrictions imposed on its independence and autonomy. Rather than giving in to the widespread inclination to view the Romantic program as a kind of remystification in the sense of a denial of knowledge, it proceeds ahead—grasping the basic undercurrent of Romantic thought, or at least the ideas of Friedrich Schlegel or Novalis, as a further increase in knowledge that may be regarded as reflexive to the extent that it continues to pursue enlightenment and enlightens with respect to itself as well. Romanticism attempts a self-criticism of Modernism—defining its own limits on the one hand and surpassing itself on the other.[37]

This idea can be expressed more clearly with reference to the difference between the Hegelian and the Romantic concepts of reflexivity. While Hegel postulates that the mind recognizes no otherness apart from itself, Romanticism establishes the foundation for a radically altered view of this other within itself. Since the Romantic period, the more metaphorical Hegelian meaning of being-with-oneself and of complete identity and self-transparency is understood as something unpreconceivable and imponderable, something that challenges reflection but never catches up with it. Although Romantic subjectivity can no longer be at home in the external, subjective world, reflection no longer culminates in the complete being-with-itself of the spirit but instead in the experience of the unavailable. Yet if the subject is neither at home in the external nor entirely with itself, reflection can never drop anchor in the safe harbor of identity and must remain therefore remain infinite and imperfectable.

This aesthetic is based upon the positioning of the subject in an irresolvable state of tension between the finite and the infinite, between the determinate and that which defies all determination. Like Hegel's, it stakes its claim to the highest, the absolute, the infinite without reservation, yet the tension between the finite and the infinite, in contrast to that described by Hegel, cannot be resolved through reconciliation. The absolute can neither coincide with the infinite as a sensual manifestation of the idea nor can it surpass the finite, leaving it behind in defeat, in accordance with Hegelian dialectics. As Friedrich Schlegel noted, "This [is] the true contradiction we harbor within our selves—that we feel both finite and infinite at the same time."[38] Irony, one of the most prominent features of Romantic art, is a product of this contradiction, which it also fosters and perpetuates. Irony, writes Schlegel, "embodies and engenders a sense of the irresolvable conflict between the indeterminate and the determinate."[39] Reconciliation of this conflict was inconceivable in early Romanticism. The absolute or the "sublime," as the Romantics occasionally referred to it, is thus not actualized in a state of perfection at rest but in the endless motion of the conflict, the continuous intensification of non-identity, the liquefaction of all that is solid, the undermining of all clarity of meaning. Thus if the infinite cannot be captured and brought to rest in a position, an object, or an image, then it becomes incapable of representation. The exclusive goal of Romantic poetry is to incorporate this non-representability *as* non-representability within itself and to put the infinite into the work of art as the product of an aesthetic process that drives the sparks of the infinite from the finite through a kind of aesthetic processing of the finite.

Novalis called this poetic operation "romanticization": "The world must be romanticized... Romanticization is nothing other than qualitative potentiation... By giving the common a higher meaning, by giving the ordinary a mysterious appearance, by giving the familiar the dignity of the unfamiliar, the finite the illusion of infinity, I romanticize it."[40] This operation of romanticization does not lead to permanent possession, however. The spark of the infinite is brief, a mere flash of lightning. In Schlegel's view, allegory is an artificial lightning generator. Lightning is the manifest form of the infinite, which reveals itself in the flash of lightning as totally resistant to representation.

Since Baudelaire, Modernism has had no room for such concepts as the sublime or the infinite, yet it is inspired by a fundamental impulse to transcend and potentiate the prosaic finite. Totally demystified Modernism, in particular, sees itself as distinct from the factual world and is thus an heir to the Hegelian legacy. It rejects that legacy wherever its dialectic demands identification with the *Weltgeist*. Post-Hegelian Modernism lives in awareness of non-identity, of difference. It derives its reflective freedom from the knowledge that that which is, is not and cannot be, all that there is.

Authors have occasionally spoken of the emptiness of Modernist transcendence. In his epoch-making book, *Die Struktur der modernen Lyrik*, Hugo Friedrich introduced the concept of "deromanticized Romanticism."[41] What Romantic Modernism since Baudelaire has retained, however, is the denial of the beauty of Modernism as representational perfection. Thus Modernists emphasized the transitory, fleeting aspect of beauty from the outset. This transitory quality is nothing specific. It is always a form of subversion of the specific, the defined, and the fixed. The modern notion of beauty is the subversion of knowledge. This has nothing at all to do with obscurantism, however, but with a pursuit of enlightenment beyond the boundaries of intractable rationalism. Manifested in the concept of "incomprehensibility" of which Friedrich Schlegel speaks in one of his most famous essays is an aesthetic program devoted to the opening of experience. That idea was and remains the most provocative feature of Romanticist aesthetics.

Second or Reflexive Modernism

Ten Theses

1 The concept of Second Modernism was introduced to the German discussion in the nineties primarily by the sociologist Ulrich Beck. In contrast to the first modern era of the industrial age, modernists of Second Modernism are much more clearly aware of the ambivalence of the Modernist project. Modernism is no longer viewed only; it is also seen as a process of crisis. Modernism engenders emancipation and material progress but also, and not by coincidence, systemic problems complexes and self-endangerment. Second Modernism recognizes its risks and limitations and reacts to that knowledge. It becomes reflexive. It recognizes the ambivalence of the system but accepts no dialectic. It admits that, if worse comes to worst, Modernism could become its own gravedigger but not, as Marx hoped, that it is capable of bringing forth the social potentials required to overcome itself and create something entirely new and different. Viewed from this perspective, there is no alternative to capitalist Modernism. And this suggests that the pluralism hailed as boundless since the Postmodern period is, in fact, not so boundless at all. Is everything possible? Probably not quite. We should not ignore the ideological undertones in the arguments of the theorists of Second Modernism. Still, this does not imply that we should blindly accept things as they are and, in doing so, increase their potential for endangerment in a spirit of naïve or deliberate denial of the risks inherent in the system. Reflection is not affirmation, but it is not critic of the system, either. And thus the words of Ulrich Beck: "not a revolution, but a new society."[42]

2 Despite several attempts, the concept of Reflexive Modernism has not yet found its way into the contemporary architecture discussion.[43] One of the reasons for this is an astounding reluctance or inability to approach the concept of Mod-

ernism in any way other than through a specific, narrow view of architectural history. Another is that society is often regarded as nothing more than a fertile ground for new trends to which architecture should respond as quickly as possible. This second position does not lead to a Reflexive Modernism but instead to a kind of supermodernism that characterizes its own attitude as "laconic acceptance of things as they are."[44] The first position was marked out in Germany during the nineties by Heinrich Klotz, founder and director of the Deutsches Architektur Museum. Klotz postulated a return to the formal repertoire of Classical Modern architecture at the end of the 20th century, a tendency he referred to as "Second Modernism."[45] Coincidentally, this terminology recalls the language of sociology, although it bears no substantive relationship to it whatsoever.

3   Every discussion of Second Modernism in architecture must distance itself from a concept of Modernism defined solely in terms of the history of style. Modernism in architecture cannot be confined, as art historians customarily do, to the 1920s but can actually be traced back to the late 17th century and the dispute between the *anciens* and the *modernes*, if not further. It is there that architectural historian Joseph Rykwert identifies the *First Moderns.*[46]

4   To single out a specific stylistic era as the zenith and epitome of Modernism, as a model for all times, would be to deny history.

5   In addition to expanding the concept of Modernism in historical terms, it is also important to discuss Modernism in architecture as an aspect of Modernism in general—that is, in its larger social and philosophical sense.

6   Consequently, the concept of Second Modernism in architecture must not be tied to aspects of the history of form. Relying more on the definition of the concept used in the social sciences, we should speak not of a repetition of the (first) era of Modernism but of an advanced, indeed radicalized form of Modernism. Modernism becomes self-reflexive by making itself aware of its own underlying principles, preconditions, and consequences. In the process, the destructive, indeed even self-destructive potential of Modernism, along with its risks and its limitations, will become visible as well.

7   Habermas referred to Modernism as an unfinished project. Modernism becomes complete (in the sense of perfection) only through critical self-reflection, through recognition and acceptance of its own boundaries. And that inevitably implies cross-

ing those boundaries. But of what do the boundaries consist? The completion of Modernism presupposes the acceptance that it cannot be completed. Or, as Adorno stated in somewhat different terms: Modernism begins at its own end.

8   Modernism itself creates awareness of its own boundaries. It "divides" itself and brings forth a second modern era from its own substance. Literary scholar Karl Heinz Bohrer has proposed a model for this process. His theory is that the subjectivity of reason and action is joined by aesthetic subjectivity, which exists in awareness of the boundary, on the boundary, and also beyond the boundary. Thus, on the basis of a divided subjectivity, modern societies enter a fundamental "amphibian" state. "Aesthetic subjectivity" (Bohrer) emerges where "transcendental homelessness" (Georg Lukacs) and historical contingency begin—at the very point, that is, where the suspicion arises that even the most advanced knowledge a society possesses with regard to action, production, and dominion still leaves a gap when all is said and done: in the recognition of imperfectability.

9   This is the signature of our historical situation: we have liberated ourselves from all of the utopias and counter-utopias of perfection. But the consequences are ambivalent. There is "sadness" (Bohrer), on the one hand, but there is also the sense of being relieved of every form of programmatic perfectionist terror and a scarcely describable feeling of freedom that permits us to gaze, at least occasionally, across the boundary. We needn't necessarily imagine modern people of the 21st century as unhappy.

10  This suggests the following perspectives for architecture:
–   Not even architecture can escape the ambivalence of divided Modernism. It must cease to dedicate itself to programs of perfection; it cannot realize utopias. What is more, even if architecture abandons all programs devoted to saving the world (including those meant to benefit the environment), it must still realize that its impact is limited, at best, even given the most intelligent use of its resources. It remains imperfect and does not try to be "everything," the "great solution."
–   "Violated Perfection": The title originally foreseen for the exhibition of Deconstructivist art in New York in 1988 thus retains its programmatic justification, although the brief history of the Deconstructivist movement shows that the formal *mise en scène* of *violated perfection,* manifested as a style, quickly exhausts its media potential.
    The point is not to present dramatic, highly photogenic, specific gestures of the violation of perfection but to over-

come the strategy of perfect design as an attitude of non-reflexive kitsch and the suppression of ambivalence through the terrorism of form. In his *Notes from a Cellar*, Fyodor Dostoyevsky cites the utopian dream of a perfect organization of happiness in the work of Russian author Nikolai Gavrilovich Chernyshevsky, who was influenced by Charles Fourier, Claude-Henri Comte de Saint-Simon, and Pierre-Joseph Proudhon. Chernyshevsky describes the life of the "new breed of humans" who live in huge crystal palaces—a symbol of historical utopia in itself. They live in a "carefully tended nature, in a huge communal palace comprised only of metal and glass—and so richly furnished: aluminum everywhere, everywhere flourishing exotic plants. Their only duties are to start the machines and watch over them while they run. Cheerful song is heard from all groups at work. And all people will live this way? Everyone? Certainly! Never-ending spring and summer, eternal joy for all."[47]

Dostoyevsky sees the crystal palace as a metaphysical swindle, an example of isolation, enclosure, shielding against everything that does not bow to the unequivocally here and now, to the present. Viewed in this light, there is still considerable currency in Eisenman's contention that post-functionalism liberates architecture from its positivist isolation and confinement and makes it receptive to the absent, the indeterminable, the evasive.

– This relieves architecture of false ambitions and obligations it cannot possibly fulfill. And this relief offers architecture the opportunity to become modern in the fullest sense of the word, to take up the ambivalence of divided Modernism and become—because it is imperfectable—truly "open."
– That is the meaning of this revival or, more precisely, this radicalization of Modernism. It describes not only the rejection of obligations to social programs it cannot meet and the rejection of grand philosophical narratives but also the denial of architecture's obligation to tell, depict, or represent anything itself. As a whole, this rejection of Postmodern narration represents a denial of the linguistic-semiotic view of architecture as a medium of signs and meanings. This relates to Venturi's model and to Rossi's as well, which works with historical signs and symbols. Architecture is more than a medium of signs and meanings; it is more than something to be *read*. Now, other qualities can emerge from it, qualities that no longer require *reading* in the traditional sense.
– A number of ideas advanced within the context of the international architecture discussion are concerned with the non-semiotic or transsemiotic characteristics of architecture.

These ideas relate to such themes as space and its relationship to the body, motion, material, sensuality, perception beyond the sphere of the visual, emotional effect, aura, monumentality, singularity, reality and virtuality, determinacy and indeterminacy, to name only a few.

A closer look at those who pursue this discussion clearly shows that it is not confined to specific forms of architectural style. The architecture of Reflexive Modernism is not a style but an attitude.

– Architecture also has a boundary at which calculated functionality and mere instrumentality comes to an end, where it is not burdened and saturated by signs and meanings, where it is open and no longer totally subject to determination. It admits the ambivalence of Modernism. Perhaps this will enable it to become Second Modernism, or at least to become a whole Modernism by reuniting its divided halves.

Ironic Enlightenment

The dilemma facing the knowledge society is that there is one thing it cannot do: create simple, indisputable knowledge. The sheer overabundance of knowledge which no one—even specialists in their own fields—has the capacity to comprehend fully, is only one aspect   the quantitative side—of the problem. The qualitative aspect is even more crucial. We no longer innocently presume today that "knowledge" corresponds to "reality." We have all become constructivists. We assume, as does Richard Rorty, that what we refer to as knowledge consists of sentences composed of changing vocabularies—linguistic experiments. The fact that these vocabularies—each associated with the highest degree of expertise—conflict with one another in the social context does not make matters any easier. What is especially difficult to cope with is the fact that these vast quantities of knowledge do not reduce the volume of ignorance but actually tend to increase it. Thus the alleged certainty of knowledge is refracted at several levels. Not only do I know that I "know," I also always know that I do not know. This knowledge of ignorance leads, as Helmut Willke points out, to a categorically irreversible uncertainty,[48] which in turn becomes a fundamental existential dilemma of the present day. Contemporary societies of knowledge now demand an extraordinary effort from their members. They must learn to live with and bear a fundamental uncertainty. But how does one do that? In the spirit of Richard Rorty, Willke recommends "enriching the ponderous earnestness of German profundity with a portion of ironic lightness.[49] How does Rorty himself characterize the "ironists"?: "… never quite able to take themselves seriously because they are always aware that the words they use to describe themselves are subject to change; always conscious of the contingency and inadequacy of their exhaustive vocabulary and thus of their own selves."[50]

"Exhaustive vocabulary" is the term Rorty uses to describe the opposite of what we refer to here as Reflexive Modernism, an advanced form of Modernism that incorporates the crisis of knowledge.

Perhaps it is true that only enlightened irony can make life in a state of fundamental uncertainty bearable and prevent us from relapsing into fundamentalisms and voluntary ignorance. "If it were possible to bring ironic enlightenment to bear on this crisis, then at least that enlightenment would not be subject to the accusation that it fails to recognize the boundaries of possible knowledge. Ironic enlightenment in this sense means recognizing that the order of the symbols of knowledge has gone awry, exposing its reverse—lack of knowledge—yet at the same time resisting despair in the face of the resulting chaos.[51] We must not think of the shallow humor of Postmodernism in this context. Irony, as the Romantics were well aware, can be a very serious matter. But of course things are not all that clear cut, as those trained in reflection will remind us. So let us admit that irony can be a serious matter—but not always.

# Architecture that Steps Forth from the Shadows

Architectural Play in the New Media World

Ernst Hubeli

The international jury that evaluated German architectural achievements of the last ten years in preparation for this exhibition emphasized the question of to what extent the designs take up or mirror socially relevant themes. Instead of concentrating on exclusive architectural objects, they were primarily interested in the didactics of an exhibition that plumbs and illustrates the possibilities and limits of architectural anticipation.

In this context the designation of German, Dutch, or Swiss architecture is misleading. It is misleading not only because the basic social conditions, the debates, and the flow of information have long become international, but because all the essential questions of architecture today revolve around themes that have arisen especially due to the dissolution of national and regional boundaries.

This does not mean that historical characteristics of countries simply disappear; yet their meaning and ranking have changed, which raises a number of questions. What has been the influence of global hyper-cultures, which are bound neither by place nor history? What correlations exist between architecture and an everyday world in which a virtual and actual reality coexist? And how have these things changed our perceptual and visual habits?

Even the questions themselves suggest that today's social framework forces a paradigm shift in architecture. It lies in a detaching of form from meanings (detaching of knowledge from understanding), an enhanced value of architecture, and a post Functionalist understanding of buildings. These signs lead to a seemingly paradoxical question with which the following essay is concerned: is it possible to think of and design architecture without objects in order to win back its objectivity?

"Ceci tuera cela"

Certainly every social change does not demand a new architecture. Change can pass it by or it can remain unrecognized; it can be falsely appraised or be only explained in retrospect. Time and again modern architecture has arisen that was conceived for new people and a new world that did not exist.

Conceptual offspring, on the contrary, stand opposed to genuine modernization, which—whether we want it or not—changes everything. Johannes Gutenberg achieved such a path-breaking invention with his moveable characters. Victor Hugo was so impressed with this reproduction technology that he traced a specter on the wall for all expressive artists: he prophesied that all old expressive forms would become outmoded. Architecture in particular, Hugo thought, would to a certain extent disappear into books because all materials had degenerated into meaninglessness: "Ceci tuera cela."

Hugo's fears were too pessimistic. They have proved themselves true only to the extent that architecture has had to reconcile itself with technical invention—for example, in the simple way that the architect Henri Labrouste did so in 1850. He attached a large number of letters to the front façade of the Bibliotheque Sainte Geneviève in order to decorate the building with the names of famous writers.

Doubled Reality

Today we often have to deal with technical inventions that suggest no architectural answer, but instead lead to a phenomenon that we can describe as a collective double life. Alongside the real there coexists a virtual world: a real and a media reality. The latter often appears as a counter-world or counter-reality. Neither of the two worlds is superterrestrial, and one can also not be separated from the other, since each everyday experience resides in the simultaneity and coexistence of both worlds.

There are now many signs that this doubled reality—even if it is perceived only unconsciously—has lasting consequences for architecture. We first notice an evident change of discourse if we call to mind previous architectural debates, which for a long time have followed the cycle of Modernism, Postmodernism, and "post-Postmodernism." The change has ranged from phases of a naïve belief in progress to phases of museum-like treatment of history, from phases of technological fascination to phases of demystified modernity, culminating in the global shock of modernization which is pessimistically accelerated or cushioned by nostalgia. Such cycles now no longer seem to take place. Literary critic Karl Heinz Bohrer and architecture theoretican Ullrich Schwarz have noted that the criticism of Modernism now passes into self-reflection—not accidentally but inevitably, because the success of Modernism obviously cannot be halted by applying a brake or by criticism. The question therefore arises as to what are the unique limits of Modernism. Where are the borders of permanent renewal and upheaval of everyday life, against which no one seriously or successfully resists, or can resist?

For architecture the question becomes more pressing: under these conditions, is there an alternative to modern architecture? Or are all architectures—like it or not— modern, reality burdened, without a utopian or unworldly superstructure?

The idea seems overdone, if only for the reason that it breaks with the former self-understanding of modern architecture. As is well known, the latter requires autonomy, which is generally formulated in an antithetical way.

Today we can insist that the distinction between non-modern and modern architecture is no longer perceptible. Several things speak in favor of this hypothesis—not due to a different perspective, but due to the displacement of levels of meaning. We see this in the fact that the question of whether architecture is old or new, genuine or false, actual or virtual, is no longer of interest to most people. In any case the hypothesis is confirmed by the fact that the distinctions (even if we had found them interesting) in every case have disappeared, because it is increasingly difficult to recognize them.

To take an example, architecture that wants to mediate history cannot escape the fact that the image of history—in whatever form—is neither history nor is it perceived as history, but only as an image, at best as a simulated image of history. Whoever still understands history as a question of the image is not up to date with his time. For the image is perceived (as a part of the everyday flood of images) first as an image and not as something else.

With this doubled reality the semiotic potential and the reception have changed in kind; architecture cannot represent unambiguous content or values by signs, images, or symbols that generally push toward an intelligible and binding meaning. Instead of a meaning-supported sign or image, a hybrid appears. This means that not only is the production and meaning of images turned upside down, but also that meanings shift from the author to the audience. For this reason no one can say with certainty how signs and objects will be read—and if they generally can be read. In any case, meanings withdraw into the public spheres.

The doubled reality does not inevitably go along with the loss of meaning in architecture, yet it compels the limits of architectural achievement and expressive power to be cultivated anew.

The Media Trap

If we first admit the journalistic relation of architecture to the media, we notice not merely a convergence but even a melding. Since the eighties architecture has stepped increasingly from the shadow of insider journals and has found a podium in almost every newspaper and magazine. In trendy global magazines, such as the London *Wallpaper,* architecture commands not only more space than lifestyle topics—it embarrasses them. Even the culture sections of German newspapers place architecture together with theater, literature, and music in considering the established cultural themes.

Almost all large architecture offices have responded to this change, and today they have at their disposal public relations specialists and whole press departments to further and control their media presence. Even many small offices attend to their publicity appearances—at comparatively high expense—for

example with a cult-like corporate identity or even self-financed monographs on never-heard-of topics, driving many offices into ruin before they are able to land a commission.

It would be a mistake to attribute this increased attention to more interesting or better architecture. The reason lies in the media itself. Certain cultural products are valuable to the media, others are not. Architecture can be so prepared that it also circulates in a successful way without complicated or long-winded explanations. Reduced to optical effects and haptic promises of pleasure, architecture can be personalized and made intimate as a creative act. In this regard notions such as "star-architects" or "author-architecture" have their origin in the new media world. They mean that personalization creates for it the presumption of being generally watched by the public (which in all other cultural branches has long been the rule). Now the question arises as to whether the increased attention on architecture itself has consequences and whether it is becoming a trap.

First we must determine what we have actually become involved with. Whether in respected journals or local newspapers—a journalistic architectural jargon has found acceptance, which formulates without explaining anything. Regarding architecture, one learns at best how it affects journalists, to what taste it belongs, or how charmed the architect is by his own work.

Public dissemination of the state of culture could indeed signify an act of liberation—if it would retire that cultural concept that was coupled to the universal educational ideal of the cultured bourgeoisie. Whether this causes culture to hedonistically broaden and become popularized, or whether the media world in any case can only serve as a distraction is left open. It is certain, however, that the media in general and its specific forms of mediation both react upon architecture.

Marshall McLuhan's thesis—the medium is the message—can today be broadened inasmuch as the message has not simply become lost in itself, it has been subjected to standardization. It matters not if it concerns fashion, art, food, drink, architecture, TV, or newspapers—the media-calculated preparation is the same. It follows a subjective equivalence of things that promises an objective indifference. The announcement is the real message. Not what, but the fact that it is announced is in the commercial interests of the media. Whether the event actually takes place or not does not matter. Thus the products of the media establish their own life beyond true reality and circulate as eternally new.

The self-referential creates an architectural genre for which the more recent architecture in Switzerland may serve as an example. Toward the end of the eighties when the Postmodern frivolity and the exuberant and flashy forms of Hans Hollein,

Michael Graves, or the Memphis Group were in the focus of the media, the super-cool forms filtered to the pure essence of material being designed by Swiss-German architects seemed like a global manifesto for a silent, anorexic counter-world—a big event within the familiar flood of images. This soon led to the global label of "radical chic," which initially described an urbane stratum of social climbers in London, and in the meantime has been established in applied arts as a stylization of Minimal Art.

What the media turned into a label surely had another origin in Switzerland. Purism in Swiss architecture has a long tradition that reaches back to factory owners, such as the shoe manufacturer Bally. Riches and luxury had never found a representative form in these circles—on the contrary, it was disapproved of, and it thus came to pass that workers' houses were often better decorated and appeared more chic than the villas of their employers. This image politics has until today granted to Swiss capital an eternal peace in labor relations that is unparalleled in Europe.

The Superficial Bang

The preparation and availability of architecture for the media consists not only in the separation of content and form. Without preparation these objects would not even exist. At the same time, as the example has shown, mediatization and museumification can combine in a curious way. History becomes an optical kick for cosmopolitan feeling.

Reproduction techniques are certainly not new to architecture. Years ago, Walter Gropius and Mies van der Rohe retouched photos of their masterpieces in order to propagate their style in an unreal perfection. Today, however, mediatization to a certain extent consists in the reverse. reproductions are increasingly the starting point of architectural design.

The Guggenheim Museum in Bilbao rises out of the rust heap of ruined heavy industry like a silver flower, an event that seems to symbolize an awakening in the postindustrial age. According to the curator, the new museum is practically unusable—which is not surprising because it was designed as a global sign that had to be recognizable as an unmistakable icon even in the micro-sphere of the internet.

The crisis-ridden city with an extremely high youth unemployment rate is gambling that architecture will bring its turnaround, that proclaiming Bilbao a cultural city will bring about a worldwide, attention-getting splash in the media. To this end there is an economy of attention. Induced architecturally, it consists in a superficial bang: a never-before-seen image that rises up from the flood of interesting images in order to land on the television screen like a punch in the eye.

Optical shows of strength can certainly overtax architecturally expressive forms. Yet up to now that spoke in favor of, rather than against, a smashing appearance on the television screen. In this way an architectural genre has been established that is developed and judged by its commercialization and effect on the media. In the case of Bilbao, it is a component of an urban-crisis management.

The small Swiss city of Lucerne indulged itself with a comparable architectural object for similar reasons. The single event that made the city known beyond its own borders was the annual music festival, which however has become less and less popular. The construction of a cultural and congress center of international stature was a last attempt to correct this. After a long and costly project development, a complex was completed with imposing presence, which gave the small town the appearance of a most significant cultural metropolis on every postcard. Yet the best concert hall in the world is usually empty, because theatrical or local functions are scarcely feasible in the highly specialized room. The price for the short-lived media success is now a continuing financial disaster for the small city.

Another example is the renovation of the Tate Gallery in London, which followed an image strategy oriented to competition with the metropolises of New York and Paris. These capitals are known for their art museums which are unmistakable monuments of architectural history. Considering this, London wagered on the uniqueness of a building that isn't even a museum. The gigantic power plant of the industrial age infiltrated all museum architecture by separating the sign from the purpose, which is merely another form of branding.

Self-Destruction of Oddities

Whether the new media world inevitably puts architecture under a specific pressure to exploit surely cannot—in light of the described examples—be conclusively answered. It is incontestable, however, that all forms have made themselves independent and that all formal problems of architecture have been automatically dispensed with. This is seen by the fact that the unique architectural object loses its effect through inflationary repetition and sinks into meaninglessness. Bilbao's Guggenheim Museum has perhaps already marked the beginning and the end point. It has less to do with the question of whether it is a good or bad building than with the conditions under which it arose. Within our present everyday reality, images and their meanings wear out rapidly, and that is even true for architectural shows of strength.

Signs and images are supplied with a materialization that leads to changes of meaning or a loss of meaning. This is certainly not new, yet increasing media penetration hastens materialization and expansion in terms of content. An obvious consequence for architecture is that its representational functions have become obsolete. Thus the unique architectural object soon earns the status of a museum-like collection of narrative forms—as chair manufacturer Fehlbaum had already anticipated by gathering objects by "star-architects" from all over the world at his factory. If necessary, uniqueness can even be industrialized, such as the "different" form of Frank Gehry or in the manner of a formal reduction, which conceptually amounts to the same thing.

No meanings can be organized with forms. As a result the last refuge into the sentiment of originality or neo-feudal luxury could not have succeeded, because the authentic experience is also felt as a media attraction and is read as a simulation. An "architecture of longing" in the heterogeneous everyday world can indeed suggest visibility, safety, and order—but only as a substitute. And *ersatz* remains *ersatz*, be it as fiction, as Disney World, or as beautiful form.

What Do You See? What Is?

An important consequence of media communication lies in our new understanding of reality, which to a large extent is independent of material conditions. Nobody asks whether the cloud icons on TV weather forecasts are real or not. And for quite a while now, people have spoken of virtual space, and thus also of the idea that there is architecture that really does not exist.

Architecture will obviously always remain material. So we don't need to ask whether it can be replaced with the virtual, but rather whether its perceptual and sensory possibilities have changed in such a way that architecture moves within a different referential frame and visual space. In it we are confronted daily with a flood of images to which we have grown accustomed, as we have regarding the inevitably increasing acceleration of perception which trigger the blending of the material with the immaterial, the apparent dissolution of the material, or the supposed reification of the immaterial. This blending, indeterminacy, and ambivalence does not mean that we surrender to them or are manipulated by them, as long we distinguish between what is and what we see. We don't even have to understand this distinction; it is sufficient to know that there is one.

The distinction between what we see and what is can in architecture only suggest an axiom, inasmuch as architecture always requires a real encounter. For media images and effects can also be had without architecture; there are reproductions of reproductions, images of images, always similar and recognizable signs—there are "bubbles of immanence" (Marc Augé).

If, however, it were a matter of measuring architecture in terms of its emotional responsibilities, then it would require forms of appropriation that would challenge and allow unique meanings. This cannot be achieved by returning to a traditional architecture, "finished" forms, or pure materials. On the contrary: when digital, artificial, and indefinable constructs are thrown out and "authentic" objects taken on, other worlds may be installed, but ones which are no less fictive, with their worn-out clichés. It doesn't matter if the revolt against the inauthentic is propagated as a sharp cultural critique or as a simple leisure-time activity.

How Does Architecture Communicate?

New forms of communication bring architecture face to face with a series of contradictions: what does it mean if architecture no longer relates to a place, to a history, or to a definite time—if place, space, and time differ so greatly? What does it mean if functions, uses, and utility values are unstable? How does architecture define itself within an interlinked, global hyper-culture? What links exist between factual and apparent form, between image and body, between material and immaterial, between sheathing and form, between construction and surface? Can a concrete house look like a glass house? A glass house like a concrete house?

In his famous painting *Ceci n'est pas une pipe*, the artist and epistemologist René Magritte pointed out very early what happens when the real object cannot be distinguished from its image. One can delude oneself and fumble into the knowledge trap. Today the knowledge trap is ubiquitous; a medium in everyday life.

Beyond pedagogy of perception, the question arises of whether architecture in general can and should answer such questions, or whether it should do nothing and just accept ambiguity and ambivalence as its reality—and not resist staging and creative wills.

In any case architecture can no longer consist of parading unique objects that put the public in the role of passively astonished subjects. Architecture that communicates looks back; it leaves the recipients to a certain extent in the lurch, in a state of uncertainty. The author and with him his creation "disappears like a face in the sand" (Michel Foucault)—in favor of the play of an open meaning that reverses the relation between author and public.

From the legitimation of subjectivity it can not be concluded that subjective creative wills are transferable to architecture. That would be a fundamentally false evaluation of Postmodern power relations. The power of interpretation has definitely shifted to the public, whether we like it or not. Thus formal intentions always turn out to be "non-reflexive kitsch that becomes a terror of perfection and design" (Ullrich Schwarz). Architecture remains only bearable without architectural suspicion.

In this regard the aesthetic formulations of the twenties are worth mentioning. Although they are not transferable because they were conceived above all in response to the conservative critique of the metropolis of that period, the considerations regarding strategies for processes of interpretation have a certain relevance today, because they are also based on an expanded framework of observation. Victor Sklovsky's "revolt of things," the alienation thesis of Karl Marx and the Surrealists, or Manfredo Tafuri's "operative criticism"—all contain strategic ideas that cushion the loss of semiotic qualities. Instead of a contemplation of the object, the act of seeing sets the standard. They experimented with disturbances in automated perception, with the insertion of unintelligible forms, with tricks and self-referential images, with the renunciation of schemes of identification, with discontinuity, with norm deviation, and with normative breaks.

The Cool Look

The requirements for corresponding image strategies have certainly changed. A review of the key events at the beginning of the media age can explain what impulses have constituted new relationships between signs, images, and their meanings. When in 1972 a large housing development in the wasteland of St. Louis was demolished, the image of the concrete slabs breaking against one another was published in newspapers all over the world. What generally signified the end of large housing complexes represented for the art historian Charles Jencks a Copernican revolution for architecture. He was convinced that the destruction of a monotonous image marked the birth of Postmodernism. Forms of Modernism were now to be replaced by a multifaceted formal language. The fatality of the allegory, which reverberated in the head of every architect, was not the unleashing of a global wave of prettiness, but rather its fallacy regarding architecture's new field of activity, which, as is well known, soon resembled a battlefield with colorfully painted corpses.

If we wanted to cite an event that characterized the changed status of architecture, then instead of the explosion of this concrete development wouldn't it be the opening of a shop in London in 1971? Malcolm McLaren and Vivienne Westwood filled the shop with old pomade boxes, heart-shaped bathmats, and stilettos—without even opening it. The shopowners' display of unsalable goods sprung from their desire to go bankrupt as fabulously as possible.

Around the same time, McLaren founded the Sex Pistols with Johnny Rotten in order to inaugurate and celebrate the musical decline of pop culture. All the well-meant songs of love, freedom, and justice—such as those by the Beatles—were replaced by a single compressed air hammer. Decorated with hammer, sickle, and swastika, their appearances were violent and empty. Part of the staging was the hindering of any reliable meaning. What became known as Punk was at the same time considered a youth counter-culture, a movement of unemployed workers, an anarchist party, narcissism, neo-Dada. The refusal to assume an identity was likewise strenuously coached, like the legendary fits of rage. The play with the irrational, falsifications, and misleading meanings required a coolly calculated artificiality.

This phenomenon mirrored far more than a *zeitgeist*. It was about the reevaluation of signs, images, symbols, and cultural standards—not in the form of a denial or renewal but in the form of their exchangeability. Through this exchangeability, the value and attribution of meanings becomes more difficult or even completely impossible. The only thing that this "Surrealism" shares with the original artistic movement of the same name is the strategy to broaden the frame of observation.

Today seeing is subjected to a ubiquitous public image that presses into private or public spaces. Some of the images function without a message; others mark a tendency toward products, life-styles, norms, and social codes. Surrealism had still infiltrated meanings and representation, and this strategy was understood as a weapon against the power of signs. Today this weapon has transformed itself from a pedagogy of perception and didactics of perception into a collective consciousness. Images and signs with pre-assigned meanings are mistrusted, or we become indifferent to them. Labels and brandings are also affected by it. In order to preserve their effect, original meanings are infiltrated or even destroyed by their own advertisings firms. Thus the Apple corporation turned on the worn-out image of the liberal, individualized lifestyle: "Think different" became "Think really different," fading out with an image of Stalin. The process has been described as "culture jamming." Certainly all strategies of images have been used as a means of advertising. Their limits however show themselves in the tendency of signs to lose power and rapidly be consumed, in such a way that the power of interpretation or the management of interpretation themselves become relative and are scarcely to be found.

Fredric Jameson sees on the horizon a "Surrealism without subconscious," which creates a "partial autonomy of language" and a "realm of aesthetics that doubles the world without being absorbed in it, and thus gains a negative or critical force, so to speak, an unworldly uselessness."

## From Form to *Überform*

The change of meaning of signs cannot be simply transferred to architecture—at least not in all respects. Yet architecture is a cultural project like any other; it cannot organize meanings for signs and forms. In addition, traditional models of representation have dissolved in such a way that architecture is confronted with its own conditions of work. What can it achieve? What can it express?

In order to answer the question, the aesthetic dimensions—apart from the forms of appropriation—have to be understood and reversed as part of a planning process. Architecture arises within a set of not always manageable decisions, which are influenced by different interests, demands, objective forces, building codes, wishes, and uncertainties. Also participating in the process are countless specialists who all emphasize their own factual concerns and preferences. Thus architects without particular authority or legacy are inevitably negotiators for a body of experts. New information systems and changing conditions impose dynamics on the decision process which suggest that the design be viewed from the perspective of permanent remodeling.

The working conditions of design therefore correspond less to inventing forms than to a strategy by which no individual form can be derived, but a multiplicity of forms with different justifications. In view of this lack of clarity, the architectural task cannot consist of determining something by means of a show of design strength, which objectively is undefined and remains so. It is however possible to give uncertainties a form, one that includes the wealth of information and necessities. Conceived in such a way, spatially structured constructs permit known and unknown appropriations and become established only through use. Accordingly, the architectural form leads no life or only a limited personal life. *The form is replaced by a form beyond forms.* You cold call it an *Überform.* It is de-automated and corresponds to something incomplete; it revolves around exciting situations, around a dynamic organized by itself, around possible and unforeseen events. The *Überform* steps beyond the architectural—not only thematically but as a consciousness of its incompleteness and uncertainty. To this extent the *Überform* (occasionally) can allow borderline experiences of perception and create play, which can be imagined as a superimposition of different levels of meaning.

This will neither "save" nor degrade architecture—but it will be freed from the weight of meaning. You could call it cynical architecture: a self-consciously uncultivated architecture that stands not in a self-sacrificial media light but in the shadows, which enables it to place itself within an open but also obscure context of justification. It is complete enough for use, but it is imperfect and open enough for the willfulness of subjective appropriation, and yet it is complex enough to be capable of anticipation.

New German Architecture
25 Projects

The texts on the twenty-five projects are by Ernst Hubeli

# Herz Jesu Kirche, Munich
## Allmann Sattler Wappner Architekten, Munich

Until well into the 1980s, efforts to secularize church architecture were devoted primarily to integrating existing buildings into so-called multifunctional parish centers. As a result, many churches ceased to exist as symbols of urban architecture. Today, we observe a reverse trend toward restoration of the sacred character of churches, for which the Herz Jesu Kirche offers an unusual example. Although the building is a "pure" church, its appearance defies characterization with respect to purpose or architectural genre. It is an indifferent glass cube that could just as easily be a hangar, particularly in view of its large gate (the architects' interpretation of the Gospel of St. Matthew: "Come unto me, all ye..."). The religious atmosphere is generated mainly within the church and enhanced by filtered light. To this end, the architects designed a room-within-a-room. The outer room is a glass shell. Its transparency decreases progressively from the side of the main portal to the altar wall. The main portal consists of 432 panes of blue glass with the text of the Passion according to St. John rendered in a stylized nail alphabet which is reminiscent of cuneiform writing. Separated by a narrow ambulatory, the inner room is enclosed by a wall of wooden slats. These are staggered and positioned in such a way that incoming light grows more intense toward the altar.

**Project:** New building for the Herz Jesu Catholic church, Munich. **Architects:** Allmann Sattler Wappner Architekten, Munich **Staff:** Project Manager: Karin Hengher; project team: Susanne Rath, Anette Gall, Michael Frank **Garden and landscape architects:** Realgrün, Munich **Artists:** Glass entrance door: Alexander Beleschenko, GB-West Glemorgan with Franz Mayer'sche Hofkunstanstalt, Munich; altar wall: Lutzenberger & Lutzenberger, Bad Wörishofen; "Five Wounds": M + M, Munich; Stations of the Cross: Matthias Wähner, Munich **Engineers:** Structural calculation: Ingenieurgesellschaft mbH Hagl, Munich; façade: Ingenieurbüro für Fassadentechnik R + R Fuchs, Munich; building utilities: HL Technik AG, Munich; acoustics: Ing. Gemeinschaft Beneke, Daberto + Partner, Munich; lighting: George Sexton Associates, Washington, D.C. **Client:** Katholische Pfarrkirchenstiftung Herz Jesu, Munich, represented by the Office of the Archbishop of the Diocese, Munich **Dimensions:** Floor space: church building, including elevated platform: approx. 1,119 m²; sacristy: approx. 456 m²; tower: approx. 22 m² **Location:** Lachnerstrasse 8, Munich-Neuhausen **Year of completion:** 2001 (dedication ceremony: 2000)
**Photos:** Florian Holzherr, Munich; Christian Richters, Münster

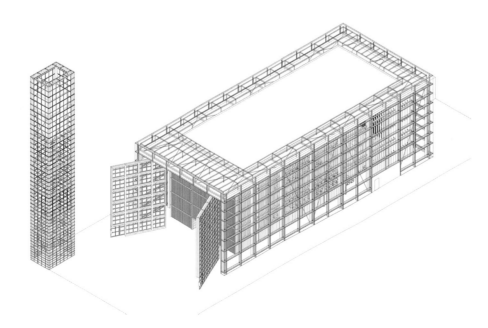

The large entrance portal can be opened hydraulically within eight minutes for special occasions

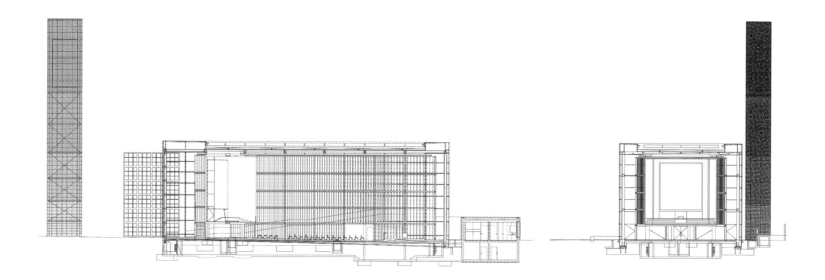

1 Church tower
2 Foundation
3 Ramp to parish center
4 Manger
5 Veneration of Mary

6 Veneration of the Five Wounds
7 Confession
8 Baptism
9 Storage room for chairs/maintenance room

10 Hallway
11 Ambo
12 Altar
13 Tabernacle
14 Sacristy for ministrants
15 Sacristy for priests

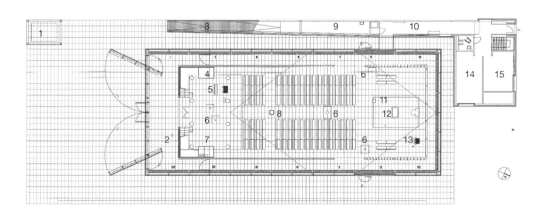

The two spatial layers: The individual glass elements in the transparent-translucent outer shell become increasingly cloudy along the façade toward the altar wall. The wooden slats of the inner shell are set at different angles, creating a nuanced light atmosphere in the church interior during the day and giving the façades a variegated appearance from the outside at night. They also have an acoustic function

Left page: View of the altar area showing the curtain along the altar wall, a web of thin rods (5 mm in diameter) of tombak, a brass-copper alloy.
This page, left: The Stations of the Cross are located between the inner and outer shells. Right: View of the entrance area and stairs leading to the organ loft

# Biosphere and BUGA Flower Hall 2001, Potsdam
## Barkow Leibinger Architekten, Berlin

Organizers of the 2001 Bundesgartenschau (National Garden Show, or BUGA) wanted to meet the strong public demand for interesting worlds of experience in which the authentic is combined with simulations, offering a continuous chain of events. With respect to the exhibition halls, it seemed logical to respond to a contemporary trend aimed at overcoming the strict boundary between building and landscape architecture—a distinction that was eliminated almost entirely in this large hall. Garden elements give way in smooth transition to architectural structures, and vice-versa. Instead of focusing on the difference between natural and artificial areas, the presentation emphasizes overlappings and seamless transitions as part of its educational objective. Thus three-dimensional geometric figures alternate with wild natural worlds. What appears wholly natural is often revealed to be an artificially modeled landscape; what looks artificial at first turns out to be a rock wall. Truly real are the ponds and fountains that regulate the climate inside the hall.

**Project:** Biosphere, flower hall for the 2001 National Garden Show, with orangery, paludarium, bar, restaurant, and offices; to open in fall 2002: Nature World **Architects:** Barkow Leibinger Architekten, Berlin **Staff:** Heiko Krech, Christian Helfrich, Dietrich Bernstorf, Giuseppe Boezi, Bernd Jürgens, Stephanie Kaindl, Jan Kircher, Volkmar Nickol, Karin Ocker, Andrea Pelzeter, Peter Rieder, Florian Steinbächer **Garden and landscape architects:** Outdoor areas: Büro Kiefer, Berlin; Nature World: Martin Diekmann Landschaftsarchitektur, Hanover **Engineers:** Structural calculation: Hörnicke Hock Thieroff – Ingenieurgemeinschaft, Berlin; building utilities: Planungsgruppe M + M, Berlin/Stuttgart; air-conditioning: Fraunhofer Institut für Bauphysik, Stuttgart **Client:** City of Potsdam, represented by the Bornstedter Feld Development Office
**Dimensions:** total floor space: 11,000 m²; exhibition space: 6,000 m² **Location:** Georg-Herrmann-Allee 99, Potsdam **Year of completion:** 2001
**Photos:** Werner Huthmacher, Berlin

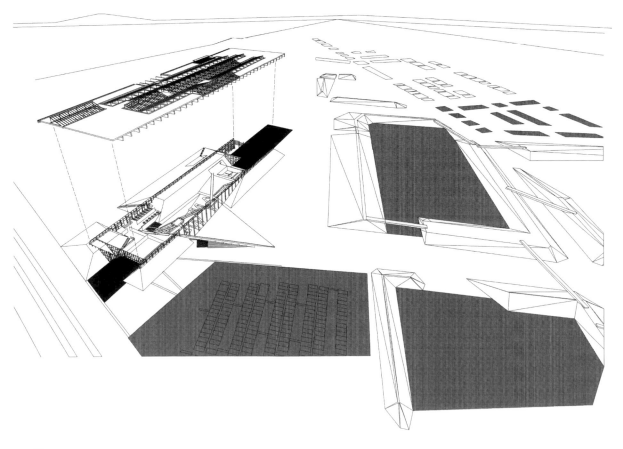

Left page: The new embankments that frame the biosphere extend the artificial topography of the former Soviet military earthworks; in the background, right: the Bornstedter Feld housing area. This page: Entrance on the east side of the biosphere

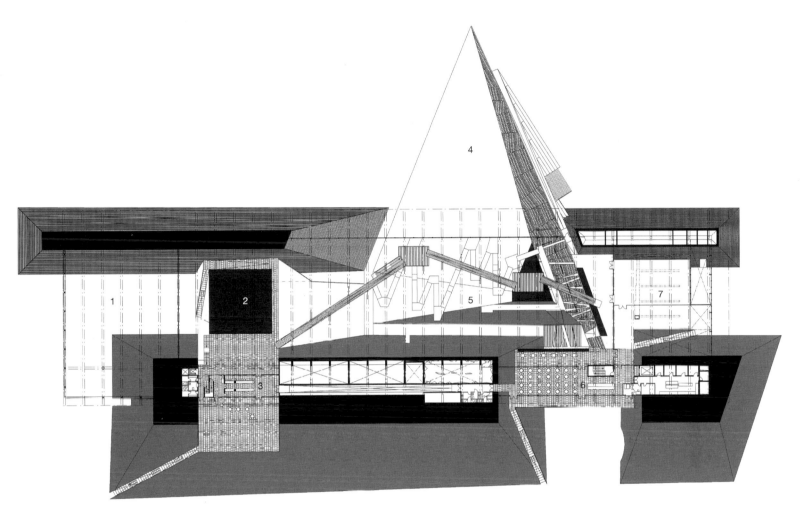

1 Orangery
2 Paludarium
3 Bar
4 Sunken garden
5 Central garden
6 Restaurant
7 Foyer

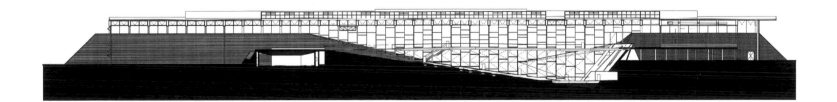

Left page, top: Upper level ground plan. Bottom: Longitudinal section. This page: Steel-glass curtain-wall façade of the central garden area and the sunken garden in front of it

Both pages: Central garden

# Nieuwe Luxor Theater, Rotterdam, The Netherlands
## Bolles + Wilson, Münster

The critique of Heroic Modernism, which was devoted to building utopias through architecture, gave rise to an architectural current oriented toward everyday themes, which often parodies the pathos of modern architectural laws with considerable irony. To a certain extent, the design for the Luxor Theater mirrors the movement of visitors on their way to the theater hall. Entering from the street, the audience "winds" its way upward over different levels and stairways that end in a loop. The loop was built around the stage and the audience seating area, making the latter the center of the theater. In this way, the motif of the moving theater visitors gives unpretentious structure to the form of the building and the directionless façade, which is faced with fiber-cement panels, a common industrial product. Thus it comes as no surprise that the truck ramp, a bold, eye-catching steel construction that had to be connected with the building for operational reasons, is the most ambitious architectural element of all.

**Project:** Music and theater hall **Architects:** Bolles + Wilson, Münster **Staff:** Project manager: James Yohe; project team: Carole Asfour, Roland Bondzio, Michael Y. H. Lin, Axel Kempers, Andreas Kimmel; model: André Pannenbäcker, Thomas Wagener, Gernot Hildebrand, Nick Adomatis **Engineers:** Construction: Bureau Bowkunde, Rotterdam; structural calculation: Gementwerken Rotterdam IBS; building engineering: Tebodin, Den Haag; acoustics: Prinssen en Bus, Uden; general contractor: IBC Van Hoorn, Capelle aan den IJssel **Client:** City of Rotterdam (OntwikkelingsBedrijf. Rotterdam), Luxor Managing Director Rob Wiegman **Dimensions:** Total floor space 16,800 m²; usable space 13,185 m²
**Location:** Kop van Zuid, Rotterdam, The Netherlands **Year of completion:** 2001
**Photos:** Christian Richters, Münster; Hisao Suzuki, Barcelona

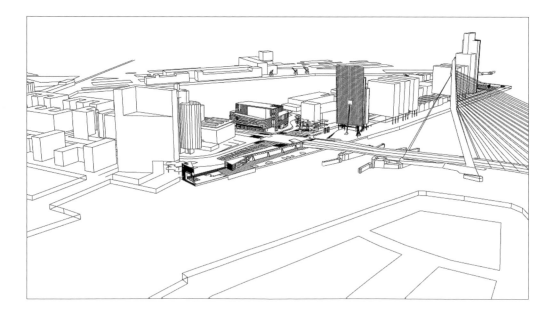

Left page: The Kop van Zuid peninsula from the north. The plans for the quay landscape with the wedge-shaped "Bridgewatchers House," located north of the theater on the Maas, were also drawn up by architects Bolles + Wilson

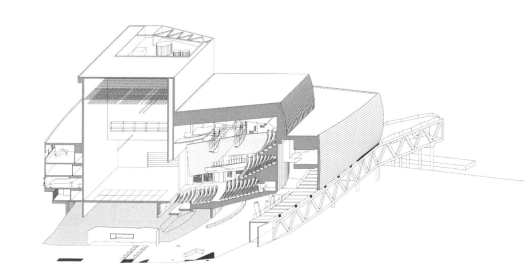

Left page, above: View of the rust-red, "integrated" loading ramp and the glass façade of the Rijn Foyer from the south. This page: Views. The façade is faced with overlapping red cement fiber panels. The use of typeface by the architects is a direct reference to the design of the Café De Unie by J. J. P. Oud. The anamorphoses of actors' portraits (planning/processing: Bolles + Wilson) on the white surfaces of the stage tower appear distorted except when approaching from the Erasmus Bridge

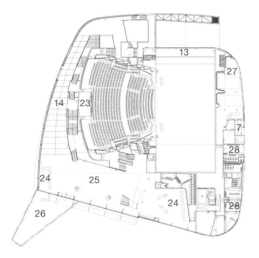

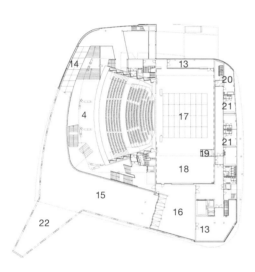

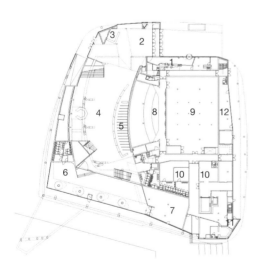

| | | | |
|---|---|---|---|
| 1 | Ticket sales | 15 | Delivery ramp |
| 2 | Entrance | 16 | Delivery |
| 3 | Information | 17 | Stage |
| 4 | Entrance hall | 18 | Side stage |
| 5 | Cloaks | 19 | Piano lift |
| 6 | Restaurant | 20 | Hairdresser |
| 7 | Kitchen | 21 | Star dressing |
| 8 | Orchestra pit | 22 | Truck turning bridge |
| 9 | Under stage | 23 | Control room |
| 10 | Orchestra dressing | 24 | Bar |
| 11 | Stage door | 25 | Rijn Foyer |
| 12 | Shop | 26 | Terrace |
| 13 | Store | 27 | Green room (cafeteria) |
| 14 | Foyer ramp | 28 | Dressing |

Left page, left (from bottom to top): Entrance level, level +1, level +2. Right: Foyer ramp. This page: Entrance lobby below the audience seating area

Theater hall: The ceiling elements, which can be adjusted to achieve desired acoustic effects, were designed by Rotterdam artist Joep van Lieshout

# Berliner Bogen Office Building, Hamburg
## BRT Architekten, Bothe Richter Teherani, Hamburg

This building is distinctly different from conventional office buildings. The large, boldly designed form marks the point of transition from the water to the city at the end of a flood-control basin—like an artificial figure protecting against the forces of nature. The glass shell covers the arching steel supports to a height of thirty-six meters. The 1,200 workplaces inside are arranged on trapezoid-shaped surfaces with a combined floor space of 30,000 square meters, which extend like balconies into the cavity between the floor and the glass shell. The concept is that of a building-within-a-building. The office areas are arranged in rows inside the glass-enclosed hall. The spaces between the outer glass shell and the interior façade form a buffer zone between outside and inside, while also serving as a winter garden with windows that can be opened. This double shell creates an internal microclimate, providing for passive use of solar energy and natural ventilation of all rooms. This cuts annual building heating costs by roughly half.

**Project:** Office building with underground flood-control basin **Architects:** BRT Architekten, Bothe Richter Teherani, Hamburg **Staff:** Alexander Maul, Michael Horn, Ilga Nelles, Claus Wendel, Beatrice Grünzig, Marcus Pape, Marcus Sporer, Grischa Todt, Bashaar Wahab, Stephen Williams, Carla Wirtz, Arne Pauer, Amelie Lerch, Ulf Kerkemeier **Garden and landscape architects:** Landscape planning: Büro Weiler/Esser, Hamburg; atrium design: H. O. Dieter Schoppe, Hamburg **Engineers:** Structural planning: Dr. Ing. Binnewies, Hamburg; technical controlling: Ridder Meyn Nuckel, Norderstedt; façade consulting: PBI Planungsbüro für Ingenieurleistungen GmbH, Wertingen; energy consulting, architectural physics, noise insulation: DS-Plan, Stuttgart; building engineering planning: RP + K Sozietät, Berlin **Client:** Becken Investitionen + Vermögensverwaltung, Hamburg **Dimensions:** Total floor space: 57,800 m² (43,000 m² above ground, 14,800 m² underground); primary usable space: 32,000 m²
**Location:** Anckelmannsplatz 1, Hamburg-Hammerbrook **Year of completion:** late 2001
**Photos:** Jörg Hempel, Aachen; Christoph Gebler, Hamburg

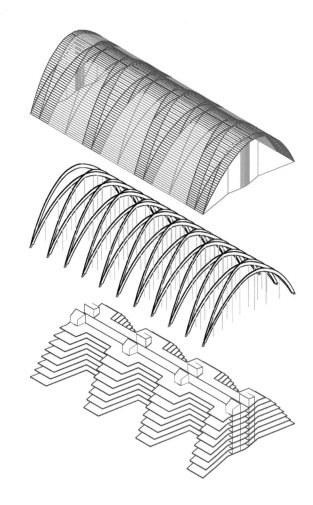

Left page: Isometric projection showing the building-within-a-building principle with ceilings suspended from the steel arches, winter gardens, and glass shell.
This page, top: Overall view

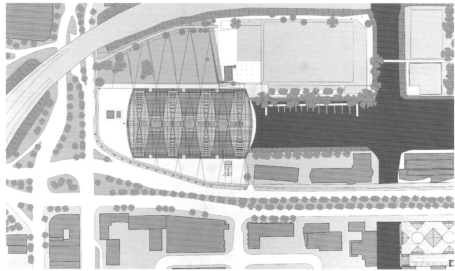

Top: The building seen from the canal. Below: Site plan. Right: The façade of the entrance side

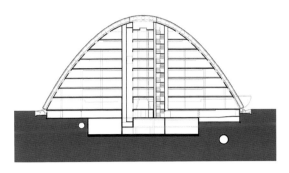

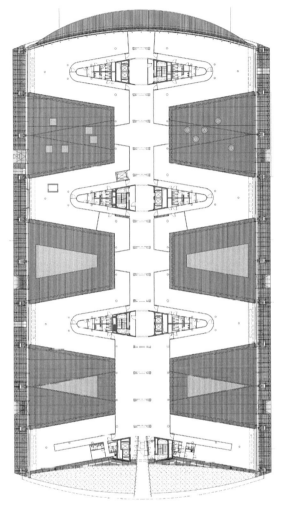

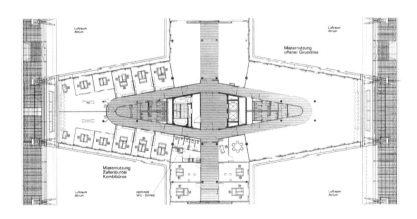

Left side: View into one of the winter gardens. This page, top: Section through one office tract. Below: Floor plan, ground floor.
Right: Floor plan of office tracts with access core

Left page: Top-hung windows provide access to the winter gardens for maintenance vehicles. The opening is flanked by bases of the arches.

This page: The main access axis of the building

# Elementary and Comprehensive School, Berlin-Hohenschönhausen
## Max Dudler Architekt, Berlin

In the 1990s, a group of Berlin architects voiced the opinion—in recollection of the *tendenza* of the seventies in Tessin—that objects of architecture should not only subordinate themselves to the urban context but should also generate cities as individual objects. This approach to design was considered an alternative to architecture which is hostile to cities. The basic idea for this school for some four hundred children involved the reconstruction of an old city wall. It was to solidify the city and its boundary at this location, where the urban periphery begins to fray. The stone conveys gravity and compactness which underscore the intent to create a clearly delineated city profile. The school shows two distinctly different sides. Toward the street, it presents itself in its full height and length; on the other side, the building blends into the landscape. The will to achieve grandeur is expressed in the interior spatial arrangement, in which seemingly endless glassed-in hallways form the structural backbone. Tracts with open and closed courtyards, containing classrooms, gymnasiums, and special-purpose rooms, complement the block along the back street.

**Project:** New elementary and comprehensive school building **Architect:** Max Dudler Architekt, Berlin **Staff:** Betti Plog, Heike Simon, Jörn Pötting, Sonja Glasberg, Jaqueline Schwarz **Garden and landscape architects:** SAL Planungsgruppe H. G. Schulten und Partner **Engineers:** Above-ground construction management: BAL Büro am Lützowplatz, Berlin; building utilities: Brendel-Ingenieure GmbH, Berlin; structural planning: Ingenieurbüro für Baustatik PCD, Berlin; acoustics: Ingenieurbüro Moll, Berlin **Client:** Hohenschönhausen District Office, Berlin **Dimensions:** Total floor space: 23,000 m² **Location:** Prendener Strasse/Falkenberger Chaussee, Berlin-Hohenschönhausen **Year of completion:** 1998
**Photos:** Stefan Müller, Berlin

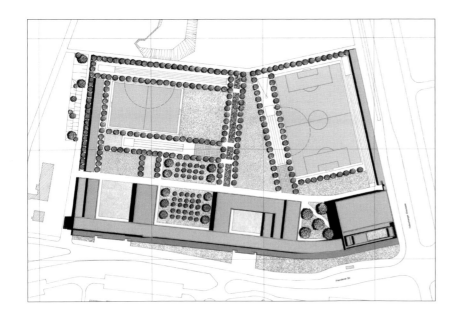

Bottom: Floor plan, 2nd floor. Very bottom: Floor plan, ground floor

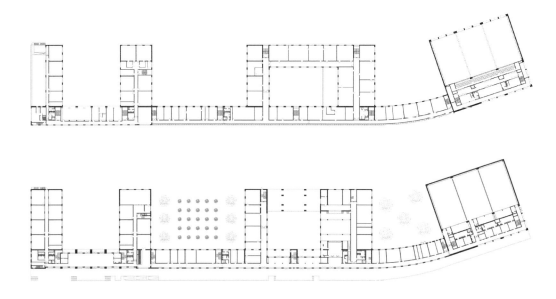

This page, left: Access hallways as glassed-in corridors. Right: Classroom

# Day-Care Center, Berlin-Karow
Höhne Architekten, Berlin
Stephan Höhne in collaboration with Christian Rapp

Buildings which serve important everyday functions (a public one in this case) offer a golden opportunity to depart from familiar architectural forms in order to highlight a specific utilitarian purpose. The day-care center has a strict geometric ground plan, but its vertical and horizontal spatial configurations are playfully intricate. Small, rather dark rooms and hallways alternate with brightly lit rooms bordering on playgrounds and large terraces. The stepped building profile may be seen as symbolizing a hill being ascended by children. Two stairways lead from the entrance along the façade to the upper floors, combining with the rooms in between to form a dense, compact building type. This, in turn, underscores the effects of the terraces and outdoor spaces as open, expansive fields of activity for the children.

**Project:** Day-care center **Architects:** Höhne Architekten, Berlin; Stephan Höhne in collaboration with Christian Rapp **Staff:** Peter Baumgärtner, Al Laufeld, Peter Eingärtner, Ullrich von Ey, Fawad Kazi **Garden and landscape architects:** Büro Kiefer, Berlin **Engineers:** Construction supervisor: Manfred Schurr, architect, Berlin; structural calcualtion: Ingenieurbüro Böske, Dülmen/Berlin; building engineering: PIN – Planende Ingenieure, Berlin; architectural physics: Dr. Ing. Manfred Flohrer, Berlin; sound insulation: BeSB GmbH Berlin, Schalltechnisches Büro **Client:** Weissensee of Berlin District Office, with official support from: Senatsverwaltung für Bauen, Wohnen und Verkehr **Dimensions:** Total floor space: 1,164 m²; usable space 740 m² **Location:** Münchehagenstrasse 43, Berlin-Karow **Year of completion:** 1998 **Photos:** Stefan Müller, Berlin

Garden façade with accessible rooftop terraces

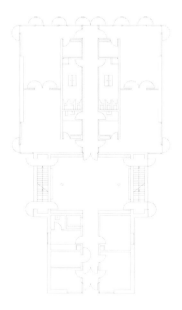
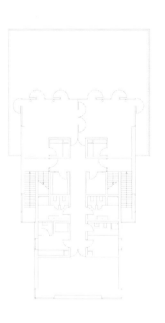
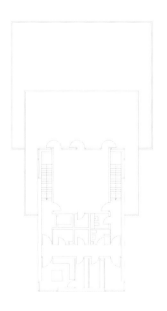

Left page, bottom (from left to right): Floor plan, ground floor; floor plan, 2nd floor; floor plan, 3rd floor.
This page: The entrance façade of the day-care center forms the southeast end of a long, park-like green area

Left page: View of the park and the surrounding buildings from the stairway.

This page, left: The central hall, with doors opening onto hallways which lead in different directions, where children can gather. Right: Group room

# RWE Tower, Essen
## Ingenhoven Overdiek and Partners, Düsseldorf

High-rise buildings make sense only where high building density is desired, since they are more expensive to build than ordinary buildings and burdened by many other disadvantages as well—high maintenance costs, problems associated with the complex façade, the loss of usable space to a large, unlighted building core, and the need for costly, complicated architectural and technical solutions for safety and fire prevention, to name only a few. The designers of this high-rise developed an innovative façade construction that does not eliminate the problems associated with this type of building but at least alleviates some of them. In addition to the standard glass façade, it also has another outer skin consisting only of a thin layer of glass. The glass is known as white glass; it does not reflect and has a non-material appearance. This dual-shell construction offers several advantages. The windows can be opened (casement windows in this case), and air circulating between the two façades is either diverted to the interior or removed. This air is either warmed or cooled by its surroundings, and the effect is a kind of natural air-conditioning system that can be regulated individually simply by opening or closing the windows.

**Project:** New headquarters building for RWE AG, Essen; international competition, 1991, 1st prize **Architects:** Ingenhoven Overdiek und Partner, Düsseldorf **Team architects:** Christoph Ingenhoven, Klaus Frankenheim, Achim Nagel, Klaus J. Osterburg, Arnd Gatermann, Peter Jan van Ouwerkerk, Martin Slawik, Roger Baumgarten, Sabine Begemann, Harald Benini, Claudia de Bruyn, Jan Dvorak, Michael Feist, Jürgen Gendrisch, Ulf Grosse, Imre Halmai, Uwe Jürgensen, Ulrich Kluth, Ingo Kraft, Martin Leffers, Jochen Müller, Wolfgang Nimptsch, Michael Paprotny, Frank Reineke, Martin Röhrig, Rudolf Rüssmann, Sakine Sahinbas, Norbert Siepmann, Elisabeth Vieira, Regina Wuff **Landscape planning:** Ingenhoven Overdiek und Partner, Düsseldorf, with Weber Klein Maas Landschaftsarchitekten, Meerbusch **Interior design:** Ingenhoven Overdiek und Partner, Düsseldorf **Engineers:** Structural framework planning: Hochtief AG, main offices, Rhein-Ruhr; Hoch- und Ingenieurbau, Essen; Buro Happold, Consulting Engineers Ltd., Bath/Düsseldorf; technical building equipment: HL-Technik AG, Consulting Engineers, Munich/Düsseldorf; IGK Ingenieurgemeinschaft Kruck, Mülheim an der Ruhr; Buro Happold, Consulting Engineers Ltd., Bath/Düsseldorf; architectural physics: Trümper & Overath Ingenieurgesellschaft für Bauphysik, Bergisch-Gladbach; façade planning: Josef Gartner & Co. Werkstätten für Stahl- und Metallkonstruktionen, Gundelfingen; wind tunnel testing: Institut für Industrieaerodynamik, Aachen; flow behavior report: HL-Technik AG, Consulting Engineers, Munich; lighting plans: HL-Technik AG Lichtplanung, Munich; fire safety: Department of Building Material Technology and Fire Safety, Bergische Universität Wuppertal; environmental engineering consulting: Geocontrol Umwelttechnische Beratung, Essen **Client:** Hochtief Projektentwicklung GmbH & Co, Essen **Dimensions:** Total floor space: 36,000 m²; usable space: 20,000 m² **Location:** Opernplatz 1, Essen **Year of completion:** 1997
**Photos:** Holger Knauf, Düsseldorf; Hans Georg Esch, Hennef **Illustration:** Peter Krämer, Düsseldorf

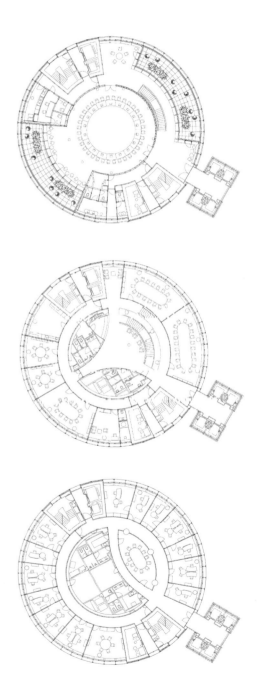

Left: Section view. Right (from top to bottom): Floor plans of conference room, conference level, normal level

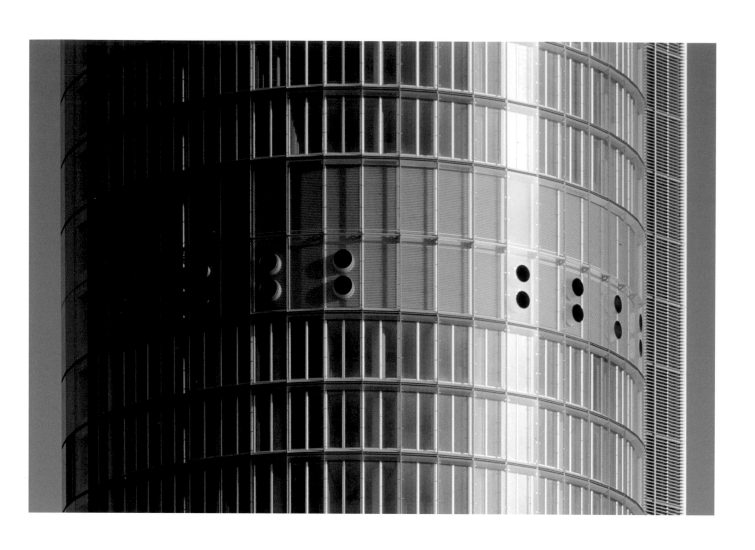

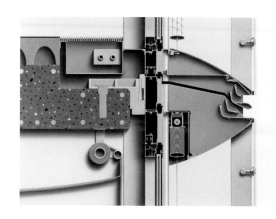

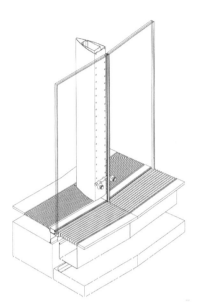 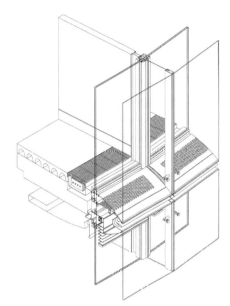 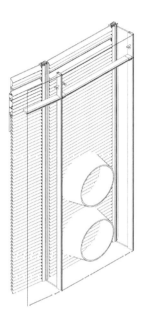

Left page, top: Façade detail showing the intake and exhaust vents of the utility level. Bottom: Detail of the double-shell façade with sheet-metal facing in the form of a fish's mouth. This page (from left to right): Isometric diagram of a ground-floor façade element, control hub, high-rise façade, utility level façade element

This page, left: Waiting area in the entrance lobby. Center: Elevator lobby on the ground floor. Right: Circular conference hall with glass dome

# Engelhardt Hof, Berlin
## Petra and Paul Kahlfeldt, Berlin

People have been migrating from Berlin—and most of the other cities of Europe—for decades. This trend is due in part to the evolution of telecommunications systems offering possibilities that make the city as a workplace only one among many options. One effect of this exodus from the city is sprawl—ceaseless development of the surrounding countryside—which raises the question of whether predominantly 19th-century urban structures can be modified and renewed in order to upgrade the city as a place to live and work. The old structures on the grounds of a former brewery were consolidated and connected through the addition of three new buildings, creating a specific configuration of outdoor space. A courtyard opens onto a street, forming a kind of bay off the roadway. The courtyard visitors enter through a narrow passage is about the same size but seems more self-enclosed and intimate. The arrangement of traditional spatial forms—rear courtyard and street—creates a modern ensemble that expresses an ambivalent relationship to surrounding urban space. The spatial concept for the offices and apartments meet the requirements of flexibility and convertibility imposed upon buildings today. Neutral with respect to function, anonymous, and formally lean, they embody architectural attributes that emphasize the urban hierarchy in the presence of the individual architectural object.

**Project:** Construction of a new apartment building and office building **Architects:** Petra and Paul Kahlfeldt, Berlin **Staff:** Anja Herold, Christoph Haag, Yves Minssart, Michael Fuchs, Jörn Pötting, Thomas Kälber, Conor Moran, Frauke Hellweg, Martin Oestlund **Garden and landscape architects:** TOPOS, Stefan Buddatsch, Berlin **Engineers:** Structural calculation: Ingenieurbüro Fink, Berlin; architectural physics: Ingenieurbüro Rahn, Berlin; lighting planning: Licht Kunst Licht, Berlin/Bonn **Client:** Brau und Brunnen AG, Berlin/Dortmund **Dimensions:** Total floor space: 6,501 m² excluding basement; usable space: 4,700 m² **Location:** Danckelmannstrasse 9, Berlin-Charlottenburg **Year of completion:** 1996 **Photos:** Stefan Müller, Berlin

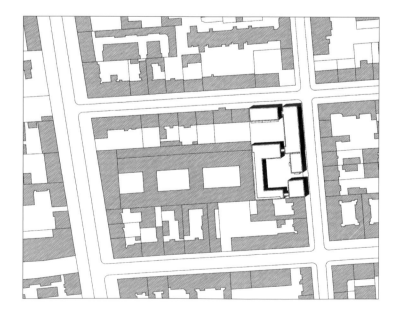

This page: Rear of the commercial building facing the apartment building courtyard. Left page: Site plan showing the square-shaped building and the two existing buildings along Danckelmannstrasse, which runs north to south, the U-shaped commercial building in the courtyard, and the apartment building facing Christstrasse

Left and center: The glass-and-steel façades on three sides of the front building lead from the street into the courtyard of the commercial building.
Right: Apartment building façade facing the street

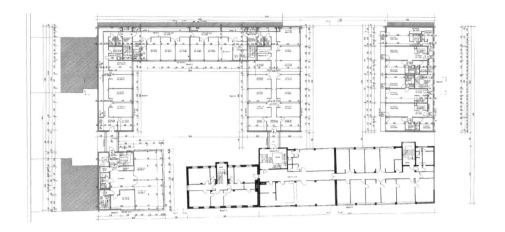

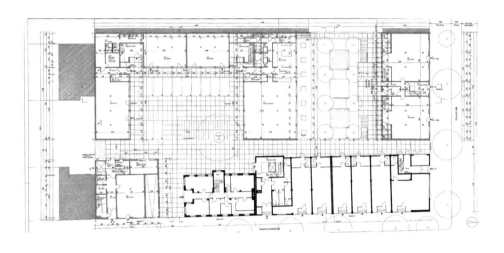

This page: Commercial building. Left page (from top to bottom): 2nd to 4th floor plan, ground floor plan, view from Danckelmannstrasse, view from Christstrasse

# DaimlerChrysler Building, Potsdamer Platz 1, Berlin
## Prof. Hans Kollhoff and Helga Timmermann, in collaboration with Jasper Jochimsen, Berlin

One current of architectural discourse in Berlin in the nineties was concerned with the relationship between urban development and architecture in our time. The debate, which was also waged internationally, soon focused in Berlin on the issue of the city profile. The design of this high-rise in the new Berlin Center responds to two iconographic motifs. As an architectural object, it reproduces the image of the brick building in the Expressionist tradition of the twenties as embodied, for example, in the Wilhelm-Marx-Haus in Düsseldorf, Fritz Höger's Chilehaus in Hamburg, and many American skyscrapers. The other motif relates to the urban landscape. On the other hand, the building is deformed, like a malleable mass, as a reciprocal image of the spatial hierarchy of street and square. The technical accessibility of modern and historical images has created a new architectural genre for the simulation of urban situations.

**Project:** Office and administrative building **Architects:** Prof. Hans Kollhoff and Helga Timmermann in collaboration with Jasper Jochimsen, Berlin **Staff:** Jens Winterhoff, Jan Burggraf, Daniel Schmid **Engineers:** Project management: Drees & Sommer, Stuttgart; structural calculation: Boll und Partner, Stuttgart; ARUP, Berlin; building engineering: Schmidt Reuter Partner, Stuttgart; ARUP, Berlin; electrical engineering: Ingenieur-büro Burrer, Ludwigsburg; elevator systems: Hundt & Partner, Berlin **Client:** DaimlerChrysler Immobilien GmbH **Dimensions:** Total floor space: 33,500 m²; usable space: 25,000 m² **Location:** Potsdamer Platz 1, Berlin **Year of completion:** 2000
**Photos:** Ivan Nemec, Frankfurt am Main/Berlin; Roland Halbe, Stuttgart

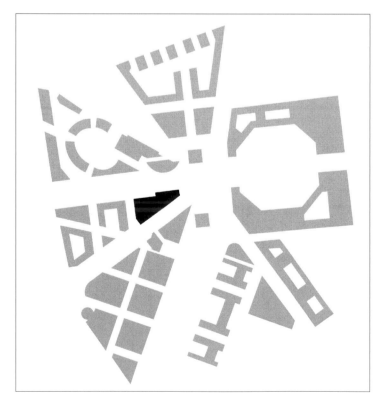

This page: Site plan. Right page: Façade along Alte Potsdamer Strasse; at the right-hand edge of the photo: the still-vacant site of Leipziger Platz

Top: Staggered building configuration. Bottom: Perspective drawings. Right page: Façade facing Potsdamer Platz

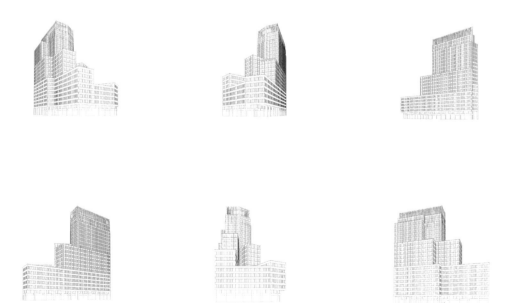

Top: Staggered building configuration. Bottom: Perspective drawings. Right page: Façade facing Potsdamer Platz

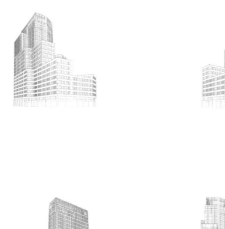

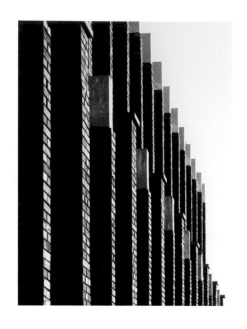
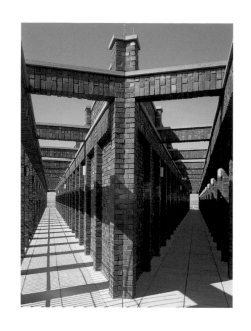

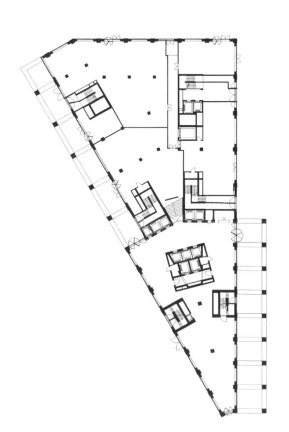
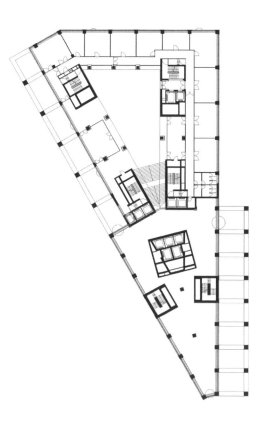
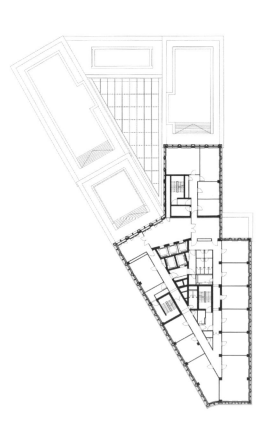

Left page, top left: On the upper levels, all façade elements emphasize the ascending vertical movement. Top right: Top of the building in the form of an accessible "crown." Bottom (from left to right): Floor plans of ground floor, 2nd floor, 14th floor. This page, left: View into the hall. Right: Foyer area

# Haus der Stille—Temporary Monastery, Meschede
## Peter Kulka with Konstantin Pichler, Cologne/Dresden

Efforts to restore religious character to church architecture have produced a current oriented toward sixties Minimal Art—insofar as that movement can be interpreted as an architectural style. The Haus der Stille (House of Stillness) presents a mute counterworld from which the superfluous and the loud are excluded in order to give expression to a sense of ascetic purity. Formal reduction and perfection, rough materials, exposed concrete, and bare walls evoke simplicity and form the background for a range of different lighting scenarios that unfold in the plain, unadorned rooms. Their shapes and openings make it possible to regulate and control incoming light. In some places the light enters from above—as one might expect in a religious setting; in others, it seems to have no direction and appears uniformly diffuse. The Haus der Stille comprises two dissimilar buildings: the long, enclosed staircase on which visitors move toward the light along a "walkable wall"; and the Seinshaus (House of Being), with its twenty cells used as living quarters. Different walkways and glass-covered bridges, which offer framed views of the surroundings, connect the two buildings.

**Project:** New guest house for the Benedictine abbey in Königsmünster **Architects:** Peter Kulka with Konstantin Pichler, Cologne/ Dresden **Staff:** Werner Gronmayer **Engineers:** Construction management: Hans Hennecke Architekt BDA, Meschede; structural calculation: Dipl.-Ing. Dieter Glöckner, Düsseldorf; building engineering: Zimmermann + Schrage, Düsseldorf; architectural physics: Graner + Partner, Bergisch-Gladbach **Client:** Benedictine Abbey, Königsmünster **Dimensions:** Total floor space: 1,941 m²; usable space: 1,053 m² **Location:** Klosterberg 11, Meschede **Year of completion:** 2001
**Photos:** Lukas Roth, Cologne

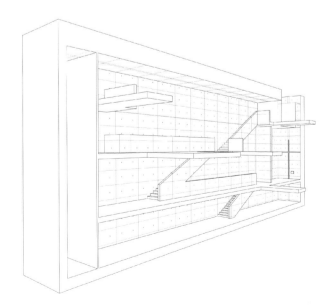

Left page: Sectional view of the "walkable wall" with the "Wayside Chapel."
This page: View uphill; in the background: Hans Schilling's Abbey Church, 1964

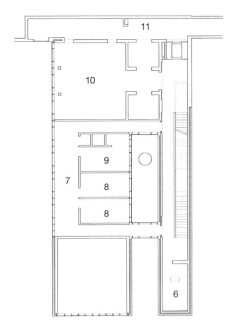
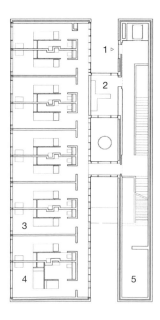

Entrance level
1  Entrance
2  Reception
3  Single guest room
4  Double room or room
   for disabled guests
5  Chapel air space

Level –1
6  Chapel
7  "Cloister"
8  Consultation room
9  Office
10 Refectory
11 Utility hallway

Left page, top: The three parts of the building (left: "Haus der Stille"; the large multi-purpose room opens toward the slope; center: "in-between space"; right: the windowless, "walkable wall"). This page, top: View of the west façade with the living cells on the two upper levels and the open, glass façade of the refectory and the "cloister" on level −1. Bottom: Sectional views of the "in-between space"

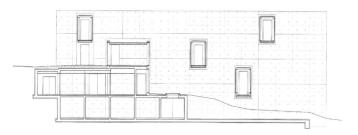

Left page: Indirect lighting from a light well in the upper southernmost corner of the "walkable wall." This page, left: The "Wayside Chapel" also receives light which is diverted through a shaft from the light well. Right: Cell; the opaque window panels can be opened

# School and Gymnasium in Scharnhauser Park, Ostfildern
## Lederer + Ragnarsdóttir + Oei, Stuttgart/Karlsruhe

The school complex—consisting of a main building, a gymnasium, and various outdoor facilities—is oriented toward the architectural configuration of the new housing development built on the grounds of a former military base.
The main building is divided along its entire length by a broad hallway illuminated by daylight from above. It provides access to classrooms on both sides and widens at one point to form an open common area. This corresponds to the concept of urban planning used in the interior: streets, squares, and buildings are interpreted as interior spaces. Although the school presents a rather monolithic outer face, a flowing spatial configuration develops inside, giving way to multistory sections and following the incline of the terrain in some places. The effect of a solemn, contemplative interior space is underscored by indirect lighting reflected by the walls. In the style of religious settings, the features and furnishings of the entire complex are also archaic—a broad landscape stairway and tower-shaped and hearth-shaped elements. The different overlapping references to architectural history give the school an aura of complexity comparable to buildings designed by Aldo Rossi or exponents of Tessin *tendenza*.

**Project:** Three-part elementary school, three-part middle school with vocational upper middle school wing and gymnasium **Architects:** Prof. Arno Lederer + Jórunn Ragnarsdóttir + Marc Oei, Stuttgart/Karlsruhe **Staff:** Alexander Mayer-Steudte, Judith Haas, Eva Caspar, Cornelia Hund, Ulrike Hautau, Marco Garcia-Barth, Pia Elser, Volker Hahn, Markus Horn, Tanja Pfahler, Annette Strauss, Daniel Trepte, Eva Wanner **Engineers:** Structural planning: Ingenieurbüro Müller + Müller, Ostfildern; heating, lighting, sanitary, and electrical planning: IG Wetzstein, Herrenberg; architectural physics consulting: Ingenieurbüro Schäcke + Bayer, Waiblingen; geology: Ingenieurbüro Vees, Leinfelden-Echterdingen; surveying: Ingenieurbüro Wagner, Ostfildern **Client:** Sanierungs- und Entwicklungsgesellschaft Ostfildern mbH **Dimensions:** Total floor space: 8,800 m²; usable space: 5,645 m² **Location:** Gerhard-Koch-Strasse 6, Ostfildern **Year of completion:** first phase: 1999; second phase: 2002 **Photos:** Roland Halbe, Stuttgart; Arno Lederer, Stuttgart

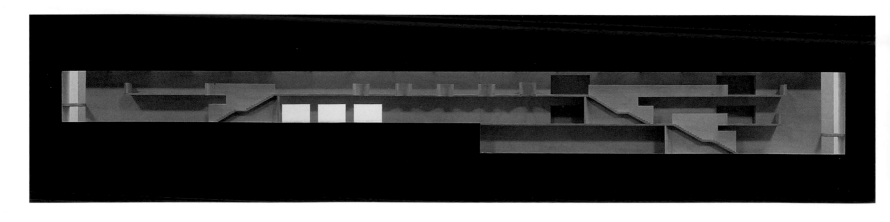

Left page: Sectional relief model of the school building, 1st phase of construction.
This page: View from the southwest toward the main school entrance, with the gymnasium in the background

This page: Exhaust chimneys for the gymnasium. Right page: Gymnasium entrance

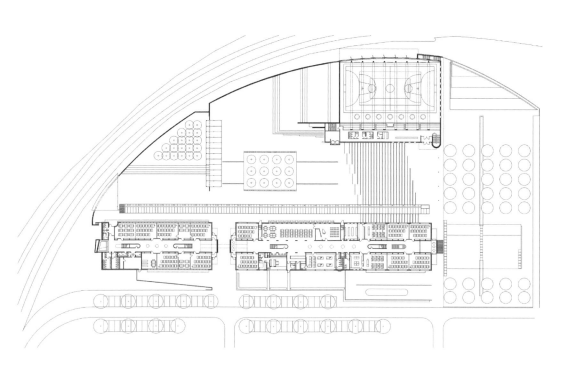

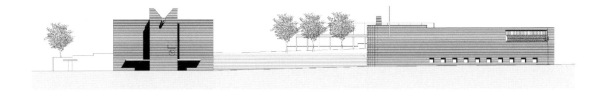

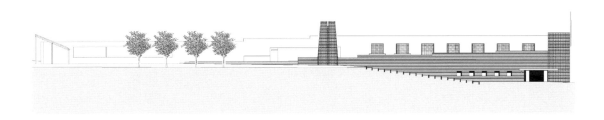

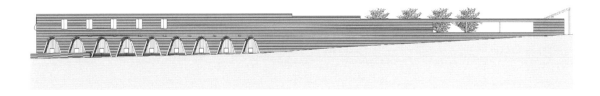

Left page, top: View of the school building from the east. Bottom: Floor plan for the central level of the school and the gymnasium. The curved end of the grounds is formed by the adjacent new streetcar line. This page (from top to bottom): South elevation of the school and the gymnasium; west elevation of the gymnasium; east elevation of the gymnasium

This page: South entrance lobby and classroom

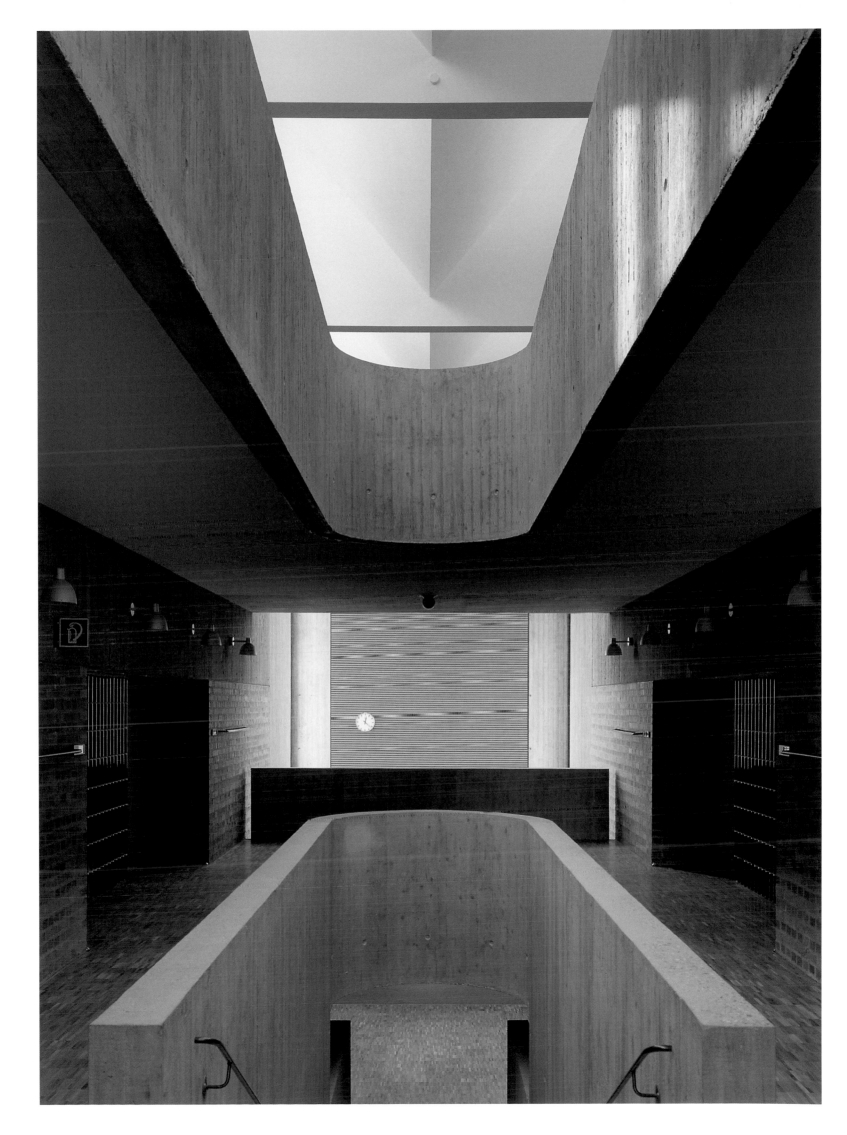

# Upper Vocational School for Social Insurance Education, Berlin-Köpenick

Léon Wohlhage Wernik Architekten, Berlin

In the age of telecommunication and the medialization of our everyday world, the representational functions of architecture have become less important, if not altogether obsolete. Symbols are increasingly becoming standardized codes with multiple, rapidly changing meanings. Architecture—as image and form at least—is hardly capable of symbolizing power relationships or social values like democracy and liberty without raising the suspicion that it has become symbolic kitsch. Any attempt to imbue architecture with more meaning than it has per se sacrifices not only style but other potentials of architecture as well. A neutral language is one of the aesthetic prerequisites of contemporary architecture. The school center embodies an appropriate presence next to the rugged Wilhelminian buildings by virtue of its mute, straightforward external appearance. Inside, however, it exhibits a spatial dynamism underscored by color. The high-ceilinged foyer draws the visitor's gaze toward a gallery and the upper floors, on which a meandering sequence of rooms characterizes the building's interior plasticity: a concept that calls to mind the spatial scheme (Raumplan) developed by Adolf Loos.

**Project:** Extension wing for a vocational school, with cafeteria, kitchen, library, administrative offices, double gymnasium, and department rooms
**Architects:** Léon Wohlhage Wernik Architekten GmbH, Berlin; Associate: Jochen Menzer **Staff:** Abdullah Motaleb, Katja Pfeiffer, Tobias Wenzel, Bettina Zalenga **Garden and landscape architects:** Weidleplan Consulting Berlin GmbH **Engineers:** Structural planning: König und Heunisch, Leipzig; project management: Schäfer Architekten und Ingenieure, Berlin; building utilities: Ridder & Meyn, Berlin **Client:** Berlin Municipal Senate, represented by the Senate Department of Building and Housing, section H VII A **Dimensions:** total floor space: 8,600 m²; usable space: 7,480 m²
**Location:** Nalepastrasse 201–209/Helmholtzstrasse 37, Berlin **Year of completion:** 1998
**Photos:** Roland Halbe, Stuttgart; Christian Richters, Münster; Konrad Wohlhage, Berlin

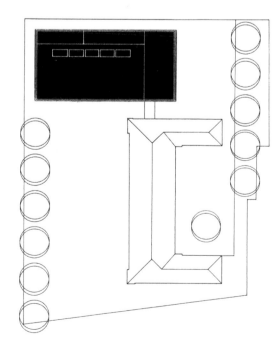

Left page: Site plan showing the old building erected in 1910 (architect: Ludwig Hoffmann) and the new wing connected to it by a glass-covered bridge.
This page: View from the east with main entrance

This page: View from the south, showing the ground-floor cafeteria and the gymnasium on the 3rd and 4th floors. Right page, top: View from the west

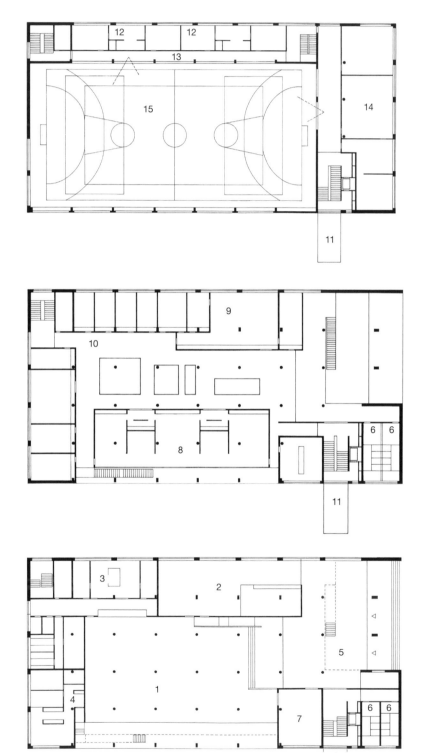

1 Cafeteria
2 Library
3 Kitchen
4 Building custodian's apartment
5 Entrance hall
6 Toilets
7 Students' common room
8 Teachers' room
9 Secretary's office
10 Administration
11 Connecting bridge
12 Dressing rooms
13 Gallery
14 Rooms for special subjects
15 Air space of gymnasium

Left page, left (from bottom to top): Floor plans of ground floor, 2nd floor, and 4th floor. Right: "Yearning Niches" by the Stuttgart artist Ulrike Böhme; right: window facing the gymnasium, left: monitor used to show videos produced by students, referred to by the artist as "Images of Yearning."
This page (from right to left): Conference room, cafeteria, gymnasium

# Senior Citizens' Housing Complex, Neuenbürg
## Mahler Günster Fuchs Architekten, Stuttgart

The small apartment complex for the elderly exemplifies "simplicity in building," a concept that has tradition in modern architecture, particularly in Germany. Simplicity denotes not only uncomplicated construction but an emphatic attention to everyday functions as well. The native Douglas fir used in the wood structure requires neither treatment (paint or varnish) nor maintenance. The innovative roof construction was built without expensive technical components. Industrial precut elements (polycarbonate panels) were used as a roof covering, which both protects and admits light, so that the energy collected by solar panels installed beneath the roof is supplemented by a greenhouse effect. This multifunctional construction is the basis for economically simple building. The most unique features of the conventional, unpretentious apartment complex are the broad walkways, which also serve as balconies and provide a setting for interaction and good neighborly relations.

**Project:** Senior citizens' housing complex **Architects:** Mahler Günster Fuchs Architekten, Stuttgart **Staff:** Heike Woller-Fuchs, Michael Peters, Karin Schmidt-Arnoldt **Engineers:** Structural planning: Ingenieurbüro Wolfgang Beck, Dennach; technical systems planning: Paul + Gampe + Partner GmbH, Esslingen; electrical systems planning: Arno Hohendorf, Heilbronn **Client:** Stadt Neuenbürg **Dimensions:** total floor space: 1,750 m²; living space: 1,340 m² **Location:** Enzring 56–62, Neuenbürg **Year of completion:** 1996
**Photos:** Christian Richters, Münster

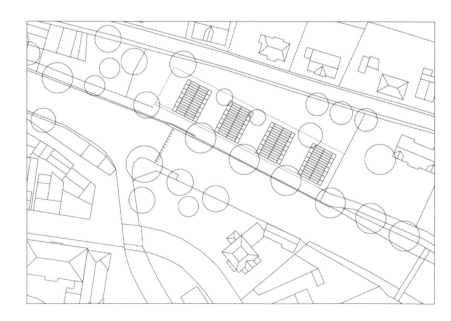

Left page: Site plan of the four individual buildings comprising the senior citizens' housing complex. This page: View from the west. The roofs are covered with transparent corrugated acrylic panels. Beneath them are the collector panels for the solar water heating and building heating support system

This page: Detail of the west façade with balconies. Right page: Detail of the south gable façade. The siding of untreated, planed Douglas fir boards is based on traditional regional principles of construction design

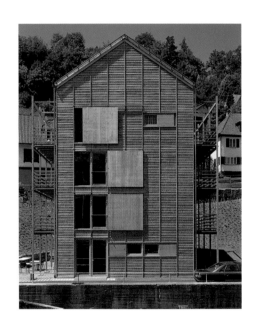

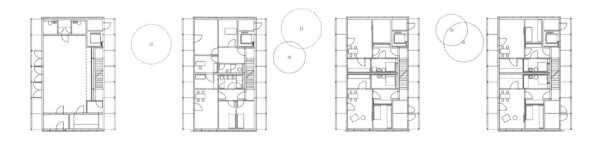

This page, top: Covered walkway and stairway on the east façade. Left page, below: Floor plan, ground floor.
This page, below: Floor plan, 2nd to 4th floors

   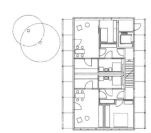

# Ochsenanger Housing Development, Bamberg
## Melchior Eckey Rommel Architekten AG, Stuttgart

Housing construction outside the cities was a focus of government policy in the U.S. during the Depression in the thirties. In part, the idea was born of the desire to promote increased consumption of cars and fuel and to raise household costs by establishing developments of single-family homes in rural areas. Today, this residential sprawl and the growing volume of commuter traffic it generates is reaching its own self-imposed limits, as European subsidy programs for more compact forms of housing developments clearly indicate. This small housing development in Ochsenanger is exemplary in the sense that, although it does not deny the dream of private home ownership, it realizes it with different, less elaborate means and a larger degree of building density. The concentration of parking lots outside the development reduces land consumption and eliminates the need for access roads. A central heating system, simple wood construction, and a modest allotment of living space are all part of the program of economical building, for which numerous outdoor areas typical of single-family homes—private gardens, front courtyards (with large storage spaces), and terraces offer welcome compensation.

**Project:** Economical housing development with private ownership and communal facilities; experimental housing project **Architects:** Melchior Eckey Rommel Architekten AG, Stuttgart; competition design: Ulrich Eckey, Marcus Rommel; project architect realization: Marcus Rommel; construction management: in collaboration with km⁺ Architekten, Bamberg **Staff:** Planning: Gudrun Ahrens, Frank Jörger, Ulrich Eckey **Landscape planning:** Melchior Eckey Rommel Architekten AG in collaboration with Brunken + Team, Stuttgart **Engineers:** Structural framework planning: Fischer + Friedrich Beratende Ingenieure, Stuttgart; heating, ventilation, and sanitary planning and architectural physics consulting: ebök Ingenieurbüro, Tübingen; electrical systems planning: Planungsbüro Pabst, Bamberg **Client:** Stadtbau GmbH Bamberg **Dimensions:** Total floor space: 4,105 m²; living space: 2,703 m² **Location:** Heinrich-Semlinger-Strasse/Ochsenanger, Bamberg **Year of completion:** 2000 **Photos:** Gerhard Hagen, Bamberg; Thomas Ott, Mühltal

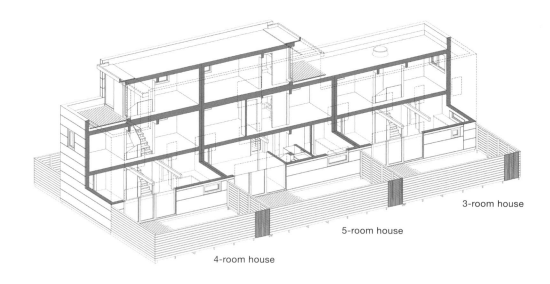

3-room house

5-room house

4-room house

Left page: Isometric diagram of a building in house group 1 in the northwestern part of the ensemble. This page: View of the green from the northwest

Left page: Entrance area: storage area (left) and courtyard perimeter (right).
This page, top: View of house group 1 from the southeast.
Bottom: Site plan of the three house groups comprising the low-energy development located on the green and near the Regnitz River

1 Garden
2 Terrace
3 Courtyard
4 Cooking/living/dining
5 Storage area
6 Living/dining
7 Kitchen
8 Rooftop terrace
9 Planted roof
10 Bicycle sheds
11 Trash storage area
12 Storage area

This page, top: Square in front of the community building. Bottom (from left to right): Floor plan of house group 1: ground floor, 2nd floor, 3rd floor.
Right page: The community building comprises the central heating plant, the building utility terminal room, a bicycle workshop or car-sharing space, a common room with kitchenette, two guest rooms, and a rooftop terrace

# Distribution Center, Bobingen
## Florian Nagler Architekten, Munich

Conventional purpose-built buildings often play a pioneering role in terms of construction design and the use of new industrial products. Such simple, cost-effective structures are then used for other types of buildings. In addition to this, the distribution center in Bobingen also exemplifies a theme of Classical Modernism: the question of the different forms and effects of transparent structures. The simple wood construction with its broadly spanned girders is covered with multilayered polycarbonate panels which achieve insulation values comparable to those of conventional glass façades. The individual panels are joined without visible seams using a tongue-and-groove system. The expansive use of this plain industrial product produces an architectural side effect in the form of an interesting translucency. The façade shell is neither transparent nor opaque, neither wall nor glass. People at work stacking boards behind the façade appear as blurred outlines and shadows. The same translucent effect is achieved from the inside out, but with a different light quality. The plastic material filters incoming light, softening it and thus creating a pleasant working atmosphere.

**Project:** Distribution center for composite wood panels **Architects:** Florian Nagler Architekten, Munich **Staff:** Stefan Lambertz, Matthias Müller, Barbara Köhler **Engineers:** Structural planning: merz kaufmann partner, Dornbirn, Austria **Client:** Kaufmann Holz AG **Dimensions:** Total floor space: 3,988 m²; usable space: 3,728 m² **Location:** Gutenbergstrasse 6, Bobingen **Year of completion:** 1999
**Photos:** Wolfram Janzer, Stuttgart

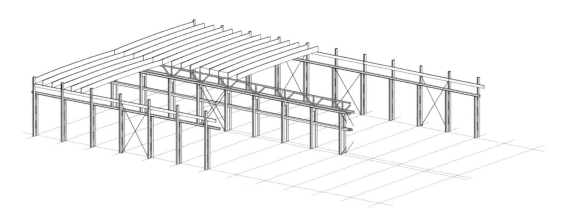

Left page: Three rows of thirteen double supports each comprise the structural framework of the two-aisled hall (total area: 46 x 76 m).
The upper half of the outer row of double supports bears the weight of the façade and the roof; the lower half serves as the mounting surface for the crane rail.
This page: Each of the six lift gates opens a passage six meters wide

This page: The translucent polycarbonate elements, the untreated yellow shutterboards of the guardrails and the doors, and the vertical double-T guide rails for the lift gates give the façade its structure, material quality, and coloration

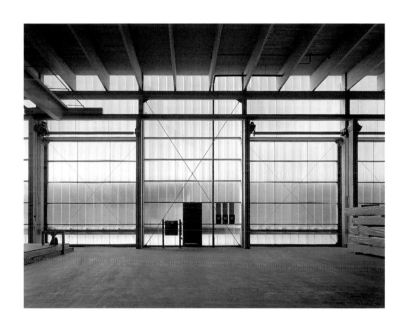

Slim, layered-board trusses, each 92 centimeters high and 12 centimeters thick, spaced two meters apart, form the main roof support system

# Saxon State Library—State and University Library, Dresden
Ortner & Ortner Baukunst, Berlin/Vienna

A prominent feature of our daily world is a seemingly endless flood of images, in which the boundaries between reality and media fiction are largely blurred. The process of distinguishing between what is and what one sees often requires so much interpretive work that people are increasingly unwilling to make the effort. Naturally, architectural images are also consumed within a context of altered visual and perceptual habits, and contemporary architects employ a variety of visual strategies. Some favor monumental optical solutions, while others tend toward hybrid images that present an open pattern for interpretation. There are two possible approaches to a reading of the library in Dresden. On the one hand, the configuration of aboveground and underground building structures, spatial sequences, and room arrangements correspond to the logic of functional organizational processes. On the other, the architectural image assumes a character of its own as a language of signs that are difficult to decipher. The non-standardized, bunker-shaped cubes are covered mosaic-style with stone panels that evoke a sculptural effect. A light-colored glaze gives the heavy material an almost transparent lightness. Thus the cubes seem familiar and strange at once. The irritating aspect of the unfamiliar is actually a deliberate allusion to bookshelves. The exaggerated motif of shelves appears to flicker in an endless series of stacks and rows.

**Project:** New building for the Saxon State Library – State and University Library **Architects:** Ortner & Ortner Baukunst, Berlin/Vienna; effective 1999: PLANUNGSARGE S. L. U. B.: ATP Achammer-Tritthart & Partner (CEO: Burkhard Junker)/Ortner & Ortner, Munich/Dresden **Staff:** Planning: Christian Lichtenwagner, Ekkehart Krainer, Ulrich Wedel, Rudi Finsterwalder, Michael Ewerhart, Michael Adlkofer, Hans Witschurke, Roland Duda, Robert Westphal, Michael Franke, Berit Grossmann; Construction management: Bernhard Eichinger, Thomas Grossmann, Thomas Heydenreich, Georgia Prätorius, Ralf Prätorius **Garden and landscape architects:** Burger + Tischer, Berlin **Engineers:** Structural planning: Gmeiner Haferl Tragwerksplanung KEG, Vienna; building engineering planning: Zibell Willner & Partner, Dresden **Client:** State of Saxony, represented by the State Construction Department, Dresden, managing director of construction: Matthias von Rüdiger **Dimensions:** Total floor space: 44,877 m²; usabale space: 30,140 m² **Location:** Zellescher Weg 18–20, Dresden **Year of completion:** 2002
**Photos:** Stefan Müller, Berlin

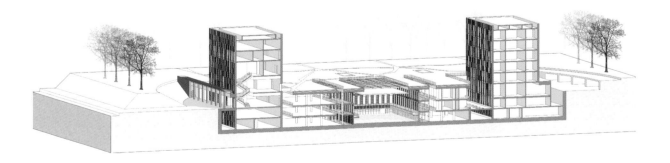

The two above-ground "stone cubes": The northern building contains primarily space intended for public use; the southern building is reserved for administrative offices

View over the glass roof of the reading room toward the northern "stone cube." Floor plans (from left to right): Level +1, Level 0, Level −1 and Level −2

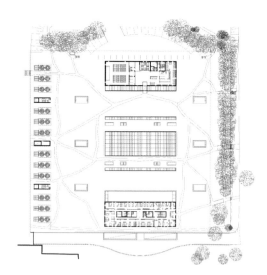

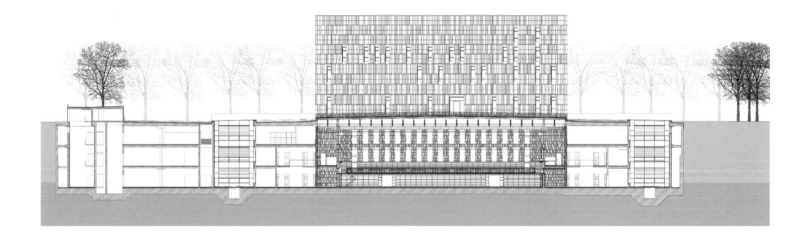

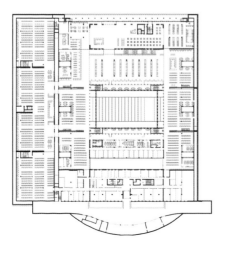
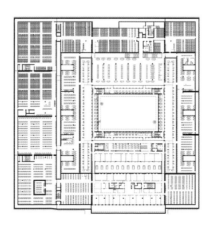
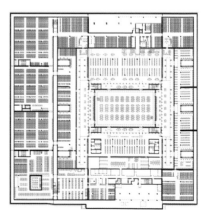

Ceilings, walls, and supporting columns in the library are covered with varnished acoustic MDF panels. This page: View from the gallery of the reference area through the reading room windows. Right page, left side: Gallery. Right side: Gallery of the reference area on the reading room level. Following double page: Reading room

# Halstenbek Sports Arena
## André Poitiers Architekten, Hamburg

The large-scale figure with its elliptical ground plan presents a contrast to the orthogonal geometries typical of buildings with similar broad-spanned supporting structures. There are no edges and no corners in this "soft space";  it seems to merge into an endless loop. This spatial impression is enhanced by a uniform concrete base that runs around the building. It forms the foundation and contains hollow spaces in which cloakrooms and utility rooms have been set up along with the forced-air heating ducts equipped with wide-range jets. Lowered to a depth of four meters below ground level, the building exploits the warmer underground temperatures, contributing significantly to a 50-percent reduction of total energy consumption. The glass roof that spans the arena like a skin is the product of a highly sophisticated architectural-engineering design. The glass-net dome must be able to withstand temperature fluctuations, high winds, and the weight of accumulating snow. The roof structure (with a crossed support system) consists of self-supporting, rod-shaped steel profiles. The tinted glass and an extendable horizontal sunshade system reduces glare to a minimum, and no artificial lighting is needed for sports events during the day.

**Project:** New sports arena building  **Architects:** André Poitiers Architekten (design and construction planning) **Staff:** Markus Röttger (Project Manager), Göran Meyer, Carsten Kiselowsky, Ulrich Engel, Sabine Eisfeld, Arnd Woelcke, Benjamin Holsten, Fabian Kremkus **Construction managment:** Rüdiger Franke, Hamburg **Garden and landscape architects:** WES Wehberg Eppinger Schmidtke, Hamburg **Engineers:** Structural planning: Schlaich, Bergermann und Partner, Stuttgart; building engineering: Berneburg und Partner, Hamburg; acoustics: Taubert und Ruhe, Halstenbek **Client:** Municipality of Halstenbek **Dimensions:** Total floor space 3,184 m²; playing surface: 2,300 m²; sports equipment storage area: 275 m² **Location:** Halstenbek **Year of completion:** 1998
**Photos:** Klemens Ortmeyer, Brunswick

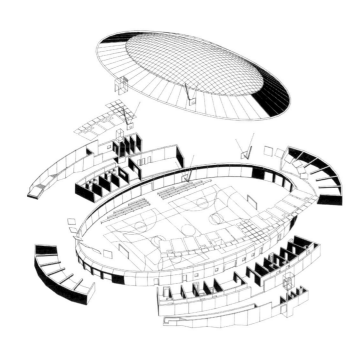

Left page: Exploded drawing.  This page: View inside the arena

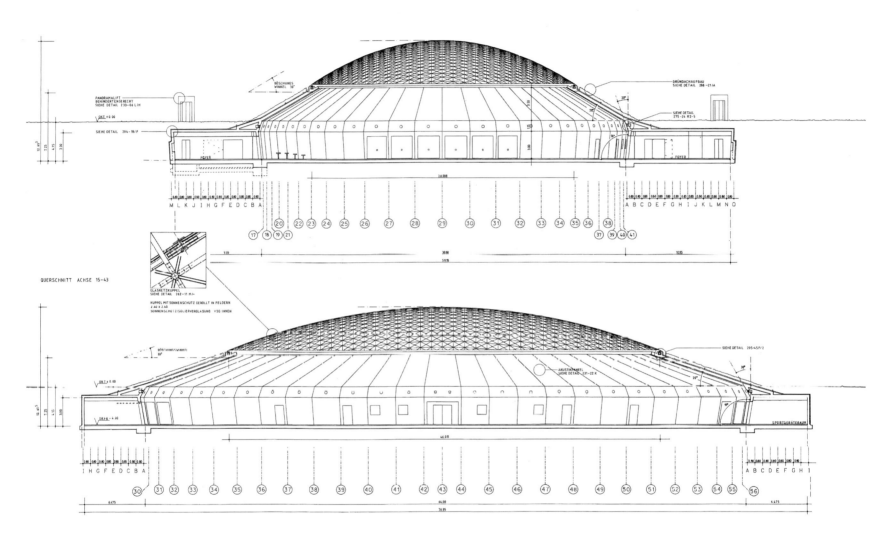

QUERSCHNITT ACHSE 15-43

GLASNETZKUPPEL
SIEHE DETAIL 262-11 H/-

KUPPEL MIT SONNENSCHUTZ GEWOLLT IN FELDERN
2.40 x 2.40
SONNENSCHUTZ/ISOLIERVERGLASUNG  VSG INNEN

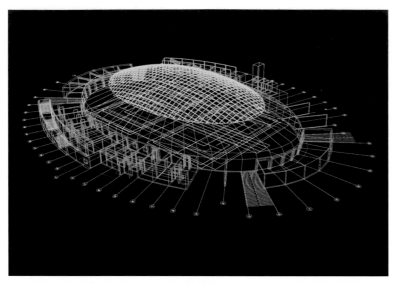

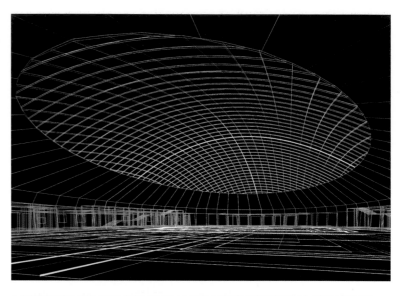

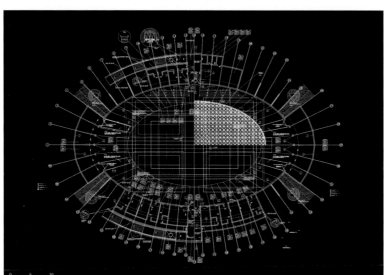

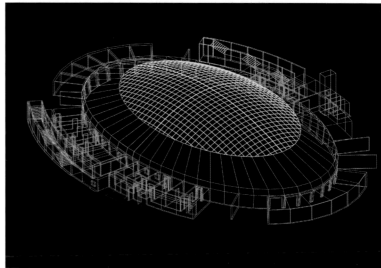

Left page: Cross section, longitudinal section.  This page: Interior and exterior perspectives, ground plan

# Printing Plant and Logistics Center, Röbel
## Carsten Roth Architekt (Logistics Center with Hampe Architekten, Ingenieure), Hamburg

Many industrial plants today offer working conditions that are hardly distinguishable from those of office complexes. This opens the way for the application of architectural principles and options previously unknown in industrial architecture. In this case, the architectural means employed resemble those of an urban ensemble. The entrance area welcomes visitors into a high-ceilinged room that gives way on the upper level to a covered arcade which corresponds to an unusual form of an atrium. This is followed by sequences of compact small and large rooms, of unexpected spatial expansions and large windows that offer a view of the poppy fields outside. The impression of interior urban architecture is underscored by the use of different materials, surface textures, and color designs. Viewed from the outside, the entire complex retains the appearance of an industrial facility. A second look shows, however, that it is also a translucent optical puzzle composed of an animated interplay of light and shadow generated by perforated metal plates.

**Project:** New building for a printing plant and a logistics center **Architects:** Printing plant and service center: Carsten Roth Architekt, Hamburg (design, detail and construction planning, construction site monitoring); logistics center: Carsten Roth Architekt, Hamburg (design, detail planning); Hampe Architekten Ingenieure, Hamburg (planning and construction site monitoring) **Staff:** Printing plant: Carsten Roth Architekt: Peter K. Becher, Juan Hidalgo, Uta Meins, Jens Merkel, Moritz Müller, Folker Paulat; logistics center: Carsten Roth Architekt: Christine Andreae, Peter K. Becher, Juan Hidalgo, Julian Hillenkamp, Uta Meins, Katja Ossmann; Hampe Architekten Ingenieure: Michel Fritsche, Siegfried Gillen, Britta Hampe, Michael Hampe, Volkmar Herrmann, Joachim Janssen, Heide Kaupp **Engineers:** Printing plant: structural planning: Ingenieurbüro für Baustatik Günter Timm, Hamburg; building utilities: RCI-Konzepte für Energie und Umwelt, Berlin; lighting technology: Lichtkontor, Hamburg; logistics center: structural planning: Werner + Wormuth und Partner, Wedel; building utilities: Klett Ingenieur GmbH, Fellbach; lighting technology: Lichtkontor, Hamburg **Client:** Optimal Media Production, Röbel **Dimensions:** Total floor space, printing plant: 5,314 m²; total floor space, logistics center: 13,140 m² **Location:** Glienholzweg 7, Röbel **Year of completion:** Printing plant: 1998; logistics center: 1999 **Photos:** Klaus Frahm, Börnsen

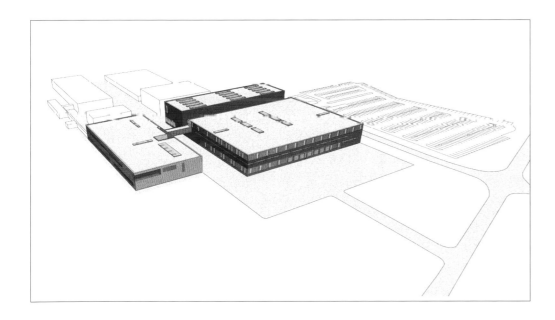

Left page: Perspective view of the entire site with printing plant (left) and logistics center (right). This page: Façade of the printing plant

View of the printing plant from the south. Right page: Glass-covered bridge connecting the printing plant and the logistics center

Left page: View of the logistics center building with main entrance. This page, left: Entrance stairway to the logistics center. Right: Detail of the printing plant façade, showing profiled aluminum sheet facing

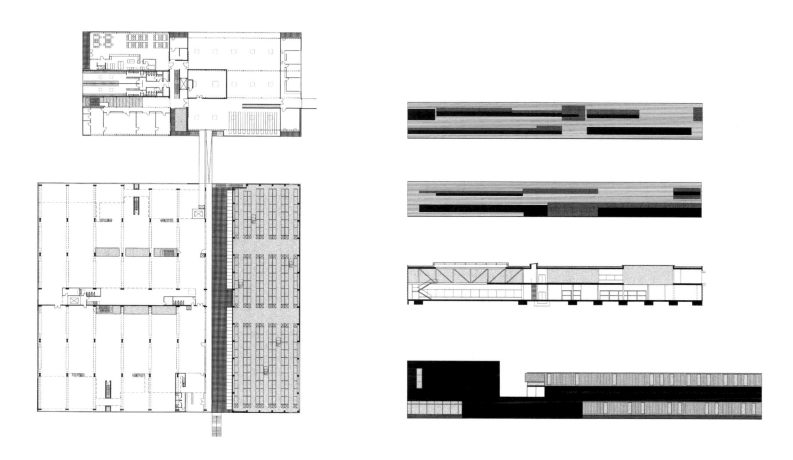

Left: Floor plan, 2nd floor of the logistics center (bottom) and the printing plant (top). Right (from top to bottom): Views of the printing plant from the north and south, longitudinal section of the printing plant, view of the logistics center from the north

Hallway on the 2nd floor, with free-standing frame construction supports and a view into the printing plant

# Federal Agency for the Environment, Dessau
## sauerbruch hutton architekten, Berlin

Environmental problems and the continuing drain on resources are attributable only in small measure to architectural aspects, building deficiencies, or obsolete building methods. Yet a kind of ecological architecture has established itself nevertheless. This approach to building involves the use of simple, proven technologies designed to exploit solar energy and other resources passively. Concepts of landscape gardening are also combined with architectural typologies to produce organic forms in most cases. The Federal Agency for the Environment building is a large, flowing figure with a colorful design that takes shape as an element of landscape architecture. The green area invades the loop-shaped inner courtyard, and the building itself appears as an integral part of the park landscape. A lake used to regulate the microclimate, native plants, a natural ventilation system, and a combined heat and power generating system are all part of the environmental standard embodied in the building complex. In its center is an atrium, which is connected to all of the departments within the agency. The offices are arranged along a central hallway which also gives access to common areas.

**Project:** Construction of a new office building with a public auditorium, library, and cafeteria **Architects:** sauerbruch hutton architekten, Berlin **Staff:** Project management: Juan Lucas Young, Andrew Kiel, René Lotz; project team: Nicole Berganski, Andrea Frensch, Frauke Gerstenberg, Rasmus Jörgensen, Mareike Lamm, Jan Läufer, David Wegener, Denise Dih, Matthias Fuchs, Andreas Herschel, Jan Liesegang, Ian McMillan, Konrad Opitz, Jakob Schemel **Garden and landscape architects:** ST raum a, Berlin **Engineers:** Contracting and property monitoring: Harms & Partner, Hanover; structural planning: Krebs & Kiefer, Berlin; technical building equipment, ventilation, heating: Zibell Willner & Partner, Cologne; technical building equipment, electrical systems: Ingenieurbüro Lehr, Dessau; technical building equipment, sanitary facilities: ITAD, Ingenieurgesellschaft für technische Ausrüstung m. b. H. Dessau; thermal building physics: Müller BBM, Berlin; Federal Energy Commissioner: IEMB Institut für Erhaltung und Modernisierung von Bauwerken e. V., TU Berlin; environmental building consulting: GFÖB Berlin mbH; building site report, foundation consulting and remediation: G. U. T., Merseburg; noise insulation and acoustics: Diete & Partner GbR, Bitterfeld; fire safety consulting and smoke exhaust simulation: Forschungsstelle für Brandschutztechnik, Karlsruhe; Hosser, Hass + Partner and the Institute of the Fire Department, Saxony-Anhalt, Heyrothsberge **Client:** Federal Republic of Germany, represented by the Federal Ministery of Finance, the Federal Ministry for the Environment, Nature Conservation, and Nuclear Safety, the Federal Ministry of Transportation, Building, and Housing, the Federal Bureau of Finance, Magdeburg, and the Municipal Construction Department, Dessau, of the Federal Bureau of Finance, Magdeburg **Dimensions:** Total floor space 40,000 m²; usable space 23,000 m² **Location:** Dessau **Year of completion:** 2004 **Photos:** Bitter + Bredt Fotografie, Berlin

Right page: Construction of planned façade: wood panel construction, cellulose insulation, wood facing of local larch, colored glass panels in the window bands

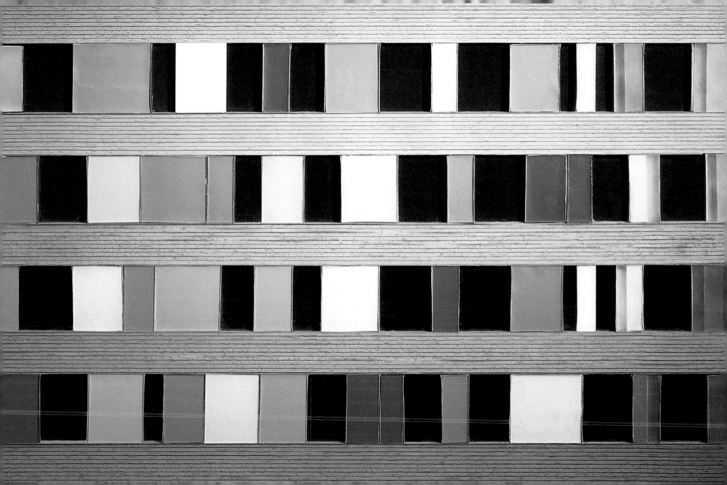

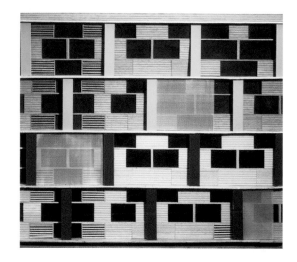
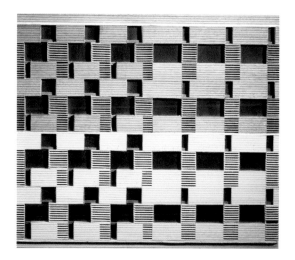

Façade studies during project development

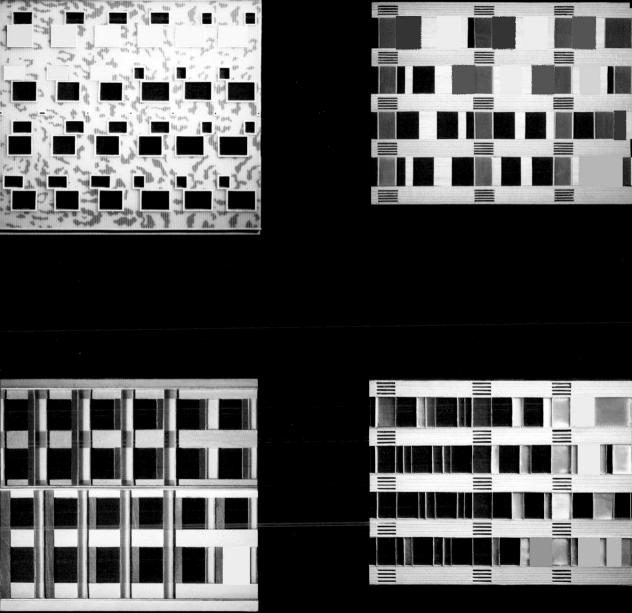

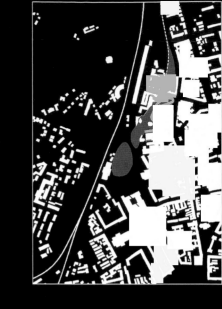

This page (from upper left): Atrium, park and main entrance, forum

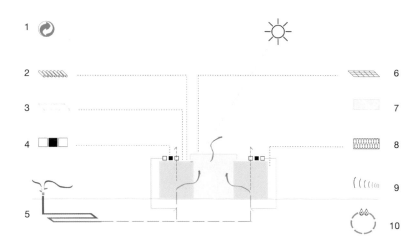

Energy and environmental concept

1 Use of ecological building materials (such as wood façade, cellulose insulation, loam interior walls)
2 Vacuum tube solar collectors, solar-aided cooling system
3 Planted roof and atrium
4 Heat recovery 74%
5 Geothermal heat pumps: system length = 5 kilometers
6 Photovoltaics
7 Optimal use of daylight through narrow building ground plan and daylight diversion; office lighting intensity dependent on daylight and occupancy
8 Achieved values 51% below minimum heat conservation levels specified in the 1995 Heat Conservation Directive, minimized transmission heat loss due to compact building form
9 Flexible exhaust system prevents noise pollution from external noise sources
10 District heating (landfill gas)

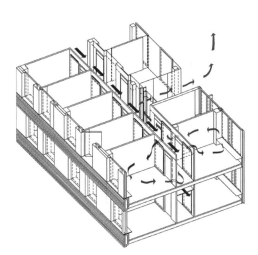

Ventilation during summer/daytime

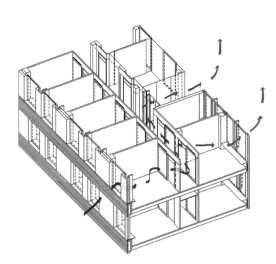

Natural cooling during summer/nighttime

Right page, top: Longitudinal section and section through the library. Center: Cross section through the cafeteria, the auditorium, and the public forum. Bottom: Ground floor plan

1 Auditorium
2 Cafeteria
3 Public forum
4 Atrium
5 Library
6 Wörlitzer Station
7 Main entrance
8 Caretaker's room
9 "Rocks" (warehouse and repro department)
10 Intake pipes for geothermal heat pump
11 Underground garage entrance/exit
12 Park
13 Pond

# Baumschulenweg Crematorium, Berlin
## Axel Schultes and Charlotte Frank, Berlin

As media influences and digitization make our world seem increasingly artificial, longing for authentic, immediate experience grows stronger as well. This yearning can also be seen as an urge to compensate for a world without enchantment. The design for the new crematorium seeks to evoke an authentic, mystical experience of life and death through architectural means developed in classical antiquity and Classical Modernism. The most prominent feature is a sequence of large and small spaces that communicate a sense of openness or enclosure, respectively. Their atmospheric quality is generated by measured lighting. Geometric configurations and the lack of a sense of scale, both traditional features of monumental architecture, play an important role in this context. The columned hall, with its twenty-nine pillars, "light capitals," and starlike ceiling spotlights symbolizes the universe—timelessness, heaven and earth—in the style of Roman temple architecture. These elements, combined with other motifs, including several Egyptian ones, gives this contemplative setting a ritualistic quality. All technical equipment is installed out of sight in the basement.

**Project:** New crematorium building **Architects:** Axel Schultes Architekten Frank Schultes Witt, Berlin; design: Axel Schultes, Charlotte Frank; project management: Margret Kister, Christoph Witt **Staff:** Daniela Andresen, Bob Choeff, Patrick Dierks, Christian Helfrich, Andreas Schuldes, Till Waninger **Outdoor areas:** Hannelore Kossel; Roads and Parks Office, Berlin-Treptow **Engineer:** Project management: Bonner Ingenieurge-meinschaft Bonn/Berlin, Dipl.-Ing. Volker Warnat; structural planning: GSE Saar Enseleit und Partner, Berlin; IDL, Berlin; building engineering: Brandi Ingenieure, Leinfelden; architectural physics: Dr.-Ing. Manfred Flohrer, Berlin; acoustics: Akustik Ingenieurbüro Moll GmbH, Berlin; construction: Bilfinger + Berger Bauaktiengesellschaft, general contractor, Berlin **Client:** Lessee: District Office, Berlin-Treptow; Lessor: DEGECIVO Grundstücksverwaltungsgesellschaft mbH, Eschborn **Dimensions:** Total lot size 9,339 m² **Location:** Kiefholzstrasse 222, Berlin **Photos:** Reinhard Görner, Berlin; Werner Huthmacher, Berlin; Ulrich Schwarz, Berlin

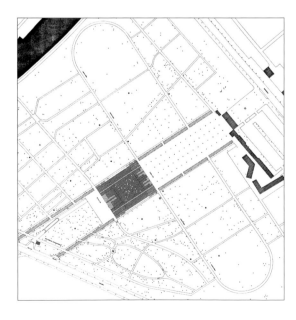

Left page: View into a front courtyard with an open stairway. This page, left: Front courtyard with a view into the Hall of Condolence. Right: View from outside into one of the two small funeral halls. Following double page: The Hall of Condolence, with twenty-nine round columns and the "light capitals"

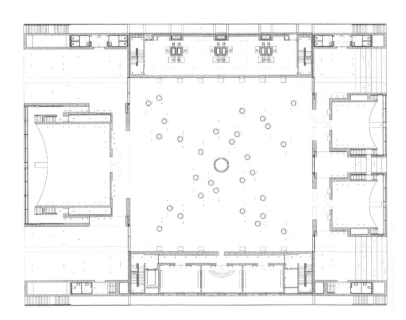

Left page, top: View into the small funeral hall. Bottom: Floor plan, ground floor. This page: The circular font, flush with the floor, and an egg-shaped form suspended above it are heathen symbols of return

# Haus R 128, Stuttgart
## Werner Sobek, Stuttgart

The unconventional, experimental aspect of this house stems from the use of brand-new materials, structural components, and high-tech electronics. In addition to the passive technologies now in widespread use elsewhere, active control elements and energy systems were employed in an effort to probe the boundaries of the possible. The form of the house itself is already an ambitious experiment. The one-room building has glass walls on all sides and appears spatially permeable from a vertical perspective as well. This hyper-transparency evokes the impression that people living in this house are more outside than inside. Computer-controlled, voice-controlled, and sensor technologies regulate all energy flows and the room climate. The refrigerator door even opens automatically; water faucets and the artificial lighting are regulated by sensors. What is more, the complicated technical system contributes to a reduction of energy consumption that makes it unnecessary to import energy from outside sources into this unusual house.

**Project:** Zero-emission, zero-energy house **Architect:** Werner Sobek, Stuttgart **Staff:** Zheng Fei, Robert Brixner, Ingo Weiss **Engineers:** Energy planning: Transsolar Energietechnik, Stuttgart; heating, ventilation, and sanitary planning and hydraulic systems: Ing.-Büro Müller, Weissach; control technology: Baumgartner, Kippenheim; steel structure and façade: SE Stahltechnik Vertriebs GmbH, Stammham; sensor technology: Jochen Köhnlein Gebäudeautomation, Albstadt **Client:** Ursula and Werner Sobek **Dimensions:** Total floor space: 320 m²; usable space: 250 m²
**Location:** Stuttgart **Year of completion:** 2000
**Fotos:** Roland Halbe, Stuttgart

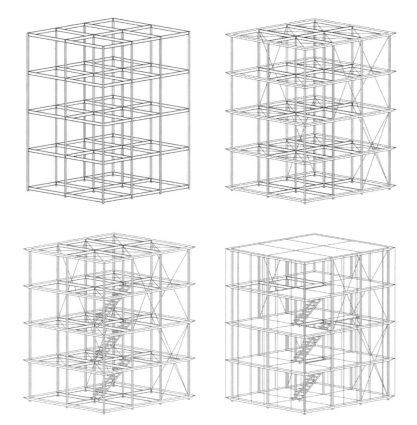

This page: The high-precision pre-fabricated framework structure was erected in four days, and tolerance compensation measures were not necessary. Right page: Residents access the entrance on the upper floor by way of a bridge (on the right in the photo) which connects the building and the sloping grounds

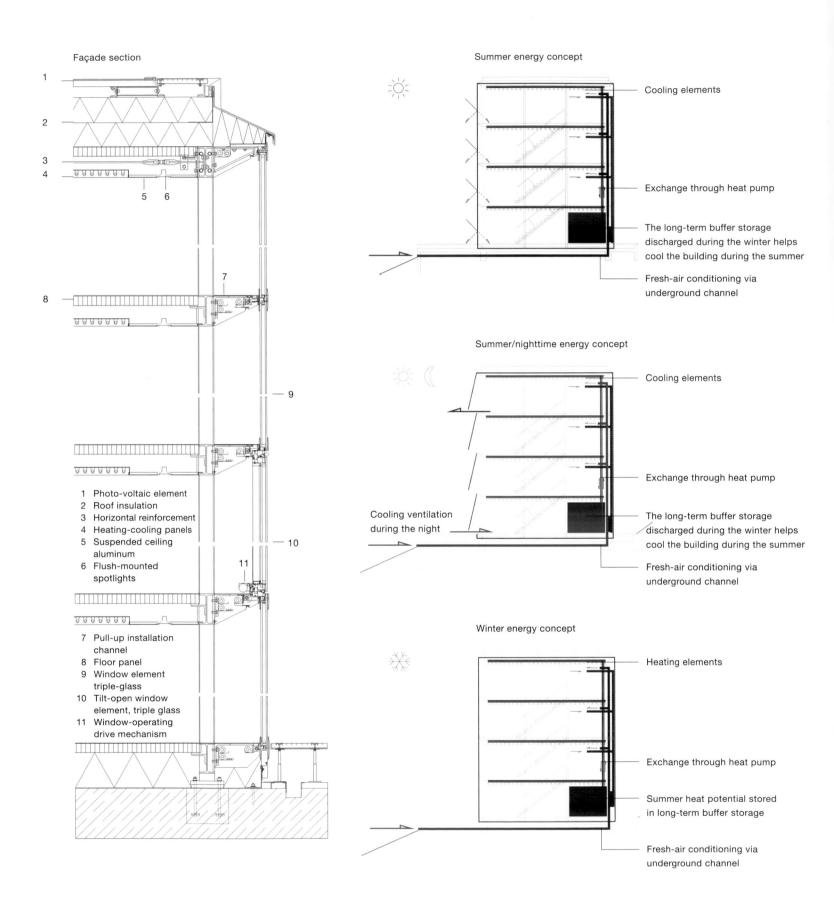

Façade section

1
2
3
4
    5   6

7

8

9

1   Photo-voltaic element
2   Roof insulation
3   Horizontal reinforcement
4   Heating-cooling panels
5   Suspended ceiling
    aluminum
6   Flush-mounted
    spotlights

10

11

7   Pull-up installation
    channel
8   Floor panel
9   Window element
    triple-glass
10  Tilt-open window
    element, triple glass
11  Window-operating
    drive mechanism

Summer energy concept

Cooling elements

Exchange through heat pump

The long-term buffer storage
discharged during the winter helps
cool the building during the summer

Fresh-air conditioning via
underground channel

Summer/nighttime energy concept

Cooling elements

Exchange through heat pump

Cooling ventilation
during the night

The long-term buffer storage
discharged during the winter helps
cool the building during the summer

Fresh-air conditioning via
underground channel

Winter energy concept

Heating elements

Exchange through heat pump

Summer heat potential stored
in long-term buffer storage

Fresh-air conditioning via
underground channel

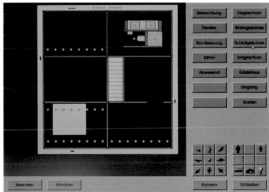

This page (from top left to bottom right): Sanitary core on the 3rd floor, kitchen block, utility area on the ground floor, building control software on a touch screen

This page: 3rd floor: Visible on the left are the bathtub, which is mobile and can be connected to the flexible installation system, and the ceiling elements with built-in heating-cooling registers. In the background is the sanitary core, and on the right the cupboard. Right page: Living and dining-room area on the upper floors

View from the playground toward the housing complex; in the middle: the community building. Left page: Isometric diagram of tho entire complex

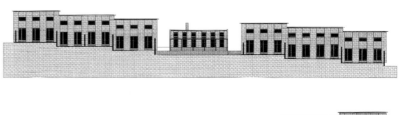

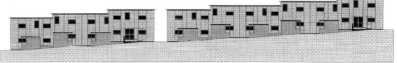

Left: Footpath through the development. Top: View into the private gardens. Bottom: Views show the grade of the complex

Top: Front door and steps to a housing unit. Bottom: The floor plans on the left show the minimum and maximum possible room configurations on the ground floor. Right: Ground plan of a building with four apartments (top: ground floor, bottom: 2nd floor). Right page: View from front door into the living room

# New Synagogue, Dresden
## Wandel Hoefer Lorch + Hirsch, Saarbrücken/Frankfurt am Main

Recent years have witnessed an increasing reorientation toward early rituals and traditional symbols in religious architecture. The new synagogue in Dresden may be seen as analogous architecture, as it addresses the fundamental architectural experience of the Jewish people in temple and tent motifs. The contrast between the permanent and the provisional also belongs to this context. From the outside, the homogeneous building looks solid and compact, while it appears to dissolve into a fragile texture inside. As objective representation is not permitted, the bronze metallic material that spans the ceiling is decorated only with a single Star of David. The complex consists of the synagogue itself and the congregation center, separated by a courtyard. Due to the geometry of the lot, the necessary east-facing orientation of the synagogue was achieved by twisting the building on its axis. The separation of the two buildings characterizes the specific significance of each: the synagogue as a place of concentration and contemplation, and the congregation center with its glass north façade as an interface to the city and the public sphere.

**Project:** Construction of a new synagogue and congregation center **Architects:** Wandel Hoefer Lorch + Hirsch, Saarbrücken/Frankfurt am Main **Staff:** Kuno Fontaine, Christoph Kratzsch, Dirk Lang, Lukas Petrikoff, Tobias Wagner **Engineers:** Project management: PM Fischer, Leipzig; structural planning: Schweitzer Ingenieure, Saarbrücken/Dresden; building engineering: Zibell Willner & Partner, Dresden; acoustics and architectural physics: Müller BBM, Dresden **Client:** Jewish congregation of Dresden **Dimensions:** Total floor space: 2,706 m²; usable space 2,120 m² **Location:** Am Hasenberg 1, Dresden **Year of completion:** 2001 **Photos:** Roland Halbe, Stuttgart; Norbert Miguletz, Frankfurt am Main; Lukas Roth, Cologne

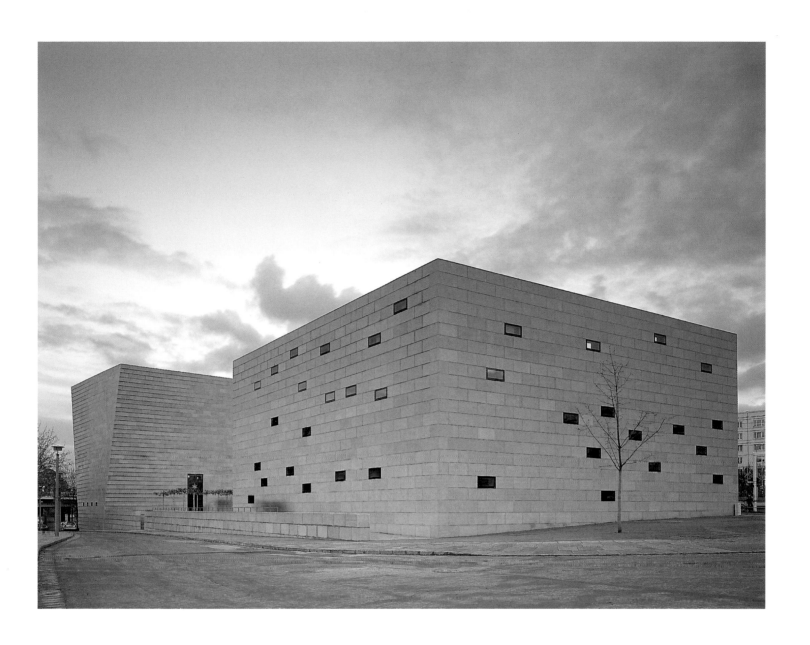

View from the southwest: The congregation center and the synagogue (in the background)

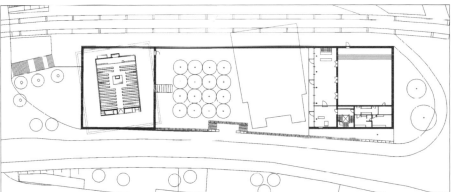

This page, bottom: Site plan with floor plan, ground floor. The site of the old synagogue designed by Gott-fried Semper and burned to the ground in the pogrom of November 9/10, 1938, is marked on the ground of the courtyard by an area covered with broken glass

This page: View of the Almemor (Torah reading stand), with the Aron Hakodesh (Torah shrine) in the background

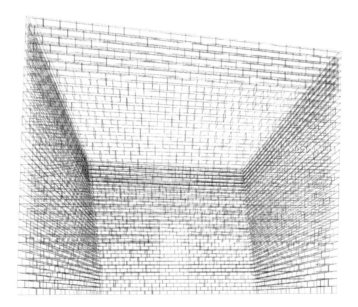

# European Youth Meeting and Education Center, Weimar
## Worschech Partner Architekten, Erfurt

The education center was built in a park on a steeply sloping hillside and consists of several different single buildings. The education center itself is housed in the old, renovated villas, while the living areas and seminar rooms are located in the four modern wooden structures. The arrangement of individual buildings as solitary pieces gives the park a look of spatial transparency. Paths and walkways through the complex provide numerous outlooks and panoramic views, making the park—in terms of its size and its own unique topography—a palpable presence at all times. Set upon free-standing supports, the narrow, elongated buildings appear to float above the slope, contributing to the impression of an ambivalent, non-hierarchical relationship between the park and the architecture.

**Project:** New building and reconstruction of existing buildings for the European Youth Meeting and Education Center, Weimar **Architects:** Worschech Partner Architekten, Erfurt **Staff:** Attila Zsoldos, Marcus Johansson, Mathias Kirchmeier **Garden and landscape architects:** Planungsbüro Wittig, Weimar **Engineers:** Structural planning: Staupendahl & Partner, Weimar; technical building equipment: EB Ebert-Ingenieure, Gera; Himmen Partner Ingenieurgesellschaft, Erfurt **Client:** Stiftung Europäische Jugendbildungs- und Jugendbegegnungsstätte Weimar **Dimensions:** Total floor space: 8,589 m²; usable space: 4,436 m² **Location:** Jenaer Strasse 2–4, Weimar **Year of completion:** 1999 **Photos:** Constantin Beyer, Weimar

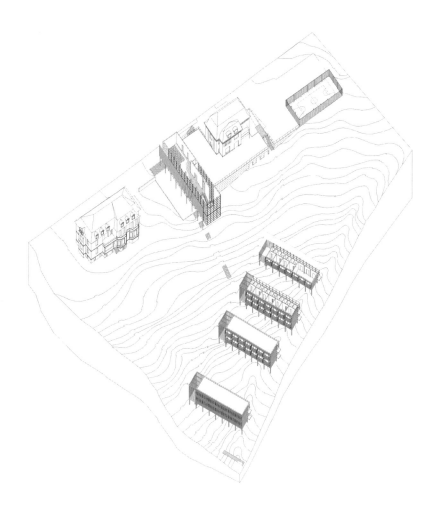

Left page: West façade of one of the four apartment buildings. This page, top: Cross section of grounds showing the western side of the ensemble. The administrative offices are located in the historical building on the left. Behind it is the new reception building, with the cafeteria and assembly hall. On the right are the four dormitory and seminar buildings. Below: Cross section of grounds showing the southern side of the dormitory and seminar buildings

This page: East façade of a dormitory and seminar building with an open stairway in the foreground. Right page: View from the reception building platform

# Neanderthal Museum of Human Evolution, Mettmann
## Zamp Kelp and Julius Krauss, Arno Brandlhuber

Museums, which since the eighties have once again become very popular cultural institutions, have to compete fiercely with one another to win the favor of visitors. Accordingly, a specific type of museum architecture has developed in the course of the past twenty years. Its ambition to attract attention is reflected in the fact that no single museum resembles another. Today, museums are being designed as unique architectural objects and as labels that also advertise for specific cities or regions. The Neanderthal Museum derives its unmistakable form from a seemingly endless spiral that runs through the entire museum. The stairways and technical equipment are concentrated in a huge, long, narrow building core made of concrete, to which the ceilings are also attached, so that supports are not needed. This, in turn, allows for the curving form of the façade, which consists of frameless glass profiles that filter the light in such a way that only soft light falls into the exhibition areas.

**Project:** Museum, exhibition building, and education center **Architects:** Günter Zamp Kelp and Julius Krauss, Arno Brandlhuber **Staff:** Thomas Gutt, Carlos Martin Gonzales, Astrid Becker, Götz Leimkühler, Marco Glashagen **Interior design:** Creamuse, Strasbourg **Engineers:** Structure: Hochtief, Essen; building engineering: Bahlmann Ingenieure, Mettmann **Client:** Stiftung Neanderthal Museum **Dimensions:** Total floor space: 3,600 m²; usable space: 2,400 m² **Location:** Talstrasse 300, Mettmann **Year of completion:** 1996
**Photos:** Peter Lippsmeier, Bochum; Michael Reisch, Düsseldorf

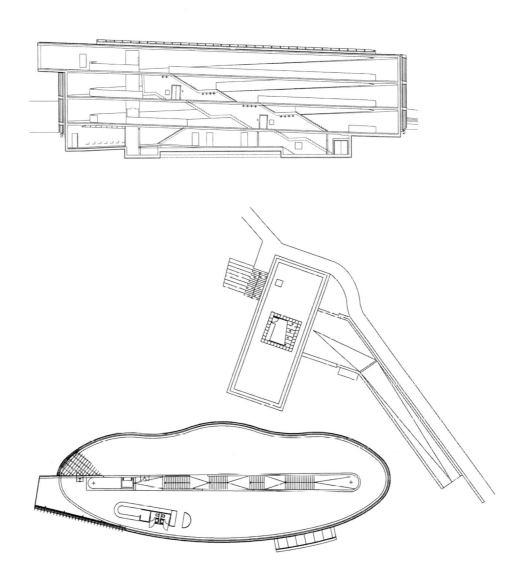

Left page: The undulating outside wall on the north face. This page: Longitudinal section and
floor plan, 3rd floor

This page (from left to right): View from the south, view into the cafeteria, stairway.
Right side: The exhibition room winds like a spiral around the entrance area

German Architecture since 1960
10 Signatures

Hysolar Institute, Universität Stuttgart, 1987

Behnisch & Partners

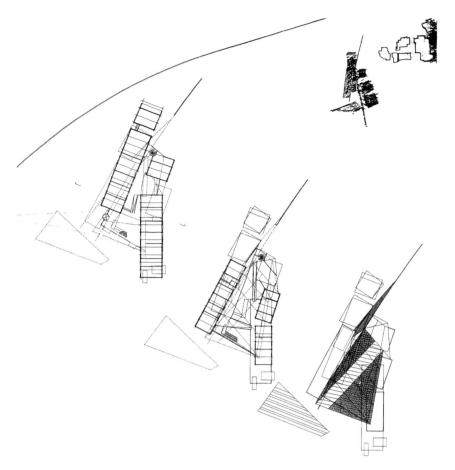

Hysolar Institute, Universität Stuttgart, 1987

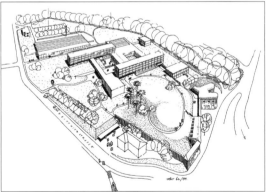

Fachhochschule Ulm, 1963, Günter Behnisch with Bruno Lambert, landscaping with Günther Grzimek

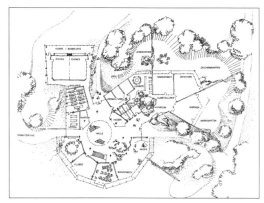

Auf dem Schäfersfeld Junior High School, Lorch, 1973

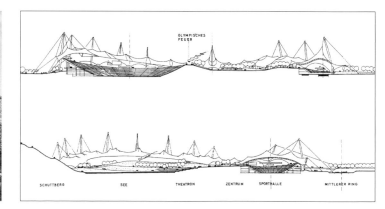

Olympic Village, Munich, buildings for the 20th Olympic Games, Munich, 1972, landscaping with Günther Grzimek,
roof construction: Behnisch & Partners, Frei Otto, Leonhardt + Andrä

Plenary Chamber of the Bundestag, Bonn, 1992, project partner and project architect: Gerald Staib, landscaping with Hans Luz + Partner

Akademie der Künste zu Berlin-Brandenburg, Berlin, competition 1994, to be completed in 2003, with Werner Durth, project partner: Franz Harter

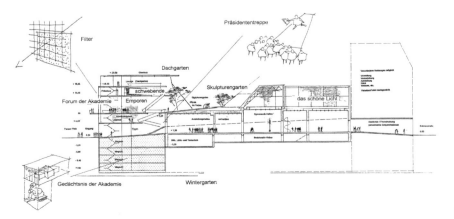

"Man is obviously capable of putting his trust even in new phenomena if he can understand them."[1]
Günter Behnisch

I first saw the junior high school at Lorch at the beginning of the seventies. The caretaker took our group around the school. He was the first caretaker on our journey who did not ridicule modern architects as having no idea about the practical aspects of a school and who also did not show us the building's shortcomings as the first thing. He was obviously enthusiastic about "his" school.

The classrooms had windows whose upper edge was higher than the room's suspended ceiling so that the ceiling had to be pulled up to avoid butting against the glass area. In addition the layers forming the ceiling had been cut off gradually—from the acoustic tile to the concrete ceiling. Thus it was possible to see each individual layer—instead of an overall package with a facing behind which the ceiling structure would normally disappear.

An architectural revelation: this architecture was self-explanatory! That is, of course, usually the case with the prefabricated concrete buildings of schools built at that time; there is nothing mysterious about them. The difference is that with this school everything is demonstrated by architectural means through the cutting open of the construction: something is deliberately being explained here. In the other buildings it is only visible by chance.

The "displacement of man from the center of his world leads to a change in relationship to the world of objects. These are wrested from human control and interpretation and stand out-of-control, strange, and silent vis-à-vis the individual, 'distinct from man': 'In the end Modernism made it possible for objects to be released from their role of *speaking for man,* to be able to *speak for themselves* of their own objecthood,"[2] writes Ullrich Schwarz, quoting Peter Eisenman, in one of his lucid analyses of the latter's architectural theories. At first sight the building details of the Behnisch office appear to be in accordance with those words: the things, the objects "speak for themselves." They are freed from their restraints, while they—like the ceiling of the classroom in Lorch—are shown and as a result acquire independence and dignity.

But Behnisch goes further than Eisenman in his theory which the latter has realized in buildings such as the Wexner Center for the Visual Arts. The support which hangs there above a staircase is to demonstrate the "equally valid object." But it must fail in these efforts because it is actually not equal—it has been thought up, formed, and symbolically charged by the architect through his explanations. (For was the support asked by anyone if in fact it wanted to make an appearance in architecture as an overhead support? Perhaps it would rather have borne a weight and the architect has simply misunderstood it?) Behnisch on the other hand sets the "emancipation of the object"—almost paradoxically—in the service of humanity. He remains the "director of operations"; *he* permits the objects to be what they are—and to explain that to the people.

The buildings created by Behnisch on his way to arriving at that point are the usual ones we expect to hear about: from the Vogelsang School in Stuttgart (1959), which still is marked by techniques of craftsmanship, to the Fachhochschule in Ulm (1963), which was built with prefabricated parts, to the buildings for the Olympic Games in Munich (1967–72), which strove for a new symbiosis of buildings and landscape, and in the roof of which, built with Frei Otto's collaboration, he also advanced by means of technology to a new freedom of architectural form. The Hysolar Institute (1987) in Stuttgart and the kindergarten in the Luginsland area of Stuttgart (1990) mark the greatest swings towards an "openness of the individual," before this openness was checked in favor of a new "discipline of the open" in the Postmuseum in Frankfurt and the plenary chamber of the Bundestag in Bonn. The building of the Akademie der Künste on Pariser Platz in Berlin may represent—and we shall have to wait for the building to be completed—a new stage in the development of the debate about historical context and present-day formal models.

This "discipline of the open" can be clearly perceived in the Bonn plenary chamber. The ground plan is of a classical order: the circle in the rectangle is one of the great historical figures in buildings whose social importance is to be stressed. From Roman classical antiquity through the Renaissance and Palladio to Classicism it formed a motif. Even 20th-century architects took it up: Le Corbusier with the parliament building in Chandigarh or James Stirling with the extension of the Staatsgalerie in Stuttgart.

Stirling's design was particularly fiercely attacked by Behnisch in those days—perhaps his plenary chamber is in fact also a late (conscious or unconscious) statement about his previous rejection. Stirling had designed the inner courtyard of the museum as a rotunda open at the top, as an inner courtyard. With Behnisch the sky above the members of parliament is simulated by the skylight because it would hardly have been possible to convey to them the feeling of having to meet in the open air—in spite of the venerable model of the Germanic tribes. But with both, Stirling as well as Behnisch, the symmetrical arrangement of rectangle and circle on a central axis is broken up: Stirling brings the passers-by diagonally up to the rotunda which then they can only pass through along the curve; the entrance on the symmetrical axis with its Egyptian-style portal ends in the underground garage. Behnisch also leads members of parliament and visitors diagonally towards the building and at the same time expects the former to descend to a lower level. One can see in this a conscious architectural gesture in the spirit of a warning against arrogance for those who are after all only to represent the people temporarily.

On the routes along which people are guided every architectural detail, from the supports to the balustrade, shows how Behnisch understands democracy (and how in his opinion the members of parliament should understand it): as an expression of the need to respect the "rights of the weak," to assert oneself independently but at the same time to adapt oneself to a common "great" form. "I see absolutely no alternative to the attempt to base one's own work on the ideals and aims inherent in our concept of democracy, which of course also change,"[3] Behnisch states. The treatment of detail—and not for instance the glazing of façades—shows in every one of his buildings what is meant by the concept of "transparency."

That then also amazingly amusing details can arise such as the wooden knot on the balustrade of the entrance steps for Rita Süssmuth, the then president of the Bundestag, relieves the architectural demonstration of its programmatic heaviness. And the initiative of Bavarian members of parliament who demanded the removal of the balustrade clearly proves its rightness.

A "democratic architecture" which Behnisch himself also rightly does not see in the "question of the externals of architecture" but "in the processes"[4] springs from an idealistic concept. It assumes that in spite of all the faults of the political and social system there is no better one: "I ... suspect secret, albeit definite poetical, almost Romantic traits.... And this longing, leaving open, searching—what is it other than a kind of blue flower, too?"[5] said his former colleague Karla Kowalski.

No man would have said that in this way, and certainly no architectural theorist. But of course she is right: to translate into architecture the image of an open society operating according to the rules of civility (and not for instance to demand an "autonomy of architecture") presents an ideal—the same kind of ideal as was implemented with the Palace of Versailles for the Sun King Louis XIV, just as the Gothic cathedral illustrated a heavenly Jerusalem, the Pantheon a perfect (Roman) world, or the Villa Rotunda the pure harmony of geometry, man, and God. In the architecture of the 20th century there is also this "architecture as an image of the world": in Tatlin's *Monument to the Third International* or in Leonidov's library, in Le Corbusier's Villa Savoye, in Mies van der Rohe's Nationalgalerie, or in Bernard Tschumi's Parc de la Villette. Behnisch's ideal of democracy, however, cannot be reduced to one particular building, precisely because it includes the genesis of architecture. So it is not represented by one individual building but by an architectural attitude; it is represented by the non-unique, the "open detail," the "open building." Behnisch's architecture of liberation from actual or supposed constraints functions because he displays the parts of the building and the spatial connections in their independence and their coherence.

Today we are surrounded by technical appliances which we do not understand. This is not only true of the really complex things such as video recorders or Saturn rockets. Even a simple light switch is to most people an incomprehensible *terra incognita*, fortunately surrounded by a well-designed box and thus concealed. How am I to believe that electricity flows in a piece of solid metal? On the other hand I can understand a bicycle: we step on the pedal and by means of a chain make the wheel turn in a rotary motion (a modern Shimano gearshift with twenty-one gears is also not really comprehensible, but we trust it out of habit).

Behnisch's architecture aims exactly at this difference; Julius Posener described it in one of his most beautiful essays as the difference between "appliance and object":[6] "Both serve us; the appliances meanwhile do it in an indirect and mysterious way," for the "objects fill us with trust ... the appliances on the other hand fill us with fear."[7] What I do not understand I find uncanny. Transferred into architecture, this poses an elementary question which has to do with the stability or instability of the environment we have constructed: how much permanent change can man tolerate? The daily banality—the world might change constantly and in the service of the economy and for the sake of our own progress we would have to adapt ourselves to this change—is confronted by the necessary constancy, which gives "security," which creates a sense of basic trust forming a firm wall to place our back against.

We have had bicycles for quite some time but not video recorders. From that we might conclude the following: if we build the old today we will find ourselves on the safe side, where a basic sense of trust is retrievable. But it only appears so. People would be torn apart between the daily pressure of change and the false security of bull's-eye panes and half-timbered construction. Therefore Behnisch does something different: he builds "bicycles with Shimano gears," up-to-date buildings which make their present-day quality understandable, understood from within themselves. For as Julius Posener says, "Man is obviously capable of putting his trust even in new phenomena if he can understand them."[8]
Gert Kähler

Ute and Kaspar Bienefeld Residence, Hohen Neuendorf, 1995

Heinz Bienefeld

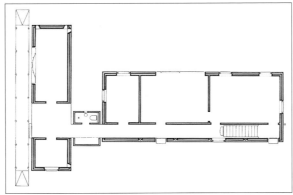
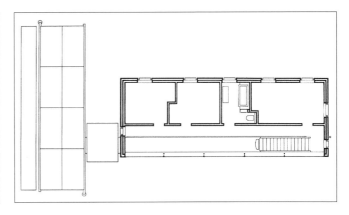

Ute and Kaspar Bienefeld Residence, Hohen Neuendorf, 1995

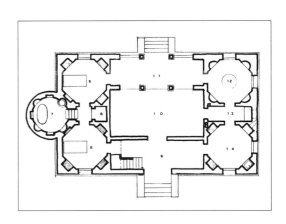

Wilhelm Nagel Residence, Wesseling-Keldenich, 1907

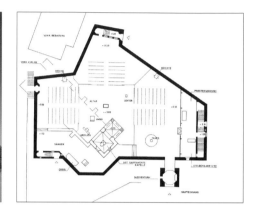

Parish Church of Saint Willibrord, Mandern-Waldweiler, 1968

Parish Church of Saint Boniface, Wildbergerhütte-Reichshof, 1974

Heinze-Manke Residence, Cologne-Rodenkirchen, 1984

Babanek Residence, Brühl, 1991

The number of buildings constructed by this architect, whom many people called the German Carlo Scarpa, was anything but extensive. Apart from four churches and a city kindergarten he left behind him fewer than three dozen large one-family houses, which is not much in thirty-three years of independent work. The son of a craftsman, well-read, but not gifted at writing and making speeches, he wrote very little and drew up no manifesto. Promoting himself in the media, so important today, was far from the thoughts of this solitary figure. Only later in life did he find the recognition he deserved. When Heinz Bienefeld was posthumously awarded the prestigious prize of the Bund Deutscher Architekten, Manfred Sack called him an "architect who was extraordinary, self-willed, self-confident, upright, always faithful to his convictions, obsessed with form, and always searching for true beauty." The stigma of the outsider had been transformed into an accolade.

Heinz Bienefeld (1926–95) was born in Krefeld and had been educated at Cologne schools of arts and crafts as a pupil and colleague of Dominikus Böhm. He was greatly influenced by the church architect Emil Steffann, whose simple churches seemed to stand completely outside the present age. The admirable independence of that loner offered a model for Bienefeld's completely independent path walked with steadfastness, quite remote from what his colleagues and the architectural journals were declaring as up to date. The price he paid for this obstinacy was high.

The postwar modern style of the fifties and sixties with which the Federal Republic tried to free itself from the resounding traditionalism of the Third Reich, appeared to him degenerate; he found the offers of the booming construction industry hideous and banal. Instead of emulating Le Corbusier and continuing to revere Mies van der Rohe which he had done at first, in the mid-fifties he began to talk of the "eternal laws of architecture," which did not gain him any friends. In one of his sketch books we find Bienefeld's polemic formula, "form is everything, function is nothing," the very opposite of Louis Sullivan's maxims. He could also have said: where space, proportion and surfaces are not in harmony, the architecture is bad, whether or not the function is right. And when he looked around in the city and the country, this was more the rule than the exception.

Whatever the "eternal laws of architecture" was supposed to mean, Heinz Bienefeld searched for and found them at the end of the fifties in old and ancient works of architectural theory—in Vitruvius and Palladio, Josef Durm and Friedrich Ostendorf. His persistent regard for sources, which almost everyone but he regarded as obsolete, was bound to estrange him from his contemporaries. Instead of traveling to Scandinavia or the United States where his colleagues were looking

around, from the sixties on he was always drawn back to Italy. Asked about models, Bienefeld even in the eighties and nineties named nature, whose solutions always seemed to be perfect in construction and at the same time beautiful, and the architecture of ancient Rome in which he recognized an exemplary connection between intelligent construction, the use of suitable materials, and a sense of beauty.

In 1967, at the age of forty, he built with amazing single-mindedness the Palladian-style residence of Wilhelm Nagel in Wesseling, with axial spatial sequences and meticulously built vaults. A Lower Rhine house on account of the dark red brick walls, but at the same time an equally unmistakable homage to Italy when one looks at the intimate garden courtyard and the three-part loggia whose openings imitate the famous Palladian motif. Like no other building of that decade in Germany the house referred back to architectural history, to building tradition and craftwork, and thus to things which had seemed banned from contemporary architecture since the arrival of the modern age.

The Nagel residence is an acknowledgement of a Lower Rhine regionalism, though in a very independent variant by Heinz Bienefeld which links the particular place with a distant fantasy landscape. Its regionalism founded entirely on form and material thus became free from the national accretions which in the Third Reich had become associated with the cult of the homeland. That this happened in the Rhineland, where Romans and Germanic tribes had already lived together two thousand years before, is perhaps no coincidence. "The Rhine flows into the Mediterranean," commented Wolfgang Pehnt ironically on Bienefeld's flexible concept of home. If one considers that the Casa Tononi in the Swiss canton of Tessin, Bruno Reichlin's variation on the Villa Rotonda, was not built until five years later, the Nagel residence could have been an event—as a noteworthy step towards a Postmodern age as yet still nameless. Derided by local architects, it remained unnoticed for a long time and only came to light for the first time in 1980 in a publication. Today it is the most frequently portrayed of Bienefeld's buildings.

Along with fame came the trend to claim him for the Postmodern period, as whose "forerunner" Bienefeld has been called again and again since 1985 in spite of his denials. He was made partly to blame for supposedly initiating a style for whose exaggerated ideas he was anything but responsible. Thus it remained unnoticed again that Bienefeld's classical Palladian period had already been at an end in 1969. What interested him after that were the "unsentimental anonymous architectural forms" which "leave the author the least possible scope for the unchecked," which liberated him from opinions and fashions of the day and which no longer exposed him to the danger of being celebrated or dismissed as the protagonist of a particular style, something important after his experiences with the mannerism of the Nagel residence.

With the Babanek residence in Brühl (1990) Bienefeld produced a didactic building, marked by antitheses and ambiguities about the nature of the house and its parts. The brick-built core, the elongated "stepped house" cut back on the second floor, is house and staircase at the same time. The façades display a dual nature: solidity and weight on the one side, transparency and lightness on the other. The brick-built garden side with dark, deep-set windows looks at first sight like a symbol of wall, massiveness, and weight. On closer examination it hovers closely above the ground, lifted off by horizontal slit windows, providing light to the cellar. The façade on the other side is the opposite: a pure glass outer shell and thereby the antithesis of a solid wall. It surrounds the two-story hall in which any person leaving the brick-built cell areas appears to be standing in the open air.

The constructional elements of a house—floors, staircase, wall, windows, roof, supports, and beams—often come over as specially emphasized, the transitions from one element to the next appearing engineered with an excess of rhetoric. This mannerism is particularly evident in the Babanek residence, where the main staircase folded out of sheet steel stands free in the hall as if on a stage, where a line of windows under the roof raises it and allows it to hover, which leads at the same time to the solid wall apparently standing by itself as if there were only it and no house behind. Such a complex building, uniting tradition and modernity, is an attempt to portray nothing less than the basic "essence of the house" while at the same time dissolving itself. One imagines an escapist idyll, as Bienefeld has been accused of creating, to be quite different. The protective home of childhood dreams is the starting point, but it is shown as an illusion which even a positive dreamer like Bienefeld could not believe in.

Bienefeld, always obsessed by detail, constantly reinvented the elements of the house, in order to make these recognizable in the Aristotelian sense in their own nature. In contrast to the culture of hardware department stores and the decline of craftsmanship, the man who would have much preferred to make everything himself put in fittings and additions of all kinds designed by himself, which often could only be produced by craftwork unusual for its time. Again and again he found intelligent clients who felt the somewhat difficult dealings with this architect to be "almost like a sacrifice but a necessary, meaningful sacrifice" (Wolfgang Pehnt).

Bienefeld was introduced to church architecture by Dominikus Böhm and Emil Steffann, two of the most prominent architects of the 20th century in this field. The extension of the parish church of Saint Andrew in Wesseling (1964) was Bienefeld's first commission after becoming self-employed. An existing Neo-Gothic church was opened up alongside the side nave and connected with the new church hall as a double church. The broad cubic building with rough brick walls and only a few round arch windows was built under the influence of his first Italian journey, when he had been especially fascinated by the Curia Iulia at the Forum in Rome.

Not until the buildings of the parish church in the village of Mandern-Waldweiler in the Eifel region (1968) did Bienefeld free himself from close dependence on classical antiquity. On a polygonal ground plan which follows the close limits of the church grounds, a gloomy church rises up, lit from above by a roof lamp. The remains of an existing sacrament chapel were added to and rebuilt—with astonishing results: the interior space offers a mystical image of an old town square with a freestanding church. On the almost completely solid walls Bienefeld produced for the first time his virtuoso composed "fugue pictures" from different layers and colors of brick, which are reminiscent of Roman walls. He also built the exterior and interior walls of Saint Boniface in Wildbergerhütte-Reichshof (1974) on the same pattern. He situated the parish church under a saddle roof resting on six freestanding columns which protects and shelters the octagonal stone building a little in the manner of Marc-Antoine de Laugier's primitive hut.

Like hardly anyone else before him Bienefeld managed by recourse to timeless "original shapes" to create archaically graceful spatial images. His churches and houses became eloquent buildings par excellence, on which the roughest yet meticulously executed detail still has something to communicate—about shape and material, about the nature of the material used, about surfaces and tectonics, about the fitting together of the parts and the connection with the whole.
Wolfgang Voigt

Bensberg Town Hall, Bergisch-Gladbach, 1967

Gottfried Böhm

  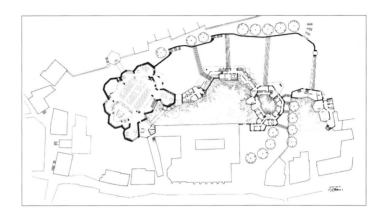

Pilgrimage Church, Mary Queen of Peace, Velbert-Neviges, 1968

Renovation of the palace area and new construction of the central pavilion, Saarbrücken Palace, 1989,
Project team: Gottfried Böhm, Nikolaus Rosiny, Klaus Krüger, and Lutz Rieger, Cologne/Saarbrücken

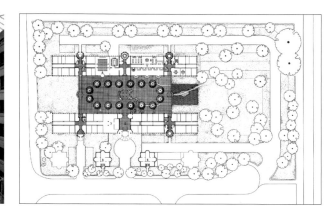

Züblin-Haus, Administration Building, Stuttgart-Vaihingen, 1985

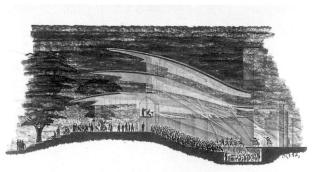

Hans-Otto-Theater Potsdam, starting 1995

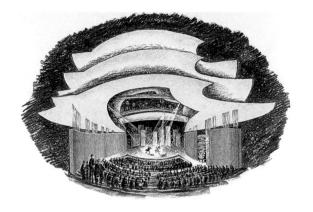

Administration Building for Deutsche Bank, Luxemburg, 1991

The rapid changes of the present day, the tempo of innovations, the increased obsolescence of all techniques and knowledge, and the fast change in lifestyles have also made their mark on architecture. In the case of many architectural projects, a building is written off after a decade, and with others, rebuilding and refurbishing at least are on the agenda by that time. It also seems natural to adapt the exterior image, or at any rate to put up the load-bearing framework for the long term but on the other hand to keep the façade replaceable and to give the buildings from the outset a character of lightness, mobility, and transitoriness. At the end of the writing-off period everything is up for reconsideration anyway.

The buildings of Gottfried Böhm (born in 1920) embody the opposite of such a nomadic concept. Germany's sole winner of the Pritzker Prize until now has gone his own way. His architecture reacts in an anticyclical way; it declares its allegiance to the stable element of building. It agrees with Arthur Schopenhauer, who says that architecture should make visible the effectiveness of gravity. Böhm's buildings have a presence; they are conspicuous, authoritative, they demand attention irrespective of how large or small they are. Where they have found a place they create the feeling that they will stay there for a long time. This impression is linked with their corporeality, materiality, and also to the manner in which these buildings are connected with the ground. They almost never touch the ground with slender pillars surrounded by space; almost always they sit on the ground with pronounced bases.

Böhm did not only study architecture from 1942 to 1947 at the Technische Hochschule in Munich, but sculpture, too, at the Akademie der Bildenden Künste. The gigantic architectural sculptures created by him in the sixties (the pilgrimage church in Velbert-Neviges of 1963–72, Saint Gertrude in Cologne of 1960–66, and the Church of the Resurrection in Cologne-Melaten of 1964–70) rise up like clumps of rock from the earth with their large, folded concrete surfaces. They are monuments directed against the inhospitable nature of cities.

With the later buildings also, which are not solid buildings but skeleton constructions, Böhm's interest lay in the physically tangible form. Strongly profiled supports, sometimes protruding in front of the façades, a wall relief casting shadows, prominent upper terminations, towers, bay windows, bridges, or roof crowns characterize every building as an individual whole. The structure of the surfaces remains tactile and contributes to the solidity of these buildings. Concrete is left rough or is worked by hand. Often aggregates are added which give it the granular quality and color of natural stone. The Böhm office has always liked to use bricks and clinkers in all its phases, because of their small-scale texture as well as their tactile qualities.

On a temperature scale of the emotions this architecture would be placed in the warm zone. Whereas in buildings by other architects perception goes directly from the eye to the intellect, Böhm's architecture demands the whole range of the senses. The surfaces and their detail beg to be sensed, the spaces and spatial sequences ask to be grasped intuitively in gravitation, dynamics, and temperature. Down-to-earth details such as entrance areas, steps, handles, and handrails receive special attention. Ornamentation is not a crime with Böhm, but an introduction to a perception of scale—and an abundance of creative pleasure.

Böhm's architecture underwent definite changes in the course of the decades. When after the death of his father, the great church-builder Dominikus Böhm, he took over the latter's office, he had to see a series of projects through. Obviously he first of all took over his father's repertoire, although he had to set it in new contexts and dimensions. In the fifties Gottfried Böhm followed the steep-hipped wire plaster ceilings which Böhm Senior had employed in his Expressionist church buildings of the twenties with "fabric ceilings" and suspended concrete shells, later with free-folded concrete slabs. With their help he succeeded in inventing buildings and space in which the boldest hopes of the Expressionist generation found fulfillment. A proud bourgeois building like the town hall at Bensberg in the Rhineland (1962–71), planted into the remains of a medieval castle, is the crowning glory of the town in the spirit of Bruno Taut's "crystallized image of human stratification."

For two pragmatic reasons he could not stay with this architecture that was rich in fantasy, even fantastic, and bore fairy-tale qualities. There was a lack of skilled workers for the complex shuttering work on the sculptured building shapes, and apart from that it was too expensive. Around 1970 Böhm went over to a style of building that worked more with rectangular and repetitive elements. Sequence and symmetry gained in significance, whereas Böhm in his concrete sculptures of the sixties had placed his hopes on free figurations.

Baroque traits appeared after the Expressionist ones: axially ordered open spaces, perspectively effective compositions, staged points of view, sophisticated, often labyrinthine intersections in the interior space. The synthesis of arts that culminated in the Baroque was something that Böhm also strove for. In some of his sacred and secular buildings not only the furniture and fittings, but also the inlaid floors and stained glass stem from him. Whenever the mood took him he would also climb onto the scaffolding and decorate the rooms and stairwells himself. Then for days—before the invention of the cellular telephone—he could not be reached from his office.

What characterizes the work of Böhm throughout all its periods is the conviction of the power and dignity of institutions. Anthropologists have defined human beings as deficient creatures. Their special place in creation rests on the lack of sure instincts which they compensate for by means of tools, cultural techniques, and institutions. In Böhm's work there are many buildings which were built as a commission from institutions: church buildings, town halls, parliament buildings, law courts, and cultural buildings. The almost naïve pathos inherent in these designs cannot be found in any other architectural office of German postwar architecture. It is as if Böhm's architecture were saying: power is nothing evil, if it remains responsible power, and as such it has a right to expression.

This is the most likely point at which opinions about Böhm's architecture may vary—above all when the headquarters of private firms profit from the aplomb of a spectacular appearance. The administration building of the construction company Züblin (1981–85) with the central nave of its mighty glass hall towers over the fields of a Stuttgart suburb. With bank buildings one is reminded of the tradition of these institutes that had their forerunners in the urban palaces of the financial nobility of Tuscany. Böhm's banks are modern *palazzi*. The Luxembourg branch of Deutsche Bank (1987–91) displays in its foyer the inventive richness of Piranesi's spatial creations. In the roof landscape with its countless conical roofs the prestigious element dissolves into the light-hearted without the authoritative gesture being lost.

Nothing characterizes this respect for the institutional better than the planning report on the German Bundestag in Berlin for which Böhm received the commission in 1988, in other words before German reunification. The reconstruction of the four-sided dome on Paul Wallot's Wilhelminian Reichstag had been suggested several times and just as often rejected again. In his unrealized project Böhm quite naturally adopted the dome as a dignified form, but he interpreted it in his own manner. Wallot had merely planned it with a view to the external effect on the city. Internally the dome did not appear and was not utilized. Böhm wanted to put it at the disposal of the parliament which was to meet there high above the earth, a little nearer to heaven than other mortals—literally an "Upper House." The representatives of the people were in his eyes entitled to a privileged place, *the* privileged place.

The unrealized Reichstag project is only one example, albeit the most prominent, of Böhm's on-going debate about the evidence of history. History for him seems to be an institution like other overarching and stabilizing institutions of life—like the state, the church, or the town and its facilities. Böhm uses types of building that had a very long life. One constantly recurring type is the three-naved basilica which he transferred back into secular building whence it originally came. Parallel office wings, on one or two levels and linked by a central hall, can be found in administration buildings, town halls, shopping centers, law courts, or hotels. With the central hall, another type of building stemming from the 19th century could be constructed: the arcade. As a built-up path it guarantees the linking of the building with the town, or, the other way round, the continuation of the town into the building, which always was very important to Böhm. With the WDR arcades in Cologne (1991–96, with Peter Böhm) the arcade breaks up the radio center complex by producing—unusually for Böhm—a really Deconstructivist and chaotic pile of containers.

Towers as landmarks visible from afar are an obvious attraction for a church builder like Böhm. He liked to make use of them in a form stemming from the industrial age, so that they remind one of water towers or blast furnaces. In museum projects for Hamburg, Stuttgart, and Cologne (1986–90) he transplanted them from a technological to a cultural context. Another topic that has occupied architects in the last decade is the use of large roof shells made of steel panels or reinforced concrete. They too have their specific weight, create a heavy load over podia and auditoriums rather than hovering like weightless clouds above them. Böhm incorporated them in projects for cultural buildings like the theater in Potsdam (planning started in 1995).

The architect, who has made himself a self-conscious servant of many institutions, lives for his part in a particular sort of institution, a family of architects reaching back for generations. Gottfried Böhm's grandfather was already active in the building industry. His father, Dominikus, has a firm place in the history of architecture. Gottfried Böhm's wife, Elisabeth, is an architect in her own right. Of his four sons three—Stephan, Peter, and Paul—have become architects with an impressive output. Varied though the works are, there nevertheless seems to be a prior understanding of what one takes on in these offices and what is better left alone. Neither the Postmodern pleasure at quotation nor the asceticism of the New Simplicity are part of the repertoire of the Böhms. In an epoch that approaches with mistrust any institutions with a well-known identity a family portrait presents itself which recalls the great architecture families of the past: names like Parler, Thumb, Bähr, and Dientzenhofer.

Wolfgang Pehnt

Jumbo Hangar for Deutsche Lufthansa, Hamburg, 1992, with Karsten Brauer

## von Gerkan, Marg and Partners

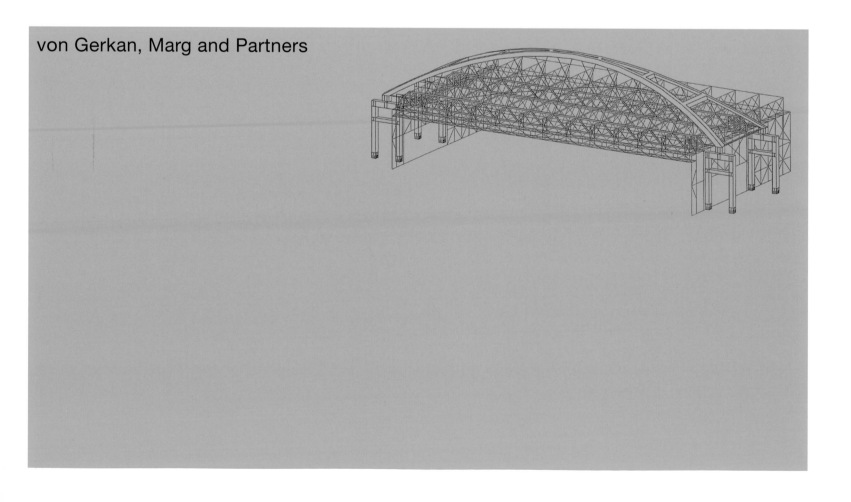

Hillmann Garage, Bremen, 1984

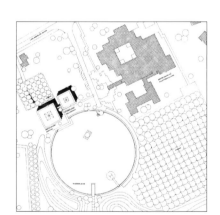

Carl Bertelsmann Foundation, Gütersloh, 1991

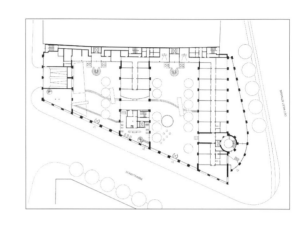

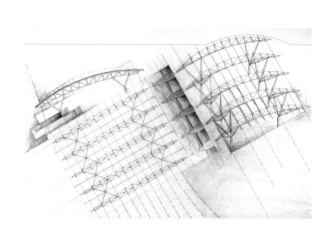

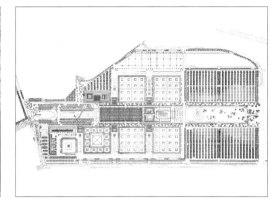

To many ears "gmp" sounds like SOM or OMA; in Germany at least it is a well-known and familiar trademark of the architectural world. Trademarks have an image, people associate them with pictures, companies, types. So what does gmp stand for, what kind of images does the abbreviation evoke? Is there a secret for its success?

For the team working with Meinhard von Gerkan and Volkwin Marg of Hamburg is successful, having branches in Aachen, Berlin, and Peking and presently employing a total of 280 colleagues. Rolf Niedballa, Karsten Brauer, Klaus Staratzke, and Andreas Sack were the partners in the early seventies. Sack left in 1982, Brauer and Niedballa in 1990. Uwe Grahl, Joachim Zais, and Hubert Nienhoff arrived in 1993–94, Wolfgang Haux, Nikolaus Goetze, and Jürgen Hillmer in 1998. Since 1964 gmp has managed to collect more than 150 first prizes in both national and international competitions. Are they sober pragmatists, are they out-and-out moderns, are they artists, are they ever-trendy fashion architects? The architects themselves evade the issue: "We have neither an individual or adopted dogma nor one integrated theoretical building to which we would be able or would want to subordinate our work of the last twelve years," von Gerkan and Marg wrote when the first report of their work appeared in 1978. No formalisms! They have (almost) always adhered to that. Another creed: no experiments! Experiments in the sense of playing at games of chance, trying out whether something goes well, taking risks, whether dangerous to themselves or to their clients.

The non-doctrinal combination of gmp out of pragmatically rationalistic fulfillment of function and attention to an aesthetic sense embedded in the mainstream of Modernism, linked with a restrained pleasure in the particular form, proved over the decades to be a guarantee for successes in the competition business and architectural practice—despite all the fashions and trends right up until the present day. There are a number of offices in Germany which have operated for a long time with similar success and which to a large extent control the complex business of construction. The gmp office has kept a decisive step ahead of them, as a result finding their way into the architectural guidebooks; this step is the creative mastering of the task which leads to a symbolic, aesthetic, often prototypical form and makes a visit to the buildings worthwhile.

If one wanted to classify gmp's architecture stylistically one would probably have to arrive at the idea of Second, Third, or Fourth Modernism—according to how you interpret it. A concise, easily detectable basic structure, often a square grid, is convenient for them; the square also surfaces very frequently as a general motif on the façades, even though they do not succumb to the obsession of their famous colleague from Cologne. "Of course an order of things can never become a recipe for the creation of works of art. The creative spark of the artist goes beyond logic and reason," as Walter Gropius had already recognized. And gmp mostly succeeds in setting off this spark. An order, the square for instance, never becomes restrictive. It is modulated, altered, and when it appears necessary the formats change, mostly to a recumbent rectangle, to gain an almost Japanese charm and elegance. Only rarely do markedly significant large shapes appear such as the tent roof of the Berlin Tempodrom folded like a flower—a leitmotif which also characterizes the trade fair building in Nanning in China. More often the (widely welcomed) distinctiveness and significance are achieved by functional or constructive decisions. As for instance in Bielefeld's civic center whose bow-shaped, fully glazed top acquired such a symbolic appearance—because of the emergency staircase covered over due to fire regulations—that the stylized view is used as a logo of the hall and is printed on all letterheads, programs, and posters.

Perhaps Meinhard von Gerkan and Volkwin Marg were fortunate that their formation as architects fell in the years before 1968. Completely open-minded as regards functional considerations and analytical methods, they would perhaps have excelled in the 1968 wave of theorizing and would have ended up in a dead-end street. Yet around 1970, when architects—particularly those in the universities—were preferring to write books rather than draw up plans, when beauty was to be replaced by "numeric aestheticism" and calculated by the computer, when functional plans were being judged by statistics and design processes and building methods broken down into elements and systematized, they had already carved out their conception of architecture and were immune to theoretical challenge.

It is not surprising that we are confronted by gmp buildings all over Hamburg: from the apartment block to the airbus factory, from the villa to the airport, and of course by their own house, a combination of architects' workshop, gallery, and residence in a wonderful location overlooking the Elbe. What is more surprising, however, is that gmp's work has also made its mark on the German capital in a way hardly any Berlin archi-

tectural firm has ever done. In this metropolis, gmp is immediately there to greet us: at the ICE station in Spandau with its light halls or in the future at Lehrter Bahnhof, the city's central railway junction, at Tegel airport or in the future at the large Berlin-Brandenburg international airport out at Schönefeld. You can stay in a gmp hotel on Leipziger Strasse or at the first-class Swissôtel in an exclusive location on Kurfürstendamm right opposite Café Kranzler, where the huge circular building designed by Meinhard von Gerkan reminds us in its formal language of such heroes of Berlin architecture as Erich Mendelsohn and in particular Hans Poelzig. A few steps further on, on the even busier Tauentzienstrasse, Volkwin Marg has made his mark with a shoe emporium.

But even in the old, now renovated business center of Berlin-Mitte they are represented by some decent buildings. Immediately to the left behind the Brandenburg Gate, on Pariser Platz which has been done up magnificently as the "showpiece of the town," there stands the capital's branch of the Dresdner Bank with its refined reserve. Inside, however, one of the most beautiful interior spaces to be built recently on the river Spree opens up with its magnificent circular courtyard. While Meinhard von Gerkan was busy at the western end of Unter den Linden, Volkwin Marg was able to make his contribution to new architecture in Berlin on Friedrichstrasse. And one might round off the evening in Vau, the top-class restaurant which von Gerkan designed for the master chef Viehhauser, who has his main restaurant in the gmp offices in Hamburg. The following day the gmp excursion might continue as follows: first to the energy-saving houses of the *International Building Exhibition* of 1987, then into the government area to the Dorotheenblöcke offices of the German Bundestag and a visit in the "embassy" of the states of Brandenburg and Mecklenburg-West Pomerania. Even a visit to a home game of Hertha BSC at the Olympic stadium does not go by without a friendly greeting from gmp, for Volkwin Marg performed the trick, during the soccer season, of getting Werner March's thirties stadium, now classified as a listed building, into shape for the World Cup. Thus there are almost two dozen buildings, and certainly not the most insignificant ones, with which gmp shows its colors in Berlin. There seems to be nothing they would not be able to do and this self-esteem also communicates itself to the observer.

There was no question of gmp not becoming involved in the capital or in the new states after reunification. Just one week before the fall of the Wall Meinhard von Gerkan had opened an exhibition in Dresden, given a lecture, and returned to Hamburg convinced that "we in the West owe our colleagues 'over there' a cultural exchange." One week later the unthinkable seemed possible and thus arose the West-East architects' workshop on Dresden as a *Gesamtkunstwerk*, presented by Meinhard von Gerkan and financed by the Jürgen Ponto Foundation. There were sixty participants. Gmp wasthen able to build in other places: the new Leipzig trade fair buildings, at the time certainly the most beautiful trade fair site in Germany, the wonderful Weimar Hall about which there had been some irritation on account of the demolition of the original listed building, further office and commercial buildings in Leipzig and Suhl, as well as a rehabilitation clinic on the Baltic coast.

Meinhard von Gerkan was also similarly occupied when in 1998 he set up a workshop for students in Brunswick and Bucharest, after winning the urban-planning competition "Bucharest 2000," to promote the exchange of ideas as well as architectural culture and personal relationships. Activities such as this, for which most colleagues believe they have no time, bear witness to the conviction that the architect's work is more than just building up as many cubic meters of space as possible at the least possible expense. At gmp they have constantly reflected about *Die Verantwortung des Architekten* (The Architect's Responsibility), to take a title from the numerous books by von Gerkan, and they have continually spoken up in the interests of architectural culture.

It tends to be the norm that architects who after their studies move into professional life together at some point or other go their own separate ways. Meinhard von Gerkan and Volkwin Marg also worked closely together at the beginning, while later at least partly taking a different direction. In 1974 von Gerkan took up a chair as a full professor in design at the Technische Universität in Brunswick, Marg was president of the Bund Deutscher Architekten (BDA) from 1979 to 1983 and took up the chair of urban design at the Rheinisch-Westfälische Technische Hochschule (RWTH) in Aachen From around 1980 they were each named separately as authors of gmp's designs. Von Gerkan accordingly works on the majority of projects at the planning stage. Certain special interests are clear: work involving the care of monuments is of more interest to Volkwin Marg, cultural buildings to Meinhard von Gerkan. Marg designed the great trade fair centers—such as the ones in Leipzig or Rimini—and the majority of stadiums; von Gerkan most of the transportation buildings, stations, airports.... Only a second, closer look reveals the author, for von Gerkan cultivates a more elegant form in structure and design, while Marg sets about the work in a somewhat more pragmatic and technical way, without on his part losing sight of the elegance of form which is for him more closely oriented on Classical Modernism. Unlike German engine and vehicle manufacturers, German architects are not among the leaders in exporting; gmp on the other hand frequently participates in competitions all over the world. In 1978 people thought they had pulled off a big coup—since the first prize in a worldwide competition of 601 participants promised a prestigious commission. Unfortunately the clients' successors who had in the meantime come to power by force showed no inclination to build the Pahlavi National Library in Tehran, named after the Shah of Iran.

Other activities were more successful. Volkwin Marg's Sheraton Hotel in Ankara was built after a competition judged by experts. In 1999 a competition victory, in 2002 the opening of a congress and exhibition center in Nanning in China—it can happen as quickly as that in far-away countries. One recent competition success won against some famous international competition (second prize went to SOM) was the Fortune Plaza development project with 700,000 square meters of floor space in Peking where the German School of gmp had been built and several apartment block projects begun.

Brilliant red and blue colored walls, orange-colored stairs, pale yellow ceilings: you have to rub your eyes in amazement on visiting the central lecture hall at the Technische Universität in Chemnitz. The colors of Luis Barragán and Vilchis Ricardo Legorreta in a gmp building? Vivid colors hardly ever came into play in the hundreds of buildings by the company, only the soft brown of wood, the warm red of brick plus steel gray, panels in white, and as an exception a red pillar as the height of frivolity. In Chemnitz, however, we are reminded once again of the roots, of the early work of gmp: Tegel airport. At the time the red, orange, yellow, and brown palette in which airport gangways, counters, and the metal bodies of the main tenance buildings had been lacquered had been given the name "pop colors."

After reacting against the current fashion for many years, gmp is obviously coming to terms with the modern trends of the age, the use of strong colors on the one hand and on the other the awareness of materials of the "New Simplicity" of German-Swiss style. A certain adaptability to the signs of the time is part of gmp's recipe for success. Let us call it receptiveness to the spirit of the age, flexibility, which has nothing to do with opportunism, since gmp does trim its sails to the wind but tries at all times to blow hard itself.
Falk Jaeger

Residence, Regensburg, 1979, Thomas Herzog

# Herzog + Partners

Residence, Regensburg, 1979, Thomas Herzog

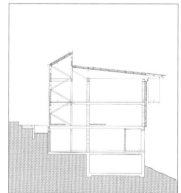

Youth Educational Center Guest House, Windberg, 1991, Thomas Herzog

Wilkhahn Production Halls, Eimbeckhausen, 1992, Thomas Herzog

Design Center, Linz, 1993, Thomas Herzog with Hanns Jörg Schrade

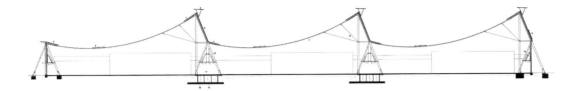

Trade Fair Hall 26, Hanover, 1996, Herzog + Partners

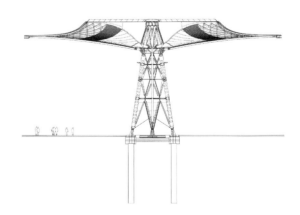

Expo Roof, Hanover, 2000, Herzog + Partners

For more than thirty years Thomas Herzog, who founded an architectural practice in 1971 with his wife, the designer Verena Herzog-Loibl, has been one of the most important advocates of energy-saving architecture. At that time the concept of "ecology" in the field of architecture was still unheard of; today it is much talked about but often reduced to a slogan: there is hardly a high-rise which is not extolled by its designers as "ecological" in order to speed up its authorization process; and hardly any building whatsoever which does not bear the label "sustainable development" familiar to us since the Earth Summit in Rio in 1992.

To a large extent it is due to Herzog that the idea of ecology in architecture has been freed from banal ideas. Costly solar panels on a holiday house generally amount to nothing more than vain symbolism like grass roofs on suburban developments of one-family houses. Again and again Herzog has proved that it is a matter of holistic understanding. In other words, thinking systematically and not making individual questions absolute. Topics for debate are the minimizing of energy costs for heating and cooling, the use of renewable energy, and the possibility of recycling building materials. Ecological building is inspired by low-tech methods as they have been preserved until today in the constructional shapes of some traditional societies, but it by no means pursues the path of a sectarian pseudo-green hostility to technology. On the contrary: Herzog, who gained his doctorate at the University of Rome in 1972 with his thesis *Pneumatische Konstruktionen,* comes from the tradition of constructive Structuralists—Jean Prouvé and Konrad Wachsmann were the important inspirational sources of his early years. For three decades the Munich architect has been pursuing with quite amazing dedication the research and development of building methods which fulfill ecological demands—as a practicing architect and a passionate inventor and as a university lecturer in Kassel, Darmstadt, and, since 1993, in Munich. In this he is unusual in Germany where this area of research has been almost completely neglected by architects. The list of the elements and building systems produced by research into materials and construction is long, ranging from terracotta façades with ventilation behind them, panels with translucent insulation, or overhead screens for buildings with glass roofs.

Like most of his colleagues Herzog also began with small architectural commissions in order to work his way up gradually to larger projects. A one-family house in Regensburg (1977–79) which after more than twenty years can certainly also be classified as an important work, brought the architect, born in 1941, fame in his specialist field: an upright wooden frame construction with a glass roof sloping down to the ground. The optimal use of solar energy (the lower parts of the building situated in front of the actual living area serve as conservatories) is combined here with maximum transparency to form a striking mass with a triangular cross-section which is skillfully incorporated into the landscape and also integrated an existing beech tree. The clarity of the structure based on a constructional grid of 90 by 90 by 45 centimeters which is expressed in the staggered arrangement of side rooms, main rooms, and greenhouse areas to the front led to a striking form which is aesthetically convincing; Herzog had proved that ecological architecture does not have to present an image of vernacular suburbanity. An experimental understanding of architecture, based on the testing, continuation, and further development of design concepts protects Herzog from being repetitive; every house is presented as a new experimental form as a response to earlier research results. Thus with the wedge-shaped houses in the northern part of Munich (1979–82) Herzog fell back on the concept of the Regensburg house, but expanded the concept with a solar installation fitted directly into the frame of the building. The time and energy going into research makes every building a unique object; it is not surprising that Herzog's work, after more than thirty years of activity with a good fifty projects and construction methods either realized or designed, can still be grasped as a whole.

The architect's buildings presuppose a thinking and carefully considered user, a client therefore who does not regard the house as a self-service shop and is prepared to learn how to deal with the building and its energy system. The separation into heated and unheated areas led to a typology of "two-zone-houses" in which the solid part with the technical installations is kept as small as possible. If this is carried out by professional architectural firms then the light building components can, thanks to prefabrication, be produced by the users themselves.

The separation of the spatial areas has found its most convincing expression in the guest house of the youth educational center in Windberg (1987–91). The dormitory area here is built of heavy materials as a thermally inert system so that the walls can function as storage areas; the façade was also provided with translucent insulation which permits the use of solar radiation without loss of heat. The information board in the entrance area explaining to overnight guests the functional principle and encouraging them to reflect on their dealings with energy testifies to the educational interests of the client and the architect.

With the production site for the chair manufacturer Wilkhahn in Eimbeckhausen near Hanover (1989–92), built a little later, Herzog succeeded in making the leap into larger-scale projects in the early nineties. For the ambitious undertaking which had already provided Herbert Hirche and Frei Otto with commissions, halls were built which have nothing in common with the usual ubiquitous trapezoid metal boxes. Natural ventilation and optimal lighting are the essentials of the complex integrated convincingly into the sequence of existing buildings. Translucent features on the façade, interrupted at eye level by a transparent strip, allow the light to penetrate deep into the halls; the green roofs give protection from overheating in summer.

Since the Wilkhahn project the building of halls and exhibition centers is one of the main types of commission for the Munich office. Pioneering work in this context was the congress and exhibition hall in Linz (1989–93) where, as the result of a specially developed light screen, they succeeded in providing the inside with a generous amount of daylight. The maximum internal height of twelve meters allowed the airspace of the mass supported by flat curved steel girders to be kept to a minimum for thermal reasons. Adapting in a contemporary way Joseph Paxton's vision of the Crystal Palace for the London World's Fair of 1851, Herzog, with his much more elegant building, was able to formulate a new type of exhibition hall after the Black Box Era. Since then the office has been increasingly concerned with large projects; in Wiesbaden, for example, a large complex consisting of four interconnected blocks of buildings is presently being built for the building industry's supplementary benefit office.

Important buildings of recent years were built especially for the Hanover trade fair site. In addition to Hall 26, Herzog's new administrative block, artistically somewhat austere, was built with which he proved that, contrary to popular opinion, the demand for an architecture that conserves resources accords very well with the high-rise type of building. Low energy consumption and the extensive use of wind and sun for controlling temperature and ventilation were the essential aims which Herzog mainly fulfilled with a ventilation tower rising up far above the body of the building: thermal lift produces the effect of a chimney which gets the system of natural air circulation going. An anthill functions in much the same way and in fact Herzog has been occupied intensively since the seventies with relationships between nature and architecture.

But the Expo roof which likewise was built on the site of the Hanover trade fair for the World's Fair in 2000 can be considered to be even more spectacular. Each of the ten huge wooden umbrellas clustered together over the central square of the exhibition measures 40 by 40 meters along the sides—an impressive construction which set new standards in the field of architecture with the renewable raw material wood and became an architectural landmark of Expo 2000: construc-

tions of trellis-like slats forming double curved concave dishes rest on solid wood supports.

Herzog's buildings may have been built almost exclusively in Germany—though mostly outside the large centers such as Munich or Berlin—but the architect has also made an international name for himself with his research and publications. This can be seen not least in the European Charter for Solar Energy in Architecture and Town Planning drawn up by Thomas Herzog in 1994–95 which was signed by such renowned colleagues as Ralph Erskine, Norman Foster, Nicholas Grimshaw, Herman Hertzberger, Michael Hopkins, or Françoise Jourda. It is urban-planning aspects above all that come more clearly into the foreground as a result of the great projects of recent years. Since 1995, Solar City near Linz, designed by Herzog along with Norman Foster and Richard Rogers, has been under construction. Even though the development is situated far away from the heart of the city, the use of public transportation is being encouraged and individual transportation is restricted where possible.

At the same time Solar City represents a model of to what extent solar energy can be used today in the building of new developments or cities. The required low energy standards should be further improved by means of direct solar radiation, solid and compressed construction methods, as well as by the insulation qualities of façade linings.

Hubertus Adam

  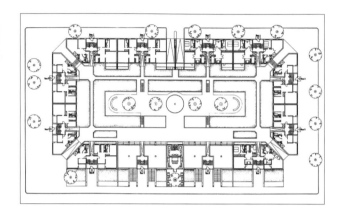

Block 270, Vinetaplatz, Berlin, 1977

Josef P. Kleihues

Main Workshop for the Berlin Municipal Cleaning Department, Berlin, 1978

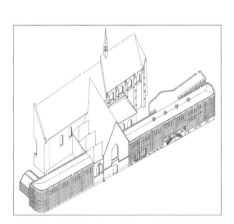

Museum of Prehistory and Early History, Frankfurt am Main, 1989

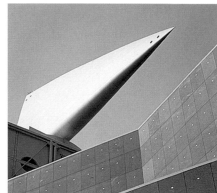

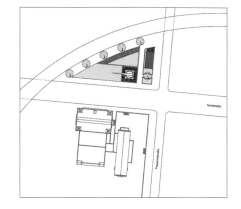

Kant-Dreieck Office Building, Berlin, 1994

Museum of Contemporary Art, Chicago, 1996

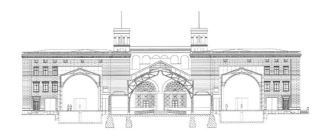

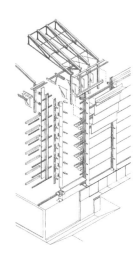

Hamburger Bahnhof, Museum of Contemporary Art, Berlin, 1996

"The worst enemy of modern architecture is the idea of space that is defined only through economic and technical demands without regard for the idea of place."
Vittorio Gregotti[1]

For a good ten years the architect Josef Paul Kleihues built relatively little and yet was ceaselessly active. In the eighties he concerned himself with the "symbolic capital" of architecture (Pierre Bourdieu), that is, with aesthetic competence in architectural matters and its acceptance in public perception. His base was the *Internationale Bauausstellung* (International Building Exhibition, known as IBA, 1984–87), where he served as the director of its reconstruction department from 1979 to 1987. Together with the journalist and publisher Wolf Jobst Siedler, he had launched it in West Berlin in the seventies and fitted it with the motto—at the time unusual, even offensive—of "the inner city as a place of living." Behind the sensational flurry of the individual "events," IBA was a special planning institute, neither completely public nor really private in its organization, a floating, equilibrated body of experts with elitist self-assurance, which performed both at the governmental and public levels. Younger architects today like to spin IBA with legends. When seen against the plausible lethargy and atomized confusion of present architectural discussions, it seems much more in fact like a remedy from a vital debate; it combined important public interests with cosmopolitan glitter. Kleihues managed all the conflicts with city authorities, the economic reviews, and the cooperative, social, or private building undertakings; he brought more than 150 international architectural elders to Berlin. They not only graced the city with excellent works, but also discussed their designs in symposia, providing a storehouse of ideas and suggestions. From the Italian *tendenza* of Rossi, Grassi, and Gregotti to the Dutch Structuralism of Hertzberger and the Anglo-Saxon Conceptualism of Rem Koolhaas (OMA), from the Luxemburg High Classicism of the Krier brothers to the American "autonomists" John Hejduk, Peter Eisenman, and Richard Meier, as well as the storyteller Charles Moore—

nearly all tendencies of international architecture were assembled in Berlin. Indeed, Oswald Mathias Ungers of Cologne was not left out, nor was the (more radical) Dioscuri constellation of Kleihues with Ungers, nor the criticism of Colin Rowe, Heinrich Klotz, and Kenneth Frampton. Young talents such as Hans Kollhoff, Daniel Libeskind, or Zaha Hadid made their first appearances on the IBA podium. It was at that time that one began to pronounce the word "Deconstructivism" without a stutter. And a few of the architects even built buildings.

In the end it must be said that looking at this IBA within the history of German postwar architecture, that no one has done more for the cultural situation, for the esteem, knowledge, and meaning of architecture in society than has Kleihues. Later it was attempted again and again, in smaller or larger matters, to tie everything to the cultural success of the 1984–87 IBA. And even if Kleihues naturally did not personally initiate everything, the broad effect of architecture, at least in Germany, is scarcely imaginable without his cooperation. Indeed that architecture over the course of the transitional nineties could even slip into the role of a "guiding medium of culture," as the critic Michael Mönninger noticed,[2] was due not just to the unexpected building boom after the fall of the Berlin Wall. It was also in good measure due to the preparatory work that Kleihues had undertaken in the years before as a capable manager in implementing changes.[3]

Toward the end of the decade, however, he seemed to suffer from the predominance of this type of journalism: "I am very familiar with the pleasure of making," he admitted in an interview in 1989,[4] and by that meant that his withdrawal had weighed down on him. Shortly thereafter his architectural practice officially exploded. From 1990 arose in rapid succession the renovation and expansion of the Hamburger Bahnhof in Berlin (museum of contemporary art), the Museum of Contemporary Art (MCA) in Chicago, the Checkpoint Arcades and the Triangle in Berlin Friedrichstadt, the Platz vor dem Neuen Tor off Invalidenstrasse, the Liebermann and Sommer buildings directly next to the Brandenburg Gate, Margrafenhaus on Gendarmenmarkt, as well as the Kontorhaus and Hofgarten buildings—called "experiments" by Kleihues himself—on Friedrichstrasse. The verdict for the central train station in Berlin-Tiergarten (Lehrter Bahnhof), in which the German railway authorities let Kleihues compete against the Hamburg architectural giant Gerkan, Marg, and Partners (gmp)—with a more fortunate result for the latter—created a major controversy in 1992. By contrast, there was the somewhat concurrent and uncommon success of Kant-Dreieck, whose aluminum sail mirrored the plan of the ensemble in the Berlin sky. Quickly it has transformed itself into an urban landmark, even

if today it has been somewhat shaded by Helmuth Jahn's new Kranzler-Eck tower.

Kleihues's architectural stature was already displayed in the early successes of the main workshop for the Berlin Municipal Cleaning Department (BSR), in Tempelhof (1970–78), and of the apartment house (Block 270) on Vinetaplatz in Wedding (1971–77).[5] Both are programmatic buildings, with which he makes it clear that architecture is not exterior façade drapery or mere fulfillment of a purported commission, but is something that grows out of the historical and aesthetic reflection on the task and place. With the truck-repair workshop of the BSR building, Kleihues finds a classically pure, almost sublime language that arises from the ingenious analysis and organization of the course of operations. And with the apartment house on Vinetaplatz he employs for the first time since World War II an urban block design instead of the high-rise or disk-shaped building preferred by architecturally economic functionalism. The historical and aesthetic, clear-cut, thought-out attempts were moreover precisely transposed into a love of detailing—elements out of which Kleihues's lifelong architectural grammar remains impressed.

Yet his cultural-historical means lies above all in the fact that he succeeded once again in bringing the urban paradigm into the architectural discourse and in having made the eventual building decisions all but unrenounceable. His most important achievement must be the rehabilitation of the city and urbanism in general as obligations to be taken seriously by designing and building architects. This fact goes far beyond the technical and constructional consequences of architecture and extends into cultural and socio-political areas. Above all it means a break with the self-conception of the modern generation, to which the 20th-century architectural discourse had sworn allegiance.[6] It means the return from an architecture of object fixation to a design of the urban space—not individual architectural icons, but that the semantically rich urban space should (again) take center stage in the architectural work. And thus the initiatives that Kleihues seized in this regard have become as multifaceted as the theme. It is therefore characteristic of his efforts not to let the break become too painful, perhaps on occasions not even all too clear. He staged and practiced it as a "dialogue between modernity and history," as it was formulated by the Munich architectural historian Winfried Nerdinger. With that, Kleihues grounded architecture with a "theoretical basic concept that he referenced to history and developed out of history."[7]

Kleihues has discussed this at length in conversations with the philosopher Claus Baldus.[8] From them it can be inferred that he has never—unlike his friendly rival and critical combatant Oswald Mathias Ungers—lashed out at 20th-century

Modernism as a disaster, but he understood and sanctioned its atmosphere of change in the 1920s. As a mediator he wanted to take it up and continue it. This double vision of a turning away from Modernism and its continuation is expressed in the theory of *critical reconstruction*, which Kleihues worked on during his years at IBA. With its formulation it is related to the "criticism" of Modernism's offending anti-historicism and the vehement negation of tradition; it is "reconstruction" yet in a way referring to its socio-political intentions and self-reflective practice—in Kleihues's understanding therefore rationalist. Later this ambitious program for pouring new wine into old skins was made banal by the production of new architecture on traditional urban lots. Yet even in this simplification we can still read in Kleihues's attempt—following up on Aldo Rossi's architecture and urban theory (*L'Architettura della città*, Padua 1966)—the desire to reevaluate the urban plan for its "memory." Suitably considered and protected, it becomes the grand road of approach, by way of which the historicity of contemporary architectural practice can be reached, as can be the understanding and meaning of urban culture. This key concept of *critical reconstruction* is joined by stereometry—the volumes, that is, the presumptive (mixture of) uses—as well as with physiognomy, that is, clothing, façade, and the aesthetic outfitting of buildings.

Kleihues's aesthetic is as paradoxical as the figure of the architect all told. Restive and playful, strict and yet seemingly off the cuff, logical and economical in means, but nevertheless inclined to a dreamy dance—like the sail on Kant-Dreieck that is dedicated to the soubrette and dancer Josephine Baker. There is a tendency for the monumental, as with the hospital in Berlin-Neukölln or the MCA in Chicago, and at the same time an obsession for precise details, for which Kleihues suffers no tolerance, as he notes not without pride. In short it is a *coincidentia oppositorium*, an ensemble of contradictions or, as one description of his aesthetics runs, a "poetic rationalism."[9]

Josef Paul Kleihues was born in 1933 in the Westphalian town of Herne, the son of a family of building contractors. He studied in Stuttgart and Berlin with Peter Poelzig and (for a short time) with Hans Scharoun. He received his aesthetic imprint, however, at the Ecole des Beaux-Arts in Paris, to which he received a scholarship in 1960. There he assimilated the rationalist tradition of Marc-Antoine Laugier, Jean-Nicolas-Louis Durand, and Eugène-Emmanuel Viollet-le-Duc. Through Karl Friedrich Schinkel he proceeded to Peter Behrens and Le Corbusier—he is closer to this artistic rationalist and Platonist than to Walter Gropius or Ludwig Mies van der Rohe, to whom he clearly distances himself.[10] The attribute of poetry in his aesthetics also signals a distance to the "Functionalist" ways of the Modernism of the 1920s. With the poetic Kleihues summoned the anarchist movement of artistic subjectivity, romantic individuality, which challenges the "rationalist" world order with the right of fantasy. And whereas the rationalist behavior in architecture is based on the pre-established harmony of the geometric basic forms of circles, squares, and triangles, Kleihues reclaims the charismatic traversing of its discipline with poetry—the contrasts and reflections that one finds in all his buildings.

The image of the architect Kleihues can be rounded off, however, only by noting the three exhibitions that he arranged. He planned the first, *Adventures of Ideas: Architecture and Philosophy since the Industrial Revolution*, in 1984 with his IBA advisor Vittorio Magnago Lampugnani.[11] Then there was *750 Years of Architecture and City Planning in Berlin*, which he organized himself in 1987 at the conclusion of the IBA 1984–87.[12] Finally, there was the exhibition *City of the ARCHITECTURE of the City: Berlin 1900–2000*, for which he collaborated with Paul Kahrfeldt and which was shown for a short summer in the atmospheric ruin of Friedrich August Stüler's Neues Museum on Museum Island.[13] In retrospect this triad of themes—philosophy, history, architecture—yield the image of an architect who has won his self-understanding and his aesthetics from a critical further development of Modernism. That basically distinguishes him from the following generation, which is confronted with a deregulated architectural market of historically liberated effects. For Kleihues architecture was (and is) always an art with a public responsibility before the historical. Cities, he once said, "have not become beautiful by accident. Battles have been waged over centuries for that."[14] But they should be beautiful—and not just in his opinion.

Gerwin Zohlen

Imperial War Museum—North, Manchester/England, 2002

# Daniel Libeskind

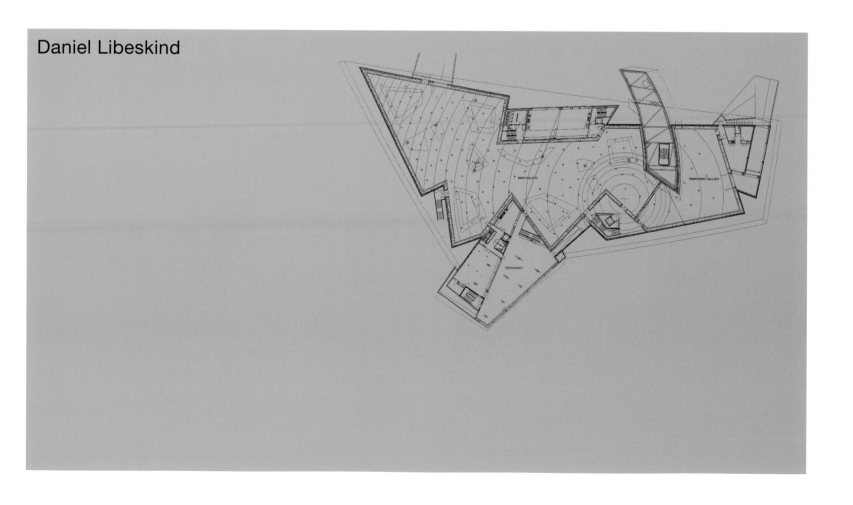

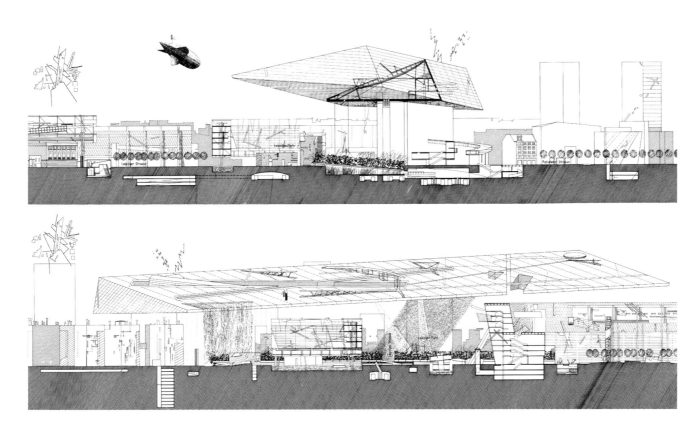

Out of Line, Potsdamer Platz/Leipziger Platz, 1991

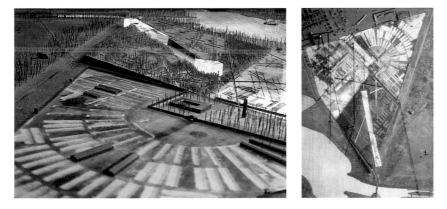

Mourning, Urbanization of the former grounds of the SS barracks in Oranienburg/Sachsenhausen, 1993

Between the Lines, Jewish Museum Berlin, 1999

  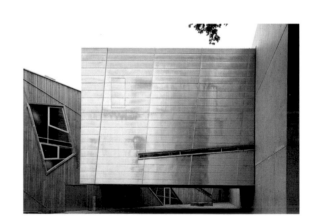

Museum without Exit, Felix-Nussbaum-Haus, Osnabrück, 2001

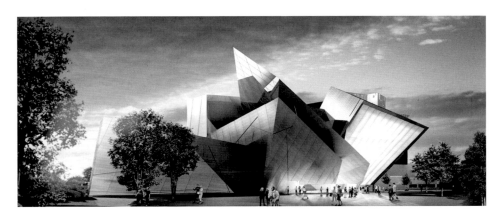

The Eye and the Wing, Extension to Denver Art Museum, Denver, Colorado, USA, 2005

"Estrangement from the world is a factor of art; so whoever perceives it as other than strange does not perceive it at all."
—Theodor W. Adorno[1]

Colossalism, Art, and Consumption

Can architects afford not to follow the trend? Can one expect architects to go underground so that their contributions cannot be taken over as slogans and robbed of their content? Should architecture be protected from market values which infiltrate everything and every one of us? From the "plots of large companies which would like to make the world into a gaming room for consumers with the mind of a child"?[2] Did architecture finally lose its innocence in 1989 (if indeed it ever had any)? With McWorld's or the global hegemony of businesses, in the caricature of culture, in a "dynamic, ruthless, and lightweight culture whose main value is its marketability,"[3] in a round of mental amusement parks? The fall of the Berlin Wall in 1989 and the end of the Soviet Union in 1991

complicated the world situation, and out of a dual opposition there evolved fragmented pieces and regional rivalry. With the age of globalization a new period of architecture began—focused on in the 1988 exhibition *Deconstructivist Architecture* at the Museum of Modern Art in New York—which wanted to rid itself of every "ism," a task it ultimately could not manage. Like no other architect, Daniel Libeskind, comparable at the most with Zaha M. Hadid and far removed from the "homemade populism"[4] of a Frank O. Gehry, abandoned the safe territory of architecture in order to liberate, emotionalize, and search for the new social relevance of city and space. No other contribution at the New York exhibition was so far removed from architectural convention and reality, from the image of building, as his City Edge project (1987) for the Tiergarten district of Berlin. A huge mass of building, tearing open the Berlin Wall and jutting diagonally into the sky, demarcates beneath it a previously unknown public area. Everything looks as if it might collapse. The people in the offices and apartments of this uprooted low tower block, rising at its highest point to only around ten stories and supported by clusters of delicate pillars, hover inescapably above an empty space which is to be filled with social life. A vivisection of city and architecture searching for truth and meaning as it had already indicated in the Micromegas of 1979. After all, in the year of the exhibition Libeskind began work on the competition for the Jewish Museum in Berlin, which is marked in equal measure by fragility and void. "In recent years," Libeskind said later, "we had the good fortune to experience the end of all unique concepts and their claims to omnipotence. If architecture does not want to enter the next century as the last bastion of the totalitarian, it has to acknowledge what is the consensus in the socio-political dimension: pluralism and the renaissance of decentralized systems, a conscious dealing with resources and above all with its own history."[5]

## Descartes, the King of Confidence Tricksters

In his book *The Twilight of American Culture,* published in the United States in 2000,[6] the American cultural historian and social critic Morris Berman, who takes as his starting point the work of the Russian-American sociologist Pitirim Sorokin in the thirties, differentiates between two fundamental categories of civilization: the "ideational" and the "sensate." "Ideational cultures are by nature spiritual or ascetic, and they concentrate primarily on the transformation of the inner life, whereas sensate cultures such as ours are materialistic and are based on the modification of the exterior world."[7] In the face of Sorokin's uncanny visions which we are already experiencing as real in the meantime—kitsch and quantitative colossalism instead of qualitative refinement, bestseller instead of classic, technology instead of genius, information instead of serious thought—Berman pleads for a "monastic option" beyond the publicity and attention of the media.

The task of the "new monks" or "native strangers" is to set against "a world of trash, uncertainty, social inequality, and mass consumption" the individual, personal example, the reality of an authentic, non-commercial way of life far away from the market and its utilitarian values. This would take place not in the hope of success and respect but geared toward a feeling for value and meaning contained in action itself and also to the safeguarding of the past ideals of the Enlightenment which after a catastrophe or catharsis perhaps (and hopefully) might come into service once again in better times. That would be in the framework of a new Renaissance or Enlightenment, in which art, science, and literature play a central role in the life of a very large part of the population.

## The Modern Age: Sexy, but Old-Fashioned

The architect with no eye for profit, power, fame, and self-promotion: a guerilla who does not only sparkle with creativity but also makes a contribution to society's continuing development? Berman names examples: not Jean-Paul Sartre but Boris Vian; not Johann Wolfgang von Goethe, but Heinrich von Kleist; not Martin Heidegger but Ludwig Wittgenstein. The references in the architectural field are, however, thin on the ground. Frederick Law Olmstedt, the landscape architect of Central Park in Manhattan, is quoted first—with his view that a democracy needs places "of unconscious or indirect relaxation" in order to function—places where there is contact and company: simple instead of ostentatious, decentralized instead of standardized, communicative instead of solemn. From a German perspective, it is surprising that Libeskind the American, a Berliner by adoption, plays no part here.

For Libeskind, whose Felix-Nussbaum-Haus in Osnabrück[8] was chosen by the American magazine *Time* as one of the top ten designs of 1998, it is not a question of styling but of the metaphysical dimension of architecture which he considers indispensable for the emancipation of society: "The vital origin of architecture lies in the substance of the soul, and its being is culture."[9] It is about the cultural matrix, the dimension of urban depth, a symbolic visible portrayal of history in a subjective artistic impulse. "This approach endeavors to explore the deeper order anchored not only in visible forms but also in invisible and hidden sources feeding culture itself—thought, art, literature, song, and movement. It regards history and tradition as a single body, whose memories and dreams cannot easily be reconstructed."[10]

"Nothing straight can be carved out of such crooked wood as man is made of."—Immanuel Kant[11]

If one follows Berman's argument, an NMI (new monastic individual) is the "puristic embodiment of the human spirit," and it has no part in anything which is classed as an "ism": "For an NMI knows the historical irony which involves movements beginning full of critical energy and ending as new (oppressive) orthodoxies, with texts, heroes, and slogans."[12] Daniel Libeskind, the "metaphysician of architects" who loves to give philosophical talks which no one understands,[13] the "juggler of thoughts, quotations, associations, connections, and references," for whom—as was acknowledged at the presentation of the Goethe medal—it is a question of a "spiritualization of hard matter in the age of a fetishistically understood materialism"[14] has not always made the meaning of his work easy to understand. Libeskind, the "theoretical nursery child, charismatic in the return to those cultural resources on which he is in a position to draw,"[15] denied his association with Deconstructivism, for example, contested the relationship between his (after an exhibition hall in Japan) second building to actually be realized—the museum in Osnabrück—and the Jewish Museum in Berlin designed earlier, somehow no longer remembered a broken-open Star of David as a stage of the design plan, and rejected a suggestion of the building as a "design for a memorial" that might restrict on thematic grounds the formal language used. With the text of his lecture "Stadt und Sein," however, he has in the meantime turned to a wider audience.[16] When Libeskind, the son of Polish Jews in Lodz, an American citizen since 1965, received the German Architectural Prize for the Jewish Museum—"the answer of humane architecture to state terrorism trying to exterminate a whole race"[17]—he had in any case made himself clear. His museum was to be a sign of hope not only pointing to the past but more importantly to the future. Otherwise Berlin's present-day architecture, as Libeskind said the next day on television, appears rather "mediocre" or "uninspired": "Good, well-known architects have built the worst buildings of their career here."[18] Rebuilding is in any case nothing other than a marketing idea. "Annoyingly a great chance has been lost. It is not an optimistic preview of the cities of the 21st century if people only ask about the number of investors and purchasers they can attract... Much more attention should be given to public areas and the different activities of the people in them.... Public life, that means experienced freedom.... Without a new cultural vision it makes little sense to play around with visitor numbers and development plans."[19]

Sliding into the Uncanny

For Libeskind future developments are more than promising, and the reports of success come in thick and fast. The reason is in the monopoly of the new which sends people like Wellington Webb, the mayor of Denver, into raptures: "Mr. Libeskind's talent will make an impressive contribution to the economic significance of the museum for the city of Denver and the state of Colorado."[20] At this point the NMI halo fades. However: "Artists and architects, if they want to represent the new world with its dynamism and constant productiveness, have to look for new languages or develop existing languages."[21] Libeskind's brand name, after a long theoretical and art-laden experimental period, is one of the worldwide concepts of a globalized architecture, as Jacques Herzog defines it: "The star system in architecture is a consequence of globalization, of globalized architecture. In order for a city or a country to position itself, it needs architects who themselves can be treated as a brand name. Architecture, art, and fashion today are interrelated in their content. In all these areas it is essential to build on authentic research, whether as an architect, fashion designer, or artist. To this extent fashion and architecture have moved close to art. As a result architecture like fashion is something we need in order to survive in this world and also to communicate."[22] Yet Libeskind, who likes to argue for his architecture and its relationship to landscape with quiet contemplation as restoration of physical and mental well-being, anticipated Morris Berman's monastic option in 1988 in the philosophical montage of his potential for seduction: "Not until I tackled the project did I discover that the weapons of architecture and the weapons of the world did not have their origins in the Renaissance—their origins lay rather in the monastery. Machine guns and parachutes and atom bombs are not inventions of Leonardo da Vinci, but of Thomas Aquinas and of an even earlier spirituality. I have tried to become the architect who is commissioned by a monastery and who would then deliver the non-objective as well as the objective counterpart to the purified, sacred experience. In other words I made a cogwheel..."[23] In a world in which "good" is equated with goods and is traded in more than a billion square meters of shopping mall, the architect occupies himself in the meantime with the new cathedrals of the city. Libeskind aestheticizes what really needs to be analyzed: for example a post-Piranesi maze of shops in Bern. But did it make sense to ignore the problem of the periphery? For Libeskind everyday life is even the true work of art; he wants to celebrate the encounter in public. The experimental distance from a Jewish museum in Berlin cannot be greater and yet it is all about the same aims—as a prototype of the (sub-)urban society on an even more relevant plane. "Art is uncanny because it obscures reality and also because it deceives. But it does not deceive from within itself; its power to deceive has its basis rather in the desire projected into it by the observer."[24]

Klaus-Dieter Weiss

  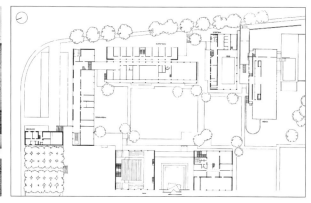

Pedagogical College, Eichstätt, 1965, with Josef Elfinger, Ingolstadt

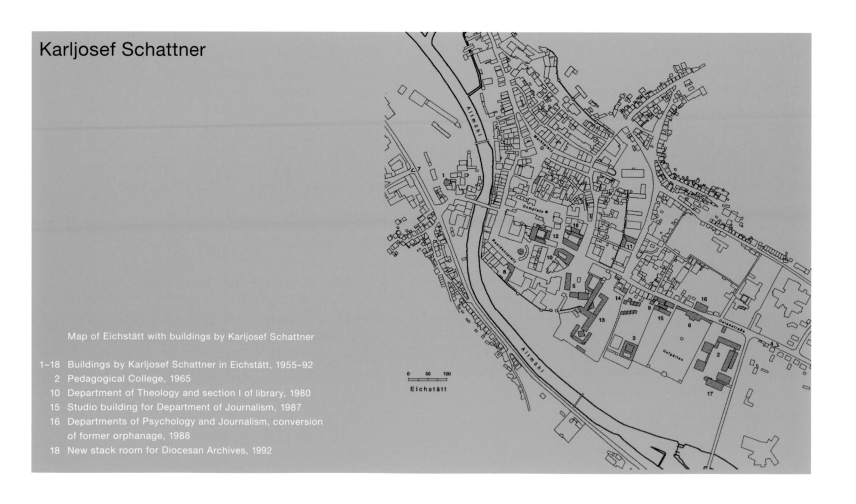

# Karljosef Schattner

Map of Eichstätt with buildings by Karljosef Schattner

1–18  Buildings by Karljosef Schattner in Eichstätt, 1955–92
   2  Pedagogical College, 1965
  10  Department of Theology and section I of library, 1980
  15  Studio building for Department of Journalism, 1987
  16  Departments of Psychology and Journalism, conversion
       of former orphanage, 1988
  18  New stack room for Diocesan Archives, 1992

Eichstätt

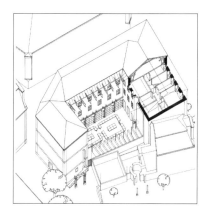

Department of Theology and section I of library, Katholische Universität Eichstätt, Ulmer Hof conversion and addition, 1980

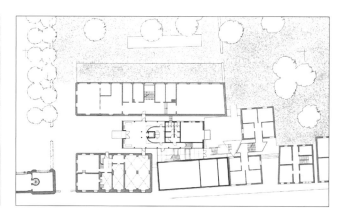

Studio Building for Department of Journalism, Katholische Universität Eichstätt, 1987

   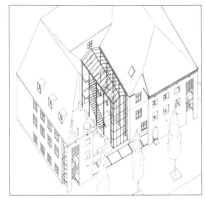

Departments of Psychology and Journalism, Katholische Universität Eichstätt, conversion of former orphanage, 1988

Mutschler Residence, Ulm, 1995, with Wilhelm Huber

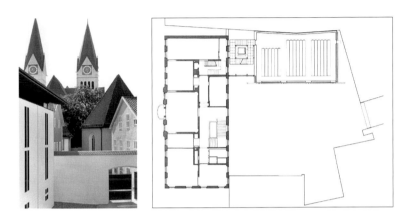

Diocesan Archives, Eichstätt, new stack room, 1992, with Karl Frey

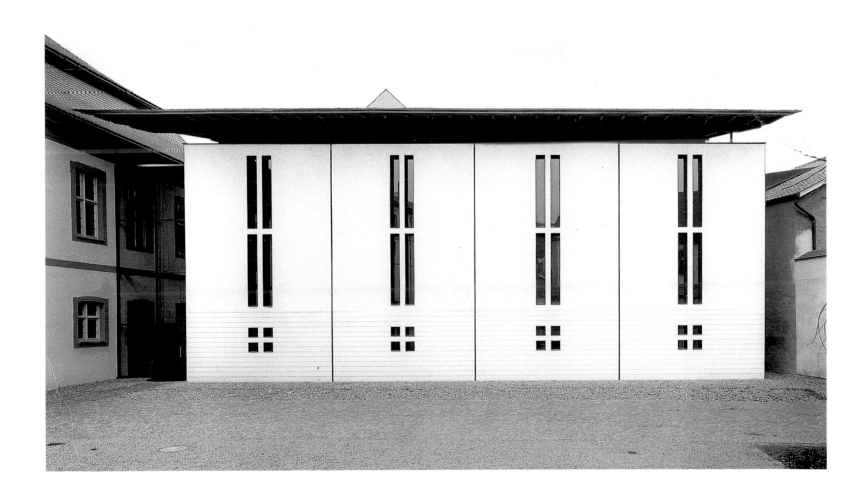

Karljosef Schattner is an exception within contemporary German architecture. His work is concentrated in and around the small Baroque town of Eichstätt in the Altmühl valley, where Schattner was active for almost thirty-five years (1957–91) as a diocesan architect. No other architect of his generation has built in such a limited area or worked with the same client for so many years; no other architect could have evolved his position so persistently and unswervingly in dealing—Schattner would say "in dialogue"—with tradition. In this regard he always describes himself as a resolute partisan of Modernism, yet without (as Günther Behnisch once expressed it) being "arbitrary" in altering the traditional townscape.

This has led to an exceptionally clear and compact statement that makes Catholic Eichstätt into a mecca for architectural pilgrims, as a much admired model for "new building in a historical context." At the same time there is a striking contradiction within Schattner's work, for strictly speaking his radically modern architecture could only prosper on the basis of an outmoded architect-client relationship that is practically a thing of the past.

The most important client was the Catholic Church, a patron with power and money personified in the bishops of Eichstätt, of whom there have been only three during Schattner's tenure. Client and architect got to know and appreciate each other. Continuity and trust also shaped the working relationship with the clerical council, the committee that oversees diocesan building and which represents the bishop's building director himself. And as the Church does not function first and foremost as a profit-oriented investor, Schattner could realize his projects without the economic pressures and time constraints so commonplace today. Thus he has always considered it a privilege to have a client who "recognizes spiritual quality as quality, and who is accessible to intellectual arguments."

By contrast, the guarantor for the handicraft quality of his buildings has been the cathedral lodge that he founded in Eichstätt. The masons, stucco workers, and metal workers—altogether ten specialists—were experts in the techniques necesary for historical buildings, and with each commission they spared him the problem of finding a labor force that met his high demands. In an exchange between architect and craftsmen—each with knowledge from which the other profits—details were designed, sometimes commonly developed, discussed, often revised, and only in a relatively late stage decided on the site.

Therefore far from the metropolises, in all the quiet and retirement of a Bavarian provincial town, work was able to arise that was able to profess itself for today in such a pronounced way because it was essentially owed to yesterday's conditions of production. It is work, moreover, that in its structure, scale, material, and form clearly relates to the place. Schattner's remark that architecture always solves the same problems—namely "to utilize the material and its structure, to use rhythm, symmetry, and asymmetry, to exploit light and shadow, to employ the tectonics of the architectural masses, their scale, and the mutual proportionality of their building parts"—leads therefore to one further constant: architecture always needs an identifiable, engaged client and good craftsmen. In Eichstätt both conditions were fulfilled.

What Karljosef Schattner found there when he assumed the diocesan building post in 1957 was a rarity in postwar Germany. The town, which is situated in the river valley of the Altmühl between two chains of hills of the Frankish Jura, had weathered the war practically intact. The last serious acts of destruction go back to the Swedes in the Thirty Years' War. That which was rebuilt in the 17th and 18th centuries by territorial rulers, prince-bishops, and the nobility is today still extensively intact—an urban Baroque work of art, created by three great architects who came to Bavaria from Switzerland: Maurizio Pedetti from Tessin, and Jakob Engel and Gabriel de Gabrieli from Graubünden. Schattner's tasks consisted above all of adapting old buildings to serve new purposes, and they encompassed the whole spectrum from renovation and restoration of old buildings to the addition of new wings to the incorporation of new elements.

The founding of a Catholic university shortly after Schattner's appointment proved to be another stroke of luck. For the institutional buildings do not lead a satellite existence outside of town, but were erected on the edge of and in the town itself, mostly in historic buildings. "A cardinal question of all monumental preservation," writes Wolfgang Pehnt,[1] namely to find a use compatible with them, is thus answered in Eichstätt almost automatically: practically all former bishopric residences, cavalier courts, orangeries, and stables today accommodate libraries, technical disciplines, and administrative offices for the university or seminaries. And the architect has brought everything into a dialogue of old and new that is as lively as it is programmatic.

Already by virtue of his Prussian extraction, above all however by his studies, Schattner has an unsentimental relation with the Baroque. In their reserved sobriety his buildings stand in marked contrast to the vivacious curves of the 18th century and make Eichstätt into a place of a very unique—of a Schattnerish kind of—Modernism: simple, rational, without the slightest trace of historicist imitation, reductive in dimensions and materials, and conceived of sparseness. The motto here is not fusion but contrast. The implements for his tasks as the diocesan architect in Eichstätt were passed on to him by his teacher in Munich, Hans Döllgast. The latter's creative restoration of the Alte Pinakothek, which confronted the traditional in both a respectful and self-assured way, impressed Schattner's architectural thinking: "His dealings with a work of historical architecture destroyed by the war became a basic law for my later work."

Yet he found his unmistakable signature in his direct confrontation of the historical building body. The renovation of the former cathedral deanery (1965–66) shows in this regard almost the whole range of his means, which had changed over the course of years (formally, not in basic attitude) under the influence of such models as Carlo Scarpa or Giancarlo De Carlo, later also the new Tessin School. An exterior sign for the completely new interior life of the Baroque building, which today houses the administration of the diocesan authorities and building officials, is a squared, one-and-a-half story stone portal. Behind it opens a two-story hall with a bridge structure made out of reinforced concrete and steel steps.

Everything that at first seems so sparing in the latter's sensual charm in truth is suggestive here of a richly orchestrated aesthetic formed on contrasts: the contrast of the opulent Baroque façade with its curved gable and a minimalist interior spatial structure, the clear distinction between then and now, the contrast of the broad surfaces of the interior walls and the visually delicate wickerwork of the stair railings and balustrades, the dull gray of the exposed concrete and the silvery glitter of the stainless steel elements. The special status of staircases in his architecture is likewise marked out here. With Schattner's staircase it is without exception as much a matter of being artistic as having an engineered and precise structure, which on the one hand pays tribute to the Baroque desire for staging the ascent and descent, while the steel installation on the other hand also contributes to it "by creating unexpected modern interior spaces in old buildings." He effectively introduces this "superimposition of primary and secondary structures," which as a solid component of his vocabulary draws through the work "to achieve a spatial intensification."

His later works also follow the principle of clearly distinguishing the building parts that have arisen in very different times, or, as Schattner describes it, of making legible new "entries" within the "document" of the building—except that the canon of the material and color has over the years become somewhat more varied and more playful, aromatized with a breath of irony. For example, in Schattner's last building as a diocesan architect, the Diocesan Archives (1989–92), the eaves are blood red; in a burlesque self-citation, the blind window turns a façade motive of his Clerical Seminar (1981–84) upside down. In the reading hall of the Ulmer Hof (1978–80), which has been converted into the department of Catholic theology, he flirts with industrial models, such as his sheet-metal roof and latticework trusses above the originally open interior court, his use of library decking, and the cylinder staircases in the corners. Brightly colored stucco accentuates the vaulted body of the radio broadcasting studio in the new building of the department of journalism, which, as a cube with a tall portal notch, is pushed between the finely articulated Baroque orangeries.

With special virtuosity Schattner has availed himself of everything relating to the "art of the joint," as his preference for the separating link between old and new would indicate. Characteristic, above all, are the glazed intermediate zones and hallways, which keep the historical and his own work apart and together at the same time—as is the case with the journalism building and the central staircase of the former orphanage. There are also linear or pointed, almost bodiless connections for supports and mounts, contrasting materials to emphasize seams, to mark intersections, to set caesuras—individually and collectively they are strategies against the "beautiful appearance of the ahistorical."

"Accommodation and even very skilled imitation will devalue existing historical architecture. We cannot avoid solving our tasks with our means and our constructions, limited by the horizon of our time." It remains surprising that despite this distancing rapport of old and new, despite this "non-Baroque architectural conception"[2] that acts contrary to the existing, therefore despite this contrariness, Schattner succeeds in creating a unity. His work harmonizes with the Baroque architecture; it enriches, enhances, and endows the built town with a historical focus. Schattner's work therefore remains trailblazing for "new building in a historical context"—even in a time that with growing enthusiasm lets itself be dazzled by "the beautiful appearance of the ahistorical." We need only to look to Berlin, where at the end of 2001 a government-appointed commission of specialists voiced itself in favor of the "reconstruction" of the Stadtschloss torn down after World War II—a new building with the fake façade of the Hohenzollern palace stuck on. Then we understand how good Eichstätt is.

Amber Sayah

Gruner + Jahr Publishing House, Hamburg, 1990, concept and design: Steidle + Partners with Kiessler + Partners, realization: Schweger + Partners

# Steidle + Partners

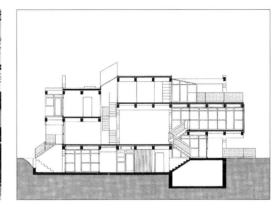

Genter Strasse 13 Housing Complex, Munich, 1972, Otto Steidle with Doris Thut, Ralph Thut, and Jens Freiberg

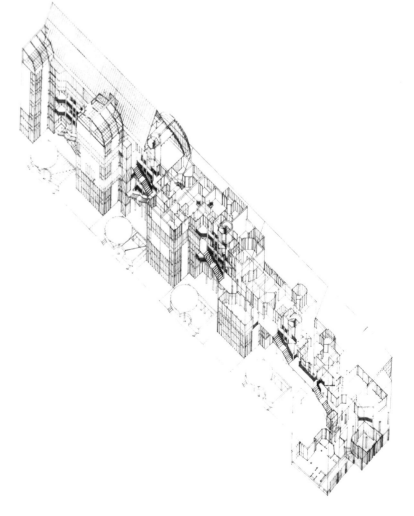

International Meeting Center for Scholars, Berlin, 1983, Otto Steidle
with Siegwart Geiger, Hans Kohl, Alexander Lux

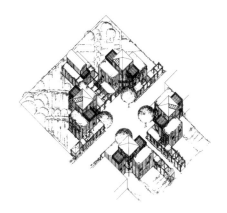

Green Buildings, BUGA National Garden Show, Berlin, 1985, Otto Steidle with Hans Kohl

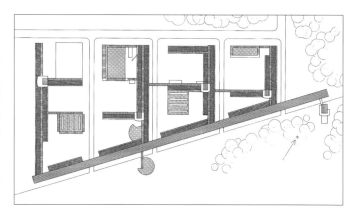

Universität Ulm-West, Ulm, 1992, Otto Steidle with Siegwart Geiger, Alexander Lux, Peter Schmitz, Thomas Standl, Johann Spengler

Wacker Building, Munich, 1997, Otto Steidle with Hans Kohl, Erich Gassmann, Martin Klein, Claudia Dias, and Martina Hornhardt

One reaches Harpfing with the train from Munich in an hour and a half, changing in Mühldorf, then further to Simbach. There Otto Steidle collects one in a sports utility vehicle with his raw hands still gray with mortar, clay sticking to his corduroy pants. Harpfing has become his domestic center of focus with a charming farm, meadows, fields, ponds, and forest. Four horses and a dog belong to the family, which is frequently augmented by co-workers and colleagues when farmer Steidle recalls his actual means of livelihood and works on a competition in his rural refuge.

Sometimes he only spends one day a week looking after his other offices in Simbach, Munich, and Berlin—the potatoes and spelt are also work! But the fact that Steidle affords himself the luxury of rural life and has not fled to Poona does not stem from a drop-out mentality. His parents had a farm in Milbertshofen. But as a youth, although he sometimes felt drawn to becoming a farmer, he did an internship in an architectural office and studied at the Staatsbauschule in Munich. After graduating in 1965 he enrolled in the Munich Akademie der Bildenden Künste, and that same year he worked on his first housing project. By the time he received his diploma in 1969 his portfolio had grown to include around twenty housing projects. He then formed Steidle + Partners, and there have always been colleagues around him, whose responsibility is concealed in meaningful conjunctions.

The Early Years: Inconspicuous and North of Munich

Steidle's buildings of the sixties have remained rather inconspicuous. The earliest buildings are in the vicinity of his parent's house (and the fact that the children were able to sell some of the land they had inherited made the start-up phase of the young office discreetly easier).

If one views these multifamily units today with their well-arranged façades that open up towards the outside with balconies and access ramps, one will not recognize the handwriting of Otto Steidle. But they are certainly—like Ungers's buildings of the fifties—worthy of study. Some are only heavy and without flourish, their year of construction undeniable, and there is little more to say about them. Others with their openness and lightness show a proximity to Sep Ruf, Steidle's esteemed teacher at the Akademie. These are buildings with lively articulation that distinguish themselves by playfully solved (or perhaps just experimental) details. Massive parapets are snapped in playfully, but naturally more beautiful are the filigree railings. The faded colors originally must have been rather powerful, far removed from the harmonies that Steidle today brings to façades with Erich Wiesner. In the examples in Obermenzing we find the first attempts at a concrete skeleton. Here appear the forms and materials corresponding to the taste of the late sixties: trapezoidal sheet-metal, bulging railings with round corners, and corrugated bars.

Improvisation and Atmospheric Social Politics

The housing complex at Genter Strasse 13, which arose in collaboration with Doris and Ralph Thut, represents a caesura: it immediately became a much-published example of Steidle's work. As if it were a practical concession to his later favorite theme of city planning, Steidle was able to advance the already-begun type of a prefabricated concrete skeletal building on adjacent properties. Genter Strasse, where he has his Munich office today, has adequately proven its flexibility and interpretability as a place of living and working; it means something more than a space delineated with characteristic concrete bones. Steidle—who certainly lived in the climate of the student movement, although without himself distributing fliers, demonstrating against the Vietnam War, or disturbing seminars—viewed his housing project as a metaphor for his image of society. He wanted to create a three-dimensional framework, but not some foreign living forms that should settle in here. The isolated small-family house and its brick bonds sprang in his opinion from the same exhausted mental image. Open stacked floors, yielding the view, are shifted into levels; they had to be able to accommodate communal living areas or they could give back collective areas to families or to single units. Yet in fact the housing units were also well suited to self-employed and working-parent-households with computer stations in live-in offices. Steidle, no social romantic, wanted more than to define the contemporary taste in dwelling in an aesthetic way; he took part in the experiment of whether architecture can also influence change. The exterior of the housing complex was never remodeled, and the free-standing concrete pillars are indicative of its unfinished and changeable nature.

The Elementa housing project in Nuremberg (1972–74) once again introduced industrialized building methods into social housing. Steidle's contribution to the *documenta urbana* in Kassel (1979–82) reminds one only in passing of the ideals of the informal extended family, but it introduces a new element that would increasingly permeate Steidle's architecture: communication. Paths and stairs, landings and passageways amalgamate the anonymous living structure with half-public spaces that encourage appropriation.

With the *documenta* project also began his teaching activity, first at the Gesamthochschule in Kassel, then at the Technische Universität in Berlin. After guest professorships in Cambridge and Amsterdam he returned again to the Munich Akademie, in whose hallow corridors he had once organized a motorcycle race as a student.

One might ask how anyone can practice three exacting callings at the same time: playing farmer, architect, and college teacher. For Steidle in no way resembles a hyperactive manager—on the contrary, no one has yet seen him with the appropriate insignia of the double-breasted suit and necktie. Instead one finds him looking rather disheveled, his hands stuck deep in the pockets of his soft wool jacket, at talks and lectures; then he speaks of his work, as if he had just come from the drawing board. It is easy to imagine that there is no computer there. His private atelier at his farm is a large room in the former barn. The light through the small windows is supplemented by a simple field of glass panes in the low ceiling, above which the old steel roof is creased with a pair of inlaid glass blocks. Below stands a colossal table, strewn with rolls of paper, color pens, and blueprints. A cast-iron stove supplies warmth in the winter when Steidl sketches—for clients in Peking, Celyabinsk, Bremerhaven, and Deggendorf. One could make a film of an architect here that conceivably could take place in 1950 or 1930. Howard Roark in Harpfing.

Behind this bohemian life is perhaps the strategy that Steidle is only concerned with what he can do, and only does as much as he wants. For he has never responded to a general invitation for designs. There are people for that who are more perseverant. He even leaves such architectural tasks as museums or industrial buildings to colleagues who are more experienced in these fields. Likewise he is little interested in single-family houses, not only out of social-political resentment but because he has no desire "to go shopping for tiles with the lady of the house." He writes the script and directs it. For this reason city planning is not a new discipline for him; it also concerns architecture—a concrete construct between building and living. For the whole must accord with the proportionality of the means. Details are somewhat valuable to him, but he would never do something only because it belongs to the performance image of the exacting architect. And he smiles: "I was never so industrious. To Kiessler I have always said: Uwe, do half as much."

In his book *Moderne und Postmoderne* (Modernism and Post-modernism) Heinrich Klotz discusses Otto Steidle in the chapter entitled "Against Perfection." He recognizes narrative motives in his "modest arbor architecture," which follow such other laws as the fulfillment of function and the greatest possible simplification of the basic forms. This improvisational reification of architecture marks the second phase of the architect's work. It was accompanied by commissions in Hamburg and Kassel, in Berlin during the IBA period, and by the end of the eighties his watershed reached to Vienna with large neighborhood projects.

This colorful architecture of the seventies and eighties left behind the coarseness of the concrete assembly elements. The buildings for the national garden show in Berlin (1982–85) are typical. The fact that the stairs here were built with seat alcoves and the railings were fabricated in the manner of cribs leads us back to the theme "Build it yourself, and do it simply." The senior citizens' home in Berlin-Kreuzberg (1982–87) stays within the context of the former shed. And why should one not allow older people something of the architecture of summer holidays when they are no longer as mobile? At the same time he built the ambitious headquarters for publishing house Gruner + Jahr in Hamburg (1983–90), with which the Bavarian had wanted to give "harbor-related elements" back to Hamburgers, and on which he let himself be guided by the creative élan expected in the editing departments. The multi-family housing on Wittelsbacher Rondell in Munich (1980–81), by contrast, remains almost unknown; the buildings display the vocal interpretation of an upper class villa neighborhood. With the international conference center in Berlin-Wilmersdorf (1979–83) a progressively composed urban architecture, whose design focuses literally on the "meeting," is resolved by an artistic staging of staircases and arbors, which serve the attractive realms of general rather than private use. In a conversation with Ulrich Conrads, who with his campaign against Postmodernism presumably views Steidle as a combatant, he explained that this architecture "does not necessarily give us more order, but it does clearly convey the ability to organize and share our urban living situation." This phase until the beginning of the nineties was perhaps the decisive one for the architect. Or does it only seem so because at that time his work could still be followed in the immediate vicinity?

International, Metropolitan—and Distrusting of Typologies

In the year 2000 we come upon Otto Steidle as a participant of the Biennale in Venice. Among his friends are Herzog & de Meuron, Jean Nouvel, Will Alsop, and Coop Himmelb(l)au— without his coming especially close to their architecture. His work rather has affinities to Adolf Krischanitz and Massimil-

iano Fukas. It even respects MVRDV—Holland's "aha effect." Now the large-scale becomes interesting. Ad-hoc architecture, messing around, as Steidle himself calls it without coquetry, is always supported by a search for balance and joint responsibility and must prove its worth in the international arena. And it is well known that the air is thinner there. Since the university in Ulm (1988–92), which has just been complemented with a library, Steidle has received the greatest attention. Erich Wiesner's color conception and the city planning figure stretching to a 400-meter entrance ramp, along with the looming curious towers, are attempts to reassess the indescribable scientific activities of a college, not with a glittering high-tech scheme, but with the comprehensible means of expression of the architect. Steidle mistrusts buildings that only fulfill one function and speak typologically. Another example of this is the office and living complex on Prinzregentenstrasse in Munich (1992–97). Neither the façade nor the plan betray the use for which it is intended. Small extra windows, which he always likes to add, break through the reason of the purely rational. Should the working places no longer pay off, the structure could with some technical modifications become attractive dwellings— with the anxious question whether after a recession anyone could afford it in this inner-city oasis. The most recent works—the Michaelisquartier in Hamburg and the office buildings on Theresienhöhe in Munich, which he will execute himself after his urban planning scheme was chosen in competition—promise a new facet: the serial element of the metropolis. Narrow, upright window units, sometimes with rhythmic disturbances, show themselves from afar as obligatory frames, and change up close by the refined play with the material (clinker, ceramics, or stucco) and color producing the lively energy that holds everything together.

If one sits together with Otto Steidle in his simple rural living room, whose middle is occupied by a monstrous corpulent stove, and wonders about the willful furnishings (which consist primarily of benches, couches, and beds), it occurs to one that there is no television set but a piano and an old record player. Then one senses how very much it is a matter of personal architecture that is created in the barn across the way. Steidle speaks and hears himself. One gets the feeling that he is explaining not only his motivation to the questioner but he is also describing it to himself for the first time, as if he is getting to know himself and checking what has already been read into him by others. And if all the hermeneutics fail, then at some point he says, "I do that for myself. I want it to be what I myself am." I build thus, "because I am unable to do it any other way." And he shouldn't be hindered in this endeavor.
Wolfgang Bachmann

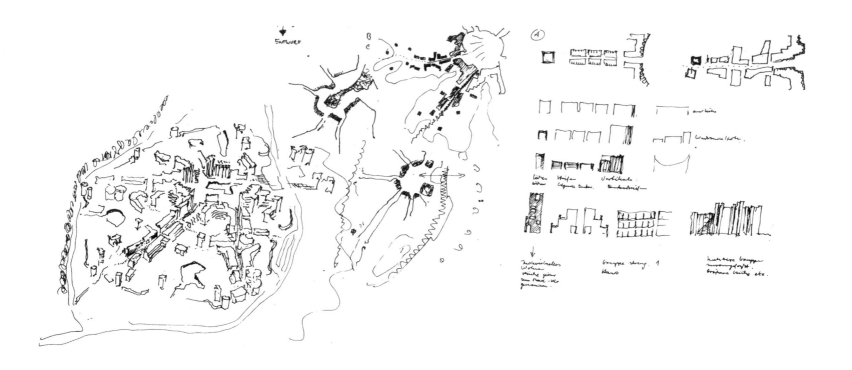

Competition design for a student dormitory of the Technical College Twente, Enschede, Holland, 1964 (top and bottom)

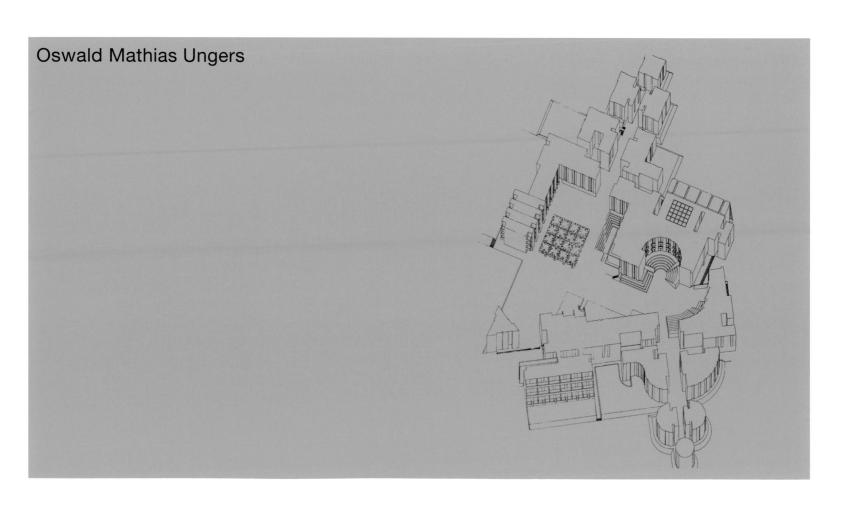

# Oswald Mathias Ungers

Multiple-Family Residence (1959) and Library Cube (1990), Belvederestrasse, Cologne-Müngersdorf

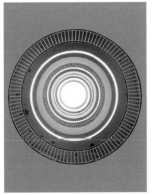

Gatehouse for Messe- und Ausstellungs-GmbH, Frankfurt am Main, 1984 and 1997 (expansion of Terminal Mitte)

Residence of the German Ambassador, Washington D.C., 1995

Ungers Residence III, Cologne, 1996

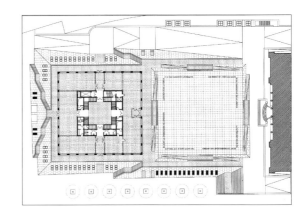

Expansion of the Kunsthalle Hamburg, Galerie der Gegenwart (Gallery of Contemporary Art), 1996

"What should one design for a place for which there is no program, yet which is impressed with the superimposition of a two-thousand-year-old urban history? In a city in which ... the history of architecture lies open like a book for everyone who knows how to read it?"
—Oswald Mathias Ungers[1]

## Coincidence of Contraries

Oswald Mathias Ungers formulated these questions in 1995 in his speech at the topping-out ceremony for the hot springs on the forum in Trier. This city of the greatest compaction in terms of architectural history has become the object of a recurrent calling for the architect born in Kaisersesch, in the Eifel Mountains, in 1926. Here in the ensemble of the cathedral, Gothic and ancient Roman styles, Ottonian and Rhenish late Romantic, Baroque movement and classical rigor are brought together in a manifold totality.[2] Not far from that sacral city

center, under the Viehmarktplatz, lie remnants from Roman and Celtic times that needed preservation. On a square plan Ungers designed a glass cabinet as "a window into the past," which lets one look down on the former layouts of the city. Trier, says Ungers, is "a perfect example of the continuous *formation* and *transformation* of an urban image";[3] in no other city will one better understand the concept of a *coincidentia oppositorum*, a coincidence of contraries, as first expressed by Nikolaus Kues in 1440. It is this concept to which the architect again and again refers; it forms the leitmotif of his architectural thinking.

Around the same time—in 1996—he built a small building in Cologne whose form could hardly be less unambiguous. To students Ungers says, "This is everything that I can offer you after seventy years. This is the house. I can do no more, but also no less."[4] The house is his own, the third in a remarkable succession. Four decades earlier, one street away, his first home created a stir: a brick building composed of raw cubes, placed on a concrete pedestal. Reyner Banham elevated it to a "confession,"[5] as a prime example of brick brutalism. In the adjacent garden in 1990 Ungers followed up with a striking library cube in basalt lava for his unique book collection of treatises and valuable first editions. It is "a stereometric body, rational and consistently logical," wrapped around "a white cubic skeleton, a basic element of architecture, the essence of building."[6] In step three, Ungers pushes the abstraction further in favor of the idea. He built a pure, white box two stories high, four window-axes wide. A two-story hall is flanked on each side by two rooms lying above one another; all technical functions are hidden in the double skin of the walls. The box without a socle or cornice rests on a severe plinth: an ideal area in which the laws of architecture are valid. This is the other pole in Ungers's work; against superimposition, it is the purification of the idea which has taken on form. The floor plan recalls houses by Palladio, Otto Wagner, Mies van der Rohe, and—even more—the Schinkel Pavilion in Charlottenburg. Ungers's goal has been "to build the same house, but polished like a gem, free from any decoration, and led back to the pure archetype."[7]

Formation of Language

What should one design in history, in a place, beyond a functional program? The Trier questions reflect a basic quality in Ungers's work, which is dedicated to the search for and transformation of universal spatial concepts. Ungers is considered *the* German rationalist; he puts it more precisely: "The formal language of architecture … expresses the aesthetic value of architecture as its own intrinsic value. It has its own ratio, and only thus is the concept of rational architecture to be understood."[8] No other German architect in the second half of the 20th century has produced such a rich body of theory and likewise sought to prove it in practice.

In this endeavor Ungers has remained true to his thought and—following a creation of the rudiments—to his formal vocabulary. The latter provokes opposition because it seems to deny all trends, for instance, of the fragile or the virtual; it resists fashions as much as the harassing fire of extra-architectural questions. In fact Ungers continues to create architecture in stone, and where he erects broad glass surfaces—as, for instance, in the Frankfurt Trade Fair (1983–84) or in the unrealized high-rise cube of the Düsseldorf statehouse (1991)—the bodies give the feeling of being no less enclosed. He proceeds from the stabilizing certitude of the square and reverts to it at every scale. Ungers does not feel constrained by it, but recognizes it as a form allowing the greatest freedom.[9] In the categories of architectural language that are based on a spatial typology, the square constitutes of course the inflection, not the actually meaning of the "spoken."

This meaning, however, has been the object of Ungers's work since he opened his Cologne office in 1950. Form is "expression of spiritual content,"[10] proclaims the manifesto *Zu einer neuen Architektur* (Toward a New Architecture), which Ungers and Reinhard Gieselmann published in 1960. This concept of form refers not to the surface area of individual building parts, but to the space formed by it, or to put it in a more abstract way, the spatial type as it remains identifiable throughout history. With Ungers architecture is raised with a claim of autonomy, which can never be reconciled with "Functionalism." Against its "mentality of purpose"[11] the former student of Egon Eiermann demands form; against the placelessness of international Modernism he early on emphasized the bond to the existing, the *genius loci*. For him this means analysis of the existing spatial structure, of its transformation and reintegration.

Since the sixties Ungers has worked toward systematization. After some early complex apartment and housing developments, the sense of scale was lost with the massive housing projects for the Märkisches Viertel in Berlin (1962). Perhaps this was one of the reasons for an intensification of theoretical pursuits.[12] From 1963 to 1978 Ungers built no project; he taught at the Technische Universität in Berlin, then at Cornell University in the United States. Yet some of his most important designs were made during this period, for example, the student dormitory in Twente (1964), the Berlin art museums (1965), and Cologne's (former) Wallraf-Richartz-Museum (1975). Untouched by the tribulations of practical building, these designs had to show no compromise; they tested the foundation of meaning in architectural relations and the basis of geometric logic. Morphological series of bodies and spatial types were tried out, axes appeared and were broken, variations established multiplicity in unity.[13] Historical models gleaned through; in the design for Twente, for example, there are residues of Schinkel's plan for the Acropolis and Hadrian's Villa. In *Das Recht der Architektur auf eine autonome Sprache* (Architecture's Right to an Autonomous Language, 1980), Ungers argued vehemently against Immanuel Kant's view that architecture be counted among "the unfree arts, of *pulchritudo adhaerens*," and that they are subordinate to the service of the function: "Architecture, to put it drastically, is free of purpose, which does not mean that it is useless, but rather that its true dimension manifests itself independently of all exterior constraints." An idea must underlie the form; architecture possesses the capability to free human existence "from the triviality of the real and to raise the material forces artistically."[14] In his book *Die Thematisierung der Architektur* (The Thematization of Architecture),[15] Ungers names the themes of architectural design—alongside transformation, of course, "assemblage" or "incorporation" (applied in the Deutsches Architekturmuseum in Frankfurt as the "house within the house," 1979–84). Ungers's designs are recognizable as a part of a single, on-going project.

New Abstraction

The dilemma that this project conceals resides within the claim of autonomy of (Neo-) rationalism in general: the work must continue to reflect on its own failure, the world of ideas is irreconcilable with the real world. Still in 1983 Ungers had to defend his return to practice "Should I perhaps say, 'No, I am an artist. I do not want to get my fingers dirty'?"[16] The proclamation applied to the Torhaus in Frankfurt; which as a tall building shaped like a giant window was the first and largest building of Ungers to confront a complex urban planning situation—here as a connecting link between the fair grounds and railway tract—with a radical purification of geometry. It is the first of a series of projects which become increasingly pure in formal terms. Ungers speaks of a "new abstraction," that is, "until the object appears in its basic structure, the concept in its clearest geometry, and the theme in its most impressive form."[17] The more basic the idea becomes, certainly all the more difficult it becomes, even to decipher the connection to the typologies found in the existing context, or as Wolfgang Pehnt put it, "The mute perfection of the later buildings, such as the high-rise buildings for Neuss and Cologne-Deutz or the latest private houses, are related to their specific surroundings only by a contrasting sense of otherness, actually by their affiliation with another aggregate condition."[18]

Yet Ungers sees his works as dealing with that basic conflict, not bringing it to a head. Increasingly he is interested in the fragment,[19] meaning each—even slight—deviation from the pure form due to what has been found. In fact, it is the city that presents itself heterogeneously, not the individual building. The two poles, purification and superimposition, find each other in urban thinking. Concepts for that—"The City as Folly," "The City of Complementary Places"—have infused city planning designs, for example, for the Euroforum in Cologne (1992) or the Humboldt Colonnades in Berlin (starting in 1995).[20] The form of the singular encroachment oriented to the ideal confers expressive power on impure structure.

This proportionality is seen in the two already notable museum buildings in Hamburg (1986–96) and Cologne (1996–2000). The Kunsthalle expansion in Hamburg is a light-colored cube—with flush windows emphasizing the doubled symmetry—which disassociates itself from the existing building by the mass of its own surface area. Standing by itself like a solitaire on a sloped socle further brings the rigor of its inner organization to the outside. Self-consciously unadorned, it reacts to the large buildings around it and becomes a dominant element between the railway station and the Alster. By contrast the new Wallraf-Richartz-Museum in Cologne is embedded in a narrow context. The references extend from the derivation of the design module from the bordering church ruins to the incorporation of a former alley in the glass staircase. The city appears not disassociated as in Hamburg, but absorbed by the building; thus the museum tract itself, all the more protected, can again approach an almost ideal cube inside. Some years earlier, with the Badische Landesbibliothek in Karlsruhe (1980–92), Ungers proceeded in a similar way: outside the building answers historical neighbors, inside it culminates in the "ideal" reading room vaulted like the Pantheon.

Precisely this subtle embedding of the ideal in the city once again makes it clear that the basic conflict remains insoluble, that the border of change is only shifted. As soon as buildings—in Cologne inside, in Hamburg already on the smooth exteriors—work toward a flawless type they appear to withdraw from the world. They lose weight and body; they become model-like, unapproachable, and therefore also placeless—a characteristic tendency which Ungers had been explicitly challenging in light of classic Modernism. The dome of the Karlsruhe library, built without squinches or spandrels, "appears not as a heavy bearing-wall Pantheon transplanted to the north," writes Pehnt, "but as a sketched, illuminated citation. It is not the heavenly realm itself but a reminder of it."[21] One can no longer interpret the permanence of Ungers as materiality in time, but increasingly as continuation of the type beyond time. Yet life cannot follow it to there, and in the end just as little can the built architecture. This is true even for the third Ungers house, which inquires about the possibility of an "objectless architecture" and—"if one takes it as strictly as Wittgenstein had taken it, or as one must take it"[22] —fails, as Ungers confesses. The fact that Ungers's concept of fragment, which is suitable to this experience, actually consolidates the ideal order standing behind it, will remain the point of departure for criticism. The making relative of this order, however, is not Ungers's theme, just as little as is the reconciliation of the idea and reality. For him, obviously, it can only be a matter of making legible as a drama the failure of architecture in this reconciliation, which itself corresponds to the performance of the sublime.

Olaf Winkler

New German Architecture since 1990
Preconditions, Topics, Contexts

# German Architecture from 1945 to 1990

Wolfgang Pehnt

Günter Behnisch & Partners, German Bundestag, Bonn, 1983–92

Volunteer Service on the Mountain of Rubble

Time passes more quickly in some eras. Or does it only seem that way to contemporaries? The fact that it is always one's own experienced present in which the clocks seem to tick faster suggests that the answer is yes. When the *Trümmerfrauen*—as the women who cleared the rubble of World War II are called—and adolescents returned to the cities after war's end and began sorting bricks and stones and shoveling debris onto trucks, people expected that it would take decades to clear the cities. But the cities of Germany were practically rubble-free by the early fifties—an achievement made possible by modernized motor and equipment pools. Estimates made for individual cities show that no more than 5 percent were cleared in "volunteer service" with picks and shovels. In many places, the rubble left behind as the legacy of catastrophe was used to build amusement parks and sports facilities. The psychic suppression of the past that became an increasingly prominent characteristic of the postwar years had its physical counterpart in beautified hills of rubble.

In May of 1945, no one could have imagined the changes the cities and countryside would undergo in the decades to come: the achievements in reconstruction of the first few years, the "economic miracle" of the fifties in the Federal Republic of Germany, and the "planned socialist urban redevelopment" in the German Democratic Republic. Inconceivable were the modernization efforts undertaken in response to the dictates of traffic and transportation policy, the rationalization and industrialization of building production, the construction of new large-scale housing projects, and the growth of completely new cities, from Eisenhüttenstadt to Volkswagenstadt, from Wolfen to Wulfen. No one could have envisioned such developments as the conversion of city centers into glamorous marketplaces for goods and capital in the West or into—less glamorous—forums of a "mature socialist society"[1] in the East. The succession of different styles that unfolded far above the political and economic base would have elicited only astonishment and disbelief among the cellar dwellers of 1945. In many cases, two or three and sometimes even more different buildings have been erected on the same plot of land in the course of the few decades that have passed since 1945.

The war came to an end in Europe with the surrender of the German *Wehrmacht* on May 7 and 8, 1945. The most important territorial decisions had already been made by the Allies by this time, or would follow at the Potsdam Conference in July and August of that year. The U.S. Morgenthau Plan, which sought to block the reconstruction of heavy industry and turn vanquished Germany into a largely agricultural nation, was soon tabled. Soviet hopes of internationalizing the Ruhr industrial region were dashed by resistance on the part of the British and Americans. The former Reich territory east of the Oder-Neisse Line fell de facto to Poland, and East Prussia went to the Soviet Union. The founding of the Federal Republic in 1949 ended the division of western Germany into three occupation zones, but the founding of the GDR that followed effectively divided the country in two for forty years.

The two states began life under very different conditions. The grand economic aid program named after U.S. Secretary of State George Catlett Marshall provided the foundation for the Western economic miracle. Credit provided through special programs for refugee housing and for fifteen ECA settlements[2] also benefited the construction industry. One out of every five housing units was built with Marshall Plan funds, as was emphasized in the accompanying propaganda campaign. Due to significantly larger reparation payments and more major demolitions, the GDR started from a much weaker position, even though most of its larger cities—with the exception of Dresden and Frankfurt an der Oder—were less heavily damaged than those in the West.

The most pressing concerns of the very first years related to infrastructure. Water, gas, and power supply had to be restored, sewer systems, streetcar and railroad lines, and bridges repaired or rebuilt. More than six million housing units in postwar Germany were destroyed or damaged. The demand for new housing was estimated at five to six million units in West Germany alone. Living space was needed for evacuees returning to the cities from rural exile and for some eight million refugees from the lost eastern territories. Highest priority was given to securing ruins and restoring damaged buildings. Temporary shelters and Quonset huts, which provided valuable experience in prefabrication, satisfied the most urgent needs for the time being. Rudimentary, ultra-low-cost buildings were erected in suburban areas, many of them using loam construction methods. Even Hermann Henselmann, who became the GDR's star architect years later, wrote a loam construction guide in 1947.

Simplicity and Validity

Yet hope did not fade. Memories of the post-World-War-I era were vivid in the minds of many: the dilemma of having only the barest essentials but still clinging to the vision of utopia. In some cases, even during the period immediately after 1945, expectations associated with building appear to have gone beyond mere provisional responses to urgent needs, encompassing such ideas as purification, truth, simplicity, a focus on the essential. "What is it that throws us to our beds in despair and sadness every evening," asked Otto Bartning, "but makes us leap up again every morning with incredible, totally unreasonable courage?"[3]

That courage was paired with impatience. Just two years later, in 1947, an appeal published by the Deutscher Werkbund (German Association of Craftsmen),[4] the first version of which was signed by thirty-eight artists, architects, and publicists, lamented the passage of two years without progress. "Back then"—two years previously!—people had been filled with a sense of liberation and ready to get on with the task at hand. Now, however, they realized just how much the collapse of the visible world is an expression of intellectual and spiritual deterioration. Reliance on temporary structures to meet the needs of the devastated cities merely intensified this sense of impatience. In many city centers, moratoriums imposed on building in the interest of keeping options open for future large-scale planning remained in effect until the Currency Reform of 1949, in some cases longer.

What the authors of the public appeal—professed Modernists all—recommended was "simplicity and validity." This "simplicity and validity" was to set itself apart from over-specialization and meager provisional form alike. Workshop associations were called for, almost echoing the declarations of the revolutionary artists' unions and the Bauhaus Manifesto of 1919. The authors' statements with regard to urban construction reflect the concept of a federation of urban districts, a "loosely structured modular city" that embodied the urbanist ideal of the next fifteen years.[5] It was a planning concept developed by progressive urban planners during the twenties and later adopted by planners in the Third Reich—often the very same people—for their own purposes. Only the substantive intent of the scheme had changed. Articles in the relevant literature of the Nazi era equated the communal cells of urban landscapes to the organizational structure of the party. After 1945, the "local groups" once again became "neighborhoods," "housing cells," "school districts," or "parishes."

Numerous studies have shown that the idea of the "zero hour," the claim of new, fresh beginning, is a myth of the postwar era.[6] In many city planning and construction offices, the same personnel could be found at work after a hiatus of only a few weeks. Cases have been reported in which these officials brought out models from the Nazi years, rededicated local party forums as culture forums, scraped the national symbol with the swastika from plaques, and presented the old Nazi plans as new proposals. Several high officials were forced to resign under pressure from the occupation powers. Yet many of those appointed later were former members of the Committee for the Reconstruction of Destroyed Cities—under the command of Armaments Minister Albert Speer—of the studio

of the General Architecture Inspector for Reconstruction of the Reich Capital—a position formerly held by Speer—and of the construction departments of the German Labor Front or the Nazi arms industry. Among their ranks were such planner-celebrities of the fifties and sixties as Rudolf Hillebrecht of Hanover, Friedrich Tamms of Düsseldorf, and Hans Stephan and Karl Bonatz of Berlin. "Regardless of whether we were planning industrial facilities, agricultural settlements, housing, barracks, military structures, or highway bridges—we all in the same brown-painted boat."[7] This self-critical confession by Alfons Leitl stands out as a rare exception.

Appointments of politically compromised experts triggered isolated public protests in such cities as Düsseldorf, Cologne, and Berlin even before the machinery of reconstruction had gained a full head of steam. The reappointment of Paul Schmitthenner—a highly esteemed educator, a leading advocate of landscape-based architecture, and a militant representative of the Kampfbund Deutscher Architekten und Ingenieure—to the Technische Hochschule Stuttgart also generated considerable controversy. Years later, no one was bothered by the backgrounds of such figures. They looked forward at the end of especially successful careers to receiving the Great Cross of Merit for their service to the Federal Republic.

These tacit continuities were more readily apparent in the architecture of those early years than in urban planning. The plans for grand avenues and assembly squares conceived during the Nazi years were actually realized at only very few locations during the thirties and either abandoned by postwar planners or transformed into broad traffic arteries. Yet the administrative buildings erected during the period prior to the phase of urban modernization and internationalization in the late fifties clearly recall, in their ponderousness and their strong axial orientation, the tradition of institutional architecture that was shaped by Wilhelmine representationalism, the pathos of industrial firms during the Weimar Republic, and the intimidation aesthetics of the Third Reich—although never expressed as bluntly as in the "Little Reich Chancellery" of the Gerling Group in Cologne (1949–60), for which Arno Breker, a sculptor who had been very active on behalf of the Nazi regime, was also partly responsible.

There were also successful efforts to transpose "simplicity and validity" into architectural form without suppressing memories of the past. Poverty was regarded as a calling, and a noble one at that. "Something new must emerge, something that does not evade the lofty appeal that is inherent in poverty, that does not seek to escape its supposed wretchedness but instead finds the eternal nobility still concealed within it today," wrote the church architect Emil Steffann at a time when things had begun to move comfortingly towards the economic miracle.[8] Examples of archetypal architecture can be found in the churches of Dominikus Böhm, Rudolf Schwarz, Hans Schwippert, Emil Steffann, and several others. The use of rubble was not regarded as a response to budget constraints but as an act of truth. Otto Bartning's provisional church program, which was funded by the World Council of Churches, must also be seen in this context. Forty-eight wood-frame churches were planned between Worms and Wismar, Magdeburg and Munich. The framework was filled with whatever material was available at the building site: stone fragments, bricks, rubble. Variations were both possible and welcome. No two churches in this series were the same.

Secular architecture also offers examples of structures in which neither the destruction nor the recollection of it were ignored. One such example was the reconstruction of the Gürzenich in Cologne (1949–55), a late-medieval market and dance hall, by Karl Band and Rudolf Schwarz. In this multipurpose structure, with Baroque-style staircases, chandeliers, and strings of lights that anticipated the playful ornamentation of the fifties, the outer wall of the destroyed Church of Saint Alban formed the inside wall of the hall. The ruined church interior, its vaulted ceilings collapsed and never repaired, could be viewed through the windows. Kneeling below are the grieving parents, a war monument based upon an original figure by Käthe Kollwitz. Another solution of the same order was the restoration of the Alte Pinakothek in Munich by Hans Döllgast (1952–57). The architect closed the gaping bomb hole in the wall of the south façade with plain masonry composed of rubble bricks. "Why hide something that is there! People should be able to see that the Pinakothek has a history and that it, too, was not spared the ravages of war."[9]

The issue of dealing with ruins—which also meant coming to grips with the past—was the theme of a characteristic debate that took place throughout Germany around 1948. The controversy concerned two buildings in similar states of ruin located only three hundred meters apart: the Goethehaus and the Paulskirche in Frankfurt. The birthplace of the Olympian Johann Wolfgang von Goethe and the seat of the first German national assembly were closely associated with the national identity—more than ever before or since in struggling postwar Germany. In the case of the Goethehaus, the advocates of a final and permanent farewell were defeated. The building was painstakingly rebuilt and restored. The Paulskirche, on the other hand, was reconstructed as a new festive venue for the Germans, its burned-out shell faintly echoing the pathos of Rome. "With its pure and impoverished form, the reconstructed Paulskirche stands as a monument to our people's will to build a new and better order out of the ashes of disaster," wrote one of the architects involved in the project.[10] Even

the Central Administrative Office of the Socialist Unity Party of Germany (SED) sent a donation of ten thousand DM.

Conflict between reconstruction and demolition arose again in Dresden—with respect to buildings that were perhaps less crucial to the public psyche than the Goethehaus and the Paulskirche yet more significant from the art-historical standpoint. Reconstruction of the Baroque Zwinger was initiated in 1945 under an order issued by the Soviet Military Mission—a remarkable development indeed, as this caprice of a feudal lord must have clashed with the ideology of the future Workers' and Farmers' State. The Frauenkirche, the bourgeois answer to the royal palace and chapel, was left in ruins as a monument. The fact that these very ruins became a symbol of recovery and a focus of yearnings for the old city profile after 1989 ultimately led to its reconstruction. The Frankfurt Paulskirche nearly suffered a similar fate in the late eighties, when the party of archivists sought to have it restored to its condition of 1848.

Official Travel Abroad

Orientation to foreign standards was seen as an avenue of escape from the Germany calamities. Planners and architects took make-up lessons in Modernism in the nations of the victorious powers and in neutral countries. Switzerland, Sweden, and, somewhat later, the Netherlands were the countries West German planners chose to visit whenever they were free to choose. Switzerland was looked upon as the country in which German Modernism had wintered over in neighborly proximity and from which it could now be recovered. As a welfare state with a Social Democratic government, Sweden held a strong attraction for the states of West Germany, which also had to rely on planned economies to solve their urgent problems. In Sweden, housing policy was social policy. Standardization was practiced on a grand scale, and rationalization of construction companies was promoted. Vällingby, the satellite city built outside Stockholm between 1952 and 1959, represented a new urban planning model that linked working areas, residential zones, and the city center, and boasted a sophisticated street system and subway connections.

The occupation powers did their part to help architects based in their zones gather experience through subsidized study tours in their respective countries. In France, German planners frequently sought out Auguste Perret, the grand old master of reinforced concrete construction, who merged Modernism and monumentality in his designs for Amiens and Le Havre. Marcel Lods was in great demand, primarily because of his (unrealized) architectural plans for the southern quarter of the city Mainz (1946–47). Lods had proposed setting free-standing, high-rise slabs in a park landscape, structures of the kind often cited in modern planning literature since the completion of Le Corbusier's Ville contemporaine (1922). Radical but unrealized reconstruction plans were not rare in postwar Germany, of course—from Saarbrücken to Hamburg, from Nürnberg to Dresden. How they might have looked, had they been carried out, is illustrated by the Grindel high-rises erected in Hamburg by a team of architects between 1949 and 1956. One of the architects had once worked in Le Corbusier's studio.

In Le Corbusier, France brought forth a 20th-century genius. His Unités d'habitation embodied a new model for urban living: the large structure with two-story maisonette apartments arranged along a *rue intérieur,* complemented by such facilities as a hairstylist's studio, a post office, and a landscaped rooftop with kindergarten. If the residents hadn't had to work elsewhere, these large complexes would have been virtually autonomous. Le Corbusier was commissioned to design a version of his "vertical city" for the *Interbau* exhibition in Berlin (1957). He had to adapt it to the requirements of the German building code, however, and it was too large to be built on the actual grounds of *Interbau* in the Hansaviertel. If it had not been noticeable even earlier, a new freedom in the use of forms became apparent at the latest in the pilgrimage chapel in Ronchamp, a building erected by the master between 1950 and 1955. Thus there were many reasons why German building experts were frequent visitors to Le Corbusier's small, cloister-style studio in Paris's rue de Sèvres.

Those who saw the U.S. as a model were attracted by the seductive power of the American Way of Life and the fascinating aura of the big cities with their towering skylines. Skyscrapers had cast a spell on virtually every European visitor to the U.S. even during the second and third decades of the 20th century. Exile architects, including Mies van der Rohe in Chicago and Walter Gropius in Cambridge, Massachusetts, served as anchors of German Modernism on the North American continent. Young German architects with the right connections sought out the offices of these German exiles. Another alternative was to join one of the highly efficient large firms that had flourished on wartime commissions from the U.S. government and were now entering the civilian market. The architectural design firm most familiar to Europeans was Skidmore, Owings & Merrill (SOM), thanks not least of all to its U.S. consulates that attracted considerable attention in Germany: grid structures with steel or reinforced concrete frames enclosed by glass curtain façades.

The filigree, transparent spatial containers designed by SOM, which fit in so well with the swing, the material mix, and the pastels typical of fifties design, paved the way for a new generation of high-rise buildings. These were the first in Germany worthy of being called "modern." Even conservative architects raised during the Speer era learned quickly. Preferred locations for the new curtain-wall buildings were Düsseldorf, where Paul Schneider-Esleben and Hentrich & Petschnigg were building, and Frankfurt am Main, which became the first and only German city to develop a U.S.-style high-rise skyline, modest though it was by comparison. Modernity was exhibited in this same type of building even on the other side of the Iron Curtain. Hermann Henselmann's Haus des Lehrers on Alexanderplatz in Berlin, the first curtain-walled building in the GDR, was conceived as a symbol of socialism's international competitive strength in the years between 1961 and 1964, after the demise of Stalinist national culture.

A tradition emerged from the experience of those years that must be classified among the unique qualities and achievements of the German architecture scene after 1945: the involvement of foreign architects in building. There are a number of reasons why so many architects from other countries found work in West Germany: the progressive internationalization of markets, construction programs launched by multinational corporations, and finally the advanced state of technological know-how in other countries, coupled undoubtedly with a certain sense of inferiority that affected German clients and politicians at the local and state level. Inviting architects from abroad was seen as evidence of a cosmopolitan mentality and receptiveness to the experiences of others.

*Interbau,* the 1957 international building exposition in Berlin, marked the beginning of a policy devoted to opening borders. The more participants from abroad, the greater the honor. Frequent guests included the Dutch team of Johannes Hendrik van den Broek and Jacob Berend Bakema, whose Rotterdam Lijnbaan shopping center (1949–53) served as a model for numerous variations in German pedestrian zones, and Arne Jacobsen, with his neat Danish functionalism. Alvar Aalto built a terraced housing block on the grounds of *Interbau,* a complex with floor plans arranged around an "all-purpose space," and later designed an undulating high-rise apartment building in the large Neue Vahr housing development in Bremen (1958–62). The Federal Republic of Germany has this Finnish architect's non-doctrinaire modernity and his sensitive use of light and organic material to thank for some of its most beautiful buildings. The Dutch and the Scandinavians were looked upon as neighbors with similar cultural backgrounds. The rise of the international jet set that made everything possible everywhere at the same time, was yet to come.

Between Stalin and Khrushchev

None of the impressions gained by German planners abroad was translated so visibly, so quickly, and with such far-reaching consequences as those acquired by GDR architects and planners on a journey through the Soviet Union in April and May of 1950. The lessons learned by architectural experts and party functionaries in Moscow, Kiev, Leningrad, and Stalingrad revolved around Stalin's dictum that culture is socialist in content and national in form. Functionalism and Modernism were equated with condemnable cosmopolitanism, and the Bauhaus tradition (or what was regarded as such) was held in contempt. The fact that such prominent GDR planners as Richard Paulick had emerged from that tradition made no difference. It was not until twenty years later that renewed concentration on rational building methods awakened interest in the Bauhaus and its methodology once again.

Given the diversity of German cultural landscapes, the concept of "national in form" meant mobilizing regional traditions. And what architectural style could have represented "national tradition" in Germany? Indeed, the Frankfurter Tor on Berlin's Stalinallee paraphrased Karl von Gontard's cupolas on Gendarmenmarkt; Rostock's Lange Strasse adapted elements of Hanseatic brick Gothic; Dresden's Altmarkt exhibited variations on Saxon Baroque. Urban planning was expressly understood as art. The task of urban planners was to shape urban centers as crowns of cities and to accent them with high-rise structures. Magnificent avenues and squares were required for political spectacles and demonstrations. The fact that construction workers on strike in June 1953 were the first to make use of Stalinallee, the most prominent "festive space" in East Berlin, gave the story an ironic and certainly unintended twist.

While still in Moscow in 1950, the group of traveling experts and officials summarized what they had learned in *Sixteen Principles of Urban Planning.* Barely off the editor's desk, the document was approved in a resolution passed by the GDR Council of Ministers and incorporated as an appendix into the Reconstruction Act of 1950. This document was widely interpreted in Western architecture circles as an embrace of diversity and color in the postwar city and as a corrective response to the Charter of Athens and its rigorous separation of functions. Architectural and urban planning practice in the GDR did not support such a reading. The separation of building and land ownership and the state's prerogative to annex and nationalize property in specified reconstruction zones did not lead to the improvement of undeveloped spaces but merely produced larger, more barren ones. Yet Western planners envied the GDR for its expropriation laws. In the FRG, the Fed-

eral Construction Act, which took effect in 1960, replaced the state reconstruction laws and their often more planning-friendly provisions. The scandal of flourishing land speculation and unrecovered planning profits remained a fact of life, although it clearly contradicted the constitutional principle of the social obligation associated with property.

Application of the *Sixteen Principles* in the GDR met with some opposition at first. Architects old enough to have experienced the burdensome legacy of 19th-century historicism feared a return to columns and frontons. They also suspected that party and state officials would use the principles as a means of disciplining architects. And they saw these fears confirmed in the case of the high-rise apartment building at the Weberwiese (1951–52). In response to strong criticism in *Neues Deutschland,* the official organ of the SED,[11] architect Hermann Henselmann had revised his plans for the building virtually overnight. A nine-story tower with a vaguely Neoclassical form, the Schinkel-style structure was welcomed with tremendous enthusiasm by the people of East Berlin, who saw it as a "beacon," a signal of better times to come.

The "people's sense of beauty" had ceased to play a role when the "public client" changed course again under the pressure of economic constraints. In December 1954—only four years after the legendary Moscow visit by the architectural tourists and eighteen months after Stalin's death—Nikita Khrushchev, the new Secretary General of the Communist Party of the Soviet Union, called in a speech at the All Union Conference for energetic pursuit of industrialization in the building sector and an end to waste in the form of superfluous decoration. A delegation from East Berlin was present on the occasion. Criticism had been voiced internally about the slow progress, the high costs, and the poor quality of building in the Stalinallee style. Industrialization and standarization became the new goals of building policy in the GDR. The principle of the crane runway began to replace the dictates of Socialist Realism and had an immediate impact on urban planning. The solid face of the architecture along Stalinallee, which was renamed Karl-Marx-Allee, gave way in the second building phase (1958–65) to clusters of high-rise slab structures   not towards the fringes of the city but near the center, where one would have expected more solid fronts and greater compactness.

East and West moved liked two wrestlers, locked in a clinch or each repulsing the other's advances. Berlin was still run by a single city administration until 1948. Hans Scharoun served first as Municipal Building Commissioner, then as director of the Institut für Bauwesen at the Deutsche Akademie der Wissenschaft in East Berlin, while teaching at the Technische Universität in West Berlin at the same time. Appeals for unity

Bridging the Rhine with the
Deutzer Brücke, Cologne, 1948

Paulskirche Planning Team (Eugen Blanck, Gottlieb Schaupp,
Rudolf Schwarz, Johannes Krahn), Reconstruction of the
Paulskirche, Frankfurt am Main, 1948

Otto Bartning, Evangelical Provisional Church,
Frankfurt-Bonames, 1949

Karl Band/Rudolf Schwarz,
Gürzenich, Cologne, 1949–55

Hans Döllgast, Reconstruction of the Alte Pinakothek,
Munich, 1952–57

Bernhard Hermkes, Rudolf Lodders, and others,
Grindel High-Rises, Hamburg, 1949–56

9

Hentrich & Petschnigg,
Thyssen Tower, Düsseldorf,
1957–60

10

Alvar Aalto, High-Rise in the
Neue Vahr Housing Development, Bremen, 1958–62

11

Arne Jacobsen, HEW Administrative Building
in City Nord, Hamburg, 1966–69

12

Hermann Henselmann Planning
Collective, Frankfurter Tor, Karl-
Marx-Allee (formerly Stalinallee),
Berlin, 1953–56

13

Gustav Hassenpflug, Raymond Lopez and Eugène Beaudouin,
Hans Schwippert, Hise-Rise Housing in the Hansaviertel,
Berlin, 1957

14

Hermann Henselmann, Haus des Lehrers on Alexanderplatz,
Berlin, 1961–64

15

Hans Scharoun, Philharmonie, Berlin, 1956–63

16

17

Egon Eiermann,
Kaiser Wilhelm Memorial
Church, Berlin, 1957–63

18

Helmut Striffler, Evangelical Church of Reconciliation
in Dachau Concentration Camp, 1964–67

19

Sep Ruf, Chancellor's Bungalow, Bonn, 1963/64

20

Ludwig Mies van der Rohe, Neue Nationalgalerie, Berlin,
1962–68

21

Ulrich Müther, "Ahornblatt" Multipurpose Building,
Berlin, 1971–73

22

Heinz Graffunder/Karl-Ernst Swora, Palast der Republik,
Berlin, 1973–76

23

Hans Hollein, Museum am Abteiberg,
Mönchengladbach, 1976–82

24

von Gerkan, Marg and Partners,
Hanse-Viertel Shopping Passage,
Hamburg, 1978–81

25

Rob Krier (general planning), Dietrich Bangert,
Bernd Jansen, Stefan Scholz, Axel Schultes, Axel Liepe,
and Hartmut Steigelmann, Ritterstrasse-Nord Housing
Project, Berlin-Kreuzberg, 1982–88

26

Schlaich, Bergermann & Partner, Max-Eyth-See
Pedestrian Bridge, Stuttgart, 1988

within the German cultural nation were standard elements of political rhetoric for some time. Architects from both sides participated in some competitions—as in the competition for the Fennpfuhl development in Berlin-Lichtenberg in 1956. Ernst May, Director of Planning for the Neue Heimat organization in Hamburg at the time, was awarded first prize—but not the commission, of course. Nothing in Berlin went on unobserved, in the most literal sense of the word, from across the sector boundary. While Scharoun was building his Philharmonie, that great bastion of music, close to the newly erected Wall between 1956 and 1963, his fellow architects in the East followed the progress of construction through binoculars.

The popular efforts of the East Berlin city administration were observed with concern in West Berlin. The idea for *Interbau* in the Hansaviertel was conceived not least of all as a vehicle for the presentation of West Berlin as a "window on freedom" but also as a "window on economic prosperity."[12] The Municipal Building Director at the time called for "a strong declaration of unbroken will to build up West Berlin that would be clearly heard in the East."[13] In 1950, East Berlin had initiated efforts to convert the Schlossinsel, whose remaining ruins had been demolished, and the adjacent terrain separating it from Alexanderplatz into an imposing skyline area with a massive central building. The long parade of alternatives, of which none was ever regarded as satisfactory, finally came to an end for the time being with the television tower proposed by Henselmann, the park around the Marx-Engels-Forum and the Palast der Republik (designed by Heinz Graffunder und Karl-Ernst Swora and built between 1973 and 1976). With its white marble façades, its fashionable bronzed reflective glass, and its two large assembly halls equipped with sophisticated technology, the Palast was meant to demonstrate East Berlin's status as a world city. Appreciation for the building among East Berliners stemmed more from the use of its amenities than from its aesthetics.

These efforts of the GDR to create a center for the city and the nation in East Berlin were answered in the West in 1957–58 by the international planning competition "Hauptstadt Berlin" (Berlin, Capital of Germany). Politically, the process of planning development of terrain that belonged to another state—albeit one not recognized by the Federal Republic—was an act of provocation. In terms of planning ideology, the competition served as an atlas of concepts of the city in circulation at the time. Most of the proposals in the upper rankings were characterized by an arrogant view of the existing city and hypertrophic solutions for traffic problems. The GDR responded that same year with a "contest of ideas for socialist redesign of the center of the capital of the GDR."

The Inhospitability of Cities

Building for the masses was an equally urgent issue in the West. A shortage of some 1.3 million housing units was estimated in 1960. Housing policy under Chancellor Konrad Adenauer had favored land-intensive home ownership in outlying areas for years. The new large-scale residential developments—together with compact, low-rise housing—were intended to counteract "widespread destruction of the countryside," as the Deutscher Werkbund referred to it.[14] The strategy was given ideological support in a campaign that equated urban density with higher capacity-utilization rates. The word "urbanity," contributed to the discussion by social scientist Edgar Salin, underwent a similar reinterpretation.[15] In combination, the two terms promised "urbanity through density."

In terms of expansion and population figures, the satellite cities of West Germany did not lag behind their counterparts in the GDR, such as Halle-Neustadt, Leipzig-Grünau, or Dresden-Prohlis. They accounted for a significant portion of the 500,000 to 600,000 new housing units built every year (the figure rose to 700,000 in 1973). Prefabrication was also used in the West. As a rule, these construction systems were not based upon linear elements (beams and supports) or three-dimensional living units (room-unit construction) but on flat structural elements in the form of load-bearing wall panels. The West had its "panels" as well, although they were less ponderous and employed less exclusively than in the GDR.

Large-scale developments built during the late sixties and seventies, such as Steilshoop in Hamburg and Wulfen in the northernmost part of the Ruhr region, were already responding with spacious interior courtyards or more loosely configured layouts to the dreary monotony of strict row construction and massive criticism it was beginning to draw. Yet their residents experienced substantial problems as well. Chains of high-rise buildings encircling parts of the old garden areas and their remaining small buildings in northern Berlin's Märkisches Viertel (1962–74) were meant to symbolize the departure from the drawing-board city. In the large developments in the southern part of the city (1964–75), to which Walter Gropius contributed both ideas and his good name, planners conceived round, spacious residential courts much like those in neighboring Britz. Due to their construction faults, their sheer density, their failure to provide for basic needs, their social problems, and their brutish aesthetics, both of these developments became lasting and shocking examples of the "inhospitability of cities,"[16] in spite of the good intentions of their planners.

First attempts were made during the sixties to give architecture a more striking visual appearance that would compensate for aesthetic and functional deficits. At the Brussels World's Fair in 1958, in which the GDR was not represented, as it was not in all other World's Fairs, Egon Eiermann, one of the great architecture educators in the Federal Republic, and Sep Ruf, who designed the Chancellor's bungalow, were still able to satisfy everyone with filigree pavilion constructions that expressed modesty, decency, and openness to the world. In Montreal in 1967, it was the bold, graceful tent landscape of Frei Otto that earned the busily-building Republic both popular admiration and acclaim from professional circles. Similarly successful were the Munich Olympics in 1972, with a lively, modeled terrain which no one who didn't know better would have suspected of concealing the slumbering rubble of the last World War beneath its rolling green lawns. Otto's principle of membrane construction, its application by the architect team of Günter Behnisch, and Günter Grzimek's landscape design contributed in equal measure to the final result.

Despite their unfavorable reputation, the sixties produced a number of memorable large architectural structures. These included Hans Scharoun's school and residential landscapes, his concert halls and theaters—works open to criticism with regard to details yet striking in terms of space and concept. Mies van der Rohe was finally given an opportunity to realize a temple of art made of steel and glass in his native city—just across from his former studio, in fact: the Neue Nationalgalerie at the Kulturforum in Berlin (1962–68). Though impractical then and now—for museum use, its strictly configured superstructure is sublime.

Exposed concrete as a visual material, which soon became an object of general contempt, was shaped into highly expressive large-scale structures. It first appeared quite early on, embellished with mosaics and jewel-like inlays, in the three-part Liederhalle in Stuttgart designed by Adolf Abel und Rolf Gutbrod (1949–56). Gottfried Böhm used it, as long as the high costs of formwork were affordable, for his sculptural churches and in the romantic feudal castle that became a city hall for the small mountain town of Bensberg near Cologne (1962–71). It was also the material with which Helmut Striffler designed his Church of Reconciliation at the Dachau concentration camp (1964–67) as a track through the earth, a "trench against isolation." Stillness and insight were achieved through the intensity of form rather than prevented by sheer magnitude.

The desire for visually striking architectural symbols that would shape the image of cities was also satisfied in several cases in the GDR. Hermann Henselmann called the series of high-rise buildings erected under his patronage *Bildzeichen* (pictorial symbols). They appeared in various forms: in Leipzig as an open book (university building, 1968–73); in Jena as a cylinder interpretable as a telephoto lens (high-rise building,

originally designed for the state-owned Carl Zeiss company, 1968–72); in the port city of Rostock as a sail-shaped structure (Haus der Wissenschaften, 1968–69). Ulrich Müther's hyperbolic-parabolic reinforced concrete shells, designed for restaurants and cafés, looked like exotic blossoms in the midst of a standardized monotony. Their origins were indeed exotic, as Müther's models—developed by Félix Candela, a pioneer of shell construction—stood in Mexico.

These were the exceptions in cities subjected to the forced industrialization of the building sector. The small, proprietary architect's office was still the rule in the Federal Republic,[17] although its existence was threatened by competition with the design departments of the major construction companies. Neue Heimat, a union-owned company that promoted its own reputation as the largest construction firm in the world, front-funded the sale of entire city centers, large clinics, and universities in the years preceding its own collapse in the eighties. Private architects no longer existed in the GDR. Planning and design services were performed by large, state-owned design offices, special building staffs, and project planning agencies within the building collectives. The prefabricated systems of early years began to give way after 1970 to a single large-panel construction process known as Housing Series WBS 70. Ultimately, WBS 70 accounted for 80 percent of total GDR construction output. Even though the roughly fifty panel factories in the various districts were not as completely standardized as theory prescribed, their system prevailed without appreciable resistance in urban construction. The hope that a universal modular construction system would ensure greater leeway for variation than combinations of multiple partial systems remained unfulfilled. The sheer impact of the standardized characteristics was so great that variations were virtually negligible.

History and Stories

The seventies witnessed a rediscovery of history. The European Year of Monument Preservation in 1975 was an unexpected success. The losses it brought to light were attributable not only to the war but, to an equal or even greater degree, the urban reconstruction efforts that followed. In West Berlin, Josef Paul Kleihues, architect and co-director of the *Internationale Bauausstellung* (International Building Exhibition, known as IBA) helped the phrase "critical reconstruction" to a certain measure of popularity. Above all, the concept expressed respect for the urban ground plan and lot structure, the most important documents of municipal history. The construction of traffic arteries along lines cut by planners through the hearts of inner cities came to a halt.

Traditional typologies of urban architecture such as courtyards, streets, squares, and blocks returned to the drawing boards. Now it was possible again to build a city block that presented a public face to the street and a private one to the interior, to the protected courtyard. The realization that urban renewal did not necessarily mean total demolition but could also go hand in hand with a gentle approach to people and building substance began to gain acceptance. The alternative section of the IBA in Berlin-Kreuzberg, for which Hardt-Waltherr Hämer, a veteran of many renewal projects, was responsible, emphasized gentle strategies developed in dialogue with local residents. The pressure that made it possible to realize a policy of non-destructive urban repair, as opposed to a scorched-earth approach, came from the "squatter scene" that had established a firm foothold in cities all over the country following the student revolts of 1968.

The GDR had its own showcase examples of protective renewal, among them sections of Berlin around Arkonaplatz and Arnimplatz renovated in the seventies and early eighties and the residential development on Ostheimstrasse in Leipzig. Yet another paradigmatic shift—how many did this make?—announced its arrival under the banner of "complex reconstruction." Its point of departure was the discovery that new residential developments in green areas required precisely the kind of infrastructure that already existed in the old, decrepit city centers. Savings achieved in outlying areas through serial construction would be offset by costs for new schools, kindergartens, shopping centers, sports facilities, and streetcar lines. If the existing inner-city structures were utilized, on the other hand, these savings could be invested in efforts to protect rapidly deteriorating old-building substance.

But the idea remained an unrealized vision. Even if it had wanted to pursue this new course, building policy in the GDR remained captive to its own system. The inner cities were neglected for years, although this was less the result of a lack of insight than of fundamental structural constraints. Where rents were fixed at a minimum level by the government, there was no incentive for private investment. Where the building sector was bound to the requirements of large-scale production, no one could afford to take on renewal projects, which always pose different requirements. How could a construction firm that worked with Load Class 2 (20,000 newtons) concrete panels be expected to employ trained construction technicians qualified to take on the painstaking chore of renovating a nearly-collapsing half-timber house in Quedlinburg or a derelict Jugendstil mansion in Dresden? Such work was restricted to model renovation projects in tourist cities such as Erfurt, Potsdam, and Weimar, which counted on attracting notice abroad. Often, however, the solution was to replace old inner-city structures with a kind of subdued panel construction. Under the influence of the desolate economic conditions that prevailed in the latter years of the GDR, most of what remained deteriorated at a rapid pace.[18] The price of bread was a catalyst of the revolt that led to the French Revolution. In East Germany, the catastrophic state of the manmade environment was a key factor in the people's uprisings that brought the regime to its knees in 1989.

While these conflicts revolved around history and how to preserve it, Western Postmodern architecture was concerned largely with individual stories. Cities conquered by banks and corporate headquarters, with centers where practically no one lived, witnessed the influx of quotable, colorful, sometimes amusing, but often merely inanely gabby forms and structures. The number of cultural institutions, including museum, involved was remarkably high. The museum had been a neglected topic for quite some time. Its turn came, so to speak, after that of churches, city halls, schools, and theaters. Museum collections were collages of eras and objects and were thus closely related to Postmodern collage technique. Museums provided spaces for creative design that were used above all by the global players in the architecture scene.

Among the leaders in this architectural campaign were Hans Hollein's Museum am Abteiberg in Mönchengladbach (1976–82) and James Stirling's and Michael Wilford's Neue Staatsgalerie in Stuttgart (1977–84), joined by the institutions along the Frankfurt Museumsufer, including those by Richard Meier, Oswald Mathias Ungers, Josef Paul Kleihues, and Günter Behnisch. The splendor of these richly inventive creations, some silently self-referential, others eager to tell their stories, contributed to the appeal of the inner cities and enhanced their commercial marketability. Cultural policy was rediscovered as urban development policy, while the stark social contrasts that have always shaped the character of public space in the inner cities were seen as detrimental to the city's image. Glassed shopping paradises—city arcades and the consumer-warehouse stores outside the cities—became protected, semiprivate terrain on which the owner's word is law: a fortress mentality. Rediscovered as an architectural type by Johann Friedrich Geist,[19] the arcade began a march of triumph through the big cities. In rainy Hamburg, half of the city center was perforated with examples of this 19th-century invention.

Toward the end of its days, the GDR also dabbled in referential historicism. Business and office buildings in the heart of Berlin were given new Baroque-style or Jugendstil concrete façades. In the Nikolaiviertel (1979–87), an architects' collective under the direction of Günter Stahn recreated a bit of old Berlin. Structures made of site-mixed concrete and façades selected from the range of available prefabricated elements complemented the restored, relocated buildings that crowded around the reconstructed medieval parish church and Ephraim-Palais, which was rebuilt very near its original location. The inflexible construction system was exploited for every picturesque effect it could possibly offer. Never had the architectural theatrics of capitalism and state socialism come so close to one another as here.

The cycle in which the material of aesthetics revolves has evidently accelerated over the past several decades. The repertoire has expanded progressively: the Deconstructive aesthetics of catastrophe, Second (or Third) Modernism, frugal Minimalism, strict, though site-specific geometries such as those of Oswald Mathias Ungers. Technological challenges to hall and bridge construction gave rise to the brilliant accomplishments of such great engineers as Jörg Schlaich and Stefan Polónyi, although the highway bridge construction departments and Deutsche Bahn appear not to have noticed. In the work of architects like Thomas Herzog, commitment to environmentally sound building no longer produces loam walls and grass-topped roofs but now features technically sophisticated and visually pleasing solutions for climate control and energy production.

Globalization and structural change in the building-client sector have accelerated the renewal of formal repertoires. Where everything is oriented towards media presentation, architecture cannot afford to put its head in the sand. Corporations no longer build their headquarters to last an eternity, nor do they require the dignified quality perpetuity deserves. Their pride no longer depends on the architectural embodiment of their enterprise. What they seek—at least until the next hostile or friendly takeover—is a prominent address, one that reads like a company logo. Depreciation periods for some enterprises in the communication industry now run less than ten years.

In interest of budgetary optics, public building clients, particularly local governments, often avoid eye-catching one-time construction costs in favor of leasing agreements, which also allows them to circumvent the tender processes prescribed by EU law. There is no longer any motivation to erect community buildings that make citizens proud. Among public clients, only the national government still allows itself the privilege of image-enhancing self-representation. Günter Behnisch's German Bundestag in Bonn, which was not completed until 1992 and then used only briefly for its intended purpose, became an icon of democratic architecture. In the euphoria of reunification, the Republic has invested in representation in Berlin, but it has also accepted buildings left over from the Nazi and SED eras. Should it be reprimanded for the one or the other? Or praised?

When the barriers went up along the Berlin Wall on November 9, 1989, relatives with very different biographies came face to face again. More than a few problems awaited them, though they would certainly be easier to bear than the ones previously endured. The belief that mistakes once made need never be made again has proven to be an illusion. Yet in the euphoria that engulfed everyone that evening and during the weeks that followed, everything seemed like paradise on earth, even Kurfürstendamm and Karl-Marx-Allee.

# The Eternal Return of the Void

German Architecture after German Reunification

Andreas Ruby

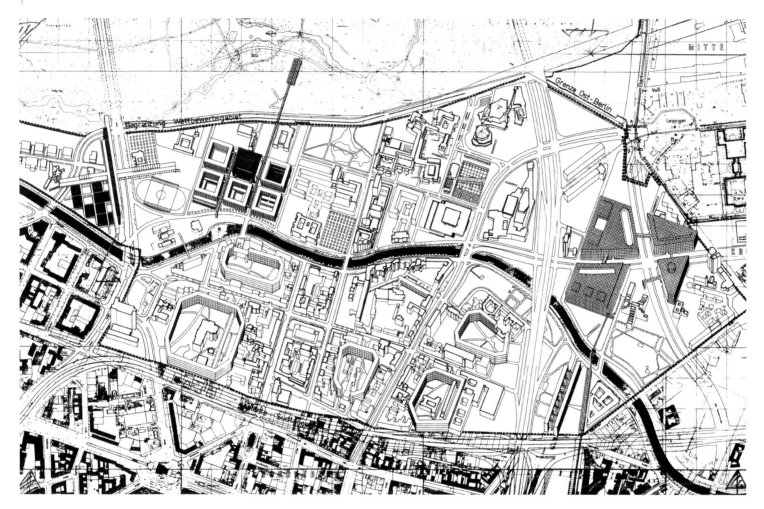

## 1

Oswald Mathias Ungers, "Berlin, the Green Archipelago," Tiergarten district competition, Berlin, 1973

In Search of a Lost National Architecture

The year 1990 represents an unprecedented turning point in the history of German architecture, for it was the year in which the term "German architecture" became meaningful again after forty years of East German and West German architecture during which *German* architecture as such did not exist. And there were other reasons for avoiding the term, apart from the division of the country after World War II. The twelve-year period of Nazi rule in which it had last been associated with meaning had made it taboo for indefinite periods of time. German postwar societies west and east had turned in horror from the specter of National Socialist world dominion, firmly resolved to build a new Germany—on both sides of the border, albeit under dramatically different circumstances, as we know.

The cultures of architecture that developed from these beginnings cannot truly be called "national," however. The architecture of the Federal Republic, in particular, was characterized by marked regional differences. Over the course of time, a number of architectural "schools" emerged which—like the "Darmstadt School" and "Hamburg Architecture"—articulated recognizable regional profiles but were much too diverse and locally motivated to contribute to the growth of a national identity.

Architecture in the German Democratic Republic (GDR), on the other hand, took shape as a unified whole in the centralized, planned economic structure of East German society, although the question of national identity played hardly any role at all in this process. Much more important were directives on architectural policy issued from Moscow. Even the planning vision of a "national tradition," the model according to which the Stalinallee in Berlin and the Altmarkt in Dresden were built, is known to have been imported from Moscow.

With the peaceful revolution of 1989 and German reunification, which followed on October 3, 1990, these forty years of parallel architectural history became at first a purely conceptual unity—without substantive content. The implication of former German Chancellor Willy Brandt's programmatic announcement that what belonged together would now grow together for the two German architectural cultures was that their unification would require a Herculean effort to bridge the gap between the opposing social systems: the civil society in the West, with its dialectic of publicness and privacy, and the elimination of that duality in the socialized East; private domestic bliss in the single-home development on the one side, collective rented housing in large socialist developments on the other. Whereas the profession was organized in the West as a system of competing architecture firms, it existed in the East in the form of huge state run planning offices. While the market economy had recourse to a highly specialized building market and individualized production methods, architects in the planned economy were forced to rely on industrialized, mass-produced, standardized construction techniques.

Berlin as a Microcosm

Nowhere did these conflicting tendencies clash so irreconcilably as in Berlin, the former Cold-War front city. Separated for decades by only the breadth of the Wall, the once hostile systems merged almost physically after the borders came down. Streets that had been cut in two by the Wall erected on August 13, 1961 reappeared in the reunited city four decades later as connected lines of a schizophrenic history. Because the Wall consisted in many places of two walls separated by a no-man's land of varying width, Berlin regained a piece of urban territory that had had only a virtual existence, so to speak, for forty years. Thus the opening of the Berlin Wall revealed a panorama of absurd urban situations that were without parallel anywhere else in the world and for which urban planners had no pat, prefabricated solutions to offer. More or less inevitably, therefore, the fusion of the eastern and western cities had to produce a new urban quality, and this opportunity for far-reaching renewal made Berlin both a symbol and a focal point of German architectural discourse during the nineties.

Yet to look back today at the Berlin that emerged after reunification is to experience a sobering revelation. We recognize in the midst of the fascinating diversity that was so typical of Berlin well into the eighties the obvious workings of a striving for order. The old center around the Gendarmenmarkt, Friedrichstrasse, and Unter den Linden, to name only a few prominent examples, have been given an architecture that radiates a certain tactile hardness, that reflects a deliberate embrace of discipline and offers no evidence of playful experimentation. The *Symphony of a Metropolis* that Walter Ruttmann intoned visually in his cinematographic homage to Berlin in 1929 has grown mute in the rigid pattern of serial block structures. Sharp-edged building blocks compress urban space into perfectly straight street corridors. Wherever our gaze falls, it is caught in the net of a leaden matrix of window-hole façades, repulsed by the hermetic texture of a constructed space that actually strives to be an accessible image: the image of an intact urbanity that refers to the city's history—though only to a very small slice of that history, as we discover upon closer examination: the era of Prussian Classicism between the late 18th and mid-19th centuries. Unwanted traces of history have been quietly obliterated, among them the architectural legacies of GDR Modernism and the Wall, which was expunged from the tissue of the urban organism within only a few years of its collapse—as thoroughly as if it had never existed.

Political Translocation

Such a glaring discrepancy between potential and actual achievement raises a number of questions. Why does a city devote itself to reconstruction of its history at the very moment it is given the opportunity to design an entirely new future? Why is that history purged of all of its inherent diversity and contradictions and reduced to a single architectural style? And what is the justification for declaring this Prussian Classicism the "typical" form of Berlin architecture at the threshold of the 21st century?

To seek answers to these questions in architecture is to seek in vain. Indeed, architecture has played no causal role at all in this development, although fundamental changes in the political landscape of the new Germany are reflected in its surface. This landscape—and with it the debate on German architecture being waged in Berlin—was altered abruptly by the resolution of the German Bundestag of June 20, 1991 to move the seat of parliament and government to Berlin in order to "complete the unification of Germany." For that resolution catapulted Berlin virtually overnight into a context of importance for which it was totally unprepared. All of a sudden, the former extraterritorial satellite of a divided German fatherland was translocated into the center of the newly united Germany. As the new German capital, Berlin became the media stage upon which the process of German reunification would be carried out. The eyes of the world now focused on Berlin to observe how the Germans would manage the reunification of the dual history of their long divided country. As a result, decisions in the spheres of culture, politics, business, and economics whose impact would hardly have been felt beyond the boundaries of Berlin before automatically took on national or, in many cases, international significance.

In this context, it was architecture in particular that assumed appreciably greater political relevance, and this at three different levels, at the very least:

– *The symbolic level:* Since the decision to make Berlin the nation's capital once again was in itself highly symbolic, the new capital needed a permanent symbolic form of representation.[1] The world was to recognize Berlin as a capital, and architecture was regarded as the appropriate medium through which to display this new function.

– *The capital-city marketing level:* The resolution to move the capital to Berlin yielded applause but raised doubts and fears as well. Would the city be able to meet the high expectations associated with its new role as the symbol and showcase of the state? Admittedly, the political biography of West Berlin prior to the fall of the Wall does not have the ring of a strong recommendation for the honor of serving as the seat of government: bastion of alternative political culture, Mecca for conscientious objectors from all over Germany,[2] magnet for the building squatter scene, birthplace of the student revolts associated with Rudi Dutschke, and the scene of violent clashes at the yearly May demonstrations—altogether an incalculable risk potential that needed to be brought under political control. Before the ministries could move from the Rhine to the Spree, Berlin had to be made "suitable for its role as a capital," as one heard in Bonn government circles, while local politicians in Berlin were frightened by the very thought that their city might be too "provincial" to stand up to the enormous pressure of expectations and the representative function. And thus a "capital-city architecture" of national stature and discipline-inducing monumentality appeared to be just the right answer at the right time.

– *The territorial level:* It is important to remember that the city regained an "orphaned" piece of territory—one that cut through its very heart—when the Wall came down. Once unattractive fringe districts were transformed almost overnight into first-class locations, and owners of property in these areas suddenly became very interested in capitalizing on that fact. Even before the collapse of the Wall, a group of investors formed around Daimler-Benz, Sony, Metro, and others purchased the derelict lot at the former Potsdamer Platz and commissioned the English architect Richard Rogers to prepare a master plan for the marketing of their property. When the Wall fell, the area became the de facto city center. Such an important part of the city, as the Berlin Senate announced with great alarm, simply could not be left to the business community alone but needed government input. The order of the day was to develop a normative overall concept for Berlin's transformation into a capital; otherwise, the state would lose control of urban development in Berlin.

Conservative Shift

To ensure political control of the process of urban development in Berlin, the Berlin city government re-established the position of Municipal Building Director in April 1991—actually a laudable decision, as it was entirely appropriate that an architect should serve as the point of contact between politics, architecture, and business. But in appointing Lübeck City Building Commissioner Hans Stimman (a member of the Social Democratic Party, or SPD) to the post, the politicians chose an advocate of conservative urban renewal—a paradigm that had guided the reconstruction of historical city centers during the eighties but must now have seemed hopelessly anachronistic in view of the impending epoch-making changes in Berlin. This anachronism was part of a program, however, as became obvious in the competition for Potsdamer Platz and Leipziger Platz, which the Berlin government hastily set in motion in the summer of 1991 in an effort to take control of the process and document its own urban development agenda. According to Wolfgang Nagel (SPD), Berlin Commissioner for Building and Housing, the most important goal was to "preserve the characteristic features of downtown Berlin ..., such as the geometric grid pattern of streets and hermetic city blocks, the sequence of streets and squares, and the existing block and lot structures, to the extent possible." The model was not to be the "American system of compact high-rise agglomeration found all over the world but the dense and spatially diverse configurations of cities like Paris, Milan, or Vienna."[3] The jury found precisely this model reflected in the proposal submitted by the Munich architects Hilmer & Sattler—an intricate colonization of space based on a rigid system of orthogonal blocks—and awarded them first prize accordingly. Other entries, which refused to kowtow to (a fictitious) history, were discreetly but resolutely passed over. The planning report prepared by Richard Rogers on commission by the investors, which was lauded by knowledgeable critics in the press as the better solution, was stricken from the agenda without a word. One of the jurors, Dutch architect Rem Koolhaas, resigned from the jury in protest against what was obviously a politically manipulated process, concluding in a remark that subsequent developments in Berlin would affirm all too emphatically, that "Berlin has become the capital at precisely the moment in which it is least equipped politically, ideologically, and artistically to assume that responsibility."[4]

This decision put an end to the Berlin architecture debate. Positions were clearly marked out and the rules defined that would henceforth determine what kind of architecture (and thus what face representing the new Germany) could and could not be built in Berlin. Architects intending to build would have to conform to these standards. No one accommodated to these strictures in a more accomplished way than the Berlin architect Hans Kollhoff, who had made a name for himself during the eighties with equally provocative and reflective architectural and urban development projects.[5] For the Potsdamer Platz competition, Kollhoff proposed an intelligent combination of high-rise cluster and park landscape that established the desired link between Kulturforum and Friedrichstadt in exemplary fashion. But the modern basic concept of his design found little favor with the jury. Kollhoff learned his

lesson more thoroughly than any other Berlin architect. In the competition for a part of Potsdamer Platz—the Daimler-Benz property—held just a year later, he submitted, as if made to order, a proposal for a standardized neo-Prussian architecture that would become the order of the day thereafter. Although Kollhoff's design did not win, it played an inordinately important role in the continuing process of forcing the city into line. It articulated the concept of the abstract city block that would come to define a more or less binding code of design for all new building in downtown Berlin in the years to come. Building alignment was to be determined by the dimensions of the construction site. The only acceptable empty spaces were those dedicated to traffic. The shape of a building emerged through the upward extension of the form of its ground plan to the prescribed eaves height of 22 meters. Roofs were to be designed as receding stepped levels but could not exceed a total building height of 30 meters. Façade configuration was to be based on the classical trinity of base, shaft, and cornice, which corresponded in functional terms to an isomorphic stacking of shops, offices, and apartments.

Space-consuming functions such as parking and delivery were to be accommodated underground and out of sight, which often resulted in a subterranean duplication of their above-ground cubature. Thus the typical Berlin city block building of the nineties is a kind of small high-rise comprising as many as twelve stories, of which half is hidden below ground level.[6]

Critical Reconstruction as Precursor

Kollhoff's coup was initially received with consternation by the informed public. The typology he proposed was actually not a new invention but instead appropriated, in careful consideration of political expedience, a type that Josef Paul Kleihues had already developed in his proposal for Potsdamer Platz and the Kontorhaus Mitte as early as 1991. Kleihues adopted a block-filling approach that he had introduced as Director of the Berlin *International Building Exposition* (IBA) from 1978 to 1987. The goal of IBA was to upgrade central urban quarters of Berlin like the southern part of Friedrichstadt and the Tiergarten, which had been relegated to the periphery of the inner city by the Wall, and make them an attractive urban setting for living and working again—and thus to pursue an urban development strategy that was markedly influenced in terms of its prerequisites by concrete historical circumstances. Yet this same strategy was surprisingly revived in the course of the turn toward conservatism in the early nineties, although the underlying historical, political, and cultural conditions were now completely different.

2

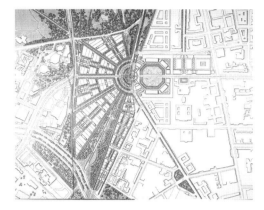

3

Richard Rogers Partnership, Master Plan for
Potsdamer Platz, Berlin, 1991

Hilmer + Sattler + Albrecht, Master Plan
for Potsdamer Platz, Berlin, competition in
1991, version of 2002

4

City of Dresden, Urban Architectural Profile, Dresden, 1993

5

Hans Kollhoff, Master Plan for Potsdamer Platz,
High-Rise Group (Comp. Stage I), Berlin, 1991

6

Hans Kollhoff, Master Plan for
Potsdamer Platz, debis area
(Comp. Stage II), Berlin, 1992

7

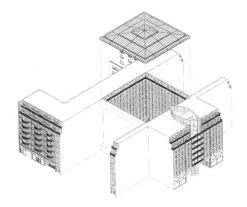

Kleihues + Kleihues, Kontorhaus Mitte, Berlin, 1991

8

Hans Kollhoff, Alexanderplatz Compotition, Berlin,
1993

9

Daniel Libeskind, Alexanderplatz
Competition, Berlin, 1993

In the course of this reapplication, however, the urban programmatics of the IBA—the critical reconstruction of the city—was simultaneously banalized and radicalized. Whereas Kleihues, during his IBA years, was concerned with a dialectical interchange between Modernism and tradition in order to achieve a balance in the city between elements of the present and the past, he now advocated an "urbanism of menotaxis." Kleihus understood this concept as "a constant urban order based upon balance among its parts which, by virtue of this intrinsic order, '*was capable of changing while remaining the same.*'"[7] With this twisted sophistry, Kleihues legitimized the methodical exclusion of otherness that was so typical of the architectural politics in Berlin at that period: the tendency to favor, over and over again, the same architects who had collaborated in the turn toward conservatism in Berlin architectural policy (most notably, aside from Hans Kollhoff, Jürgen Sawade, and Max Dudler), while architects of different persuasions were not even invited to participate in competitions whose juries had already adopted the dogma of (un)critical reconstruction under the influence of Kleihus's compatriot Hans Stimmann. It was as if the unification of Germany (and Berlin) so recently achieved demanded a similar uniformity in architecture and city planning. The least one can say is that architectural reality in Berlin supported the conclusion that only a uniform architecture could appropriately serve as a symbol of unity.

The connecting link between the new German architecture of the nineties and IBA must be seen in the approach to the issue of emptiness. Morphologically speaking, critical reconstructionism wages war on Berlin's emptiness, on the gaps in the urban tissue and the city's open spaces, regardless of whether they were the product of modern urban development or the years of war and reconstruction. This emptiness is threatening because of its indeterminacy. It is open to the future and implies the possibility of creating something new. But the new is ideologically taboo for those who dictate urban policy in the new Berlin, Stimmann and Kleihues. The new represents the hubris of Modernism, the ambition to make everything different and better. But what new solutions are left after the recently proclaimed death of all utopias? The fall of the Wall and the subsequent collapse of socialism in its realized form, as the conservative argument goes, exposed all leftist hopes for an alternative to existing society as dangerous illusions. Given the failure of Modernism, there is only possible course of historical development: back to the point that predates Modernism in order to restore the history it sought in vain to overcome.

The Potential of Emptiness

In terms of urbanism, this revisionist approach implies in a general sense the restoration of the historical outline of the city and, in particular, a return to the block as the omnipotent ordering principle of the European city. This answer to the failure of Modernism has become a stereotypical strategy in the Berlin's restorative urbanism. Yet that did not necessarily have to be. Berlin's unique situation, the compression of the geopolitical balance of the Cold War into a new urban condition, has fascinated architects and planners ever since the Wall went up, inspiring them to seek new approaches to the contemporary city. One of these was expressed in a series of research projects conducted by Oswald Mathias Ungers during his tenure as a professor at the TU Berlin in the sixties. Ungers saw the situation created by the artificial division of Berlin as a laboratory for experimentation with a new kind of urban architecture. Accepting the lack of cohesion in the existing urban tissue, Ungers sought new ways to permit the historical and the contemporary to coexist, rather than attempting to synthesize them. These studies culminated in an urban design competition project—"Berlin, the Green Archipelago" (1973)— which Ungers placed in the hands of the young Dutch architect Rem Koolhaas working in his office at the time. Koolhaas, who would leave for New York shortly therafter to begin research for his book *Delirious New York*, later remarked that the unique aspect of this project was that Ungers "took Berlin, just as it was, as a model for the city of the future, in which the alternation of concentration and emptiness was systematized and all subdivisions of the city were intrepreted as islands floating in a sea of emptiness."[8]

Within the context of this vision, which anticipated several characteristics of Koolhaas's own concepts of urban architecture, emptiness is not a threat but a promise. It emerges as the true potential of the city. This reassessment would have a lasting impact on the definition of the city block per se. In traditional urbanism, the block typology is ultimately defined as a specific configuration of solidity and void—the solid perimeter block building and the enclosed void of the courtyard within. In modernist urbanism, this relationship is reversed. The building is conceived as an object that floats freely within the open (green) space of the city. Ungers and Koolhaas overcame this dialectical opposition at a higher level. Instead of compulsively filling the gaps between existing buildings simply for the sake of restoring the integrity of the block, they saw the porosity created by war and reconstruction as an opportunity to liberate the emptiness of the open courtyard from the stifling grip of the block face and connect it to the empty space of the street. This created fluid urban spaces from one block to the next, while the gaps between buildings serve as hinges for this urban communication. In other words, precisely what Kleihues saw as Berlin's problem—the discontinuity of its urban tissue—is seen by Ungers and Koolhaas as its most important self-transforming potential.

Thus the entire theoretical framework of the IBA was exposed as a highly specific perception of Berlin that could not grasp the actual condition of the city, because it held the filter of its (selective past) like a pair of sunglasses in front of its eyes to protect against the all-too-glaring light of the present. Just as the cyberjunkies in Wim Wenders's film *Until the End of the World* (1991) were no longer able to see the "real" world around them as they stared like addicts at LCDs showing recorded scenes of their past dreams, the dream of a bygone Berlin kept Kleihues from ever truly seeing the Berlin of his own present.

To this extent, the ideological struggle underlying the Berlin architecture debate, this Germanic re-enactment of the *querelle des anciens et modernes*, was waged primarily at the level of perception. For the point was obviously the conflicting perceptions and interpretation of the city of Berlin. For the one side (Kleihues), the city was the retrotypical embodiment of the past, for the other (Koolhaas), the prototype of the future. Kleihues thought it perfectly natural and proper to "seek orientation toward the spirit and the historical examples that stand for the better side of Berlin and Prussia: the Age of Enlightenment and Humanism and the 1920s..., a period in which the tendencies of Rationalism were playfully balanced by the dimension of poetry and a metaphysically exaggerated ideal image of nature and the world, [and] in which Prussia and Berlin discovered those specific qualities that revealed their wealth of intellectual and cultural innovation."[9]

While Kleihues believed that Berlin's true (that is, *classicistic*) identity had merely been painfully distorted, Koolhaas saw the *dirty realism* of divided Berlin as anticipating the ultimate contemporary (i.e. *Chinese*) city. Berlin had showed him, he said, "how entirely missing urban presences or entirely erased architectural entities nevertheless generate what can be called an urban condition. The Center of Shenzen, for example, is not a built substance but a conglomeration of golf courses and theme parks, basically unbuilt or empty conditions. And that was the beauty of Berlin even ten years ago, that it was the most contemporary and the most avant-garde European city because it had these major vast areas of nothingness."[10]

Koolhaas was not alone in adopting this dissident view of Berlin. A number of other architects, many of them foreign, spoke out with notorious vigor during the government building boom for those qualities in Berlin that ostensibly stood in the way of a symbolic rise to the status of a national symbol. Thus the British architect Will Alsop expressed admiration for Berlin's "extraordinary robustness," which made it possible for potential beauty to stand side by side with absolute ugliness.[11] Jean Nouvel argued against simply eradicating the Wall, contending that the "space of the Wall" could become the "weld" joining the two halves of Berlin, "a zone of encounter and reconciliation" that would make the previously "forbidden" place a "gathering point for the entire city."[12] Dominique Perrault was also astounded to note "that Berlin has no real center and no real suburbs." This distinction, which was distinctly evident in the urban, political, and social tissue of France, was hardly noticeable to outsiders in Berlin: "This capital city is really one big suburb. This strikes me as a unique quality that is worth considering."[13]

This reflection on the unfamiliar as a possible component of local heritage has never taken place, however. The fact that Berlin has been unable to respond to these perceptions of outsiders raises distinct doubts about the ambitions of its city marketing strategists to achieve the status of a world city. At least one of the characteristics of a world city is that it allows the world to participate in the process of shaping it; it owes its existence to the encounter between local energies and perceptions from abroad. Yet this cultural reaction between the proximate and the distant has not taken place in Berlin. Certainly one reason for this was the climate of diffuse fears of cultural influence from abroad which, in view of the violent incidents of hostility to foreigners in the early nineties and the de facto elimination of the right of political asylum by the German parliament in 1993, take on extremely questionable connotations. Although Berlin did allow foreign architects to build, the city obviously found the risk of allowing itself to be inspired by them too great.[14]

The Extroverted Discourse

What made the Berlin debate a German debate was the fact that it completely dominated architectural discourse in Germany during the nineties. While the German discussion revolved around provincial mock battles on such issues as whether glass or stone was an "appropriate" building material for democratic architecture, the international architecture debate focused on the true changes that were taking place during the decade. High-tech architecture turned to the urban-environmentalist approach of sustainable development; urban theory discovered the dynamics of urban sprawl as a formative aspect of the contemporary city; deconstructivist architecture articulated a critical response to Postmodernism and moved from there to an architecture of topological surfaces and the discovery of the computer as an instrument of design, while a new pragmatic architecture of metropolitan density was emerging in Holland. Yet the more the outside was excluded in the German heartland, the more it became an oasis of longing for the younger generation of architects. The success of Deconstructivist architecture as a critical answer to Postmodernism, heralded by the 1988 exhibition at the MOMA, began to draw notice in Germany as well. In 1991, Daniel Libeskind was awarded the contract to design the Jewish Museum in Germany, and Peter Eisenman won the urban development competition for the design of Frankfurt's Rebstock Park the same year. Erected in 1993, the fire department station in Weil am Rhein was the first building designed by Zaha Hadid in Germany. At the same time, the architecture journal *Arch+* began to confront the German architectural community with new themes from the international debate.[15] The persistent stagnation of discourse in Germany, prompted many young German architects to go abroad during their student years. Popular sources of experience since the late eighties were the high-tech architecture firms of Foster, Rogers, and Grimshaw in London. Architects more concerned with conceptual issues, on the other hand, tended to prefer Holland, where they discovered a subversive approach to architectural design camouflaged as pragmatism in such firms as MVRDV, NL-Architects, One Architecture, van Berkel & Bos and, of course, OMA. Those with stronger interests in theory drifted to such institutions as the London Architectural Association to Ivy League universities in the U.S., such as Columbia, Princeton, and Harvard, in order to focus on computer conceptualization and new scientific insights of relevance to architecture.

Eastern Expansion

In the meantime, the basic mood of restoration spread beyond the boundaries of the capital in Germany, expanding into the newly incorporated eastern provinces. Planners began searching for historical city ground plans in Saxony, Thuringia, Brandenburg, and Mecklenburg-West Pomerania as well. The disappearance of the GDR as a political entity from the map of history appears to have stripped its planning culture of all legitimacy overnight. City planning directors called hastily from the West bemoaned the consequences of "four decades of misguided urban development." And the logical remedy for the damage incurred was the process of "urban repair," which had been tested often enough in the West. Large-scale "urban development plans" were quickly drawn up, schemes that showed how to rebuild the past and dismantle the present in order to pick up the thread of history where it had been lost through negligence in 1949. Actually, as Postmodern architect Rob Krier suggested with reference to Dresden, a city destroyed in 1945 and later rebuilt in a largely modern style,

there was really no need to develop new plans at all. In his view, the ideal solution would be to rebuild the city as it had been in 1944. Although only very few went quite that far, the idea of a broad-based restoration of former GDR cities to their protosocialist identities gradually solidified into a tacit consensus in municipal planning departments in Dresden, Leipzig, and Magdeburg. In this way, the principle of national reunification—the more or less friendly takeover of the GDR by the old and new Federal Republic—could be realized at the level of architecture and urban development. The application of western values covered the acceding territory like a silent tabula rasa that declared the historical legacy of GDR building culture invalid, creating a vacuum that needed to be filled again.

This filling of the vacuum amounted to colonization of the former territory of the GDR with conservative values, as became evident in Hans Kollhoff's winning project in the competition for Alexanderplatz in Berlin in April 1993, if not sooner. The proposal called for the nearly total demolition of the existing architecture, all of which, with the exception of two buildings by Peter Behrens, had been erected during the GDR era. The only structures to be spared were the Behrens buildings and Hermann Henselmann's Haus des Lehrers. Everything else was regarded as architecturally unworthy of preservation. Kollhoff covered the virgin ground thus created with an ensemble consisting of thirteen high-rise buildings representing a thought-provoking retrotypical amalgamation of New York skyscrapers of the thirties and the traditional Berlin city block. Kollhoff treated Alexanderplatz like a white spot on the map, as a place without history that supposedly needed this *creatio ex nihilo* in order to establish an identity of its own. In his submission, which won second prize, Daniel Libeskind took the opposite approach. All of the buildings were to be preserved and appropriately complemented by conversions, extensions, and new structures. History was to be respected (and not judged) in its totality, taken up, and written from there. The diverse traces of past history were to be brought together and incorporated into a contemporary constellation. In this rare balance of East and West, yesterday and today, found and invented, one recognized a culture devoted to negotiating political and cultural differences, of which united Germany was certainly in need. Yet it was not negotiation, the weighing of alternatives, and exchange that determined the modus operandi of the unparalleled convergence of two divided entities, but dictated policy. In this sense, Kollhoff's design was undoubtedly more appropriate for the time. He gave material shape to the relationships and shifting patterns of power during the period in which East and West were growing together, making them clearly visible for all.

The same roll-back approach to urban development was pursued in the five new German states. There, however, planners of retroactive reconstruction had access to an older historical heritage than had been available in comparatively young Berlin. Thus it came as no surprise that in Dresden, for example, emphasis was placed on the city's magnificent Baroque past. Gratefully embracing the doctrine of the historical city layout, planners dreamed here of rebuilding entire city districts and restoring their historical building structure (in terms of lot and cubature) as authentically as possible—as in the case of the reconstructed Frauenkirche at the Dresden Neumarkt. While historical structures destroyed during the war but preserved in plans and drawings began to reappear everywhere, architectural ensembles from the socialist era were placed on the condemned list without a word of discussion. Had they stood in Cologne or Rotterdam, they would probably have been seen for what they were: characteristic and in many cases outstanding examples of quality in postwar European architecture. But given where they were, their historical complicity with the political system of the GDR alone was apparently sufficient to justify declaring them *architectura non grata*.

From the European City to the City of Europe

Preoccupied with this debate over the conversion of historical city centers to museums, planners meanwhile neglected to develop model solutions for the real structural urban development problems of eastern Germany. Hundreds of thousands of people left the eastern part of the country in search of work in the West during the nineties, wreaking havoc on the housing market. One million housing units in eastern Germany were vacant in 1999, many of them in prefabricated panel-construction developments, which in the collective society were still embedded logically but now stood up to 30 percent empty and had to be torn down as too expensive to maintain. But housing vacancy is now virulent in city centers as well, as the majority of Germans in the east dream of owning homes of their own in the suburbs. And as the suburban landscape fills, the body of the city empties. While overburdened urban planning strategists devote themselves to reconstructing the urban tissue (by continuing to employ the now obsolete intrumental repertoire of the West Berlin IBA in the process), the urban landscape in eastern Germany has been shrinking for some time (a development that has been selected as the theme of the next IBA in 2010). Following a long historical phase of growth—in industry, population, and cities—we are evidently now approaching a period of stagnation and regression. This process, which does not halt outside the gates of the capital—now remodeled at such great cost—casts grave doubts on the reconstruction efforts of the IBA period. The emptiness that once existed in urban public space has simply been transformed into empty building space—at exemplified, for example, in the two million square meters of office space that now stand vacant in Berlin.[16] In light this situation, the planning efforts for the capital of Berlin during the nineties appear as an obviously symbolic attempt to give the divided city a new heart. It is interesting to note that this city project runs parallel to the campaign waged by the political parties to establish the "new center." Once recognizable distinctions between left-wing and right-wing political tendencies have evaporated in favor of an discourse of consensus that says everything and nothing at all, a discourse that avoids clear positions at all costs in the interest of capturing as many votes as possible. Berlin's new center is similarly empty. Its only statement is its refusal to come to terms with the real changes that are taking place beyond its self-imposed boundaries. And that is why a new German architecture worthy of the name can no longer be concerned with the reconstruction of the (bygone) European city but must focus instead on the constructing the urban conditions of the Europe of today, which is assuming entirely new contours in the course of the EU's eastern expansion. This is also the context of the challenge to Berlin to develop an identity more appropriate to its heterotopic history and urban culture than the questionable embodiment of a new, central German sovereignty—an identity that Philip Johnson envisioned as early as 1995 and passed along to Hans Stimmann's German capital planners: "Berlin will become the capital of the East, and the East is not at all like the West. Whether you like it or not, you are the westernmost capital of the East, and not the easternmost capital of the West."[17]

# The Next Generation: New German Architects?

Werner Sewing

In contrast to lawyers and physicians, architects see themselves faced with the problem that the need for their rendered services is hardly accepted as a matter of course. Things can also be built without architects—not only the widespread construction of standardized one-family homes in Germany attests to this. Architects must both cultivate the cultural environment from which the need for good architecture arises and produce the built object. So it is all the more surprising to observe a discrepancy that has existed for some time between the public architectural discussion on the one hand and the built—the "good"—architecture on the other. As Hanno Rauterberg demonstrates in this publication, a climate of cultural restoration has for some years been spreading in politics and the public media. The longing for the beauty of old cities, for columns and ornaments, for the surrogate of history, can no longer be ignored. The Frauenkirche in Dresden and the Schloss in Berlin are only the most prominent examples of this desire for a future that was considered past. That this attitude is not about history or a concern for landmarks is clear from a plea that the architectural director of the Berlin Senate made in 2001 for reconstructing the Schloss: "Berliners have a right to some beauty in their city." And the latest slogan of the Schloss advocates reads: it is not a matter of history, but of beauty.

In the past year Hanno Rauterberg in the *Zeit* and Heinrich Wefing in the *Frankfurter Allgemeine Zeitung* have explicitly called attention to the growing disjunction between these social outlooks and opinions, behind which is concealed a deep mistrust of the achievements of modern architecture, and the self-image of professionals—although without appreciable resonance. At the same time the only serious architectural discussion of the nineties, the so-called Berlin architectural dispute, was not about glass or stone but the image of the old city. Influenced by this anti-modern vengeance, it concerned the question of how to undo the "devastations" of Modernism.

If we compare, by contrast, typical architecture production beyond the retro-metropolis of Berlin, there is a surprising lack of such conservative tendencies. To be sure, the many "Neoclassical" buildings of Hans Kollhoff outside of Berlin, as well as the publications of his faculty office at the ETH in Zurich, bow to the conservative lifestyles of their clients. Even Frankfurt am Main now has a miniature thirties-style New York skyscraper, designed by Kollhoff. Nevertheless, united Germany is dominated by an unspectacular continuation of the modern architecture that was considered "finished" in the seventies by the assault of Postmodernism.

Let us remain with appearances: whereas ever since the seventies concrete has been discredited by the public as a raw and brutal material, it has again become a favorite. Stefan Braunfels even describes concrete as the "marble of the 20th cen-

tury." In Minimalist architecture today, concrete—ennobled and smoothed—has left its Brutalist origins far behind. In the work of Peter Zumthor, as one critic said, concrete is like velvet. Many younger architects, by contrast, exploit the rawness of the material again as a subversive element against the high cultural aestheticism of Second Modernism. The fact that this revival of the discourse of Brutalism also represents a retro-attitude seems to confirm the diagnosis of the artist Thomas Eller, who in 1997 already noticed that we in our general artistic development are slowly beginning to accept the fact "that the nineties will never have taken place, but represent an oddly timid revival, chiefly of the seventies."[1]

Has the matter-of-factness with which Modernism in recent architecture again advances to the level of an uncontested canon now become an index for the strength and sovereignty of this position, which can be shaken neither by the traditional taste of the masses nor by Berlin architecture nor by retro-reservations? Or is it just a sign of mindless self-contentment? The pragmatism of Second Modernism appears at least to need no great theoretical reflection.

When in 1998 the journal *Arch+* proposed a debate on the return of Modernism, it had difficultly in getting discussion started over two issues and the idea was not met with any response. Then there was the attempt of Heinrich Klotz, the earlier mentor of Postmodernism, to connect the art-historical creation of "Second Modernism" with the sociological efforts toward a "Reflexive Modernism" (Ulrich Beck, Anthony Giddens), which remained at the level of criticism.[2] This is why Dietmar Steiner in this catalogue rightly complains that there is virtually no feedback between theoretical discussion and architectural practice. Whether this resistance to theory is genuinely German remains unclear. Even in the Netherlands no conceptual disputes have taken place, as some years ago the North American theorist Sanford Kwinter noticed in a polemic against the pragmatism of MVRDV.[3] Yet since the late eighties Dutch architecture has proven itself to be the spearhead of Western European architectural development. And the Swiss with their national architectural production enjoy a similarly successful reputation as Holland: *SuperDutch*, yet do we need a *SuperGerman*?

The Swiss Minimalists also place less value on theoretical conciseness than on the aura of buildings. Peter Zumthor, for example, cultivates the habits of a theory-resistant craftsman by letting his work speak for itself. This seems contrary to the efforts of Jacques Herzog and Pierre de Meuron—working conceptually and experimentally—to leave behind the "taint" of the Swiss and to find their connection to the global theoretical discourse. The latter is situated between Columbia and the AA, between SCIArch and Harvard, that is, in the academy rather than in the normality of modern practice. Similarly, young German architects are always more strongly influenced by their educational stays at elite schools, although it is not all that evident in their native production. In this regard Germany is indeed no special case, but rather the rule.

Two quite recent publications offer a good overview of younger German architects. Early in 2002, the AKJAA, a group of young architects of the Bund Deutscher Architekten (BDA), published a selection of examples of largely realized projects by young German architects, divided by regions.[4] The architects organized in this association cannot be older than forty-four years of age. In 2001, the Berlin architectural critic Angelika Schnell published a still more exacting, smaller sampling in her book *Junge Deutsche Architekten* (Young German Architects). Only twelve offices are presented, which in her view stood as models for a new generation—the "Strategic Generation."[5]

The architects of this generation were born in the sixties, completed their studies in the eighties, and opened their own offices in the nineties. All had realized at least one project, but at the same time none are firmly established and therefore are represented with a full range of unbuilt designs. Angelika Schnell first of all confirms the impression "that especially with the younger generation everything is allowed except Postmodern architecture." She notes, however, that the German "scene" is certainly a "somewhat dull reflection of what is found in all the important schools and tendencies that have become influential here after some delay." She lists the Neominimalism of Switzerland, "High-Tech with eco-extras" from Great Britain, "synthetic nature" from France, "kasbah architecture" from Holland, "computer-generated blobs" from the USA. In contrast to the many regional and national movements in Western Europe, Germany is like a sponge which "absorbs local and international impulses equally and works it into a *mélange* which is difficult to define." So is Germany in fact going its own way? Does not this *mélange* more than ever epitomize the actual International Style? Interestingly enough, according to Angelika Schnell's long interviews with the architects, the Strategic Generation is not engaged in an explicit discussion of style or form. However, it does raise the question of whether the range of conceptual designs between amorphous "blobs" and geometrical boxes is not indeed based simply on formal decisions. For example, a project of the Darmstadt Netzwerkarchitekten for the local office of environmental protection in Oppenheim bears a striking resemblance to the biomorphic form of the Berlin Photonikzentrum by Sauerbruch and Hutton.

Still clearer is the preference for formal decisions in the publication of the young BDA architects. Here the work is clearly dominated by boxes, adorned with the usual vocabulary of louvers and sliding shutters—everything of a high quality, solidly executed, and with a reserved elegance. The Strategic Generation does not simply avoid explicit disputes and theoretical formulations in its style discussions; they work with an implicit canon that is self-evident within the profession itself. The Strategic Generation is a self-conscious, pragmatic, and straight-forward generation that focuses on its projects and withdraws all ideological, political, and philosophical reflections into the private realm—if these are explicitly formulated at all. Only the ecology theme is recognized as an encroaching problem, which is also translated on the project level into a situational concept.

With their pragmatism, young German architects differ only little from their young Dutch colleagues. The Dutch also feed off the conceptual and political preparatory work of avant-gardist Rem Koolhaas, who belongs to the Generation of '68. The German youth scene not only lacks this programmatic "locomotive" but also the support of urban architectural politics. The weakness of the German scene lies in its programmatic and political blaséness, but this is also spreading today in the Netherlands—to the extent that the old master Koolhaas is quickly disappearing into the Olympus of global architecture.

Young German architects—educated in the era of declining Postmodernism, impressed by the ephemeral nature of Deconstructivism, and supported in their professional "start-up-phase" by the tail wind of the post-unity building boom—could afford (perhaps as the last generation) to combine Modernism with pragmatism. Upon closer inspection, their strategies are identical to those of the more straightforward everyday Modernism of the fifties and sixties: a Modernism that had left behind the heroic ideologies of the twenties in order to proceed into the smooth waters of professional entrepreneurship.

The historical success of young German architects documented in both publications took place in the nineties, and it seems questionable at present whether it will continue in the new century. With the softening of the economic and architectural situation, with the fiscal crisis of the German government and its cuts in architectural support, as well as with the conservative climate in the public, the young generation also seems to have lost some of its luster. Or to put it differently, similar to the New Economy, whose representatives were in fact younger than the young architects, this generation suddenly looks very old—as old as they are in fact. After football players and models have long fallen back on their old-age pensions, architects mature in their mid-forties; often well into their fifties they are still considered young. Only a few are able

b & k+ brandlhuber & kniess +, Kölner Brett, 2000

Grüntuch / Ernst Architects, Apartment and Commercial Building, Hackescher Markt, Berlin, 2000

to build in their late twenties or early thirties. The Düsseldorf architect Christoph Ingenhoven, who began his successful career at the age of twenty-five, represents the great exception within this profession. With this advantage in the eighties he paralleled the careers of the stars of early Modernism, for instance, that of Walter Gropius or Mies van der Rohe. Oswald Mathias Ungers also opened his office in 1950 at just twenty-four years of age.

The Strategic Generation of today, by contrast, did not get their chance until relatively late, but they must now notice at the end of the building boom that their predecessors have at their disposal better access to the market and wield more successful strategies. The latter can depend on well-established networks, clients, political contacts, and management capabilities. In Germany this palette extends from Gerkan, Marg and Partner to Ortner & Ortner. The elders who frequently run large offices can make use of the pool of young workers, while the still younger architects—the actual Next Generation in their mid-twenties to thirties—are hired for their computer skills, yet only as cost-effective "visualizers" and network administrators. From the latter, whom Holger Liebs in *Süddeutsche Zeitung* has labeled "Generation Nix," there could still come an unexpected push of innovation, which indeed would change the field of classical architecture into the culture of the life-style animator and event manager: the Next Generation?

The profile of a generation therefore does not depend only on its own "self-creation," but essentially on the constellation in which various generations struggle for their real and symbolic survivals, and for social dependencies and framing conditions beyond their reach. Against this backdrop the situation of the young is obviously precarious.

Some years ago the sociologist Heinz Bude successfully launched a notion of "generation" that emphasized the social-Darwinian motive. Generations compete with each other over influence, power, symbolic recognition, and prestige.[6] Yet even if the social background is ultimately more decisive for the acquisition of these scant social goods, we cannot within a professional class overlook the network-forming influence of generational membership. In architecture up to now the patriarchal rule of succession has naturally dominated as a normal form of generational succession. Large offices in the United States during the long Beaux-Arts period are a prime example of this. Early employment in a prestigious office and support from the boss were crucial to a successful career there.[7] In Europe of the early 20th century, by contrast, the avant-garde elite was formed above generational conflicts. Yet even these young architects as a rule began their careers in respected offices, then organized themselves in generation-specific alliances—with the goal to change radically the self-conception

of their professional class. From that time forward to the beginning of early Postmodernism in the United States we can show that conceptual changes of architecture were always battles in which a generation fought to win acceptance of its style. The sociologist Magali Sarfatti-Larson, in fact, interpreted the rise of American Postmodernism as a coup of younger smaller offices against the established large offices of late Modernism. That this strategy was pushed to its limits was later seen when large offices such as Skidmore, Owings & Merrill adopted the vocabulary of Postmodernism.[8]

Even recent German architectural history can be decoded by the generational concept. In his book *Deutsche Architekten*, for instance, Werner Durth has written about a generation that, during the crisis of the Weimar Republic, made a technocratic understanding of architecture serve as a basis for its professional opportunism and assumed strategic positions, both under Albert Speer during the Nazi era and in postwar times in several city administrations. Whether it be Friedrich Tamms, city architect of Düsseldorf, Helmut Hentrich and Hubert Petschnigg with their successful large office, or Rudolf Hillebrecht, city architect in Hanover—they all possessed leading positions in architecture and city planning in postwar Germany.[9]

The reconstruction of the Federal Republic was sustained above all by the still younger "Flak-Assistant Generation," born between 1926 and 1930, and also known as the "Skeptical Generation."[10] Their disillusioned break with all basic ideological issues and their inclination toward pragmatic solutions within the problem's given parameters mark the well-intended yet uninspired architecture of the postwar years with its compromise of Functionalism and the "vernacular," as inspired by the Heimatschutz movement. The theoretical abstinence then so dominant also hindered German participation in the international criticism of Modernism proceeding from CIAM, which started shortly after 1945.[11] The rediscovery of the city, functional mixtures, and public spaces within the circle of Team Ten did not take place in Germany and was misunderstood during the period of late Functionalism; within the framework of the large housing settlements it was interpreted as urbanism through high density. From Dutch Structuralism and the Japanese Metabolists to English Brutalism, the Pop architecture of Archigram, and the utopian projects of Paolo Soleri—this self-revision of Modernism was only later to inform the student generation of the mid-sixties.

The abrupt end of this possible new beginning can be attributed to the victorious march of international Postmodernism, which expropriated without hesitation the urban discourse of Team Ten and cast it into the traditional forms of the historic city, which at the time was still not called the "European City." The key generation during the cultural upheaval of the Federal Republic during the sixties—the so-called Generation of '68—approximated a fundamentalist critique of Modernism with their criticisms of urban destruction, slum clearance, and large housing developments. For an innovative architectural revision in Germany was not accomplished by the Generation of '68; its architecture was "not building," wrote Dieter Hoffmann-Axthelm.[12] At the same time many of them were getting a taste of the cultural conservatism of Postmodernism.

The architectural discourse was transformed under this influence into a salvation program for the historical city. City planners, social planners, cultural critics, and the literary intelligentsia romanticized—fully in the sense of Jane Jacobs—the historical city neighborhood with its variegated social mixture. Small urban elements versus the large form: this cultural battle defeated the utopian ideas of late Modernism, although these continued to be advanced by a persistent minority. Particularly English High-Tech architecture was a special path accompanying Postmodernism, late Modernism was linked with the ecology movement and provided continuity from the sixties to the eighties. Even an outsider like Rem Koolhaas, who at that time was not yet a practicing architect, denied himself the idyll of the historical city. In retrospect he must be seen as the most important bridge between the late Modern utopian departure and Second Modernism.

In Germany, however, the architectural discussion withered away in the shadow of urban reconstruction, as necessary and as meaningful as this was for the renaissance of inner cities. Here lies the key to Berlin's special path in Germany today. Whereas in the international and German architecture discussions of the eighties Postmodernism had already become defensive as the architectural discussions of the sixties and seventies were again taken up, it was possible to bring this process to a halt in Berlin after the fall of the Wall.[13] The colonization of the Mitte section of Berlin made it possible for a network of '68ers and older IBA elites to break away from Second Modernism which in the meantime had already taken shape. The young Berlin architects who felt duty-bound to the latter lost their cultural and economic terrain. The stylization of Modernism into an actual force of destruction of the 20th century by the Berlin planners signaled the dramatic attraction of the aging Generation of '68 to cultural restoration. Wilhelminian city planning was restaged as a blow of liberation against socialism and Modernism. Yet while the rationalism of the critical reconstruction in the early nineties still represented an attempt to place limits on both the colorfulness of the old Postmodernism and on the emerging neo-historicism, Berlin politics in the last years seems to be moving in the wake of these tendencies. The Tacheles project in Berlin (2001), following the master plan of the American New Urbanists Andres Duany and Elizabeth Plater-Zyberk, marks the first visible closing of ranks behind neo-traditionalism and a no longer critical reconstruction.

It was the city planning discourse that above all weakened the effectiveness of Second Modernism, and not only in Berlin. The invocation of "dirty realism" by Rem Koolhaas, the reference to the "generic city," and automatic urbanism indeed provided a diagnosis from empirical observation; as a position for designing urban-planning concepts, however, they were applicable only conditionally. Now that ecologists have succeeded in establishing their long-standing preoccupation with the idea of the compact European city, the more recent urban projects of Dutch Second Modernism—for example, Borneo-Sporenburg in the east harbor of Amsterdam, or the projected HafenCity in Hamburg—also bear a striking resemblance to the typology of traditional city planning.

Yet most architectural projects of young German architects remain below the threshold of urban dimensions. The reason for this could simply lie in the nature of their clients, who prefer smaller objects or free-standing solitary buildings. Yet it is also conceivable that young German architects, similar to what Claus Käpplinger has observed with young French architects,[14] mistrust large projects generally and fear the loss of their professional control. This could also be a rationalization. City planning seems to be firmly in the hands of the representatives of the "European" model, and is therefore politically inaccessible to the younger Neomoderns.

The Western world seems to limit the Young Generation of Second Modernism in their activity by neo-traditionalist planning parameters that were set up by the successful politics of the previous generation, and that are supported by the present conservative cultural climate. Since this preceding generation is in no way interested in the resumption of Modernism, the "Modernism of Modernism" widespread among the Young Generation genealogically refers rather to the generation of their grandfathers, such as the Brutalists of the sixties.

It is therefore worthwhile to describe contemporary architecture from the vantage point of generational constellations. In 1926 the art historian Wilhelm Pinder proposed an "art history according to generations."[15] The cultural-historical intervals of generations are generally shorter than the biological ones. With the analysis of *zeitgeist*, Pinder was drawn to the problem of the "non-simultaneity of simultaneous events," the concurrence of seeming incompatibles, which seems to defy the idea of continuous progress. In our case this could correspond to a simultaneous retro-mix of the sixties and the 19th century. Pinder proposed a "three-voice polyphony of generations," as a conflict about the power of interpretation in the sphere of art. Conspicuous to it is a "recurrence of the grandfather in the grandson." In fact the "Strategic Generation" of young architects today identified by Angelica Schnell has a parallel in the skeptical pragmatism of the postwar Reconstruction Generation. The sociologist Helmut Schelsky has interpreted the indifference of what he calls the "Skeptical Generation" toward social morality and political engagement as a reaction to the misuse of these virtues in the ideologies of totalitarianism. In a similar way, we could interpret the comparable motives of today's Strategic Generation also as a reaction to the previous overheating of political and moral discussions by the Generation of '68: professionalism as a cultural cooling-off and social distancing. Morality and politics are detrimental to careers, therefore "uncool."

At the same time the Young Generation profits from the cultural-liberational achievements of their predecessors. They even see a positive continuity with the Generation of '68 and therefore do not seek a confrontation with them. The "Strategic Generation" does not even seek a confrontation with Postmodernism within the inter-architectural conflict, but rather pursue a practical negation of Postmodern through their projects. The negative outcome of these completely successful "cold" strategies of conflict-avoidance is seen in the content-deflation of the project of Modernism, whose original and moral-political impulse was sacrificed to an autonomous concept of architecture, one of the legacies of Postmodernism. Whether this generation will withstand the tensions that arise from its increasing estrangement from its cultural environment is rather questionable. As avoiders of conflict, young architects cannot respond to a counter-strategy, which likewise pushes aside disputes and sets the practice of the mainstream against the foundational force of Modernism. In declining the enlightened pathos of Classical Modernism in a Postmodern manner by marketing Second Modernism as an attractive, aesthetic concept of lifestyle, Second Modernism surrenders to the aesthetic logic of lifestyle Darwinism. If the majority wants Baroque, they get Baroque.

A foretaste of this cold liquidation of Second Modernism is found in a rather harmless architectural critique in the *Frankfurter Allgemeine Zeitung* of April 12, 2002. It praised a solid, minimalist building addition to the Bayerische Architektenkammer in Munich by the architects Manfred Drescher and Dieter Kubina. The praise concealed a warning: "The narrow, drawn-out structure of exposed concrete, steel, and glass turns its façade towards the street. Almost completely sheathed in glass, the building opens up at the end of Nymphenburg Canal onto park-like grounds. Its perfect proportions and polite reserve are captivating. To those for whom it seems all too serious to be indicative of today's architecture should look at its context: the Neo-Baroque villa, the headquarters of the Kammer, and the old city orphanage of 1899. All have the picturesque playfulness of southern German architecture, which today has given way to an international unity style." The reference to the elegant, well-proportioned speechlessness of an international unity style always offered a welcome occasion for a fundamental critique of Modernism. This sort of picturesque playfulness of a regional architectural dialect that is conceded here only to the old architecture is one of the qualities of tourist attractions such as Vienna or Prague. A Modernism that avoids this confrontation foregoes on a long-term basis not only its language capability but also its political capability. It fails in the politics of images. It was Postmodernism that served this politics professionally for the first time. Thus architecture became a lead medium for a while. Second Modernism, as a purist and minimalist counter-movement to the inflation of images, can and wants to avail itself of the potential of images but only in a limited way—although in public it still lives off the credit of Postmodernism.

Seen in this way, it could be that with the Next Generation of the very young—those in their twenties or thirties—who seem to have no chance professionally and have been trained knowing this, a revival of a playful and commercial intercourse with images—preconceived by Pop and Postmodernism—will for the first time become an integral component of living designs. Obviously accustomed to moving in the 3D world of the computer, to surfing the lifestyle worlds, and to weaving the everyday with cultural events, the very young are helping themselves to a reanimation within the living world—an architecture fully in the sense of the Situationists or the Pop avant-garde of the sixties. Whether this is still architecture as defined by Aldo Rossi or Peter Zumthor is another matter.

The emerging fusion of architecture, design, and animation today is certainly a sign of commercialization. With it the very young inherit the consumer-oriented side of Archigram's Plug-in City or Cedric Price's Fun Palace, and thus the ambivalent utopias of their grandfathers. Today public relations, marketing, branding, and self-marketing are taken just as for granted in the youth scene as is the subversive refusal in terms of an exclusively strategic self-conditioning: "No Logo!" The utopian and hedonistic messages of the cultural revolution of the late sixties again gain ground.

Even the devaluation of the architecture of the sixties by "Generation Planwerk" meets the continued resistance of the very young. This first became visible in the late nineties with the final failed attempt to save the Ahornblatt in Berlin, a daring concrete-shell construction of the GDR architect Ulrich Müther from the sixties.[16] Prefabricated concrete-panel buildings as well as the urban periphery, the heterotophias of the "European City", are being rediscovered as potential; the "dirty realism" of the late eighties celebrates its resurrection as "city without form." This reevaluation is accompanied by a new interpretation of Trash and Camp—the trivial codes from the everyday culture of the sixties—in advertisements and in lifestyle magazines such as *Wallpaper*.

The question of whether the subversion from the edge, the mobilization of the marginal, can meanwhile break the interpretational sovereignty of the older aesthetics remains open. Although the power of beauty requires no argument, the aesthetics of ugliness needs justification. Yet there is no room for it in the politics of images.

# History—That Was Yesterday

The Germans Are Building a New Normalcy. They Want to Preserve the Past, but without the Memories

Hanno Rauterberg

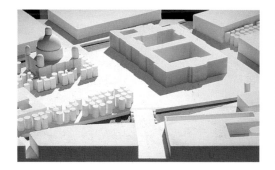

Berliner Stadtschloss, 1906

Ingenhoven, Overdiek and Partners, Design for Central Park, Berlin, 2001

Axel Schultes Architekten,
Model of the Berliner Stadtschloss

Axel Schultes Architekten,
Horseshoe instead of Schloss cube, Berlin, 2001

Axel Schultes Architekten,
Humboldt Forum with Schlüterhof façade, Berlin, 2001

"To all those who tell us we should choose art that is new and a product of our times, we say: Then do your part to ensure that we can forget this vast body of knowledge and criticism; give us new institutions cast from a single mold, a way of life and standards of taste that have nothing to do with the past. Allow us to forget everything that was. And then we will have a new kind of art, and we will have accomplished what has never been done before. It is hard for people to learn, but even harder for them to forget."
Eugène-Emmanuel Viollet-le-Duc[1]

They wanted a new kind of art, and they wanted to forget. At long last, 19th-century visions of liberation were to become glaring reality, the demands of Viollet-le-Duc, von Vischer, and Nietzsche finally to be fulfilled. "Instead of allowing our mind to explore the endless continent before us in freedom, we lock it in the chains, traps, and prison cells of memory,"[2] wrote Le Corbusier at the dawn of the 20th century—and propagated in unison with his colleagues the architecture of new beginning, purified of all forms of the past, liberated from obsolete constraints. Today we refer to this architecture as Classical Modernism, and it has long since become a part of the historical past. Back then, however, just after the turn of the century, it was regarded as the expression of a present that was to grow so powerful that it would overcome history altogether and even herald the future. "Look! The time is near. Fulfillment awaits us. Soon the streets of the cities will shine like white walls! Like Zion, the holy city, the capital of heaven. Then we shall be fulfilled."[3] A smooth, naked, white fulfillment it was to be. Adolf Loos, who wrote these words, was as firmly convinced of this as many of his radical contemporaries.

A good fifty years later, those apocalyptic hopes had given way to apocalyptic hopelessness. There was talk of the murdered city, of the limits of growth, of vast desolation. And the shock of the oil crisis ran deep. It was unthinkable to go onward as before. Project "Future and Forgetting" had become project "Past and Remember." "If very broad and effective measures are not applied now, we shall soon find ourselves standing frightened, naked, and shorn as if in a new colony in a formerly uninhabited land," wrote Karl Friedrich Schinkel in 1815. His words are a strangely vivid description of the mood of the 1970s.[4]

In response to a recommendation by the European Council, the European Architectural Heritage Year was celebrated in 1975. Embroiled in a lively discussion regarding the value of historical structures, the "throw-away society," as it referred to itself, rediscovered the old city center as living space, occupied buildings from the *Gründerzeit* of the late 19th century in order to prevent their demolition, discovered monuments of technology and industry as important historical documents, and

even warmed to the idea of protecting entire ensembles. As early as 1900, experts had pleaded for a policy that would not only protect individual buildings as monuments but would also focus on their importance as integral parts of cities and urban milieus—yet it is only now, seventy years later, that monument preservation has amassed the support and power required to establish the architectural biotope on a foundation of law. Fuelled by numerous popular initiatives and history workshops, interest with the architectural past became a broad movement. Thanks to such sympathetic support, the number of registered historical monuments tripled—in a mere thirty years.[5] "The alternative to Modernism is a civilization of memory," as Thilo Schabert summarized the motives underlying the new concern for historical monuments in 1990.[6]

The past took on new meaning not only in the West but in the GDR as well. While the eastern state had previously sought to preserve only those monuments that would support its socialist ideals and anchor it firmly in history, it now discovered a "national heritage" in which there was even room for the monuments of the enemy of the working class. Well-trained restorers were recruited, primarily from Poland, to renovate medieval churches and city walls—and even to rebuild them entirely. In East Berlin, for example, even the old *Bürgerhäuser* in the Nikolai Viertel were reconstructed in 1980 in an effort to give the capital of the GDR an appealing center of its own.

Yet the state was not alone in its concern for monument preservation. In the East, as in West Germany, there were many people willing to commit themselves, albeit less openly at first, to the preservation of endangered buildings. When medieval housing areas were once again threatened with demolition and replacement by prefabricated panel-construction projects in Görlitz and Stralsund in the late eighties, for instance—despite a great deal of state rhetoric to the contrary—open opposition formed to these attempts to extinguish the past, opposition that lent added strength to the broader protest against the SED regime and eventually culminated in the peaceful revolution of 1989. The preservation of history had actually made history.

Yet despite the drama and significance of these events, love of monuments and dedication to one's own historical heritage are not specifically German phenomena. People rediscovered their architectural past in other European cities as well. Lists of buildings in need of protection were made; old edifices became symbols of local identity and signs of hope for growth in tourism. The origins of monument preservation in the 19th century were much the same all over Europe: many people— French, German, and British alike—experienced the Age of Enlightenment as a shock; the old systems of rule began to erode, a new thirst for knowledge emerged, industrialization swept away all of the customary modes of living, and a new historical consciousness—the primal mother of monument preservation—grew forth in Europe. The people were in great fear of losing everything that was familiar. As early as 1800, Friedrich Schlegel expressed concern that the "prevailing barbarity and greedy compulsion to destroy will lay waste to all of the old monuments."[7] For many people, that statement has lost nothing of its currency even today. Monument preservation was and still is borne by a sense of the need to hold on to whatever is still there to hold on to; and sometimes it is an expression of the hope that old ways of life can be preserved along with the buildings.

Monument preservationists have responded to these impulses everywhere in Europe, and thus the history of monument preservation has followed much the same course in almost every European country. Yet there is a specific, truly German form of preserving the past, and it is found precisely where the German past is uniquely German. The fall of the Wall in 1989—comparable in terms of its impact to the French Revolution that preceded it by two hundred years—was for many people an event that shook the foundations of their existence and changed both their own sense of self and the general view of monument preservation. The complacency nourished through decades of practice, the widely accepted rational approach to the legacy of their country's history, gave way within only a few months to a powerful wave of irrationality. In an attack of collective amnesia, the Berlin Wall, undoubtedly the most powerful political monument of the 20th century, was pulled down and destroyed. "Wallpeckers" smashed it into thousands and thousands of colorful souvenirs, and the city wasted no time moving in demolition equipment. Visitors to Berlin today wander through the city searching in wonder for the last traces of divided Germany, which, but for a few exceptions, have been eradicated almost entirely.

This urge to wipe away the past shaped a pattern of behavior that would persist during the years that followed. Just recently, twelve years after the political turnabout known as the *Wende,* controversy arose in Halle an der Saale over a heroic GDR sculpture that rose high above the square in front of the railway station, the fist of the figure raised in a gesture of confidence in the ultimate triumph of socialism—a monument that had become unbearable for the city fathers and which they therefore decided to eliminate. Similar cases could be observed in many cities in eastern Germany after unification, most notably in Berlin. The idea was to cast off the uncomfortable history of the GDR by removing all evidence of its existence. The GDR Foreign Ministry, one of the finest buildings in the capital ensemble, was condemned and razed, as was the Ahornblatt, or "Maple Leaf," a restaurant built in shell-construction that had become a symbol of the heart of East Berlin for many

people. Alexanderplatz was quickly planned over with lofty visions, since its sheer breadth of urban space design to accommodate mass assemblies was looked upon in highly individualistic western German society as a symbol of inhumanity. Nor was any further use envisioned for the Palast der Republik. The former conference and event center, where the GDR legislature had convened, was ridiculed in Western media as a department-store box. All memories of the Palast were dismissed as "Eastalgia" [a play on "East" and "nostalgia"—*transl.*]. Thus in almost no time at all, most of the significant legacies of the GDR either disappeared from the Berlin city profile or were threatened with removal.

This wave of iconoclasm slowly began to ebb two or three years after German reunification. Following a phase during which the signs and symbols of the vanquished system's rule were eliminated, a period of reconciliation began. Yet a persistent longing for harmony and normalcy continues to influence the relationship of Germans to their past even today, as the following discussion will show.

It all began with cautious probing, as many Germans, especially those in the West, were completely in awe of Berlin and its buildings. A long debate was waged on the question of whether the Republic should move its capital from the Rhine to the Spree, and there were many who equated a return to Berlin with a return to the grand illusions of imperialism. For those who had regarded the architecture of past eras as harmless—architectural history, a matter of local color—the past suddenly seemed uncomfortably close. Seldom have monuments been attributed such a powerful and influential, indeed politically determining role as in those years. Every step in the process of becoming a capital, every reconstruction project, every demolition, every new plan, was associated with the German people's striving for a new self-image. Many looked on with great anticipation to discover what foundations the Berlin Republic would lay for itself.

Given the chance, the political institutions would happily have fled into neutrality, and thus the first plans called for construction of new buildings for all of the federal ministries. It soon became obvious, however, that it would be impossible to escape the past with this strategy devoted to a new beginning. Germany had been quite rightly accused of attempting to evade its historical responsibility and to present a pure white face of innocence. And so the decision was made to accept the legacy, although how this was to be done remained a matter of dispute. The reconstruction of the Reichstag became the first test case, as every single stone in the walls of this government building dedicated in 1894 seems to bear witness to a history full of evasive maneuvering and of wounds—to a parliament that once bowed to the will the Emperor and later, during the Weimar

Republic, became hopelessly entwined in legislative infighting; to a fire that consumed the Reichstag and then democracy itself; to the impact of bombs and grenades, to the flags planted on the building by Red Army troops; to plans to tear it down before it was eventually rebuilt again—as a Western bastion in the Cold War and the symbol of a long-awaited reunification. Though Hitler never governed and never spoke in this immense, stocky building, it is impossible to escape the past century with all of its inconsistencies here. Or is it?

Great hopes were placed in Lord Norman Foster when he was commissioned to redesign the Reichstag in 1994. Here was an architect who plans airports and bank towers, who manages fifty projects at once, and whom the entire world admires as an ingenious devotee of technology. Such a man should have sufficient stature and detachment to avoid losing his way in the confusing tangle of history and the dense thicket of conflicting competencies. Foster began his reconstruction project from the inside. He tore the intestines out of the Reichstag. Forty-five thousand tons of rubble were removed, including everything the architect Paul Baumgarten had had carried in during the sixties in order to convert the wartime ruin into a functional parliament building again. An internationally recognized form of Modernism was to replace the old national version. There had been entirely enough Germanic formal babble—Baumgarten was in full agreement on this point with all of the other architects who had searched in Bonn for a new, objective language for the buildings of the democratic state.

There were surely a number of practical reasons for removing his interior work and thus tearing down a third of the building. The objective was to convert the Reichstag for new use, and many floors were too confining and complicated to meet the anticipated needs. Added to this was the problem of asbestos emerging from virtually every crack. But the merciless rigor with which Baumgarten was banished from the building also suggested a desire to get rid of a few tons of ideology along with the rubble. The FRG now followed the GDR to the landfill; the evidence of division was destroyed. Baumgarten stood for the transitional and the unpretentious; his was the architecture of the old Federal Republic. It is no longer present in the new Reichstag—almost as if it had never been part of a history worth preserving. Gone was the Berlin branch of a Bonn tradition that was bound by its loyalty to the transparency of Modernism (especially until 1972) and had achieved a striking degree of autonomy in Günter Behnisch's new Bundestag.

Foster cannot be accused of seeking a return to pathetic pomp with his Reichstag project. Yet enclosed by the historic shell of walls up to three meters thick, his elegance seems somehow lifeless. Nothing of the uplifting cheer of Behnisch's building in Bonn has survived here; every playful, unconstrained aspect was lost—along with every trace of eccentricity—on the road to Berlin. Those who feared that the parliament building would succumb to the rush of neo-Teutonic national feeling were relieved. If there was anything here to fear, it was administrative, bureaucratic boredom: the avoidance of meaning or statement at all cost. Instead of seizing the opportunity for a vital integration of history, Foster gave the historical the status of a museum exhibit. Thus, for example, the vaulted ceiling dating from the Wallot era, with its rustic decorations, was exposed and impressively illuminated, so that visitors passing by it over a walkway can stop and gape at it. Many of the gaps and holes that served as reminders of the iconoclastic wave in which pictures and ornamentation were removed during the fifties were painstakingly covered over with light-colored plaster, leaving behind joints and spots but no cracks or signs of desecration. A monument with the character of a tapestry. Even the many greetings and mementos written on the walls by Russian soldiers in charcoal and wax crayon during the storming of the Reichstag in 1945 seem like mere decorations in this otherwise so sterile-looking building.

Only the dome of the new Reichstag offers visitors a prominent symbol that calls attention to the building's dramatic history by highlighting the tension between old and new. Foster originally wanted no dome at all, but a majority of members of the two Union parties spoke out in favor of a reconstruction of the old Wallot cupola as a way of giving form to the continuity of Germany history. Ultimately, the Bundestag agreed on a glass dome that quickly etched itself into the visual memory of the nation and became the symbol of the new beginning in the midst of the old. Inside the building, however, Foster was defeated by the gravity of the Reichstag's history. Though he smoothed and tidied, he did not muster the courage to take an artistic position of his own.

He can be given credit, at least, for having treated architectural history with earnest respect. Plans for many other federal building projects were pursued with considerably fewer scruples. By the mid-nineties—the so-called Berlin architecture dispute was in full swing, and discussion focused on the right guiding symbol for the city and on such matters as eaves heights, block edges, and high-rise buildings—the fate of most government buildings had already been sealed. Nearly all ministries and national political organizations had moved into existing buildings, most of them built during the *Gründerzeit* or the Nazi era. With a very few exceptions, there was no interest in using the architectural ensemble erected by the GDR government.

As in the Reichstag project, the few new buildings and extensions actually realized reflect a deliberate rejection of the guiding ideals of architecture in the Bonn Republic. The rhetoric of transparency was not abandoned entirely, and the new Foreign Ministry (architects: Müller/Reimann), for example, was given a glass-enclosed foyer in order to preserve at least the illusion of approachability. Yet architects strove at the same time for the pathos of eternal universality and wanted nothing to do with the fragile, incidental, and modest qualities that characterized government buildings in Bonn. The Office of the Federal President, for example, the first constitutional body to move from the Rhine to the Spree, flirted openly with perfection. Actually, it is not a building at all, as its two architects Martin Gruber and Helmut Kleine-Kraneburg point out. It is really an object, a work of art in the form of a shimmering black ellipse. Stringent perfection rules both inside and out. The building is all smoothness and shine, and even art bows to the prevailing order. The architecture is so precise and predetermined, so fully transposed into universal ideal forms, that it would seem to need no people, no life at all. This building is a self-enclosed system that recognizes no historical progress.

The old capital, with its barracks, its improvisations, and its temporary solutions, was mercilessly sanitized. Everything has been liberated from the past, and change is not foreseen. Gruber and Kleine-Kraneburg did not want to erect a House of Democracy, and they refused to build political architecture. Instead, they tried to create a building without past or background that is content with its own aesthetic nobility and avoids all forms of rhetoric. This apolitical minimalism was bound to fail, of course. Anyone who believes he can evade tradition altogether in the middle of Berlin betrays his own naiveté. Yet many younger architects did put this naiveté to the test in Berlin. Examples include the reductionism of a Gesine Weinmiller, who built the Federal Labor Court in Erfurt, or the austere Neoclassicism of the firm of Krüger/Schubert/Vandreike, whose proposal advanced along with that of Axel Schultes to the final round of the competition for the Chancellor's Office in 1995. Both examples show that the old forms of state representation had become acceptable in Berlin again.

They were not above dispute, however. In a flight of hysteria, particularly during the years preceding the government's move to Berlin, people criticized these buildings as examples of neo-Nazi self-indulgence—though without good reason, for their petrified rationalism was not an homage to the Nazi era but instead an appeal for normalcy in the German public sector. The age of self-effacement is over, these buildings tell us. The time has come to assert national pride, with dignity and solemnity, as other nations do. Forms per se are innocent, and the Germans no longer play a key role in world affairs, anyway—so why take recourse to the canon of Classicism? Simply because of those twelve years in which these forms were exploited for the wrong purposes?

Such questions can only be posed by those who no longer view architecture as a vehicle of meaning but see it instead as pure form, liberated from the trappings of history. The same arguments could be used to create a fashion collection adorned with beautiful, yellow stars. Then, of course, both the color and shape of the star would be innocent and timeless. One need only do one thing to transport it into everyday life: forget history.

Another project that took part in this project devoted to forgetting—which, as shown above, is firmly established in the tradition of Modernism—was the reconstruction of the Foreign Ministry planned by Hans Kollhoff. In this case, the architect was confronted by a building beset like virtually no other by the horrors of German history. A sandstone bulwark originally built for the Reichsbank, it was Hitler's first showcase project and later served as the ruling headquarters of the SED dictatorship. Instead of responding to the complex history of the building, Kollhoff, a habitual critic of postwar architecture who fervently embraces the ideals of Classicism à la 1800, declared that he wanted to "show respect for buildings like the former Reichsbank as well, not because of but in spite of the past they had."[8] He said *had*, rather than *have*, revealing in his choice of words that the past has obviously long since bid farewell in his view, that it no longer extends into the present, and that obsession with history conceals a denial of history. Stone is innocent, Kollhoff affirms as clearly as the young Neoclassicists cited above. And he, too, wishes to strip architecture of all meaning that accrues to its forms. Kollhoff recognizes neither democratic nor dictatorial architecture—his concern is with art, not politics. And thus he sees the Reichsbank building not as a historical monument but as the document of style.

There is no other explanation for the nearly total absence of a personal architectural signature in the reconstructed building. There is no irony, no articulation of new ideas—Kollhoff emphasizes an architecture of formal affirmation. The building exterior shows no sign of re-appropriation and conversion to other use, and the urge to restore prevails within as well: dignified splendor and a strange bias toward upper-class *Gemütlichkeit*. This is the ambiance in which Germany wishes to present itself to the world: built-in cupboards, window recesses, doors, and often entire walls are lined with rustic cherry moldings; important public spaces have deep, dark walnut floors, and conference-room walls are covered with the finest materials. These interiors recall a history already regarded as past two hundred years ago. Kollhoff even rediscovered the radiant splendor of chandeliers and designed different variations for the various halls, rooms, and foyers, among them a massive rosette measuring nearly two meters across.

Yet Kollhoff's intent was not to rehabilitate the architectural aesthetic of the Nazi era. The Reichsbank building, erected between 1934 and 1939, is not a typical example of the vulgarly monotonous architecture that came into vogue somewhat later with the New Chancellery of the Reich. Indeed, the building exhibits elements of a conservative Modernism in such details as horizontally divided windows, for example. And that is a tradition, as Kollhoff stated, worthy of pursuing. Yet in doing so, he ignored the fact that it was Hitler himself who approved this design by the architect Heinrich Wolff, a decision that marked the end of classical Bauhaus architecture. An international competition organized in February of 1933 was the last open competition held before 1945 and the last encounter between tradition and Modernism, between Heinrich Tessenow and Ludwig Mies van der Rohe. Anyone who builds on or inside the Reichsbank today will find himself involved in this field of conflict between competing aesthetic ideals and will have to take a position. Kollhoff opted for "respect"—he took refuge in a supposedly neutral stance, deliberately refusing to comment on Hitler's decision that meant the beginning of the end for Mies and other modern architects.

This odd distinction between form and content, this decoupling of history from its setting, amounts to an attempt to neutralize the architectural structure. It is transported into a sphere in which only aesthetics count and architects are absolved of all accountability. This same strategy of sanguine appropriation was pursued at the Aviation Ministry of the Reich built by architect Ernst Sagebiel and converted for the Federal Ministry of Finance by Hentrich-Petschnigg & Partner. This building was also stylized into a timeless work of art. The architects blithely overlooked its totalitarian posturing; in fact, they even went so far as to reconstruct them or to liberate them from the concealing trappings of the GDR era. The classical concept of the monument, which regarded a building as a storehouse of experienced life, an eloquent document of the past, is taken here to the point of absurdity.

One might be inclined to believe that Berlin suffered most under the yoke of this new approach to monuments and that the rest of the Republic remained dedicated to an honest attempt to come to grips with the historical value of its monuments. This may be true, since curiosity about the past certainly did not disappear overnight at the end of the eighties. On the contrary, there were more museums than ever before at the turn of the 21st century, more books on historical topics, more films, and more television programs devoted to historical themes. What was true in the 19th century remains true today: the faster the world turns, the more rapid the pace of development, the greater the desire of many people for permanence, for the reliable and the authentic. And monument preservation benefits from this mania for the past, which is actually a suppressed form of mania for progress—millions of visitors flock to the Open Monument Days every year to view castles, factories, and old houses.

Berlin is not an island, however. The process of dehistorification observable in many government buildings also affects other genres, other parts of the country, and has even begun to contribute to a new public consciousness with respect to monuments. This becomes particularly evident in a report commissioned by Antje Vollmer, cultural-policy spokeswoman of the Green Party and vice-president of the Bundestag, which triggered vigorous debate on the future of monument preservation in the year 2000.[9] This report—actually a pamphlet—written by urban scholar Dieter Hoffmann-Axthelm talks about a kind of monument preservation that has abused its responsibility and become meaningless. Most monument preservationists, the author argues, are obsessed with principles, self-righteous, and ignorant of the facts. Hoffmann-Axthelm even refers to them as "rag-pickers," who are incapable of distinguishing between true value and everyday junk. They continue to expand their sphere of authority, declaring even factories, hospitals, and residential settlements of the twenties and even the fifties as parts of the public heritage: "a perversion." Only a rigorous purge can stop this uncontrolled growth, the author argues. The state should end its involvement with monument preservation and concern itself in the future only with buildings owned by the government. The "culture of national monuments" must be separated once again from the sphere of "private building freedom," as was the case in the 19th century. In other words, the owner of an apartment or office building should be allowed to modify or demolish as he sees fit in the future—unless a sufficient number of other people are willing to commit themselves to saving the building. Thus the free will of the people should decide the question of preservation or demolition. "If it touches no hearts, why should it be saved?"

The chance for reason, the report argues, is to be found precisely in the possibility of destruction. The business community, still intent today upon ridding itself of the excess baggage of architectural culture in the interest of maximizing profits, must first feel the loss itself in order to develop its own will to preserve the historical heritage. One hears here a vague echo of the early Modernist manifestos of liberation and their appeals for abandonment of the old in order to begin building the new at last. The visions of the report are not far removed from those of the "Plan voisin de Paris" drafted by Le Corbusier in 1925, which proposed leveling the city center and eliminating everything old except for a few national monuments. Although Hoffmann-Axthelm and Vollmer do not dream of a *tabula rasa*, they are concerned—like Kollhoff and some of his colleagues—with a reassessment of ideals. It is not buildings that should disappear, but what overlays them. The focus in the future should

6

7

8

Lord Norman Foster, Reichstag Building, Berlin, 1999

9

10

11

Martin Gruber/Helmut Kleine-Kraneburg,
Office of the Federal President, Berlin, 1998

Müller/Reimann, Foreign Ministry, new building,
Berlin, 1999

Gesine Weinmiller with Michael Grossmann,
Federal Court of Labor, Erfurt, 1999

Hans Kollhoff, Foreign Ministry, restoration of the former Reichsbank, Berlin, 1999

Axel Schultes Architekten, Office of the Federal
Chancellor, Berlin, 2001

George Bähr, Frauenkirche, Dresden, 1931

Reconstruction of the Frauenkirche,
Dresden, 1994–2006

be on the beauty of a building and not on its historical statement. "There is no more direct measure of the value of a monument than its beauty," states the author of the report. And this topos also calls to mind the early years of Modernism, when Karl Scheffler demanded that "nothing be tolerated but the significant, beautiful old, an open-air museum of urban history, and the essential representative buildings and institutions."[10]

According to Hoffmann-Axthelm's recommendation, the only buildings worthy of protection in the future are those erected before industrialization, for only that form of the old ensures the desired degree of immediacy. A welcome side effect would be the dramatic reduction of the number of buildings listed as monuments. One could safely predict that the number of privately owned monuments would decline appreciably if the recommendations in the report were taken to heart. And thus the state, despite its retreat, would assume a more important role after all. The resulting decrease would amount to an increase for the state, and its share of the whole inventory of monuments would rise accordingly. What is more, the so-called national monuments would shine forth so much more brightly when separated from the architectural manifestations of everyday culture. The state would once again become the true protector of the national heritage—its monuments the only true monuments: "tourist attractions, focal points of historical self-discovery, standards of beauty, milestones of culture, accessible to experience, palpable, and useful," as the report states. Everything ugly, incomprehensible, and political—such as the Berlin Wall or the industrial ruins of the Ruhr region—would be eliminated from consideration. Dreary modernist architecture would have to give way, blunt manifestations of the everyday would be left to the Darwinian mechanisms of society, and the noble rest would be remystified. The nation must rediscover itself through culture.

Thus history is no longer a vehicle of reflection but of adoration; culture is no longer criticism but comfort for the soul. It is no coincidence that Vollmer and Hoffmann-Axthelm are among the most prominent supporters of a project that shaped the architectural debate of the nineties like virtually no other. Only a few months after the fall of the Wall, the possibility of reconstructing the old Hollenzollern residence that had been razed by the SED regime in 1950 at the Schlossplatz in Berlin was addressed in open discussion for the first time. The advocates of such a return referred to it as a national mission, citing the need to give a torn and tattered German society a new center, a new intellectual and spiritual middle at this location. As did the Vollmer report, the Schlossplatz discussion involved a great deal of talk about beauty and the desire for a return to an original state of wholeness that would help people forget the wounds of history. To allow Walter Ulbricht the last word—

thus went a very popular argument—and accept his decision to demolish the palace as binding today was simply unacceptable.

Pain must be silent and history must finally grant us peace—this guiding principle motivated great numbers of people throughout Germany during the nineties to commit themselves to the reconstruction of buildings destroyed long ago. Many buildings were rebuilt during the postwar years, of course, and several initiatives devoted to recovery of lost legacies emerged during the eighties and nineties—in Hildesheim as well as in Frankfurt and Munich. But the longing grew stronger with reunification. Germany had acquired a new capital, a new currency, a new list of spelling rules, and so at least the new architecture should be the old: the Stadtschloss and the Garnisonskirche in Potsdam, the Paulinerkirche in Leipzig, the Bauakademie and even the mediocre Kommandantenhaus in Berlin. All of these are buildings that recall history but deny memory. And the desire to preserve these survivors continues to grow, as if self-deception had become an addiction that must be fed in order to shield one's own illusions against reality. "Where historical truth and integrity are abandoned in a work of art, where the intent is to veil and conceal, there can be no reasonable expectation of uninhibited participation or general interest. As the creation of a vain and self-possessed age, such a work must inevitably fall to ruin with it."[11] These words of Schinkel fell for the most part on deaf ears in post-reunification Germany.

Next to the Hollernzollern residence, the second most celebrated reconstruction project was the Frauenkirche in Dresden. This was also the focus of lengthy debate, for although people missed the proud dome in the Baroque city profile, they were unwilling at first simply to clear away the hill of ruins and thus to eliminate a striking memorial to the city's destruction during World War II. Finally, it was agreed that at least a portion of the rubble, the gable torso of the west portal, would be preserved—as a reminder that the memory of the horrors of wartime destruction must never be eradicated completely. But as reconstruction progressed, the urge to achieve perfection grew increasingly stronger. The council of the Frauenkirche foundation ultimately resolved that even the very last readily recognizable warning finger of history should be integrated once again within the great whole.

"If we are to assure our country a future, we must preserve its cultural identity and make it accessible," declared German President Roman Herzog in 1997 on the occasion of the award of the National Prize to the foundation.[12] Yet pacification of the last piece of rubble means that at least a part of the German past is no longer "accessible." Fascism has been eliminated as a part of German "cultural identity," as has been the history of the GDR peace movement, for which the ruin was both a meeting place and a symbol of protest against militarism in the period beginning in 1982. That this eradication was a deliberate political objective was affirmed by Theo Waigel, federal minister of finance at the time, who had three commemorative coins minted as a means of generating funds for reconstruction. Today, Waigel declared at the coin presentation ceremony in 1995, Germany "stands for the first time on the side of the winners of history."[13] With these words, he indirectly declared the Frauenkirche a work of architecture whose magnificence would erase all memory of the defeats of the past.

The debate regarding the Schlossplatz in Berlin also revolved around questions of national identity, although the discussion was also influenced by aspects of local patriotism and nostalgic obsession. Yet the state's relationship to its own past was also defined in the process—through the country's own determination of its place in history. It remains unclear even today which history it is that is evoked at the Schlossplatz. The federal government appointed a commission tasked with breaking a path through the confusing tangle of arguments, and the commission issued a recommendation passed by a bare majority in late 2001: the Baroque façade, the historical dome, and several of the interior rooms were to be reconstructed along with the Schlüter's interior courtyard. Only very few politicians felt bound by this recommendation, however. A number of others openly voiced opposition to the commission's plans even before the final report was presented.

Thus the fate of the Schlossplatz remains to be determined, a situation that surely has something to do with continuing dissension between eastern and western Germany. If the Baroque structure with its two courtyards is to be restored, then the Palast der Republik will have to make way, for the GDR House of the People and the Government has stood since 1976 at precisely the spot once occupied by the Schlüterhof, the most precious part of the palace. Although West Germans have never felt much enthusiasm for their parliament buildings and probably have only vague memories of them, at best, the Palast der Republik remains a living reminder of the past for many people in eastern Germany even today. Only about 10 percent of the events held there had anything to do with party politics, and the building popularly known as "Erich's Lamp Shop" was primarily a venue for concerts, cabaret performances, and bowling tournaments. Here in the Palast, the East seemed quite Western; everything was available in abundance, and culture became a vehicle of popular sympathy for the SED. A recent poll indicates that 46 percent of East Berliners want to see the building preserved, while only 26 percent favor a castle. It seems obvious that, in the eyes of many people, the Palast still symbolizes a GDR as it might once have become in the distant future—at least in a material sense. But the Palast also wrote

political history: during a long six-month period from April to September 1990, the first German legislature born of a successful revolution met in the assembly hall of the former GDR national assembly. The historical significance of this part of the Palast is rivaled only by that of the Paulskirche in Frankfurt. It is one of the most important public memorials to the peaceful revolution of 1989. Though one may find this state building ugly and monstrous, it is a monument and a model nonetheless. It serves as a reminder that circumstances can be reversed, even while they exist, without destroying everything that was.

"It is a high and certainly late stage of culture that recognizes relative justification and necessities and sees phases of historical development even in decline and barbarism where earlier centuries were engaged in heated partisan dispute," wrote Jacob Burckhardt in the mid-19th century.[14] At the dawn of the 21st century, we are nowhere near such recognition of uncomfortable truths, and destruction has once again become an option. Consideration is given to demolishing a multidimensional monument in order to recreate another. To build a castle, one has to clear away history—and that seems to be what many advocates of the Hohenzollern residence want to achieve. Elke Leonhard, a former chairwoman of the Bundestag Culture Committee, openly confessed her sympathy for Ulbricht-style gestures. She would have been "happy to see the Palast blown to bits with a loud bang."[15] And in this respect she belongs to a growing segment of the public that wants nothing to do with the bulky legacy of the Schlossplatz. This group accepts history only if it is comfortable; and it is willing to eradicate the traces of an uncomfortably colorful history. In the minds of these people, the artistic value of a monument is not crucial to memory or to the intensity and significance of history. "If history can teach at all, then only as a voice of criticism," as Jürgen Habermas argued. We can learn from history how things should not be done. "It is from negative experiences that we learn the most."[16]

Yet the Schloss enthusiasts are not concerned with lessons but with aesthetics. Only the Schloss can make the square a "site of national remembrance," states publisher Klaus Wagenbach. Only thus will a symbol of the unification of East and West be created, and only thus will we be able to recover our "broken national pride" (Goerd Peschken) at last—as if one could reunite only in some distant past, eliminating all intervening history. The Berlin Senate declared through its building director Hans Stimmann that the Schlossplatz was to be transformed into a "setting of cultural and political reunification." The goal in this case is "national self-affirmation and nothing more than the return of a European city center to normalcy."[17] The idea is to construct an intact, organic national history.

Anomalies must be eliminated, and the two-faced character of German history is to be surgically corrected.

It would be comforting to dismiss the Schlossplatz debate as an isolated case, but it is—as has been demonstrated—part of an comprehensive process of intellectual change that aims to replace recollection with uplifting and to achieve the sublime. History—that was yesterday. Today we are liberated from imprisonment in the past. The difference between truth and falsehood, between fact and fiction, seems to be important to fewer and fewer people at the dawn of the 21st century. Why is that so? Why are our needs with respect to history changing? And what impact will this change have on the future of monument preservation in Germany and other European countries?

Many people experience the simultaneity of the non-simultaneous every day. The ever-present availability of all forms and styles is demonstrated in advertising, in fashion, in pop music, in design. Even the eighties (of the 20th century, of course) have been reheated and served up again. The legendary Zero series of the Leica camera was recently revived, mechanical watches are selling well once again, and even tube amplifiers have returned to the market. The more dominant high-tech becomes, the greater the longing for low-tech, for things comprehensible, things that can be controlled. It has become difficult to distinguish between "retro" and "futuro." Everything can be copied, and there seems to be nothing wrong with that. The possibility of reproducing human beings or human body parts has become real—and more than a few people see reason and purpose in doing so. And thus it comes as no surprise that the distinction between the authentic and the counterfeit in architecture hardly matters anymore. A trend toward neo-historicism is becoming increasingly evident. A growing number of architects—from Oranienburger Strasse in Berlin to Hamburg-Blankenese—are turning to an adoring embrace of the 19th century. Why shouldn't we be allowed to do today what our fathers' forefathers could do back then? Why can't we design buildings with bay windows, tympanums, cross gables, and aedicules again? These are the earnest questions posed by the neo-historicists, who have already formed broad movements in the U.S. and England.

In the early 19th century, the urge to historicize, to subject many areas of life to the rigors of science, was still guided by motives born of the Enlightenment. Humankind struggled for knowledge about itself. History was viewed less and less as something absolute, something God-given. Interest focused increasingly on the freedom of the subject and the extent to which it is determined by social conditions. Today, discussion revolves around the power of genes. The watchword is transhumanism, and belief in great societal change is on the wane. Yet as interest in society and its implications for the individual

declines, curiosity about its history and its monuments also ebbs accordingly. Though genetic engineering is still no more than a weakly burning utopian light, one has the sense that some of its early forms are already firmly rooted in the general historical consciousness. The human as an autonomous being, programmable in all of his physical and mental qualities and independent of all historical development—this image of mankind, which is shaped by a sense of omnipotence and a new absolutism of the present, appears to underlie many contemporary discussions regarding monument preservation.

The desire to preserve the impermanent is an outgrowth of the industrial age. That age is now nearing its end, and one may presume with good reason that the need for monuments as we know it is also changing—not only in Germany but everywhere in Europe. At the very least, it is clear that the Enlightenment concept of the unique and irreplaceable character of the individual is receding into the background—and with it belief in the unique identity of every individual work of architecture. The Enlightenment view that history is an irreversible linear process, that everything is created and mediated through history, that there can be no natural continuity of tradition, but that memory must be self-reflective—this view no longer appears to be firmly anchored in our thinking. In its place we observe the spread of a new attitude toward the past that is strongly reminiscent of pre-Enlightenment eras: denial of the temporal character of history and an appeal for a return of timeless standards of perfection and regularity.

It is a view that poses a substantial danger to monument preservation. For monument preservation does not take place outside the boundaries of society. The new old buildings compete with the truly old, as only very few people are capable of distinguishing between the genuine and the counterfeit, and because the question will arise sooner or later whether the old really must be preserved at such great effort and expense at all, since it is much cheaper and more practical to build things new. Restoration, reconstruction, and neo-historicism of every kind must be the enemies of every effective form of monument preservation, as they imply the total availability of everything that ever was.

And it is precisely the unavailable, the unique, and the irreproducible that make up the most important capital of monument preservationists. They must resist the "can-do" mania of our society, which is devoted to building not only a better future but a better past as well, and remain steadfast in their insistence on preserving what is true and authentic. Monument preservation must "be constantly reminded of its knowledge of the relativity of momentary forms of public interest in specific kinds of monuments. Like impartial referees, it must seek to preserve, and thus make accessible, even things that no one wants to have at a given time," wrote Georg Mörsch some twenty years ago.[18]

Surely, the task of monument preservation in these struggles on behalf of the genuine and the original will not be an easy one. For even monument preservationists must admit that the original is no longer there. Monument preservation contributes to a product of art; it is not an objective science, not a discipline in which scholars in white gloves pour through volumes in archives, never touching the real world. Monument preservationists do indeed touch reality, in fact, they alter it. They cannot rescue the things they seek to protect—the monuments—from time, but are compelled instead to help design the changes made in them, or at least to accept their share of responsibility for them. And they must remain true to their own guiding principles, their own projections, the own desires with respect to the past. "Historical research presupposes the awareness that the substance of our ego is also mediated in many ways, that it, too, is a product of history," wrote the historian Johann Gustav Droysen in 1857.[19]

But wherein lies the difference between the professional monument preservationist and the layman, between defenders of the original and advocates of reconstruction? If the original does not exist, if all there is to work with is a product of art, if the representatives of both sides seek nothing more than to have their own guiding principles materialized in the monument, then how can one distinguish clearly between a reconstruction, an openly neo-historical new building, and a protected monument converted to a new form of use? Are the differences qualitative or merely qualitative? Can we define a fundamental difference, or do the guiding principles differ only in that some articulate their historical wish-images openly and dramatically while others try, at least, to take a critical approach?

Monument preservation faces a dilemma that increases in magnitude the more it is willing to engage in self-reflection and the more rigorously it investigates its own historical practice. What can it offer in opposition to the counterfeiters if it is no longer certain of its own truth? How can it defend its picture of history against the many alluring images of longing presented by the others? How can it stand up to those who accuse it of relic-worship and adoration of wounds only because it cannot accept duplicates and random alterations?

As a symbol of a supposedly historical atmosphere, a copy may be as good as the original, whatever it may be. Either may even be regarded as authentic, since authenticity, like a work of art, takes form in the eyes of the beholder—and such eyes are easily deceived. The idea of the original, at least, is irreplaceable, however. For it is only the idea that has resisted transience, survived the passage of time; and it is only the idea that

I can trust to tell me about more than the present. Ultimately, such trust cannot be justified in rational terms. It is more a matter of faith—faith in the possibility of encountering an unavailable piece of history.

What remains to monument preservation is to voice an appeal for thinking in the conditional. And to warn against adopting a view of history as mere pleasureful compensation for an earth-shaking present, as nothing but a comfortable, attractive decoration for a barren here and now, as just a feel-good setting. Thinking in the conditional means approaching the monument as a means to achieving an understanding that the world was once very different, that it could have become very different, and that it could also be very different in the future. It means grasping the past as something unavailable that does not affirm my existence but enriches it. The past cannot do that, however, if it is only a part of a self-created present. A monument can be valuable only if it is allowed to retain its traces of history and if we follow its traces of history without being ashamed of our own historical past as well.

Many people hope to find something like meaning and origins in monuments, although such meaning never has a reliable foundation. It develops only through exploration of the many possible meanings. The real value of monument preservation lies precisely in the fact that it cannot be an objective science and because the monument cannot be a self-enclosed object—because it promises no pat answers and no final solutions but instead always invites new questions: questions that a reconstruction can never generate with the same degree of urgency. At least not in the year 2002.

# All Quiet on the Eastern Front

Viewed from this Perspective, the Real Adventure Is Yet to Come for the "New States"

Wolfgang Kil

1

Philipp Oswalt and Klaus Overmeyer, "Less Is More: Experimental Urban Reconstruction in Eastern Germany," intervention in urban districts with crumbling economies, 2001

The Akademie der Künste of Berlin-Brandenburg regularly organizes exhibitions devoted to contemporary developments in architecture in the countries of Central and Eastern Europe. The series began in 1994 with *Construction Site Poland*, followed by *Construction Site Hungary*, *Construction Site Czech Republic*, *Construction Site Moscow*, and *Construction Site Estonia*, the most recent exhibition presented in December 2001. All of these shows have been very well received, as they have offered revealing insights into the relationship between the growth of a new (or an old, newly rediscovered) building culture and significant societal movements and upheavals in these countries.

As yet, the idea of putting on a similar show dedicated to *Construction Site Eastern Germany* has occurred to no one. And the reason is not hard to find. Curiosity about a kind of architecture in the so-called "new states" that might be different or unusual in some way is lacking, simply because there is no uniquely eastern German architecture. At best, one might say that there is new architecture in eastern Germany. The space shown on maps as a somewhat "threadbare" country known as the GDR until 1990 has been occupied for nearly a decade by the most substantial investment region in Europe. The united country even began sprucing up its old capital city midway through that decade. Myriad construction cranes towered above a genuine paradise for developers, planners, architects, engineers, and building firms. Thanks to a virtual torrent of money, billions of German marks, an endless array of buildings in all conceivable variations popped from the ground like mushrooms. Viewed from a purely formal perspective, all this cacophony of architectural diversity reveals is that every contemporary architectural tendency known to the *old* states has spread across the former border into the *new* states—and not in the form of copies made in great numbers by former GDR architects from Western-style models. Indeed, nine out of ten new buildings are genuine "originals," products created by architects from western Germany. The number of eastern German architects involved in the unprecedented construction boom that spread like a tidal wave over their country after the political turnabout in 1990, known as the *Wende*, as a direct consequence of rapid reunification with the Federal Republic is virtually negligible.[1] Measured against the total volume of investment, the architects of the former GDR have practically disappeared from the market or, to be more precise, they never truly even entered it.

Part 1: The Architects: The Arduous Task of "Producing a Homeland" in New Territory

In June 1997, in the seventh year of reunification, the Hamburgische Architektenkammer (Hamburg Chamber of Architects) undertook a review of progress in the preceding years. In his report for the Chamber, architecture critic Gert Kähler posed an interesting question: "Shouldn't a specifically eastern [German] biography, combined with the task of rebuilding an entire country,"[2] give rise to some kind of an independent style of architecture? Strangely enough, this question had never been publicly expressed before in united Germany. In order to pose it at all, one had to have regarded the *Wende* of fall 1989 as more than a necessary prelude to the real "miracle" of reunification. One had to have appreciated the achievement of democratic rights and civil liberties through popular action as an equally incomparable and unforgettable collective experience—an experience history tells us has inspired equally compelling architectural expression in similar situations before.

Yet from the Western perspective, the East has generally never been regarded or taken seriously at all as an autonomous cultural landscape shaped by its own historical experience— which is why it must have seemed utter nonsense to imagine a new building culture in the East that would be different from the smoothly functioning building culture of the West, which had suffered no irritation from social upheaval. As was true of the German media landscape in general, the leading architecture journals published in Munich, Stuttgart, or Gütersloh were concerned with one question only: "Are they like us yet? Have they finally reached our level?" As if the complete absence of difference were the only guarantee of success in the "experiment in unity."

And as the country goes, so goes its people: nothing and no one in sight! Architects in the East were regarded more or less as an extinct breed. According to a now infamous pronouncement by Berlin's building director Hans Stimmann, they were "victims of a radical deforestation of architectural culture," barely professionally qualified "to calculate a simple heavy-concrete beam." Given such a degree of retardation, it was unreasonable to expect "that someone could be capable of cultural articulation at all, of sophisticated thinking in terms of colors, forms, spatial dimensions, lighting, furnishings and furniture, and so many other things.... The educated middle-class and its advanced concepts of dining culture, clothing, consumption, etc. are simply gone."[3]

Such callous remarks were indicative early on of the attitudes—and the behavior—the majority of people in eastern Germany have grown accustomed to from their western compatriots over the past ten years. And especially in Berlin, of course: "Probably the best thing about the fall of the Wall is that this incomparably beautiful square is now ours again!"[4] Uttered with no malice whatsoever by the manager (from the West) of an exclusive restaurant at the Gendarmenmarkt (in the East) in a radio interview, this enthusiastic response is typical of planning activity in Berlin during the past decade. The entire center of eastern Berlin was declared devoid of ideal value, a fallow ground whose fate was to be negotiated with shameless audacity, as if the districts in question were completely unpopulated. Not only were official buildings of the GDR promptly given over to reconstruction (ministries and embassies on Unter den Linden) or condemned entirely to demolition (Foreign Ministry, World Youth Stadium), numerous symbols of "civilian" architecture from the postwar period, among them the Lindencorso, the Hotel Berolina, and the irreproducible shell construction of the "Ahornblatt" (Maple Leaf), have also disappeared from the city panorama. The "new mind-set of building clients" proclaimed by Hans Stimmann was expressly dedicated to "restoration of our urban architectural tradition, which had been destroyed by war and the division of the city." Should resistance to the attempted appropriation emerge, Stimman suggested, "then we shall indeed have to engage in dispute with the East Berliners, because the buildings erected during the postwar years are simply all wrong."[5] As a consequence of these deliberately engendered controversies, the most prominent plans for the eastern part of the city in the years after the *Wende*—Hans Kollhoff's high-rise cascade at Alexanderplatz, the years-long dispute over a replica of the royal palace to replace the Palast der Republik, and the decidedly anti-modernist repartitioning strategy of the development concept known as "Planwerk Innenstadt" (Inner-City Planning Model)—were viewed and criticized as contrary to the interests of the people of eastern Berlin.

These East-West controversies were not restricted to Berlin but came to the surface more quickly and more violently there than elsewhere. In reality, those eastern German architects who hoped finally to make their mark with unrestricted competence under the new conditions of "liberation" were duped everywhere by the unabashed gesture of expropriation by the new decision-makers. This was the chance they had been looking for, the chance they had patiently awaited in their own country, as idealists of the old school: *"Architecture as a whole is and will always be an attempt to produce a homeland for mankind."* Not as a direct quotation but as an unspoken consensus, this conviction voiced by philosopher Ernst Bloch had served as the underlying foundation of teaching and learning at the three architecture schools in the GDR and had equipped the architects educated there with strong moral motivation. According to their concept of the profession, building culture was ultimately an outgrowth of processes of self-enlightenment and learning in society at large: architecture as the vessel of social relationships and the mirror in which they are reflected. Now they were compelled to learn that architecture is nothing but a highly mobile service devoted to following freely mobile capital wherever it may wander. The money, technology, and legal framework suddenly came from the West, and with them, inevitably, came the requisite aesthetic standards as well.

From this point on, attempts to "produce a homeland" were undertaken only rarely in the new states. The tremendous construction boom that unfolded before the eyes of the public and often transformed familiar living environments to the point of unrecognizability, especially in the larger cities, took place under conditions that were difficult for those affected to grasp and were based on concepts of utilization and benefit in which they played, at best, the role of a potential client. Plans and projects were negotiated on the basis of laws that had been enacted in ignorance of the very different conditions prevailing in the East. And all of this was paid for with money they had not provided. Moreover, the aesthetic expression, the architecture of this construction boom, reflected the conventions and the finesse of a colorful history of changing artistic styles in which East Germans had played no cultural role whatsoever, since it had unfolded in the "old" Federal Republic beyond their own horizon.

After building a secondary school in Wurzen in the state of Saxony, one Stuttgart architect described this gap in aesthetic standards and cultural expectations in particularly drastic terms: "Whereas we ... tend more towards reduction, those on the other side of the former 'curtain' favor precisely the kind of animation and excitement that reunification brought to everyday construction over there. Rounded forms of all kinds, structurally complicated overhangs and extensions, and 'noble,' high-gloss facing materials are extremely popular there. From a *human* point of view, this desire to make up for the deficit is understandable, but *as architects*, we were always intent upon resisting it ... "[6]

A truly classical gesture: the architect as the conveyor of culture. Yet by insisting upon his own standard—a more advanced one, in his view—he denied people precisely what they most urgently needed in a period of unparalleled stress brought on by a change of systems: time to grow in step and the opportunity to become involved. As it was, the new circumstances remained foreign to them, and more than a few complained that they felt like visitors in their own country—a feeling the "new" architecture never sought to soothe. Indeed, the forcibly exhibited "Westernness" of this architecture often made it worse. Such spontaneous dissatisfaction as that expressed in notoriously conservative Dresden in response to Günter Behnisch's deconstructivist-style St.-Benno-Gymnasium or Coop Himmelb(l)au's "crystalline" UFA cinema palace may be viewed as typical of the controversy generally associated with any manifestations of the "avant-garde." That the people of Eberswalde, a small town in Brandenburg still badly scarred by gaps left from the war, preferred the sentimental references to the *Gründerzeit,* or the late 19th century, by Patzschke & Klotz to the "abstract boxes" of the local technical college designed by Herzog & de Meuron, should be easier to understand, however—from a psychological point of view, perhaps, rather than in the sense of cultural criticism.

The situation was exacerbated by the influx of "reconstruction helpers" from the West into government agencies and administrative offices in major cities in the new states. Like the private building clients, they tended to maintain their old contacts with architectural firms "back home"—a process as banal as it was widespread: as long as Bitterfeld had a mayor imported from the town of Düren in Westphalia, signs at construction sites from the new city hall to the downtown apartment complex announced the involvement of an architectural firm from Düren. Similar symbiotic partnerships could be observed in Hoyerswerda between a building commissioner from "left of the Rhine" and his planning team from Bonn, which was invested with comprehensive authority. That the overwhelming majority of architects working in Wismar are from Lübeck surely has a great deal to do with the close proximity of the two Hanseatic cities. But why Halle an der Saale came to be an El Dorado for the architecture scene in Cologne, of all places, is a secret known only to the powers that be in the Halle planning department.

Even competitions did nothing to break this vicious circle. After all, participants—and jurors, of course—must be invited. Thus only those whose names were entered in the right notebooks got into these competitions (and only very few architects from eastern Germany managed to find their way into those notebooks). The juries judged as they always have: on the basis of standards established in their own debates and in keeping with their own stylistic preferences. As far as anyone knows, the fact that these competitions were taking place on soil with a different cultural history never played a role at a single jury meeting anywhere in the East.

Neither the invited jurors nor the outsiders who took part in the competition can be blamed for this particular constellation. This was business as usual for them. In Western debates on architecture, from which most of them still come today, local identity in the sense of insistence on aspects "somehow unique" to the local setting tends to be regarded as provincial or short-sighted. In the East, familiarity with a locale is looked upon as a virtue. In the West, ambitions are focused on something quite different: the *art of building* is the standard, and it is set very high. Clients, mayors, and jury members join in bowing to the universal judgment of "that grand school, the fame and aura of a traveling architectural nobility."[7] And they even

submit pliably to the aesthetic tendencies associated with this development. It is no coincidence that the most successful architectural celebrities are past masters of abstract or self-referential typologies. It is not necessary to know everything there is to know about a construction site, since—as the motto of all traveling architects makes clear—"True class stands on its own anywhere."

The facile transposition of these principles to the East could only have dire consequences for local architects. They had spent years, often under the most difficult circumstances, trying to counteract the progressive devastation of their cities through deterioration and the roughshod technologies of the GDR building industry—in the hope of some day being able to repair the destruction and establish a new order through their own efforts—and now they were forced to stand by passively, watching world-wise celebrities or cool masters of routine enlarge or contract a market square here, cut swashes through unseen city ground plans, or create other *faits accomplis*—much too often characterized by the banal mediocrity that is typical of every form of mass production. Was it really necessary to have the performers flown in for that?

Small cities in the states of Saxony, Thuringia, and Saxony-Anhalt are now beginning to resemble their sister communities in Lower Saxony or Westphalia more and more. Every move toward self-discovery and self-development in architectural culture in the new states was smothered beneath this imported architectural avalanche. Not even the newly erected showcase buildings of the young eastern German democracy—neither the county government building in Bitterfeld nor the city hall in Dessau, nor even the new state legislature building on the banks of the Elbe in Dresden—to name only three out of many such cases—were built by architects who were directly involved as citizens in the creation of that democracy.

In the early nineties, a competition was held for the design of the Dessau City Hall, and first prize was awarded to Dieter Bankert, a local once regarded one of the most creative minds in the GDR architecture scene. His proposal exhibited markedly expressionist features and was intended to "offer threshold-free, yet uplifting access to counsel and action. The people were to play a role, and the building was to be a manifestation of the turn toward democracy,"[8] as Bankert himself commented. But this sole surviving piece of "revolutionary architecture" was never realized. Instead, a "grand master" from the former West Berlin set an administrative container devoid of all expression on this prominent site.

Less scandalous than problematic in this same context is the case of the new state legislature building in the state of Saxony. Peter Kulka's main assembly hall is quite rightly one of

2

Riedel/Greiner/Murzig, Town Hall, Naundorf, 1993–94

3

Junk/Reich/Wiehl, Savings Bank, Weimar, 1992–94

4

Andreas Kottusch, Studio Building, Zwickau-Ebersbrunn, 1993

5

Dieter Bankert, Design for City Hall Expansion, Dessau, 1991

6

Appel, Behzadi, Bohne & Partner,
Famulus-Haus, Leipzig, 1998

7

Kirchner + Przyborowski, Möser Local Administration
Building, Magdeburg, 1999

Saalepark Shopping Center, Günthersdorf, 1995

Prefabricated panel-construction building before
demolition, Schwedt

Zimmermann + Partner, Urban villas constructed from
concrete elements of a high-rise, Cottbus, 2001–02

Philipp Oswalt and Klaus Overmeyer, "Less Is More: Experimental Urban
Reconstruction in Eastern Germany," intervention in urban districts with
crumbling economies, 2001

KARO-architekten, "Concepts for Leipzig-Ost"
Competition, 2001

the most highly acclaimed new structures built anywhere in Germany during the nineties. However, it draws its motifs and aesthetic power from discussions that accompanied the Bonn Republic through both good times and bad over a period of forty years (which is why its close resemblance to Günter Behnisch's assembly hall in Bonn, completed at virtually the same time, is surely no coincidence). In light of those discussions, it is undoubtedly a masterful accomplishment. But what does the new legislature building in Dresden tell the citizens of Saxony about *their* revolution?

Though there was certainly a great deal of goodwill involved at first, it became evident early on to those who could read "between the lines" how the roles would be distributed in the future. After his first trip to eastern Germany in 1990, Meinhard von Gerkan, for instance, returned from Dresden "convinced that we in the West owe our colleagues 'over there' a cultural exchange."9 He actually used the words "cultural exchange," but what he meant, of course, was a cultural *transfusion.* "I doubt that a single western German architect went there with the idea of really listening to the people and learning from *their* experiences," recollected Gert Kähler four years later. "One arrived knowing the 'right' way to do things and intending to pass that knowledge on—and thus it was not long before the consultants formed their own branch offices and began to pursue entirely different interests."10 At this point, if not sooner, the "case of eastern Germany" took on exemplary significance. Somewhere along the line, the architectural double lives of even the most well-intentioned advisors and reconstruction helpers began to split apart. The preserver and promoter of culture soon gave way to the freelance professional, with all of his specific entrepreneurial ambitions. Once this shift was accomplished, colleagues in the East were nothing more than competitors.

It is therefore fitting and necessary at this point to call attention to a fundamental failure on the part of professional institutions, trade associations, and architects' chambers. "It is not and cannot be considered fair to organize contests between well-trained participants and convalescents competing under the same starting conditions. We ignore this standard of civilized society when we deny solidarity to those who are weaker,"11 as economist Klaus Noé recently commented in his essay on the economic practice of German unification, aptly entitled "Die grosse deutsche Illusion" (The Grand German Illusion). There must have been quite a lot of wishful thinking involved among those in architectural chambers and associations who believed at the outset that establishing the same legal framework for all would automatically guarantee equality of opportunity. This premature hope for "normalcy" was of no use at all to the many newly founded architectural firms in eastern Germany. Although the prevailing ideology of the profession asserts that nothing matters but "quality," ingenuity (that is, culture) is only a very small part of architecture; the rest is business. Ignoring this base fact of life, the eastern German architects' chambers stood by and watched as their local members were eliminated with predictable regularity from every competition to which any significance at all was attached. Since they could rely on no bonus whatsoever even in the early years and in limited local competitions, they never had even the hint of a chance. Years later, this "lack of success" produced a double-jeopardy effect, as "it is often necessary in major construction projects to show evidence that entrants have previously planned building projects on a comparable scale. Yet even now, ten years after the *Wende*, very few offices [in eastern Germany] can produce such references. This is another case of the cat trying to catch its own tail."12

In comparable countries in transformation, such as Poland, Hungary, Estonia (and most recently China, where international architects are now competing vigorously), the national associations have achieved at least minimum mandatory involvement of local architects in competitions for projects funded by foreign investors. Until these protective barriers fall—in the course of EU expansion, for instance—stable architecture scenes (meaning economically sound ones, as well) can develop under the shield of protectionism, and along with them a nationally anchored—and therefore identifiable—building culture. In eastern Germany, the community of architects has been rendered virtually powerless following the import of a new elite under Western influence. The fact that they have been almost completely excluded as a recognized professional group from significant participation in the reconstruction and development of their own country must be regarded as a scandal unparalleled in recent European architectural and cultural history.

Or was this process simply an economic one? For more than ten years, there was somehow enough for everyone. Vigorously active large firms like RKW, based in Düsseldorf, were involved in planning projects accounting for investments of several billions in Leipzig alone, in contrast to which "the ambitions of eastern German architects stop at a ceiling of around ten million marks,"13 as an anonymous architect sarcastically summed up his colleagues' situation in the East as late as 2001. The incredibly large cake known as "Recovery East" has been divided up and shared by others.

Part 2: Creative Destruction?
The Attempt to Eliminate Work and Still Hope for Revenue

The Hamburgische Architektenkammer selected a rather revealing slogan for its symposium in June 1997: "Recovery East, or Writing Off a Country." The experts were not unanimous in their findings: "Americanization," said some, "Mezzogiorno," prophesied others. The focus of these extremely concerned investigations was the fate of the cities of eastern Germany, which after years of neglect during the GDR era were now threatened with substantive deterioration caused by unbridled peripheral growth. The government-dictated housing policy of the GDR had largely prevented the uncontrolled growth of endless developments of single-family homes typical of the West by decree. Consequently, most eastern German cities still conformed to the ideal of the "compact city" when the great transformation began: cities with clearly defined edges, beyond which were meadows, fields, and forests not separated from the urban boundary by diffuse intermediate zones. These clearly delineated city figures were the first things lost under the massive pressure of investment during the first years after reunification. Speculative "residential parks" and single-family homes, most of them of the cheapest quality, flooded the countryside surrounding even small and medium-sized towns with the same insipid residential sprawl that has infested the rest of the world. What is more, many outlying communities generated catastrophic competition with a succession of increasingly gigantic shopping centers—competition among themselves and above all with the old city centers, whose commercial structures were powerless to resist such merciless "waves of modernization."

This unholy alliance of home-builders and supermarkets in the outlying countryside threatened the existence of the "old European cities" that were still found in surprisingly large numbers. Buying power and tax revenues shifted increasingly into neighboring communities, and thus many urban governments had difficulty maintaining even their own infrastructure. Some cities, most notably Leipzig, which was particularly hard-hit by these developments, launched desperate counteroffensives and began putting up shopping malls, one more grandiose than the other, in their centers. (The main railway station in Leipzig was converted in this way into a "huge department store with direct rail connections.") Although the strategy worked in some cases, and buyers were lured back into the city, this form of "driving out the devil with Beelzebub" ultimately intensified the general commercial overkill effect: eastern Germany surpassed the West in per-capita shopping space in less than ten years, exceeding it by well over 100 percent in some heavily populated areas. The consequences of

this fateful race were not long in coming. Shopping streets with small retail businesses that had retained their vitality at great effort through the GDR years and beyond or had come to life again after the *Wende* were now threatened once again with desertion. At less favorable locations, signs of genuine urban blight began to appear.

This development actually should have come as a surprise to no one. As early as June 1990, the signers of the *1. Dessauer Erklärung* (First Dessau Declaration) called attention to the danger that "without flanking support measures ... the GDR [threatens] to become a playground for an early-capitalist elbow mentality—with all of the social consequences that implies." Heedless of such warnings, office buildings had been produced in a fit of speculative fever virtually at random and far in excess of actual demand. Commercial zones of grotesque proportions were established on the fringes of even the smallest country towns, a trend that prompted the president of the Administrative District of Dessau to comment sarcastically in the summer of 1993 that these were "extremely problematic times in which ten commercial zones battle over a single firm."[14] And now the same misguided development planning consultants had so urgently warned against began to affect the service and supply sector as well. Accordingly, the *2. Dessauer Erklärung* (Second Dessau Declaration) confirmed that all of the dire predictions had come true: "Due to the increasing loss of their central function, the existence of the cities and communities is endangered.... A second wave of decentralized development has followed, ignoring the available old-building potential. This supply of housing [on the fringes of the city] draws the middle-income groups out of the city centers, narrowing the social base and threatening to turn the inner cities into slums. The reversal of the traditional settlement structure—the shopping center on the edge of the city as the new center—is turning the history of the Central European city upside down. People who are willing to assume community responsibility and the city itself, as a place of social, economic, and cultural encounter, are disappearing."

As the example of eastern Germany clearly showed once again: the wisdom and good intentions of planners had nothing to do with how radically the general process of transformation affected the fate of the cities and rural areas of eastern Germany. If it is true that ultra-modern capitalism needs shopping centers in outlying areas to remain efficient, and if it is equally true that shopping centers in outlying areas are the natural-born killers of the tradition-rich "European Cities" with their market squares and shopping streets, then we must ultimately admit that ultra-modern capitalism no longer needs the "European City." The system could not be outsmarted, not even with the best of therapeutic intentions. Indeed, viewed from an objective distance, everything was logically consistent. The total reconstruction of eastern German society (including its constructed spatial environment) exhibited no "early capitalist" characteristics but was intended to produce a decidedly "future-oriented" result. The radical market strategies of German unification recognized only one concept for the eastern states—"retroactive modernization" without regard for costs or losses. Eastern Germany would either succeed in becoming a region strong enough to survive in the international climate of competition for business and industrial locations, or it would not.

Apparently, no one was prepared to believe that the experiment of neo-liberal system transformation pursued so ruthlessly could fail. Wasn't it possible now, after several years, to celebrate the "Recovery East" with reference to grandiose new construction projects? Often held up as shining examples were the Neue Leipziger Messe (gmp), the Saxon State Parliament in Dresden (Peter Kulka), the Juridicum (Law School building) of the university in Halle, or the Musikschule Weimar (both designed by Thomas van den Valentyn). And wasn't there a great deal of other architecture worthy of presentation? In many cases, government agencies and ministries had established themselves in attractive new buildings in the capital cities of the newly created German states or—following the lead of the federal government in its move to Berlin—reconstructed old buildings at considerable expense. Indeed, since they were obliged to award commissions on a competitive basis, federal, state, and local governments were responsible for a great many standard-setting buildings, particularly in the school sector (noteworthy examples being the high schools in Flöha, by Allmann/Sattler/Wappner, and Bernau, by Quick/Bäckmann/Quick) and higher education (the Heeresoffiziersschule Dresden by Auer & Weber, the Fachhochschule Anhalt in Dessau by Kister/Scheithauer/Gross, or the Fachhochschule in Wildau by Otto Steidle). Comparatively speaking, enthusiasm for the immense wave of shopping centers and office complexes built with private investment was low, particularly in view of the fact that unbridled overproduction in this sector and a surplus of empty office space was becoming more evident year by year. "Write-off architecture," was the verdict of the director of building affairs in Dresden on the majority of such projects presented to him by clients "who had never seen their construction site but had the figures of the tax authorities at their fingertips."[15]

At the same time, however, a crisis was brewing in the housing sector, which was equally overheated by speculation, the proportions of which would dwarf all of the preceding disastrous developments. For while investment funds continued to lure investors with euphoric promises for a succession of new "residential development," "residential parks," and "first-class renovation objects," and while communal housing societies and cooperatives in large-scale developments invested substantial sums in renovating their prefabricated panel-construction buildings and in beautifying their surroundings, the residents of such areas made an entirely different move. They migrated to villages in the surrounding countryside and built homes for themselves. And beginning in 1997, they migrated in significant numbers to where there was still work—in the West.[16] By the time alarmed statisticians finally focused their attention on the unprecedented low birth rates of the preceding years, the scenario of a demographic catastrophe was complete. In 2000, a government commission compiled the devastating statistics and presented them as a social time bomb of inconceivable dimensions to the public: one million housing units in eastern Germany were vacant, and the trend was expected to rise unhindered; vacancy rates (expressed as statewide averages) soon ranged between 10 and 15 percent.

The first warning signals had come from Leipzig, where nearly a third of all housing units in certain residential areas were no longer occupied. This vacancy crisis was not specific to the prefabricated panel-construction developments, such as the old towns districts of Halle, at 28 percent, and Görlitz, whose valuable Renaissance and 19th-century buildings were 48 percent vacant following renovation, clearly show. The nearby prefabricated panel-construction development of Königshufen was at nearly full capacity with a vacancy rate of only 7 percent.[17] In 2001, the first housing cooperative folded in Leipzig due to a vacancy rate of 33.6 percent. By this time, the depopulation process had taken on a dynamic character that prompted housing policy-makers and financial experts alike to warn of the destruction of the entire eastern Germany housing market.

The government commission proposed "withdrawing" three to four thousand housing units "from the market." Since that time, such terms as "deconstruction," "demolition," and "panel death" have been liberated from taboo; architects and planners, like politicians, have been compelled to adopt a practice that had long been alien to them: planning to shrink cities. The strategies for which they now call with increasing frequency are described by such terms as "deconcentration," "down-sizing," and "deceleration." Where the goal was once growth (in terms of density, residential space, facilities, etc.), the objective today is to tap the potential for reduction. Planners must decide whether compact areas are to be deconcentrated from the center or reduced from the outside in. Also at issue are complex social processes, intelligent interim solutions for residual utilization in the foreseeable future, and less radical concepts like "reconstruction instead of deconstruction." In Cottbus, for example, exemplary experience has been gained in the consolidation of typical housing units in prefabricated panel-construction buildings and in using construction materials from demolished high-rise buildings to build several "city villas" (Frank Zimmermann). The small city of Leinefeld in Thuringia drew praise for the conversion of a five-story housing block into a single-story flat-top structure which now provides office space for the housing management staff and makes rooms available to the remaining residents for meetings and events (Meier-Scupin & Petzet).

The population crisis that finally became the focus of public debate in late 2000 resulted in an unexpected turn of events in the recent history of planning and building in the eastern German states. Europe's first landscape produced by unbridled neo-liberalism took shape east of the Elbe. Investor confidence in the boom region, which offered uncommonly favorable tax incentives until only recently, has more or less collapsed. New housing construction is virtually at a standstill, and bank loans for the renovation or reconstruction of prefabricated panel-construction buildings are granted only in exceptional cases. Architects still find work reconstructing and renovating old buildings in isolated projects undertaken by private clients or the government (the latter to a decreasing extent) in response to specific demand. Following the boom years and the billions invested in the "Second *Gründerzeit*," this restraint may be viewed either as a necessary cooling-down process for an extremely overheated economy or simply as a return to normalcy.

Since the pendulum has not swung to a moderate middle position but instead to the other extreme, the tasks facing architects have not become fewer. Instead, the profession finds itself faced with new challenges, with only the vaguest of notions about how to meet them. It appears as if the brief bloom of individualized building aesthetics has now given way to a revival of "functionalism." In the course of the difficult process of shrinking, the cities are again becoming an increasingly important field of activity for social, traffic, and infrastructure planners. Landscape planners will also be needed urgently, since one of the most pressing problems involved in reducing urban density and utility space is the redefinition of the unoccupied terrain thus created as acceptable (and affordable) public space. Neither models nor strategies for acceptable conversion of housing property to post-housing landscapes have yet been developed for the extreme case in which entire housing developments are abandoned.[18] A whole culture of workshops and competitions for creative ideas has begun to take shape in this context, the first fruits of which still have the charming appeal of freely inspired "paper architecture."[19]

What the new states need in terms of imagination in planning and architecture in order to master their current crisis now and in the foreseeable future resists comparison to traditional modes of architectural endeavor. Will architecture in eastern Germany have to be viewed and assessed as a special case once again? If building culture has anything at all to do with the solution of real problems of life, then the highest cultural mandate in this "experimental region" must be to achieve the smoothest paradigmatic shift possible: away from an expansive model for development toward a truly sustainable one. A housing policy expert from Hoyerswerda once referred to the now impending process as a "a retreat with decency and dignity."[20] In this quest for existential balance among post-industrial landscapes, every form of new architecture can only serve as an arabesque, at best. Such modest ambitions are likely to find little favor in the nation's capital and its surrounding belt of intense growth (including a few "islands of new productivity"), where people will stubbornly continue to reach for the stars. But things will presumably grow quieter in the rest of the country. A paradise for gardeners—would that really be such a terrifying vision?

# A Short History of Ecological Architecture in Germany

Wilfried Dechau and Christian Holl

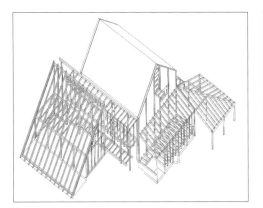
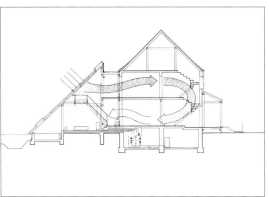

Thomas Herzog, Latz Building, Kassel, 1982

"It is high time that we adopt the laws nature has always used to control processes as complicated as those that have only recently begun to cause us such major problems with respect to the complex interplay of energy use, production, consumption, waste accumulation, traffic, urban concentration, stress, and civilization-induced illnesses. We must abandon our technocratic view, our linear, tunnel-vision thinking in favor of a new approach to reality modeled on the control cycles of nature."
Frederic Vester[1]

"Ecological architecture"—the term has already become a historical concept.[2] Usage of the phrase falls within a period for which the time frame is fairly clearly marked out. First of all, it describes a type of architecture that did not exist until the early eighties.[3] Secondly, the term is no longer used with reference to new buildings in current architectural discourse. It now serves as nothing more than a marketing argument for the real estate business. It no longer denotes a concept of architecture that is worth disputing or the effort required to reach agreement on its meaning.[4]

That is surely no coincidence. An analysis of the underlying context, the origin, and the meaning of the term shows that its emergence and disappearance is the consequence of the history of an entire movement that was fueled by much more than the desire for a different kind of architecture and the demand that architecture should assume a specific responsibility. Architecture meant something more in this case. It was to become the cornerstone of a new way of life and a new society. Or, expressed differently, ecological architecture was part of a general critique of the social system and culture that no longer exists in its original form today. Reluctance to use the term is more than a subtle sign of that fact.

A history of ecological architecture in Germany cannot be confined to a few isolated aspects. Essential to an understanding of the form given to this kind of architecture is an awareness of the cultural ambitions of the generation that promoted its development: known in Germany as the "Generation of '68." It is also impossible to overlook the question of why the aftermath of the events of 1968 produced different results in Germany than in other countries—and, above all, why architecture assumed a role of such importance in Germany after 1968.

The exceptional character of the situation in Germany may have been the product of a reliance on democracy born of the experience of an unusually brutal dictatorship that was still very much alive in the collective memory. Added to this was the fact that direct confrontation with the model of the GDR left no fertile ground for the development of socialism as a pos-

sible alternative. The prevailing climate of oppression and the absence of civil liberties were too familiar to have gained even marginal acceptance in the West.[5]

This may well have contributed to the lack of a perceived alternative to democracy as it was practiced in western Germany and the desire to change the system from within in a "march through the institutions" in keeping with the ideals of the student movement. From our perspective today, this may explain not only the movement's extraordinary success but a number of other developments as well. Very soon after 1968, public involvement in matters such as urban planning increased, and success had been achieved in resident-friendly urban renewal projects. Environmental compatibility reviews were conducted as a part of building planning procedure. All in all, however, this strong reliance on the system was responsible for the movement's downfall, as becomes clear in retrospect.[6]

The idea was to develop a different approach to human and interpersonal relations and to people's attitudes towards their natural environment and to make it an integral part of a new kind of life.[7] Forms of cultural expression were expected not only to communicate chosen objectives to the outside world but to become an inseparable part of the new life as well. And thus it is no coincidence that early ecological architecture in Germany was linked to forms of living that contrasted strongly with familiar modes. One is reminded in this context of the "drop-out" models of the seventies: urban communes which occupied entire buildings, rural communes whose members strived for a maximum autonomy in communities of life and work.

What may seem naïve from our point of view today was not without justification, for the goal was not merely to develop new architectural parameters—to conserve energy or extend the life of a building—but also to create an image that conformed to the concept and reflected a sense of involvement in natural cycles. This approach to a reading of architecture was broadly accepted in the general architectural discourse of Postmodernism. Architecture was to serve as a medium for the expression of a fundamental attitude and be permitted to make statements about a society's condition.

This attitude was reflected not only in the demonstrative planting of grass on building roofs, the use of untreated wood in façades, or in unruly, overgrown gardens. The ambition that encompassed the broader social context also explains why the functions originally attributed to ecological architecture were as diverse as the terms used to describe them. Architecture sought harmony with nature and reliance on regional traditions which, unlike international styles, were attentive to such things as the local availability of materials and regional

### Architectural biology

Architectural biology focuses holistically on the relationships between living beings and their immediate environment. Architectural biologists are concerned primarily with "healthy living environments" composed of "healthy housing materials." Emphasis is placed on the subjective sense of well-being, with less attention given to conserving resources. The criteria for assessment are subjective, and sometimes dubious. The proximity of architectural biology to non-scientific methods —such as geomantry—tends to encourage a skeptical view of this discipline.

### Architectural ecology

Ecological architecture seeks to reduce interventions in natural systems to the extent possible. In other words, air, water, and soil pollution are to be kept to a minimum. Important parameters include resource conservation, reduction of pollution and energy consumption during manufacture, transport, and use of materials and reuse or recycling of materials recovered from demolished buildings.

### Bionics

Derived from the words "biology" and "technology," the term denotes a young field of research involving the disciplines of biology, engineering, architecture, and mathematics. Bionics attempts to find solutions for technical problems (construction details or systems) in models from nature.

### Biotecture

This term generally attributed to Rudolf Doernach combines "biology" and "architecture." Even if he did not actually coin the term himself, he is its most prominent representative—in his demand, for example, that people should "let their houses grow" (or, in other words, leave building to the [tamed] growth of nature).

### Sustainability

Originally applied only to forestry, the term "sustainability" was charged with new meaning—analogous to such phrases as "sustainable development" in 1992 (World Environment Summit in Rio de Janeiro)—and has rarely been left unspoken in any debate since then, although it is still no less vague and ambiguous than it ever was. Sustainability described the interaction between economics and environmentalism in pursuit of the goal of ensuring that all opportunities for development remain open to future generations. The basic principles underlying the concept of sustainability: The use of renewable resources should not exceed the natural growth rate. Exhaustible resources should be consumed only when they can be replaced by others. Pollutant levels should not exceed the environment's capacity to tolerate them. That all sounds quite noble but remains vague and noncommittal in the absence of binding guidelines.

### Low-energy building

The term is used to describe buildings that require less energy for heating than conventional ones. Scientific consensus has settled on a maximum value of 70 kWh/m²a (applied to net floor space per story) for heating and utility energy consumption. The government definition used to determine eligibility for subsidies establishes that the low-energy standard is given when the heating energy consumption value for a building is at least 25 percent lower than the value specified in the Heat Insulation Directive. It is not clear how the official definition of the low-energy standard will be affected by enactment of the Energy Conservation Directive (EnEV).

### Passive building

A passive house provides a comfortable interior climate without an active heating or air-conditioning system. It "heats" and cools passively. The principle works only where specific annual heat energy needs do not exceed 15 kWh/m²a. This is not to be achieved at the expense of higher addition consumption of other forms of energy (such as electricity), as the total specific primary energy consumption level per square meter of living space in a European passive building must not exceed 120 kWh/m²a (for room heating, hot-water heating, and household power needs). This forms the basis from which remaining energy needs can be covered by renewable forms of energy.

### Solar architecture

Solar architecture relies on the sun. Incoming solar radiation is used as a direct source of heat and light. Passive use of solar energy is achieved by installing large windows oriented toward the sun in combination with large heat-retaining masses in the building interior.

climate conditions. With respect to residential development, the intent was to oppose the anonymous, technological city with a community model. Architecture, many believed, should serve as the vehicle and the medium for a responsible way of life that would meet the needs of both human beings and the natural environment. The concept of ecological architecture was always associated with aspects of emancipation, grassroots democracy, and a critique of the powers that be. The heavy freight carried by the definition is surely part of the reason why the term now tends to be avoided. It was too closely bound to attitudes typical of the time, attitudes no one shares in quite that form today.

Health-conscious building using natural, alternative materials, living communities, alternative farming methods, and experiments in self-sufficiency—these ambitions reflect the broad spectrum of the holistic approach within which architecture operated. And they also illustrate the diversity of concepts used to communicate the postulate: natural construction, health-conscious building, vital architecture, building with the sun.

Yet alternative rural communities, "drop-out" models, and the appeal for decentralization were only a part of the total reality. The response also focused on the city and involved criticism of their present form, which in turn led to demands for urban redesign and reconstruction wherever cities estranged people from nature and their environment (which includes other people as well)—in traffic policy, for example, in new residential developments, in the dictate of separation of functions—but also for preservation, in places where urban forms were conducive to the reversal of this separation of functions and to the restoration of a direct relationship between human beings and nature: in late-19th-century structures with green courtyards and reconfigured street space. As early as 1965, Alexander Mitscherlich condemned the "inhospitability of our cities" in his book of the same title, *Die Unwirtlichkeit unserer Städte*. The book's subtitle, *Eine Anstiftung zum Unfrieden* (An Appeal for Civil Disobedience), is also quite revealing. In 1971, the Neue Sammlung in Munich presented the exhibition entitled *PROFITOPOLI$ oder der Mensch braucht eine andere Stadt* ("PROFITOPOLI$, or People Need a Different Kind of City),[8] to which the alternative model (presented on a touring exhibition) made specific reference in 1985: *Ökotopolis—Bauen mit der Natur* (Ecolopolis—Building with Nature).

Possible approaches to construction-project development without expert supervision were explored in planning studios. The idea behind the concept of advocacy in planning adopted from U.S. practice was to give a voice to those who were unable to articulate their needs within the framework of the planning process. Public participation was integrated into building planning. Efforts dedicated to the improvement of living environments, traffic reduction, old-building renovation, and preservation of existing structures were interwoven. But squatter actions in protest of building overproduction sponsored by the political system and controlled by speculators, which went hand in hand with the destruction of old buildings, low-cost housing, and traditional neighborhoods are also part of this tableau of diverse activities with which people strove to oppose the system from within.

Housing was a central concern in this context—to a degree that is perhaps peculiar to the Federal Republic of Germany. Housing policy assumed a very special, unique significance in postwar Germany—a situation due at least in part the consequences of war, for the massive wartime destruction and the flood of returning refuges for whom housing was needed posed a great challenge to government. This was one—if not the most important—reason why housing and home-ownership policy consistently played an important role in political debate on an ideological level.

The Christian Democratic Union (CDU) took the lead in defending the view that the promotion of ownership in the real estate sector was an effective means of counteracting popular radicalism and forms of communist or socialist collectivism. In 1965–66, just prior to the outbreak of student unrest, the "second assistance program" was instituted, establishing a basis for the systematic promotion of single-family homes. Thus it seems only logical that anti-establishment protest was also directed against the standard models of the normal family in its appropriately standardized home propagated by campaigning politicians.[9]

Urban communes, squatter actions, and household communities were not the only examples of community-oriented projects or new forms of communal living. Housing models such Schafbrühl in Tübingen or Laher Wiesen in Hanover also belong to this category.

Euphoria soon waned, however. Tensions no one had anticipated during the "heroic phase" soon became evident—the conflict between comfort and self-denial, between community and privacy, between "healthy" and environmentally justifiable materials (examples include such materials as cork, coconut fiber, and tropical woods).[10]

Thus the ecological architecture movement was exposed to multiple stress and strain that eventually led to disillusionment. For one thing, the communities themselves often failed to withstand the pressure of self-imposed discipline. The goals of self-fulfillment and the attraction of individualized lifestyles often contradicted the ideal of community, which offered only limited leeway for the fulfillment of individual wants and desires. The practice of self-imposed isolation also drew criti-

4

5

6

Gernot Minke, Minke Residence, Kassel, 1985

7

8

9

Eble, Ambeth, Haefele, and Oed, Schafbrühl Housing Development, Tübingen, 1984

Boockhoff + Rentrop, Laher Wiesen Housing Development, Hanover, 1985

Rolf Disch, Heliotrope – Solar Tower, Freiburg, 1995

10

11

12

Hegger, Hegger, Schleiff, Educational Center at the
Ecological Center, Hamm, 1996

LOG ID/Dieter Schempp, Office Building, Dresden, 1997

13

14

15

Assmann/Salomon, Low-Energy Building,
Berlin-Marzahn, 1998

Hegger, Hegger, Schleiff, Founders' Center, Hamm, 1998

cism, as it became clear that it also excluded those without whom a restructuring of society could not be accomplished.

The excessive burden imposed on ecological architecture also exposed the fundamental discrepancy between the reality of the microcosm composed of living environment and small neighborhood, on the one hand, and the larger political and structural reality of the prevailing system, on the other. There was no way to stem the expanding tide of housing space consumption.

The guiding image also proved to be a trap. The very power to communicate ideas that made it so seductive also ensured that the complexity of the environmental context ultimately diminished. The simple image abandoned its reference to the all-encompassing utopia. As a distinct and easily understandable part of the whole environmental message, it soon became more important than the message itself. The goal of restoring streams in the urban environment to their natural beds became a surrogate battleground of great visual potency. The traffic diversions required to give urban centers a photogenic aura merely shifted the burden of traffic elsewhere. Flight from the city into ecological neighborhoods and homes confirmed and strengthened planning principles based on the separation of functions. Environmental consciousness became fashionable. Structural, economic, and social considerations that resisted striking media presentation were neglected and disappeared from view.

In much the same way, one-sided concern with environmental housing reform ultimately proved to be counterproductive, as it obscured the social circumstances that affect living situations and caused them to be neglected in another context. Industrial, commercial, and administrative construction remained strangely untouched by ecological architecture for a long time.

Of the three fundamental principles of ecological architecture—the *social* objective devoted to changing behavior, the *urban-architectural* principle of creating the compact, hybrid city of short access routes, and the *technical* goal of minimizing consumption and increasing efficiency—the technical component received the most attention. The two other principles fell victim to the disillusionment cited above, which emerged because the lofty ambitions could not be achieved in the real world. All of the successes gained at the local level were offset by opposing developments on a larger scale. Energy and land consumption, environmental destruction, and traffic volume increased despite all efforts to the contrary. No increasing sense of responsibility or willingness to adopt new behavior patterns was evident at the popular level, nor did government legislation have an appreciable impact on the progressive fragmentation of neighborhood and functional structures.

Even the triumph of the technical principle of ecological architecture ran counter to the expectations of idealists. It provided politicians with impressive arguments in support of their hush-hush tactics, without encouraging criticism of the economic system. It did nothing to diminish hopes of increasing prosperity or to foster self-discipline; in fact, it even developed into an industry in its own right—and thus became a part of the very growth ideology the environmental movement had sought to escape with its alternative model of an economy based on recycling and renewal. Criticism of this shift of emphasis soon grew silent.[11]

Nevertheless, the technical principle succeeded to the extent that it continued to serve as a motor for development. The concept of the passive building was developed in 1987, and the first such structure was built as a row house in Darmstadt-Kranichstein in 1991. A new heat insulation law took effect in 1995, and the Energy Conservation Directive to be enacted in 2002 covers not only heating but with the entire building energy budget. All of this is accompanied by publications that raise hopes for increasing prosperity and diminished energy consumption.[12] The perversion that underlies such a narrow focus on building engineering is reflected in the fact that numerous subsidies are available for energy-saving new construction, while comparatively little support is provided for much more important modernization projects for buildings.

This emphasis on pursuit of the technical approach dedicated to efficient energy use is evident in recent developments in architecture as well. The original desire to reduce dependence on technology through the use of natural materials (wood, loam, grass roofs, etc.) has given way to enthusiasm for efficient means of harnessing high-powered technology. Glassed patios as heat traps, buildings positioned facing south, slanted south-facing façades consisting entirely of glass, and thick, heavily insulated northern faces symbolize one thing above all: the desire to achieve optimum use of renewable energy without sacrifice to environmental safety.

Appeals for energy conservation tend to force both structural problems and distrust of technical approaches to such problems into the background. But the structural conflict cannot be resolved with engineering solutions. As strange as this may sound, the prospects for resolution become dimmer with every international conferences on environmental protection. While the increasing use of the term "sustainable development" at such summits (it was first heard in Rio de Janeiro in 1992) may appear to signal a new departure, a closer look reveals that it serves to cement the structural laws that have governed economic policy up to now. Agenda 21, for example, does not question the economic goal of continuous growth but actually promotes it. Participatory processes are not supported from the bottom up; instead, consultation processes are encouraged from the top down, which automatically diminishes their effectiveness. And the problem of exhaustible resources is not even mentioned!

Yet even the "political panacea" of sustainability is problematic. It is extremely vague and offers no opportunity for concrete commitment in contemporary political action. The definition of sustainability as a state in which future generations have all options open to them is more than dubious, for the risks associated with actions in the present—provided they are even recognized as such—are rarely calculable or quantifiable. And that is why there is no answer to the question of what may or may not restrict the options of future generations.

Later conferences (especially the Kyoto meeting) have confirmed, at least for the time being, that the skeptics were right. A commitment to environmental goals for which compliance can be monitored and sanctions would be imposed for noncompliance is nowhere in sight. Effective self-obligation also seems far beyond reach at present.[13]

In Germany, the weak impact of the Green Party alliance on government policy has contributed to further disillusionment. And this, too, is evident in architecture. In this country, it is no longer possible to distinguish between architecture that meets stringent environmental requirements in terms of resource conservation and architecture that does not. This is true in both a positive and a negative sense.

It takes a considerable amount of specialized knowledge to recognize that such buildings as those recently designed by Thomas Herzog, for example, reflect a more serious attitude toward responsibility in architecture than others. These buildings also have considerable aesthetic value, but not because they emphasize the environmental issue. Thomas Herzog represents an architectural aesthetic in which the theme of ecological architecture converges with the wider architectural discourse. Here we note the rebirth of the architect and engineer who explores the essence of architecture at all levels to produce a coherent result. Yet structures of management, regional development and housing policy, cultural identity, and social responsibility are not addressed.

Thomas Jocher and Dietrich Fink explicitly point out that, in one of their projects—their Solar House, a multistory apartment building in Coburg—they used a conventional building as a reference model. In this case, superior architectural quality is achieved within the framework of a familiar, conventional building type, although the outcome also shows that architecture that saves resources and energy need not "stick out" simply because it does so and can work with conventional means.[14]

The tendency suggested by these examples may offer some solace—and is perhaps entirely in keeping with the abandonment of Postmodernism, which had come to be regarded as overly verbose and banal, that culminated in the early nineties. Yet the other side of the coin is revealed in the everyday context, in the single-family home built as a passive building in the suburbs, for example. It, too, is hardly distinguishable in its insipidness from others: superfluous gambrel roofs, bay windows, and dormers are as inappropriate in passive buildings as they are in other single-family houses.

Ecological architecture is sold—with the same mélange of ingredients from which it once emerged: health-conscious construction, natural materials, a healthy living climate. And sold along with it is a history and a faded image of a time we recall as one in which people still believed in visions. It is a bitter-tasting form of retro-architecture.

Ecological architecture has now disappeared from architectural discourse. All that we can do today is learn from its failure. Yet the circumstances from which it emerged are still evident everywhere. Voices have warned of the structural effects. One such prophet is Hermann Scheer, who has analyzed the interrelationships between energy supply and housing development structures and identified the consequences for urban development planning that derive from the need for a decentralized supply of alternative energy.[15] Do-it-yourself building initiatives have also been rediscovered within the context of the IBA Emscher Park projects. The governing Social-Democratic/Green coalition is now promoting such initiatives, which once again address the structural aspects of the significance of social stability, urban planning, and housing construction.

And it would appear that awareness of the injustice of and the danger posed by the prevailing global economic system is once again emerging as a mass movement—in a form that is as pluralistic as that of the sixties and seventies.

It is entirely conceivable that a new architectural aesthetic will develop on the basis of this awareness, but something more is needed as well. Architecture must be rediscovered as a medium. Architecture must be understood again as surface and depth—surface that speaks and appeals for communication, that gives insight into depth; depth as part of a complex pattern of interrelationships and interactions. The dominant reductive aesthetic of our day seeks to negate the intermediary character of architecture by reducing the building to its essentials and strips it of all narrative references.[16] Only when architecture once again recognizes and accepts its intermediary character (which it cannot shed), will it make sense to speak of something like ecological architecture. That something will need a new name, however, in order to avoid being mistaken for what failed before.

# New German Architecture in the International Context

Dietmar M. Steiner

What is new German architecture? It is modest, middle-class, yet fairly good architecture that plods along in a somewhat boring, uninspiring style. Everything is very clean, very decent and orderly, and meets the technical standards; everything works and seems to fit somehow. New German architecture has no brilliance, no glamour, no stars, and whenever scandals or disputes arise between so-called camps, the neighbors are astonished at these sham battles (in Berlin). New German architecture has large, efficient, economically successful firms, perfectly organized service organizations that rake in enormous revenues, but the world of architecture ignores them no less than it does the equally efficient architecture firms of the United States. But new German architecture also has a number of small lone wolves helplessly training for survival through merciless self-exploitation—in total devotion to the ideal of Truth, Beauty, and Goodness—although hardly anyone knows them by name. Yes, there is a new German architecture, yet it is somehow absent at the same time. New German architecture is one of the biggest puzzles of contemporary architecture in the world, or perhaps only in Europe.

This is surely a polemically incorrect assessment that emerges from the very *zeitgeist* that sees its achievable objective in sustaining the Postmodern state of architecture and exploiting its value for the culture industry—a state German architects generally want no part of. They want to go about their work in earnest, nothing more. But this "nothing more" is the problem.

Switzerland, Spain, Portugal, France, the Netherlands, Finland, and even the province of Austria to the south of Germany cut a better figure in the vanity fair of architecture than the huge, economically powerful colossus of Germany, which is evidently in the midst of a profound architectural identity crisis comparable today only to that of Italy, the giant of European architectural history and the real object of German longing. And where, may I ask, since we're talking about history, is Greece?

So new German architecture is not alone with its feelings of inferiority. It would be better to focus on its causes, however, than to persist in blaming the arrogant media, malicious, backstabbing, know-nothing critics, and investors obsesses with international stars. My objective here is to expose some of the roots of the current dilemma—as theses, not as analytical findings, and definitely not as certainties. Protest is welcome.

I have been concerned for many years with this phenomenon of committed German architecture and its non-relationship to international architectural production, and I have still not arrived at a satisfactory explanation. The simple fact is that contemporary German architecture has played no role at all in international architectural discourse or in international developments in architecture for decades. Much too long, certainly, for a nation of its size and wealth and one whose contribution to the growth of Modernism in the 20th century is unrivalled by that of any other country. After all, one of the birthplaces of Modernism was located in Germany. From the Bauhaus to Heinrich Tessenow to the Stuttgart Weissenhofsiedlung and beyond the Nazi era to the modern period of reconstruction, German architecture and the positions of its representatives were forces to be reckoned with in international architectural discourse. But German architecture retreated into a kind of inner emigration as early as the fifties. The positions of such architects as Rudolf Schwarz had no impact beyond the borders of Germany. The Anglo-Saxon debate on New Towns was hardly noticed here, which explains why no German positions were articulated at subsequent CIAM conferences or in ongoing discussions of themes raised at these meetings. Nor did Germany play a leading role in formulating the theories of New Brutalism.

Potential resistance against prevailing architectural practice and late-Functionalist architecture began to take shape in the U.S. and Europe in the late sixties, but no corresponding attitude developed in Germany. Constant in Holland, the Situationists, Yona Friedman in France, New Urban Landscape in Italy, with Archizoom, Cedric Price, and Archigram in England, the American alternative movement and the "Austrian phenomenon" in Austria—initially with Hans Hollein and Walter Pichler, then with Haus-Rucker-Co, Coop Himmelblau, and Missing Link. A worldwide movement dedicated to alternative architecture emerged, but Germany remained mired during these years dominated by the student revolts of 1968 in fatal sensory ignorance. Germany's position was that of total political refusal to make any kind of aesthetic statement regarding contemporary architecture of the time. We recall the "written diplomas" that gathered together all late-capitalist scenarios of doom and resistance and thus served as justification for refusal to take any kind of a position on contemporary architecture.

The only developments of a lasting nature during those years were the investigations of Frei Otto. His constructions in Montreal and Munich, realized in collaboration with such architects as Rolf Gutbrod and Günter Behnisch, and his scientific experiments represented the most important contribution to the identity of a new German republic in the world of international politics. And Mathias Ungers pursued his typological studies largely outside the official limelight, spending many years in the United States.

The international movement that ultimately traumatized German architecture was Postmodernism. Heinrich Klotz dared to violate the taboo. The Achilles heel of German architecture was wounded. What is your position on history and its forms? A history that could only be modern, as every other historical reminiscence would inevitably be associated with the Nazi era. That Postmodernism and accusations of Fascism were linked only in Germany is typical. The spectrum ranging from anti-capitalist statement to real socialist euphoria represented by such figures as Aldo Rossi or the young Leon Krier was largely ignored in the German debate.

The artificial Postmodernist experiments in deconstruction undertaken by the New York Five—John Heijduk, Peter Eisenman, Charles Gwathmey, Michael Graves, and Richard Meier—found as little echo in Germany as the studies of everyday culture pursued by the Greys associated with Robert Venturi, Denise Scott-Brown, and Steven Izenour in Philadelphia. And the typological operations of the Tessin *tendenza* were covered over with political propaganda posters in Germany during those years of the seventies. German schools of architecture also disappeared from the international stage, which was left in Europe to the Architectural Association School in London and the ETH in Zurich. These two university institutions were also the only ones that pursued intensive transatlantic dialogue.

Yet West Berlin became the grand stage of Postmodernist world architecture in the eighties nonetheless, thanks to the *Internationale Bauausstellung* (International Building Exhibition, known as IBA). This large-scale project and the stylistic and moral conflict between old-building and new-building IBA, which was regarded as rather scurrilous by outsiders, have yet to be rigorously analyzed from the perspective of architectural sociology. At first glance, however, it would appear that this international architectural presentation brought nothing to the German scene. The guardians of the Holy Grail and functionaries of eternally modern German architecture roused themselves briefly and then proceeded in their unshakeable conviction that architecture has no style and no form, that it needs no intramural debate within the discipline, since it is concerned with nothing but the planning of better living spaces by morally upstanding architects—with due consideration given to matters of fees, secondary costs, and legal provision regarding construction damage claims settlement.

A great sigh of relief was heard in Germany in the late eighties, once Postmodernism had exhausted itself as a style and a compulsive concern with new technological possibilities had begun to dominate architecture. Now we are finally permitted to be technologically modern, the German architects said. The era of stylistic, historical darkness has finally come to an end. Finally, we no longer need theories to explain why what we do is architecture. German architects now became obsessed with the new reductionism and rationalism. The technology of building itself was now acceptable once again as an argument for progress and needed no further reflection. Accordingly, the journal *Detail* quite rightly assumed a leading international position. And reunification reactivated those old virtues of the German building industry that Albert Speer once claimed as his true achievement. In 1969, he wrote in his memoirs that he had succeeded in the course of building the arms industry in developing the German construction industry into an efficient, powerful machine. The reunification of Germany after the collapse of the Wall in 1989 offered an ideal opportunity to apply these virtues and achievements in the new German states—while pulling rational German architects along behind them.

An architectural debate involving disputable positions and worthy of being taken seriously took place in Germany during the nineties only on the surface. The so-called Berlin Debate—reconstruction of the historical city versus pursuit of the free dynamics of globalism—produced only rhetorical results. Potsdamer Platz was rebuilt under the dogma of the reconstruction of historical Berlin, and what one sees there now is the incarnation of a suburban shopping and business mall in the empty center of Berlin. Anyone who expected a different outcome deserves to be called a numbskull. The history and values of GDR architecture, which—viewed once again from the outside—certainly did exist, were quickly destroyed. Yet for me, the Palast der Republik remains an important monument of cultural history—more important for the new Germany, at least, than the ghost of the Berlin Stadtschloss.

Architecture media in Germany did precisely what they had been doing for decades. *Bauwelt, Baumeister,* and all the others remained late-Modernist magazines which reviewed selected individual accomplishments of German architects in a spirit of critical commitment, so to speak, but without success. Germany is still the only country among the great nations of the modern era that does not have a truly international journal of architecture—like *Domus* in Italy or *L'Architecture d'aujourd'hui* in France. Only the perpetually struggling *Arch+* takes part at a learned level in the international debate and is also taken seriously in that context. Born of the sociological discourse of the seventies, this journal made the shift, though somewhat late, to the cultural debate on architecture. But even *Arch+* has never achieved the position it deserves in Germany, one that would have enabled it to exert a significant influence on academic and university discourse. It would seem that the international importance of *Arch+* has always been greater than its local standing. *Daidalos,* the forum for academic theses on architecture, served for many years as a colorful background prop suggesting expensive taste and erudition in the executive offices of German business architecture firms. When *Daidalos* attempted a revival with a new concept and considerable international attention and sought financial support, no one came to its rescue. The publications of the architects' chambers and associations draw practically no international notice at all.

This, then, is the visible media and intellectual face of a German architecture that sees its strength within Europe—comparable at best with that of Norway—in the provision of services. Yet it denies this categorization at the same time. German architects, if one pays heed to the statements and the modest policies of their professional organizations, want to be good bakers, mechanics, or carpenters, and they long for suitably objective performance criteria. A baker who bakes good bread that also tastes good needn't submit to price competition to demonstrate his cultural quality. But how does one recognize good architecture that also "tastes" good? Only in that it regards itself as cultural and artistic achievement and communicates this attitude.

This phenomenon is becomes strikingly evident in the German approach to architecture competitions. The architecture competition per se in its present form is an invention of the modern era based on the political consensus that decisions about the award of building contracts are best made by involving the entire profession and having submissions judged by representatives of the profession on the basis of their own quality criteria. One basic premise of the competition is that all architects are motivated by artistic interest and will submit proposals for building projects for nothing. Thus architects contribute work without pay in the general public interest and contribute to the development of a broader building culture. Although it is quite obvious today that the public they serve in this way is rather indifferent to that service and that this system can no longer do justice to the realities of architectural work, German architects insist upon maintaining it. I contend that there is an ideological reason for this. German architects deliberately expose themselves to the lottery of the architecture competition because they believe it is the only way to achieve a democratic equality of average results that immunizes German architecture in the long term against individual decisions that could be open to attack. The German architecture competition virtually guarantees that there are no outstanding results. It ensures democratic normalcy and mediocrity. It is a political program—devoted to the principle that the powerful must never again be allowed to decide alone—and has nothing to do with the quest for architectural quality; indeed, it does quite a good job of preventing it.

Before concluding, I would like to call attention to a positive perspective in the interest of finally giving the existing gifts and talents of the new German architecture, which exist beyond doubt, the freedom they deserve. German architecture will never achieve the kind of Calvinist-rational strength that leads to a rational covenant of quality between clients and architects without the protective umbrella of professional trade associations in such countries as Switzerland or the Netherlands. Thus in my view there is only one preferable solution. Only when we achieve a situation in Germany in which architecture is no longer the domain of professional trade organizations and federal and state building departments but is regarded as a cultural and artistic discipline worthy of support will there be a chance for structural change. And then a reform of architectural education must follow. There must be at least *one* school with an international orientation and international standing. And there should be at least *one* learned journal of architecture willing and capable of taking the offensive in the international debate. German architecture is not alone in its reliance on this intellectual, artistic, and cultural offensive. It is Europe that needs this—currently dormant—strength from Germany in order to assert itself in opposition to the prevailing U.S. East Coast discourse. This will require a network of efficient, contemporary cultural institutions. In the present environment, every German state should have a functional, independent, publicly funded museum, institute, or architecture center now.

And my last wish for a new debate on German architecture is addressed to everyone—politicians, the media, and the general public: Let us honor the aging gods as great artists without question; they have achieved great things. And let us love the no longer quite so young architects of the new German architecture in all their autonomy and individuality. Now as always, only creative and obsessive personalities have the capacity to give us the gift of an architecture of the future.

Appendix

Notes
Architects
Authors

Pages 12–17
Ullrich Schwarz
"New German Architecture—An Exhibition"

1  See Karl Heinz Bohrer, *Nach der Natur: Über Politik und Ästhetik*, Munich and Vienna 1988, pp. 209 ff.

2  Heinz Schlaffer, *Die Kurze Geschichte der deutschen Literatur*, Munich 2002, p. 8.

3  Heinz Bude, "Wo steht die Soziologische Theorie heute?" in Eva Barlösius, Hans-Peter Müller, and Steffen Sigmund, eds., *Gesellschaftsbilder im Umbruch: Soziologische Perspektiven in Deutschland*, Opladen 2001, p. 74.

4  Jürgen Habermas, "Rede zur Verleihung des Friedenspreises des Börsenvereins des Deutschen Buchhandels," *Frankfurter Allgemeine Zeitung*, 15 October 2001, p. 9.

5  Peter Sloterdijk, *Eurotaoismus: Zur Kritik der politischen Kinetik*, Frankfurt am Main 1989, p. 292.

Pages 18–31
Ullrich Schwarz
"Reflexive Modernism"

1  Matthias Kellner, "Thesen zur Bedeutung des Globalisierungsbegriffs," *Deutsche Zeitschrift für Philosophie* 6 (1997), p. 917.

2  Karl Marx and Friedrich Engels, *Manifesto of the Communist Party*, English version of 1888 authorized by Friedrich Engels, in Marx and Engels, *Collected Works*, New York 1976, vol. 6.

3  Ulrich Beck, *Was ist Globalisierung?*, Frankfurt am Main 1997, p. 182.

4  Vittorio Magnago Lampugnani, "Eine Architektur der Zukunft ohne Visionen?", *Neue Zürcher Zeitung*, July 7, 1997, p. 24.

5  Heinrich Klotz, ed., *Revision der Moderne: Postmoderne Architektur 1960–1980*, Munich 1984, p. 8.

6  Jürgen Habermas, "Die neue Unübersichtlichkeit: Die Krise des Wohlfahrts-staates und die Erschöpfung utopischer Energien," *Merkur* 431 (January 1985), p. 1.

7  Wolfgang D. Brönner, *Blondel—Perrault: Zur Architekturtheorie des 17. Jahrhunderts in Frankreich*, Bonn 1972, p. 9.

8  See Hans Freier, *Kritische Poetik: Legitimation und Kritik der Poesie in Gottscheds Dichtkunst*, Stuttgart 1972, p. 140.

9  On this point see Georg Germann, *Einführung in die Geschichte der Architektur-theorie*, Darmstadt 1987, 2nd ed., Darmstadt 1980, pp. 195 ff.; Antonio Hernandez, *Grundzüge einer Ideengeschichte der französischen Architekturtheorie von 1560–1800*, Basel 1972, pp. 50 ff.; and for a general overview: Alberto Perez-Gomez, *Architecture and the Crisis of Modern Science*, Cambridge and London 1984.

10  Hernandez 1972 (see note 9), p. 116.

11  Jan Assmann, *Das kulturelle Gedächtnis: Schrift, Erinnerung und politische Identität in frühen Hochkulturen*, Munich 1997, 2nd ed., Munich 1999, p. 165.

12  Ibid., p. 30.

13  Peter Eisenman, "Editor's Introduction," in Aldo Rossi, *The Architecture of the City*, Cambridge and London 1982, p. 7.

14  See Manfredo Tafuri, *The Sphere and the Labyrinth: Avant-Gardes and Architecture from Piranesi to the 1970s*, Cambridge and London 1987, pp. 273 ff.; see also Manfredo Tafuri and Francesco Dal Co, *Gegenwart* (Weltgeschichte der Architektur), Stuttgart 1988, p. 186.

15  Christian Norberg-Schulz, *Genius loci: Paesaggio, ambiente, architettura*, Milan 1979; quoted from German edition: *Genius loci: Landschaft, Lebensraum, Baukunst*, Stuttgart 1982, p. 190.

16  Ibid., p. 191.

17  Ibid., p. 23.

18  Kenneth Frampton, "Kritischer Regionalismus. Thesen zu einer Architektur des Widerstands," in Andreas Huyssen and Klaus Scherpe, eds., *Postmoderne: Zeichen eines kulturellen Wandels*, Reinbek 1986, p. 158.

19  Ibid., p. 168.

20  Viktor Sklovskij, "Kunst als Verfahren," in Jurij Striedter, ed., *Russischer Formalismus*, Munich 1971, p. 15.

21  Theodor W. Adorno, *Ästhetische Theorie*, Frankfurt am Main 1970, p. 55.

22  See *Das virtuelle Haus*, Cologne 1998; also Ullrich Schwarz, "Das virtuelle Haus: Architekten und Philosophen auf der Suche nach den Potentialen des Neuen," *Werk, Bauen + Wohnen* (June 1997), pp. 45 ff.

23  See Jeff Kipnis, "Towards a New Architecture," *AD* (March/April 1993), pp. 41 ff.; Sanford Kwinter, "Der Genius der Materie," *Arch+* 119/120 (1993), pp. 44 ff.; Greg Lynn, "Architectural Curvelinearity," in Kenneth Powell, ed., *Folding in Architecture* (Architectural Design, 102), London 1993, pp. 8 ff.

24  Peter Eisenman, *Aura und Exzess: Zur Überwindung der Metaphysik der Architektur*, edited and with an introduction by Ullrich Schwarz, Vienna 1995, pp. 295 ff.

25  Ibid., p. 182.

26  Hans Ibelings, *Supermodernism: Architecture in the Age of Globalization*, Rotterdam 1998, p. 89.

27  Ibid., p. 69.

28  Ibid., p. 33.

29  Andreas Ruby, "Von der Avantgarde zur Arrièregarde und zurück," *Werk, Bauen + Wohnen* 10 (2001), p. 44.

30  Ernst Hubeli, in *Definite Indefinite: Riegler Riewe*, ed. Architekturstiftung Österreich, Vienna and New York 2002, p. 61.

31  See Urte Heldhuser and Johannes Weiss, eds., *Die Modernität der Romantik: Zur Wiederkehr des Ungleichen*, Kassel 1999, pp. 12 ff.

32  Charles Baudelaire, "Was ist Romantik?", in *Sämtliche Werke: Briefe*, ed. Friedhelm Kemp and Claude Pichois in collaboration with Wolfgang Drost, Munich and Vienna 1977, vol. 1, p. 198 ff.

33  Georg Wilhelm Friedrich Hegel, *Vorlesungen über die Ästhetik II*, in *Werke in zwanzig Bänden*, Frankfurt am Main 1970, vol. 14, p. 221.

34  Ibid., p. 220.

35  Ibid., p. 223.

36  Ibid., p. 221.

37  See Heldhuser and Weiss 1999 (see note 31), p. 12.

38  Friedrich Schlegel, quoted from Manfred Frank, *Einführung in die frühromantische Ästhetik*, Frankfurt am Main 1989, p. 287.

39  Friedrich Schlegel, "Über die Unverständlichkeit," in Friedrich Schlegel, *Schriften zur Literatur*, ed. Wolfdietrich Rasch, Munich 1972, p. 338.

40  Novalis, *Werke: Tagebücher und Briefe Friedrich von Hardenbergs*, ed. Hans-Joachim Mähl and Richard Samuel, Darmstadt 1999, vol. 2, p. 334.

41  Hugo Friedrich, *Die Struktur der modernen Lyrik: Von Baudelaire bis zur Gegenwart*, Reinbek 1964, p. 22.

42  Ulrich Beck, "Das Zeitalter der Nebenfolgen und die Politisierung der Moderne," in Ulrich Beck, Anthony Giddens, and Scott Lash, eds., *Reflexive Modernisierung: Eine Kontroverse*, Frankfurt am Main 1996, p. 30.

43  See *Arch+* 143 (October 1998).

44  Ibelings 1998 (see note 26), p. 133.

45  Heinrich Klotz, *Architektur der Zweiten Moderne*, Stuttgart 1999.

46  Joseph Rykwert, *The First Moderns: The Architects of the Eighteenth Century*, Cambridge and London 1983.

47  Cited in Hans Walter Poll, "Nachwort," in Fyodor Dostoyevsky, *Aufzeichnungen aus dem Kellerloch*, Stuttgart 1984, pp. 155 f.

48  Helmut Willke, *Dystopia: Studien zur Krisis des Wissens in der modernen Gesellschaft*, Frankfurt am Main 2002, p. 11.

49  Ibid., p. 39.

50  Richard Rorty, *Kontingenz, Ironie und Solidarität*, Frankfurt am Main 1989, p. 128.

51  Willke 2002 (see note 48), p. 47.

Pages 32–38
Ernst Hubeli
"Architecture That Steps Forth from the Shadows"

–  Franz Dröge and Michael Müller, "Musealisierung und Mediatisierung: Strategien urbaner Ästhetisierung und der Widerspruch von Ort und Raum," *Werk, Bauen + Wohnen* (Zurich) 7/8 (1996).

–  Ullrich Schwarz, "Vom Ort zum Ereignis," *Werk, Bauen + Wohnen* (Zurich) 12 (1999).

–  Ernst Hubeli and Andreas Herczog, *Bilderpolitik: Architektur im Spannungsfeld von Städtebau, Denkmalpflege und Politik* (Stadt und Verkehr, 54), Zurich 1995.

–  Ernst Hubeli, "*Ceci tuera cela:* Von der Gattung zur Strategie: Über die aktuelle Antizipationsfahigkeit der Architektur," *Wert und Mehrwert* (HAD Dokumente), Graz 2001.

–  Ernst Hubeli and Andreas Herczog, *Öffentlichkeit und öffentlicher Raum* (Stadt und Verkehr, 48), Zurich 1995, rev. ed. Zurich 2000.

Pages 218–223
Gert Kähler
"Behnisch & Partners"

1 Julius Posener, "Apparat und Gegenstand," lecture given in 1967, in Posener, *Aufsätze und Vorträge 1931–1980*, Brunswick and Wiesbaden 1981, pp. 152 ff.

2 Ullrich Schwarz, "Das Erhabene und das Groteske oder Michelangelo, Piranesi und die Folgen," in Gert Kähler, ed., *Schräge Architektur und aufrechter Gang*, Brunswick and Wiesbaden 1993, p. 125; Peter Eisenman quotation in Eisenman, "The Graves of Modernism," *Oppositions* 12 (1978), p. 25.

3 Günter Behnisch in an interview by Klaus-Dieter Weiss, *Werk, Bauen + Wohnen* 9 (1990), p. 2.

4 *Architekten Behnisch & Partner: Arbeiten aus den Jahren 1952–1987*, Stuttgart 1987, p. 150.

5 Karla Szyszkowitz-Kowalski, in Dominique Gauzin-Müller, *Behnisch & Partner: 50 Jahre Architektur*, Berlin 1997, p. 21.

6 Posener 1967 (see note 1).

7 Ibid., pp. 155, 157.

8 Ibid. p. 157.


Pages 248–253
Gerwin Zohlen
"Josef P. Kleihues"

1 Vittorio Gregotti, lecture at the New York Architectural League, 1983, cited in Kenneth Frampton, *Die Architektur der Moderne: Eine kritische Baugeschichte*, 7th ed., Stuttgart 2001, p. 275 (1st ed. Stuttgart, 1983).

2 Michael Mönniger, "Der Aufstieg der Architektur zum kulturellen Leitmedium," in Ingeborg Flagge, ed., *Streiten für die menschliche Stadt: Texte zur Architekturkritik*, Hamburg 1997; see also Peter Neitzke, Carl Steckeweh, and Reinhart Wustlich, eds., *Centrum: Jahrbuch Architektur und Stadt 1998–1999*, Brunswick and Wiesbaden 1998.

3 On IBA 1984–87, see Gerwin Zohlen, "Die IBA *est divisa in partes tres*," in Paul Kahlfeldt and Josef Paul Kleihues, eds., *Stadt der ARCHITEKTUR der Stadt: Berlin 1900–2000*, exh. cat. Neues Museum, Berlin, 2000.

4 Josef Paul Kleihues and Claus Baldus, "Begriff und Praxis der Erinnerung," in *Josef Paul Kleihues im Gespräch*, Tübingen and Berlin 1996, p. 83.

5 See Andrea Mesecke and Thorsten Scheer, eds., *Joseph Paul Kleihues*, Basel 1996, pp. 76 ff., 124 ff.

4 See Dieter Hoffmann-Axthelm, *Die Rettung der Architektur vor sich selbst: Zehn Polemiken* (Bauwelt Fundamente, 108), Brunswick and Wiesbaden 1995.

7 Winfried Nerdinger, "Dialog zwischen Moderne und Geschichte," in Mesecke and Scheer 1996 (see note 5), p. 10.

8 Josef Paul Kleihues, ed., *750 Jahre Architektur und Städtebau in Berlin: Die Internationale Bauausstellung im Kontext der Baugeschichte Berlins*, exh. cat. Neue Nationalgalerie, Berlin, Stuttgart 1987, pp. 264 ff.

9 See Thorsten Scheer, "Poetischer Rationalismus," in Mesecke and Scheer 1996 (see note 5), pp. 13 ff.; Gerwin Zohlen, "Der Regent: Josef Paul Kleihues," in *Baumeister des neuen Berlin*, 5th ed., Berlin 2001, pp. 87 ff.

10 Kleihues and Baldus 1996 (see note 4).

11 Internationale Bauausstellung Berlin 1984, *Das Abenteuer der Ideen: Architektur und Philosophie seit der industriellen Revolution*, exh. cat. Neue Nationalgalerie, Berlin, ed. Vittorio Magnago Lampugnani, Berlin 1984.

12 See Kleihues 1987 (see note 8).

13 See Kahlfeldt and Kleihues 2000 (see note 3).

14 "Ich bin doch keine Architekturfabrik: Josef Paul Kleihues im Gespräch mit Christian Bauschke," *Wochenpost* 44 (27 October 1994).


Pages 254–259
Klaus-Dieter Weiss
"Daniel Libeskind"

1 Theodor W. Adorno, *Ästhetische Theorie* (1970), Frankfurt am Main 1998, p. 274.

2 John Updike, *Bech in Bedrängnis*, Reinbek 2000, p. 265 f.

3 Todd Gitlin, "The Liberal Arts in the Age of Info-Glut," *Chronicle of Higher Education*, May 1, 1998, cited in Morris Berman, *The Twilight of American Culture*, New York 2000, published in German as *Kultur vor dem Kollaps? Wegbereiter Amerika*, Frankfurt am Main et al. 2002, p. 165.

4 Anthony Vidler, *unHEIMlich: Über Unbehagen in der modernen Architektur*, Hamburg 2002, p. 178.

5 Daniel Libeskind, cited in *Du* (November 1994), p. 54.

6 Berman 2002 (see note 3).

7 Ibid., p. 131.

8 See also Thorsten Rodieck, *Daniel Libeskind: Museum ohne Ausgang*, Tübingen and Berlin 1999.

9 Daniel Libeskind, cited in DeutschlandRadio-Online, 25 March 2000.

10 Daniel Libeskind, "Symbol und Interpretation" (1981), cited in Libeskind, *Radix Matrix: Architekturen und Schriften*, Munich and New York 1994, p. 176.

11 Immanuel Kant, "Idee zu einer allgemeinen Geschichte in weltbürgerlicher Absicht" (1784), in Wilhelm Weischedel, ed., *Immanuel Kant: Werkausgabe* (1968), Frankfurt am Main 1977, vol. 11, p. 41.

12 Berman 2002 (see note 3), p. 170.

13 Thomas Lackmann, *Jewrassic Park: Wie baut man (k)ein Jüdisches Museum in Berlin*, Berlin and Vienna 2000, pp. 15, 20.

14 Ibid., p. 44.

15 Ibid., p. 48.

16 Daniel Libeskind, "Stadt und Sein," in Stefanie Carp, Daniel Libeskind, and Jan Philipp Reemtsma, *Alles Kunst? Wie arbeitet der Mensch im neuen Jahrtausend, und was tut er in der übrigen Zeit?*, Reinbek 2001, pp. 223 ff.

17 Federal President Johannes Rau on the occasion of his speech at the conferment of the German Architectural Prize in 1999, cited in *Der Spiegel Online*, November 16, 1999.

18 Daniel Libeskind, cited in *Der Spiegel* 3 (January 18, 1999).

19 Interview with Daniel Libeskind, *Der Tagesspiegel*, 20 November 1999.

20 BauNetz report on the Denver Art Museum, July 18, 2000.

21 Charles Jencks, "Die Architektur des springenden Universums," *Arch+* 141 (April 1998), p. 26.

22 Interview with Jacques Herzog, *Süddeutsche Zeitung*, February 21, 2002.

23 Daniel Libeskind, "Architecture Intermundium" (1988), cited in Libeskind 1994 (see note 10), p. 154.

24 Vidler 2002 (see note 4), p. 57.


Pages 260–265
Amber Sayah
"Karljosef Schattner"

All unreferenced citations are those of Karljosef Schattner and are from his writings, lectures, and newspaper interviews with the architect.

1 Wolfgang Pehnt, *Karljosef Schattner: Ein Architekt aus Eichstätt*, new edition, Stuttgart 1999, p. 21.

2 Ulrich Weisner, *Neue Architektur im Detail: Heinz Bienefeld, Gottfried Böhm, Karljosef Schattner*, exh. cat. Kunsthalle Bielefeld, Bielefeld 1989, p. 99.


Pages 272–277
Olaf Winkler
"Oswald Mathias Ungers"

1 Oswald Mathias Ungers, "Rede zum Richtfest Thermen am Forum, Viehmarktplatz, Trier (1989–1998)," in *Centrum: Jahrbuch Architektur und Stadt 1997–1998*, Brunswick and Wiesbaden 1997, p. 141.

2 See Heinrich Klotz, ed., *O. M. Ungers 1951–1984: Bauten und Projekte*, Brunswick and Wiesbaden 1985, p. 25.

3 Ungers 1997 (see note 1).

4 Jürgen Sawade, "Wohnhaus Ungers 3, in Köln-Müngersdorf," in Anja Sieber-Albers and Martin Kieren, eds., *Sichtweisen: Betrachtungen zum Werk von O. M. Ungers*, Cologne 1999, p. 141.

5 Reyner Banham, *Brutalismus in der Architektur: Ethik oder Ästhetik?*, Stuttgart 1966, p. 126.

6 Martin Kieren, "Von der Sinngebung—oder: Der allgemeine Typus," in Architektur Forum Rheinland, ed., *Rheinisches Jahrbuch für Architektur 1*, Wuppertal 2000, p. 246.

7 Sawade 1999 (see note 4), p. 140.

8 Oswald Mathias Ungers, "Das Recht der Architektur auf eine autonome Sprache," in *Architektur 1951–1990*, Stuttgart 1991, p. 239.

9 Oswald Mathias Ungers in conversation, Cologne, July 2001.

10 Cited in Klotz 1985 (see note 2), p. 17.

11 Ungers 1999 (see note 8), p. 237.

12 See Fritz Neumeyer, "Architektonisches Enigma: Ein Ganzes für sich und eine Einheit aus Einzelheiten," in Ungers 1991 (see note 8), p. 9.

13 See Klotz 1985 (see note 2), p. 21.

14 Ungers 1991 (see note 8), pp. 237 ff.

15 Oswald Mathias Ungers, *Die Thematisierung der Architektur*, Stuttgart 1983; published in Italian as *Architettura come tema*, Mailand 1982.

16 To Leon Krier in Charlotteville, N.C., November 1983, cited in Martin Kieren, *Oswald Mathias Ungers*, Zurich 1994, p. 32.

17 Oswald Mathias Ungers, "Die neue Abstraktion—ein Versuch, Stellung zu beziehen," cited in Ungers 1991 (see note 8), p. 237.

18 Wolfgang Pehnt, "Nutrimentum Spiritus," in Sieber-Albers and Kieren 1999 (see note 4), p. 131.

19 Oswald Mathias Ungers in conversation, Cologne, July 2001.

20 See Oswald Mathias Ungers and Stefan Vieths, *Die Dialektische Stadt*, Cologne 1999.

21 Pehnt 1999 (see note 18), p. 128.

22 Oswald Mathias Ungers in conversation, Cologne, July 2001.

Pages 280–293
Wolfgang Pehnt
"German Architecture from 1945 to 1990"

1 Gerhard Krenz, *Architektur zwischen gestern und morgen: Ein Vierteljahrhundert Architekturentwicklung in der DDR*, Berlin 1974, 2nd ed. 1975, p. 139.

2 ECA = Economic Cooperation Administration.

3 Otto Bartning, "Mensch ohne Raum," *Hefte für Baukunst und Werkform* 1 (1947), p. 20.

4 "Ein Aufruf: Grundsätzliche Forderungen," *Hefte für Baukunst und Werkform* 1 (1947), p. 29; reprinted in several publications.

5 Johannes Göderitz, Hubert Hoffmann, and Roland Rainer, *Die gegliederte und aufgelockerte Stadt*, Tübingen 1957.

6 See also Werner Durth, *Deutsche Architekten: Biographische Verflechtungen 1900–1930*, Brunswick and Wiesbaden 1986, 2nd ed. 1987; Winfried Nerdinger, ed., *Bauhaus-Moderne im Nationalsozialismus: Zwischen Anbiederung und Verfolgung*, Munich 1993.

7 Alfons Leitl, "Anmerkungen zur Zeit," *Baukunst und Werkform* 1 (1949), p. 3.

8 Emil Steffann, "Können wir noch Kirchen bauen?" (1958), in Gisberth Hülsmann and Manfred Sundermann, eds., *Emil Steffann*, 2nd ed., Düsseldorf 1981, p. 107.

9 Hans Döllgast, *Münchener Merkur* 153, June 26, 1952, quoted from Emil Altenhöfer, "Hans Döllgast und die Alte Pinakothek," in *Hans Döllgast 1891–1974*, ed. Bund Deutscher Architekten et al., Munich, 2nd ed., Munich 1988, p. 78.

10 Rudolf Schwarz, *Kirchenbau: Welt vor der Schwelle*, Heidelberg 1960, p. 94.

11 Rudolf Herrnstadt, "Über den Baustil, den politischen Stil und den Genossen Henselmann," *Neues Deutschland*, July 29, 1951.

12 Ernst Reuter, mayor of West Berlin, 1949, quoted from Johann Friedrich Geist and Klaus Kürvers, *Das Berliner Mietshaus 1945–1989*, Munich 1989, p. 354.

13 Karl Mahler, "Internationale Bauausstellung 1956 [sic!]," *Bauwelt* 35 (1953), pp 681 ff.

14 Title of the 1959 Werkbund conference in Marl.

15 At the Day of German Cities in Augsburg, 1960. Edgar Salin, "Urbanität," in *Erneuerung unserer Städte: Vorträge, Aussprache und Ergebnisse der 11. Hauptversammlung des Deutschen Städtetages*, Stuttgart and Cologne 1960, pp. 9 ff.

16 Alexander Mitscherlich, *Die Unwirtlichkeit unserer Städte*, Frankfurt am Main 1965.

17 According to estimates made around 1980, 40 percent of these offices were one-man companies, another 40 percent employed staffs of no more than four. See Gernot Feldhusen, *Architekten und ihre beruflichen Perspektiven*, Stuttgart 1982.

18 See Thomas Topfstedt, *Stadtdenkmale im Osten Deutschlands*, Leipzig 1994.

19 Johann Friedrich Geist, *Passagen, ein Bautyp des 19. Jahrhunderts*, Munich 1969, 2nd ed., 1978.

Selected Bibliography

– Beyme, Klaus von, Werner Durth, Niels Gutschow, Winfried Nerdinger, and Thomas Topfstedt, *Neue Städte aus Ruinen: Deutscher Städtebau der Nachkriegszeit*, Munich 1992.

– Bund Deutscher Architekten, DAI, and BDGA with Alois Giefer, Franz Sales Meyer, and Joachim Beinlich, eds., *Planen und Bauen im neuen Deutschland*, Cologne and Opladen 1960.

– Bundesministerium für Raumordnung, Bauwesen und Städtebau et al., eds., *Ideen, Orte, Entwürfe: Architektur und Städtebau in der Bundesrepublik Deutschland*, Berlin 1990.

– Burchard, John, *The Voice of the Phoenix: Postwar Architecture in Germany*, Cambridge, Mass., and London 1966.

– Conrads, Ulrich, Werner Marschall, and James C. Palms, *Neue deutsche Architektur 2*, Stuttgart 1962.

– Durth, Werner, *Deutsche Architekten: Biographische Verflechtungen 1900–1930*, Brunswick and Wiesbaden 1986, 2nd ed. 1987.

– Durth, Werner and Niels Gutschow, *Träume in Trümmern: Planungen zum Wiederaufbau zerstörter Städte im Westen Deutschlands 1940–1950*, 2 vols., Brunswick and Wiesbaden 1988; abridged version: Munich 1993.

– Durth, Werner, Jörn Düwel, and Niels Gutschow, *Architektur und Städtebau der DDR*, vol. 1: *Ostkreuz*, vol. 2: *Aufbau*, Frankfurt am Main 1998.

– Düwel, Jörn, Werner Durth, Niels Gutschow, and Jochem Schneider, *1945: Krieg—Zerstörung—Aufbau: Architektur und Stadtplanung 1940–1960*, Berlin 1995.

– Düwel, Jörn, *Baukunst voran! Architektur und Städtebau in der SBZ/DDR*, Berlin 1995.

– Feldmeyer, Gerhard G., *Die neue deutsche Architektur*, Stuttgart et al. 1993.

– Flagge, Ingeborg, ed., *Geschichte des Wohnens*, vol. 5: *1945 bis heute*, Stuttgart 1999.

– Geist, Johann Friedrich and Klaus Kürvers, *Das Berliner Mietshaus 1945–1989*, Munich 1989.

– Gleiniger-Neumann, Andrea and Hans-Peter Schwarz, eds., *Bauen heute: Architektur der Gegenwart in der Bundesrepublik Deutschland*, exh. cat. Deutsches Architektur Museum, Frankfurt am Main, Stuttgart 1985.

– Hatje, Gerd, Hubert Hoffmann, and Karl Kaspar, *Neue deutsche Architektur*, Stuttgart 1956.

– Klotz, Heinrich, *Architektur in der Bundesrepublik: Gespräche mit sechs Architekten*, Frankfurt am Main et al. 1977.

– Krenz, Gerhard, *Architektur zwischen gestern und morgen: Ein Vierteljahrhundert Architekturentwicklung in der DDR*, Berlin 1974, 2nd ed. 1975.

– Koenig, Giovanni Klaus, *Architettura tedesca del secondo dopoguerra*, Rocca San Casciano 1965.

– Nestler, Paolo and Peter M. Bode, *Deutsche Kunst seit 1960: Architektur*, Munich 1976.

– Pehnt, Wolfgang, *Neue deutsche Architektur 3*, Stuttgart 1970.

– Topfstedt, Thomas, *Städtebau in der DDR 1955–71*, Leipzig 1985.

– Schneider, Romana, Winfried Nerdinger, and Wilfried Wang, eds., *Architektur im 20. Jahrhundert*, vol. 8: *Deutschland*, exh. cat., Deutsches Architektur Museum, Frankfurt am Main, Munich 2000.

Pages 294–303
Andreas Ruby
"The Eternal Return of the Void"

1 The resolution of the Bundestag regarding the seat of the new capital was the outcome of a long, embittered struggle between pro-Berlin and pro-Bonn lobbies. In the end, the Berlin advocates won by a bare majority of 18 votes (338 for versus 320 against). Seventeen "yes" votes came from the PDS, the legal successor of the SED (Sozialistische Einheitspartei Deutschlands, the German Unity Party), which had been the governing party in the GDR for forty years. The pro-Bonn faction took the view that Berlin's historical burden made it unsuitable as a representative of a reunited Germany. The pro-Berlin camp contended that Germany could present its history more credibly in Berlin. The PDS believed that placing the capital in Berlin would be more beneficial to the interests of eastern Germany and would perpetuate the role East Berlin had formerly played as capital of the GDR.

2 From the standpoint of national sovereignty, West Berlin was a zone of occupation under the control of the Allied Powers after the Second World War: the U.S., Great Britain, and France. This explains why the Federal Republic was not permitted to station an army in Berlin or draft recruits for military service from Berlin.

3 Wolfgang Nagel, "Paris, Mailand oder Wien als Vorbild," *Tagesspiegel*, October 17, 1991.

4 Rem Koolhaas, "Massakrierte Ideen," *Frankfurter Allgemeine Zeitung*, October 16, 1991.

5 This process of transformation can be traced in detail in Rudolf Steger's precise analysis, "Konversion zur Konvention. Hans Kollhoffs Rückkehr zur Halbzeit der Moderne," *Arch+* 117 (June 1993), pp. 12–14.

6 This insistence on ideological principles came at the risk of grave environmental problems. The groundwater level in Berlin is unusually high, at about twenty meters. In order to conform to the outdated eaves height while accommodating the parking spaces required today (which naturally did not have to be taken into account when the eaves height was specified in the 19th century) at the same time, the groundwater level had to be artificially reduced. This was economically unjustifiable and environmentally irresponsible, as it would have a severe negative impact on the green biotopes of the city, such as the Tiergarten, as the roots of plants in these areas would be unable to draw as much water.

7 Josef Paul Kleihues, "Kritische Rekonstruktion: Auf dem Weg zur Metropole Berlin," *Deutsche Bauzeitung* 5 (1993), p. 78.

8 Rem Koolhaas in an interview with Hubertus Siegert, March 16, 1996; from the series entitled *Gespräche ohne Kamera*, conducted by Hubertus Siegert as an accompaniment to his film *Berlin Babylon* (Germany, 1996–2001), and published in the Internet (http://www.berlinbabylon.de/Pages/bb-koolhaas.html).

9 Kleihues 1993 (see note 7), p. 77.

10 "Rem Koolhaas in Conversation with Hans-Ulrich Obrist," *Art Orbit* 4 (1999); see http://www.artnode.se/artorbit/issue4/i_koolhaas/i_koolhaas.html.

11 Will Alsop, in Hans Stimmann, ed., *Babylon, Berlin etc. Das Vokabular der europäischen Stadt*, Lapidarium Conferences, 1995, Basel et al. 1995, p. 108.

12 Jean Nouvel, in Stimmann 1995 (see note 11), pp. 204 f.

13 "Cette capitale est une banlieue dans son ensemble." Dominique Perrault, in Stimmann 1995 (see note 11), p. 212.

14 Under the shadow of official planning activity, a number of efforts were undertaken to work with the Berlin "as it was" and to develop it from there, without becoming caught up in historical projections. See Philipp Oswalt, *Berlin—Stadt ohne Form: Strategien einer anderen Architektur*, in collaboration with Anthony Fontenot and the "Automatic Urbanism" team, with contributions by Rudolf Stegers, Munich et al. 2000.

15 *Arch+* was also the only German journal of architecture that exposed the latent tendency to ideologize the Berlin architectural debate and subjected it to critical examination. See in this context *Von Berlin nach Neuteutonia* 122 (June 1994).

16 Leo Klimm, "Wer mietet mehr? Berlin als Zentrum der Immobilien-Krise," *Süddeutsche Zeitung*, March 19, 2002.

17 Philip Johnson, in Stimmann 1995 (see note 11), p. 48.

Pages 304–311
Werner Sewing
"The Next Generation: New German Architects?"

1 Thomas Eller, "Endstation Comeback," *Der Tagesspiegel*, July 23, 1997.

2 *Arch+* (Die Moderne der Moderne) 143 (October 1998); *Arch+* (Die Debatte) 146 (April 1999).

3 Sanford Kwinter, "La Trahison des clercs (und anderer moderner Mummenschanz)," *Arch+* 146 (April 1999).

4 Bund Deutscher Architekten, ed., *AKJAA: Positionen junger Architekten in Deutschland*, Basel 2002.

5 Angelika Schnell, *Junge Deutsche Architekten*, Basel 2000.

6 Heinz Bude, *Deutschen Karrieren*, Frankfurt am Main 1987; *Das Altern einer Generation: Die Jahrgänge 1938–1948*, Frankfurt am Main 1995; *Generation Berlin*, Berlin 2001.

7 Roxanne Kuter Williamson, *American Architects and the Mechanics of Fame*, Austin 1991.

8 Magalei Sarfatti-Larson, *Behind the Postmodern Façade: Architectural Change in Late Twentieth-Century America*, Berkeley 1993.

9 Werner Durth, *Deutsche Architekten: Biographische Verflectungen 1900–1970*, Brunswick 1986, paperback ed. Munich 1992.

10 Helmut Schelsky, *Die skeptische Generation: Eine Sociologie der deutschen Jugend*, Dusseldorf 1957, 2nd ed. Frankfurt am Main 1975.

11 Eric Mumford, *The CIAM Discourse on Urbanism 1928–1960*, Cambridge, Mass., and London 2000; Sarah Williams Goldhagen and Réjean Legault, eds., *Anxious Modernisms: Experimentation in Postwar Architectural Culture*, Cambridge, Mass., 2000.

12 Ulf Meyer in conversation with Dieter Hoffmann-Axthelm, "Die Architektur der 68er ist das Nicht-Bauen," *Der Architekt* 7 (1997).

13 Werner Sewing, "Berlinische Architecture," *Arch+* (Von Berlin nach Neu-Teutonia) 122 (June 1994).

14 Corinne Jaquand-Goddefroy and Claus Käpplinger, *Young French Architects*, Basel 1999.

15 Wilhelm Pinder, *Das Problem der Generation in der Kunstgeschichte Europas*, Munich 1926, 2nd ed. Leipzig 1928; Frederic J. Schwartz, "Ernst Bloch and Wilhelm Pinder: Out of Sync," *Grey Room* 3 (spring 2001).

16 See the contribution of Wolfgang Pehnt in this publication, ill. on p. 289.

Pages 312–323
Hanno Rauterberg
"History—That Was Yesterday"

1 Eugène-Emmanuel Viollet-le-Duc, *Entretiens sur l'architecture*, Paris 1863–1872, vol. 1, reprint, Brussels 1977, p. 324 (from the author's translation).

2 Le Corbusier, *L'Art décoratif d'aujourdhui*, Paris 1925, cited in Le Corbusier, *The Decorative Art of Today*, London 1987, p. 189.

3 Adolf Loos, *Trotzdem*, Vienna 1931, p. 80.

4 Cited in Karl Friedrich Schinkel, *Die Denkmalpflege*, vol. 3, 1901, p. 6.

5 Gottfried Kiesow, *Einführung in die Denkmalpflege*, 2nd, revised edition, Stuttgart 1989, p. 39.

6 Thilo Schabert, *Stadtarchitektur: Spiegel der Welt*, Zurich 1990, p. 111.

7 Friedrich Schlegel, *Sämtliche Werke*, vol. 6, Vienna 1823, p. 257.

8 Hans Kollhoff in an interview with Sebastian Redecke and Hans Wilderotter, in Hans Wilderotter, ed., *Das Haus am Werderschen Markt*, Berlin 2000.

9 Dieter Hoffmann-Axthelm, "Kann die Denkmalpflege entstaatlicht werden? Gutachten für die Bundestagsfraktion von Bündnis 90/Die Grünen," documented in *Entstaatlichung der Denkmalpflege? Von der Provokation zur Diskussion—Eine Debatte über die Zukunft der Denkmalpflege*, ed. Vereinigung der Landesdenkmalpfleger in der Bundesrepublik Deutschland, Berlin 2000.

10 Karl Scheffler, *Die Architektur der Grossstadt*, Berlin 1913, p. 15.

11 Cited in Bernhard Schmid, *Oberpräsident von Schein und die Marienburg*, Halle 1940, p. 225.

12 Roman Herzog, "Zur Verleihung des Nationalpreises der Deutschen Nationalstiftung," *Bulletin* 32 of the Presse- und Informationsamt der Bundesregierung, April 29, 1997, p. 346.

13 Theo Waigel, "Die Dresdner Frauenkirche—Symbol der Hoffnung auf Frieden," *Bulletin* 39 of the Presse- und Informationsamt der Bundesregierung, May 15, 1995, p. 341.

14 Jacob Burckhardt, *Über das Studium der Geschichte*, Munich 1982, p. 83.

15 "Rekonstruktion und Modernität sind kein Widerspruch—ein Interview mit Elke Leonhard," *Die Welt*, June 21, 2000.

16 Jürgen Habermas, *Die Normalität einer Berliner Republik*, Frankfurt 1995, pp. 14 f.

17 Hans Stimmann, "Reurbanisierung der historischen Staatsmitte," in *Die Berliner Schlossdebatte—Pro und Contra*, ed. Wilhelm von Boddien and Helmut Engel, Berlin 2000, p. 67.

18 Georg Mörsch, "Wer bestimmt das öffentliche Interesse an der Erhaltung von Baudenkmalen? Mechanismen und Problematik der Auswahl," *Deutsche Kunst und Denkmalpflege* 38 (1980), p. 127.

19 Johann Gustav Droysen, *Historik*, text edition by Peter Leyh, Stuttgart 1977, p. 399.

Pages 324–333
Wolfgang Kil
"All Quiet on the Eastern Front"

1 The findings of a survey conducted by the architects' chamber of the state of Saxony in 1996 showed that local firms were involved in only 20 percent of total construction volume, including straight engineering projects, in the state.

2 Gert Kähler in an address to the conference "Aufbau Ost oder ein Land als

Abschreibungsobjekt?" hosted by the Hamburgische Architektenkammer on June 19–20, 1997 in Hamburg; unpublished manuscript.

3 Hans Stimmann during the panel discussion "Pro Bauakademie—Argumente für eine Neugründung" at the "Constructa '92" trade fair in Hanover, published by the Senatsverwaltung für Bau- und Wohnungswesen, Berlin 1992.

4 Cited in Dietrich Mühlberg, "Von Schlossfreiheit und Burgfrieden," in *Die Zeit* 47, 15 November 2001.

5 Hans Stimmann, cited in *Spiegel* 42, 1994.

6 Christian Knoche, "Gymnasium in Wurzen (Sachsen): Erfahrungen in den neuen Ländern," in *Deutsche Bauzeitung* 3 (1997), p. 70 (italics added by the author).

7 Dorothea Parker, in *Bauwelt* 16 (1995).

8 Dieter Bankert, *Traditionen und Visionen—4. Internationales Architekturforum Dessau*, Cologne 1994.

9 Meinhard von Gerkan, in *Archithese* 3 (1993).

10 Kähler 1997 (see footnote 2).

11 Klaus Noé, "Die grosse deutsche Illusion," in *Lettre International* 50 (fall 2000).

12 "Erneut alarmierender Rückgang des Auftragsvolumens," in *Deutsches Architektenblatt*, Ausgabe Ost, 7 (2001).

13 Torsten Birne, "Eine Frage des Stils," in Wolfgang Kil, ed., *Neue Landschaft: Sachsen*, Dresden 2001.

14 Cited in Gerhard Lenz, *Verlusterfahrung Landschaft*, Frankfurt am Main and New York 1999, p. 192.

15 Cited in Heidrun Hannusch, "Die Moderne am Katzentisch," in *Dresdner Neueste Nachrichten*, June 18, 1999.

16 All available economic data point to the year 1996 as the zenith of "retroactive development" in eastern Germany. After 1996, the economic indicators (investments, gross domestic product, productivity, income) began to fall; structural unemployment stagnated at a high level. Polls begin to show an increasing mood of resignation in the new German states in 1997.

17 City Planning Office, Görlitz: concept for integrated urban planning, dated August 2001.

18 The "return of housing land to the forest" has already begun in parts of the new city district of Schwedt. It may also be regarded as a realistic option for numerous other cities, including especially those comprised entirely of new buildings and is seen as particularly urgent for Wolfen-Nord, for several housing complexes in Hoyerswerda and—in the author's view—in at least the fringe areas of Halle-Neustadt.

19 The original study entitled "Less Is More" by Philipp Oswalt and Klaus Overmeyer was the triggering impulse for the seminar with the same title held at the Bauhaus Dessau in December 2001. KARO-architecten energized the local debate in Leipzig with their provocative "forestation" proposals for the eastern part of downtown Leipzig in the summer of 2001.

20 Margitta Fassl, managing director of the Hoyerswerda Housing Association, cited in *Frankfurter Allgemeine Zeitung*, July 12, 2000.

Pages 334–341
Wilfried Dechau and Christian Holl
"A Short History of Ecological Architecture in Germany"

1 Frederic Vester, *Neuland des Denkens: Vom technokratischen zum kybernetischen Zeitalter*, Stuttgart 1980.

2 As there is no adequate translation of the German term *ökologisches Bauen*, we have chosen to use "ecological architecture." *Ed.*

3 One of the first publications in which this term appeared in the title was *Ökologisches Bauen* by Dirk Althaus, Ingo Gabriel, and Per Krusche, Wiesbaden and Berlin 1982.

4 A review of current publications confirms this. The relevant titles no longer read *Ökologisches Bauen* or *Ökologische Architektur*, but identify practical guides or information for building clients: *Ökologische Bausanierung, Der Ökologische Bauauftrag, Handbuch ökologische Siedlungsentwicklung*, or *Kindergärten ökologisch bauen und gestalten*. Scholarly journals, in particular, have ceased using the words "ecological" in their titles.

5 Socialism was of course discussed as an alternative to capitalism, and the issue was pursued in publications and activities. These initiatives soon ebbed, however, in the absence of a political force willing to respond to them. Neither the German Social Democratic Party (SPD) which was strongly devoted to the promise of prosperity for the working classes and, as a governing party during the seventies, was compelled to remain aloof from such alternatives, nor the German Communist Party (KPD), whose influence in the West was never more than negligible, showed signs of responsiveness to encouragements toward environmental policy. In this regard, see Jost Hermand, *Grüne Utopien in Deutschland*, Frankfurt am Main 1991.

6 The Green Party was ultimately the political force that brought environmental concerns into the political arena, although it was subject from the outset to the conflict between affirmation of the system as a party and the recognition that the prevailing system could not really be expected to eliminate the threat of environmental destruction. What is more, the political ambitions of some party members—those of Otto Schily (who left the party in 1989) and Joschka Fischer, for example—were more closely related to social responsibility than to green utopias. Relevant to this context is Thomas E. Schmidt, "Nach der politischen Utopie," in the special issue ("Zukunft denken: Nach den Utopien") of *Merkur* 9/10 (September/October 2001).

7 See in particular the writings of Herbert Marcuse, especially *Eros and Civilization*, New York, 1962, or "Kulturrevolution," in Herbert Marcuse, *Nachgelassene Schriften*, vol. 1: *Das Schicksal der bürgerlichen Demokratie*, ed. Peter-Erwin Jansen, Lüneburg 1999.

8 The subtitle reads "Eine Ausstellung über den miserablen Zustand unserer Städte, über die Notwendigkeit, diesen Zustand zu ändern, damit der Mensch wieder menschenwürdig in seiner Stadt leben kann" (An exhibition on the miserable state of our cities and on the necessity of changing it, so that people can once again live in dignity in their cities).

9 "The suburban single-family house, the successor to the urban villa of the late 19th century, is the epitome of urban irresponsibility: The client is permitted to confuse his dream images with his identity." Alexander Mitscherlich, *Die Unwirtlichkeit unserer Städte*, Frankfurt am Main 1965.

10 In this regard, see Norbert Gestring, Hartwig Heine, Rüdiger Mautz, Hans-Norbert Mayer, and Walter Siebel, *Ökologie und urbane Lebensweise*, Wiesbaden 1997.

11 "These technical solutions are feasible in isolation and thus suitable for display. Ecology becomes 'positive' in the wink of an eye." Dieter Hoffmann-Axthelm, "Untergehende Städte," *Arch+* 94 (April 1998). See also Gestring et al. 1997 (see note 9), p. 56: "Staking everything on technical restructuring and improvements in efficiency is problematic for several reasons. Orientation to what is technical feasible often leads to the reduction of ecological architecture to the issue of energy conservation. Important fields of action are thus eliminated from consideration from the outset."

12 See Ernst Ulrich Weizsäcker, *Faktor Vier: Doppelter Wohlstand, halbierter Naturverbrauch*, Munich 1997, and Friedrich Schmidt-Bleek, *Das MIPS-Konzept: Weniger Naturverbrauch, mehr Lebensqualität durch Faktor 10*, Munich 2000.

13 See, for example, Christoph Spehr, *Die Ökofalle: Nachhaltigkeit und Krise*, Vienna 1996.

14 Thomas Jocher and Dietrich Fink, "Niedrigstenergie als Geschosswohnungsbau," *Bundesbaublatt* 3 (2002).

15 See Hermann Scheer, *Solare Weltwirtschaft*, Munich 2000.

16 See Boris Groys, *Unter Verdacht*, Munich 2001. Retro-architecture points to the lack of such narrative elements, yet it creates nothing but easily saleable atmospheres. And for that reason it will never produce architecture that questions the prevailing power system, since it relies on it. See in this regard Walter Prigge, "Inniges Verhältnis, untrennbar," *Deutsche Bauzeitung* 2 (2001).

administrative building for Lufthansa AG, Frankfurt am Main; International competition (1st prize, 1999). – "Uptown München;" International competition (2nd prize, 1993). 2013 Main railway station in Stuttgart; International competition (1st prize, 1997)

**Recent Publications** Kristin Feireiss and Hans-Jürgen Commerell, eds., *Ingenhoven Overdiek und Partner: Evolution – Ökologie – Architektur,* Berlin 1996. Kristin Feireiss and Hans-Jürgen Commerell, eds., *Ingenhoven Overdiek und Partner: Hauptbahnhof Stuttgart,* Berlin 1999. Ingenhoven Overdiek und Partner, eds., *Ingenhoven Overdiek und Partner: Hochhaus am Olympiapark,* Düsseldorf 1999. Till Briegleb, ed., *Ingenhoven Overdiek und Partner: Hochhaus RWE AG Essen,* Basel et al. 2000. Ingenhoven Overdiek und Partner and KMS Team, eds., *1/1: Architektur und Design: Neue Synergien,* Basel 2001. Kristin Feireiss, ed., *Ingenhoven Overdiek und Partner: Energies,* Basel 2002

**Contact**
Ingenhoven Overdiek und Partner
Kaistrasse 16a
40221 Düsseldorf
Postfach 190046
40110 Düsseldorf
Tel.: 0049-211-3010101
Fax: 0049-211-3010131
info@ingenhoven-overdiek.de
www.ingenhoven-overdiek.de

## Petra and Paul Kahlfeldt

**Petra Kahlfeldt** (Dipl.-Ing. Architekt). 1960 Born in Kaiserslautern. 1979–85 Studied architecture at the TU Berlin. 1981/82 Studied architecture at the University of Florence. 1985 Degree. 1985–87 Worked at various architectural offices in Berlin. Since 1987 Collaboration with Paul Kahlfeldt in their joint architects' office. 1990–95 Member of the academic staff, Chair of Design and Architectural Engineering, at the TU Berlin. 1997/98 Scholarship to the Deutsche Akademie, Villa Massimo, Rome. Since 2000 Member in the Design Advisory Board of the city of Ostfildern and member of the State Monuments Council of the city of Berlin. Since 2001 Chairman of the BDA State Association, Berlin

**Paul Kahlfeldt** (Prof. Dipl.-Ing. Architekt). 1956 Born in Berlin. 1976–78 Training as a carpenter/cabinetmaker. 1979–84 Studied architecture at the TU Berlin. 1984–87 Worked at various architecture offices in Berlin. Since 1987 Collaboration with Petra Kahlfeldt in their joint architects' office. 1988–92 Director of the Berlin office of Pro-

fessor Josef P. Kleihues. 1998 Instructor at the Hochschule für Technik, Wirtschaft und Gestaltung, Bernburg. 1999–2001 Coordinator for the architectural reconstruction of the Festspielhaus Hellerau in Dresden, appointed by the Heinrich-Tessenow-Gesellschaft. Since 1999 Professor of Design, Architectural Engineering and Building Engineering at the TU Kaiserslautern. 1998 Member of the Board of Directors of the Deutscher Werkbund Berlin

**Office** 1987 Founding of the joint office of Kahlfeldt Architekten. 1996 BDA Prize Berlin, honorable mention. 1997 Architecture Prize from the Deutsche Ziegelindustrie, honorable mention

**Major Building Projects** 1994 Haus Bastian, Berlin-Dahlem. 1996 Bank building, Baruth (near Berlin). – Engelhardt Hof, Berlin. 1997 Housing development on Sophienstrasse, Berlin-Mitte. – Bank building, Grossbeeren (near Berlin). 1998 Rosmarin-Karree, new building complex with 72 apartments, Berlin-Mitte. 2001 Reconstruction and conversion of a former large transformer station in Berlin-Charlottenburg for MetaDesign. – Housing development on Elbchaussee, Hamburg. – Exhibition architecture for *Mies van der Rohe und Berlin,* Altes Museum, Berlin

**Contact**
Kahlfeldt Architekten
Kurfürstendamm 58
10707 Berlin
Tel.: 0049-30-3277980
Fax: 0049-30-32779829
mail@kahlfeldt-architekten.de
www.kahlfeldt-architekten.de

## Prof. Hans Kollhoff
## Architekten Kollhoff und Timmermann

**Hans Kollhoff** (Prof. Dipl.-Ing. Architekt). 1946 Born in Lobenstein. 1968–75 Studied architecture and earned degree from the Universität Karlsruhe. 1975–78 DAAD scholarship and study at Cornell University, New York. Since 1978 Independent office in Berlin. 1978–83 Assistant, Chair of Building Theory and Design, TU Berlin. Since 1984 Partnership with Helga Timmermann. 1983–85 Guest professorships for Building Theory and Architectural Engineering, Hochschule der Künste Berlin. 1986/87 Interim for Chair Professor of Urban Design and Industrial Architecture at the Universität Dortmund. 1987–89 Guest professor at the ETH Zürich. Since 1990 Professur of Architecture and Engineering Design at the ETH Zürich. 1999 Founded the Atelier Prof. Hans Kollhoff GmbH, Rotkreuz, Switzerland. 2000 Established the Kantoors Kollhoff, Rotterdam, Netherlands

**Helga Timmermann** (Dipl.-Ing. Architektin). 1953 Born in Aachen. 1971–73 Studied architecture at the RWTH Aachen.

1973–79 Studied architecture at the TH Darmstadt. 1979 Degree under Prof. Romero, TH Darmstadt. 1979/80 Worked at the office of Büro Kiemle, Kreidt & Partner, Berlin. 1981 Worked at the office of Oswald Mathias Ungers, Berlin. – Worked at the office of Kollhoff & Ovaska, Berlin. 1981–84 Assistant, Chair of High-Rise Construction and Design, TH Darmstadt. 1984 Worked at the office of J. Sawade, Berlin. Since 1984 Partnership with Hans Kollhoff. 1999 Founded the Atelier Prof. Hans Kollhoff GmbH, Rotkreuz, Switzerland, with Hans Kollhoff. 2000 Guest professor at the Hochschule für bildende Künste Hamburg

**Jasper Jochimsen** (Dipl.-Ing. Architekt). 1964 Born in Freiburg. 1984–92 Studied architecture at the TU Berlin (Dipl.-Ing.) and the University of Miami (Fulbright Scholarship, Mag. arch.). 1989 Freelance work for the architects' office of Müller Reimann, Berlin. 1990–99 Project director at the office of Prof. Hans Kollhoff, Berlin. – Guest lectures and critiques at the ETH Zürich, TU Berlin, TU Dresden. Since 2000 Member of the academic staff of the Universität der Künste Berlin, Chair of Prof. Benedict Tonon. 2000 Founded the office of Behles & Jochimsen with Armin Behles

**Major Building Projects** 1986 Wohnpark Victoria (housing complex), Berlin-Kreuzberg. 1987 Wohnen am Schloss (housing complex), Berlin-Charlottenburg. 1994 Housing development, KNSM-Eiland, Amsterdam. 1996 Block 208, Hofgarten am Gendarmenmarkt, Berlin-Mitte. 1999 Daimler Chrysler Immobilien GmbH, Potsdamer Platz 1, Berlin. – German Ministry of Foreign Affairs, refurbishing of the former Reichsbank building, Berlin-Mitte. 2000 Villa Gerl, private home, Berlin. 2002 Hochhaus am Deutschherrnufer, apartment building, Frankfurt am Main

**Recent Publications** *Hans Kollhoff,* Barcelona 1991. Hans Kollhoff and Fritz Neumeyer, *Der Friedrichswerder – Die Bauakademie: Ein retroaktives Manifest für die Arbeitsgemeinschaft Friedrichswerder,* 1992. Hans Kollhoff and Helga Timmermann, *Berliner Projekte,* Antwerp 1994. Max Hetzler, *Hans Kollhoff,* Berlin 1995. Annegret Burg, *Architekten Kollhoff und Timmermann: Beispiele,* Basel 1998. Martin Kieren, *Hans Kollhoff: Werke und Bauten 1976–2001,* Stuttgart 2002

**Contact**
Prof. Hans Kollhoff
Architekten Kollhoff und Timmermann
Kurfürstendamm 178–179
10707 Berlin
Tel.: 0049-30-8841850
Fax: 0049-30-88418596
buero@kollhoff.de
www.kollhoff.de

## Peter Kulka with Konstantin Pichler

**Peter Kulka** (Prof. Dipl. Architekt). 1937 Born in Dresden. 1958 Completed studies in engineering, concentration in architecture. 1964 Completed studies in architecture at the Hochschule für bildende und angewandte Kunst in Berlin-Weissensee. – Assistant to Hermann Henselmann at the Institut für Typenprojektierung, Berlin. 1965–68 Work at the office of Hans Scharoun, Berlin. Since 1969 Independent architect. 1970–79 Partner in the architects' partnership of Herzog, Köpke, Kulka, Siepmann and Töpper. 1977 Group exhibition at the Museum of Modern Art, New York. Since 1979 Established his own office in Cologne. 1986–92 University professor of Constructive Design at the RWTH, Aachen. Since 1991 Runs his own office in Dresden. Since 1996 Founding member of the Sächsische Akademie der Künste. – Member of the Berliner Akademie der Künste

**Konstantin Pichler** (Dipl.-Ing. Architekt). 1963 Born in Cologne. 1989 Completed studies in architecture at the FH Köln. Since 1990 Member of the staff at the Atelier Prof. Peter Kulka. 1997/98 Instructor of Architectural Design at the FH Köln

**Office** 1994 German Steel Construction Prize for the parliament building, state of Sachsen. 1995 Awarded the German Architecture Prize for the parliament building of Saxony. – Exhibition at the Mies van der Rohe Pavilion, Barcelona, Award for European Architecture. 1996 Awarded the Heinrich Tessenow Medal. – Exhibition of the Chemnitz Stadium project, Galerie Aedes East, Berlin. 2000 European Museum Award of the Year, recognition for the NS-Dokumentationszentrum, EL-DE-building, Cologne. –*Architektur im 20. Jahrhundert,* Deutsches Architektur Museum, Frankfurt am Main

**Major Building Projects** 1999 Parliament building of Saxony, Dresden, new buildings, renovation of and addition to the existing building, redesign of the parliament building square. 1997 Nazi documentation center in the EL-DE building Cologne. 1999 Galerie für Zeitgenössische Kunst, Leipzig. 1995 Chemnitz sports stadium 2002 (with Ulrich Königs). 2001 Haus der Stille – Temporary Monastery, Meschede. 2002 Concert Hall on Gendarmenmarkt, Berlin-Mitte, conversion and redesign of the audition hall and the foyer in the north wing. 2003 City rail station, Bayerischer Bahnhof, Leipzig. – Multimedia Center on Rotherbaumchaussee, 2. BA, Hamburg-Rothenbaum. – Education and training building for the Robert-Bosch GmbH, Heidehofstrasse, Stuttgart

**Recent Publications** *Peter Kulka: Bauten und Projekte 1990–95,* Cologne 1996. Andreas Denk and Josef Matzerath, *Die drei Dresdner Parlamente,* Eurasburg 2000

**Contact**
Peter Kulka Univ. Prof. Dipl. Architekt BDA
Neusser Strasse 27–29
50670 Köln
Tel.: 0049-221-9730400
Fax: 0049-221-7390819
atelier@peterkulka.de
www.peterkulka.de

## Lederer + Ragnarsdóttir + Oei

**Arno Lederer** (Prof. Dipl.–Ing.). 1947 Born in Stuttgart. 1966 High school diploma ("Abitur") in Stuttgart-Bad Cannstatt,. 1968–76 Studied architecture in Stuttgart and Vienna. 1976 Degree. 1977 Worked at the office of Ernst Gisel, Zurich. 1978 Worked at the office of BHO (Berger Hauser Oed), Tübingen. Since 1979 Independent architect. 1985–90 Professor of Constructive Planning and Design at the FH für Technik in Stuttgart. Since 1985 Office partnership with Jórunn Ragnarsdóttir. From 1992 Expansion of the office partnership to include Marc Oei. 1990 Appointed Professor of Architectural Engineering and Design I at the Universität Karlsruhe. Since 1997 Director, Chair of Building Theory, Faculty of Architecture, Universität Karlsruhe

**Jórunn Ragnarsdóttir** (Dipl.-Ing.). 1957 Born in Akureyri, Iceland. 1975 High school diploma in Reykjavik. 1976–82 Studied architecture in Stuttgart. 1982 Degree from the Universität Stuttgart. Since 1982 Freelance work for the office of Arno Lederer. Since 1985 Partner in the office partnership. 1990–92 Instructor at the Universität Stuttgart. 1999–2001 Design of several stage sets at the National and State Theater in Reykjavik

**Marc Oei** (Dipl.-Ing. [FH]). 1962 Born in Stuttgart. 1981 High school diploma ("Abitur") in Fellbach. 1984 1988 Studied architecture in Stuttgart. 1988 Degree from the Hochschule für Technik in Stuttgart. 1988–91 Employed by the office partnership of Lederer Ragnarsdóttir. Since 1992 Partner in the office partnership. 1993–96 Instructor at the Universität Karlsruhe. Since 1999 Instructor at the Hochschule für Technik in Stuttgart. 2001 Instructor at the Universität Stuttgart

**Office** 1997 Hugo-Häring Prize (BDA) for the EKZ office building with warehouse in Reutlingen. 2000 Hugo-Häring Prize (BDA) for the main administration building of the EVS (EnBW) in Stuttgart. 2000–02 *Lederer + Ragnarsdóttir + Oei.: Drinnen ist anders als draussen*, Galerie Aedes, Berlin; Architekturgalerie München; Architekturgalerie am Weissenhof, Stuttgart; Haus der Architektur in Dresden. 2001 German Architecture Prize (BDA), award for the school and gymnasium in Scharnhauser Park, Ostfildern. – Nominated for the Mies van der Rohe Award for Contemporary Architecture, Fundació Mies van der Rohe

Barcelona, for the school and gymnasium in Scharnhauser Park, Ostfildern

**Major Building Projects** 1991 Finance Office building with cafeteria, Reutlingen. 1997 Main administration building for the EVS (EnBW), Stuttgart. 1999 Katholische Akademie, Stuttgart-Hohenheim. 1999/2002 School and gymnasium in Scharnhauser Park, Ostfildern. 2000 Salem International College, Überlingen am Bodensee. 2001 Catholic parish center, St. Antonius, Stuttgart. Since 2001 Renovation and conversion of the Hessisches Staatstheater, Darmstadt. – Renovation and remodeling of the Helvetia insurance building, Frankfurt am Main. – Gustav-von-Schmoller Vocational School, Heilbronn

**Recent Publications** Arno Lederer and Jórunn Ragnarsdóttir, *Wohnen heute*, Stuttgart and Zurich 1992. Wolfgang Bachmann, ed., *Lederer Ragnarsdóttir Oei*, texts by Haila Ochs, Munich 1995. *Lederer + Ragnarsdóttir + Oei: Drinnen ist anders als draussen*, texts by Falk Jaeger and Hans-Jürgen Breuning, Berlin 2000. *Lederer + Ragnarsdóttir + Oei: Drinnen ist anders als draussen*, text by Winfried Nerdinger, Baunach 2001

**Contact**
Lederer + Ragnarsdóttir + Oei
Kornbergstrasse 36
70176 Stuttgart
Tel.: 0049-711-2255060
Fax: 0049-711-22550622

Lederer + Ragnarsdóttir + Oei
Schumannstrasse 3
76185 Karlsruhe
Tel.: 0049-721-5694667
Fax: 0049-721-5694669

mail@archlro.de
www.archlro.de

## Léon Wohlhage Wernik Architekten

**Hilde Léon** (Prof. Dipl.-Ing.). 1972–78 Studied architecture at the TU Berlin. 1978 Degree. 1979–81 DAAD scholarship to the University of Venice. Since 1987 Member of the BDA Berlin. 1990–95 Member of the academic staff of the Hochschule der Künste Berlin, Chair of Urban Design and Architecture, under Prof. A. Grazioli. Since 1996 Member of the Design Council of the city of Berlin. 1997–99 Interim professorship at the Hochschule für bildende Künste Hamburg. Since 2000 Member of the Design Council of the city of Salzburg. – Professor at the Universität Hannover. 2002 Commissioner for the German Pavilion at the Venice Biennale

**Konrad Wohlhage** (Dipl.-Ing.). 1975–78 Studied architecture at the TU München. 1978–83 Studied architecture at the TU Delft. 1983 Degree from the TU Delft. 1987–90 Member of the academic staff, Chair of Design and Architectural Engineering, at the TU Berlin. 1996–2000 Member of the Design Council of the city of Münster. Since 2000 Member of the Design Council of the city of Munich. – Member of the BDA Berlin and the Deutscher Werkbund

**Siegfried Wernik** (Dipl.-Ing.). 1972–78 Studied architecture at the RWTH Aachen. 1978 Degree. 1979–90 Associate partner in the office of Stirling, Wilford & Associates, Stuttgart/Berlin/London. 1991–94 Office partnership with Brands und Kolbe, Berlin. Since 1994 Collaboration with Hilde Léon and Konrad Wohlhage

**Office** 1983 Founded the office léonwohlhage in Berlin. Since 1994 Léon Wohlhage Wernik Architekten GmbH. 1988 *Denkmal oder Denkmodell: Projekte für die Zukunft Berlins*, Kunsthalle Berlin. –*Berlinmodell Industriekultur*, symposium and exhibition, Berlin. 1992 *Bauten und Projekte léonwohlhage*, Architekturgalerie Aedes, Berlin. 1994 Architecture Prize from the BDA and the Berlin Senate. 1995 Exhibition at the Fragnera Gallery of Architecture, Prague. –*Architekturmodelle*, Galerie Hetzler, Berlin/Düsseldorf. 1996 German Critics' Prize for Architecture. 1997 *Projekte für Berlin-Adlershof*, Galerie Aedes, Berlin. – Particpated in the International Biennial of Architecture and Urban Design in São Paulo. – Exhibition at the Galerie Kammer, Hamburg. – German Architecture Prize, honorable mention. – German Architecture Prize, Concrete Construction. 1998 Architecture Prize from the BDA and the Berlin Senate. 1999 *kunstbaukunst. Oberstufenzentrum Sozialversicherungen in Berlin-Köpenick*, Galerie Aedes, Berlin. –*Botschaften und Landesvertretungen*, Deutsches Architektur Zentrum, Berlin. – Architecture Prize from the BDA Hamburg. 2000 Exhibition at the Hamburg City Hall in conjunction with the "Hamburger Architektursommer." – Exhibition in conjunction with the German Festival in India, New Delhi. 2001 *Made in Berlin*, Nederlands Architectuur Instituut, Rotterdam. – *Just Arrived: Indien und Bremen in Berlin*, Galerie Aedes, Berlin

**Major Building Projects** 1998 Upper secondary school center for social insurance, Berlin-Köpenick. 1999 State offices of the Free Hanseatic City of Bremen, Berlin-Tiergarten. – Administration building on Halenseestrasse, Berlin-Wilmersdorf. 2001 Embassy building of the Republic of India, Berlin-Tiergarten. 2002 New city district center in Stuttgart-Vaihingen: Schwaben-Galerie, office building, hotel, auditorium, adult education center, market hall and shopping center with underground garage on the former grounds of the Schwaben

Brewery. – Historical Borsig grounds, restoration of the former administrative building of the Borsig AG (listed historical monument) and extension, with office and residential buildings, Berlin. 2003 Schillerhaus, office and commercial building with apartments, Frankfurt am Main. 2004 Haus Dönhoff, renovation and vertical extension of the building and planning for an adjacent residential and commercial building, Berlin-Mitte

**Recent Publications** Friederike Schneider, ed., *léonwohlhage: Bauten und Projekte 1987–1997*, Basel et al. 1997. *léonwohlhage: Projekte des Büros 1987–1997*, Zurich 1997. *"kunstbaukunst": Oberstufenzentrum Berlin Köpenick*, Berlin 1999. *Just Arrived: Indien und Bremen in Berlin*, Berlin 2001

**Contact**
Léon Wohlhage Wernik Architekten GmbH
Windscheidstrasse 18
10627 Berlin
Tel.: 0049-30-3276000
Fax: 0049-30-32760060
post@leonwohlhagewernik.de
www.leonwohlhagewernik.de

## Mahler Günster Fuchs Architekten

**Klaus Mahler** (Prof. Dipl.-Ing.). 1940 Born in Stuttgart. Studied architecture at the TU Stuttgart. 1968 Degree from the TU Stuttgart. 1975–81 Professor at the FH Köln. 1981–2001 Professor at the Universität Kaiserslautern

**Armin Günster** (Dipl.-Ing.). 1959 Born in Weitersburg. 1978 High school diploma ("Abitur") in Bendorf. 1979–86 Studied architecture in Kaiserslautern and Darmstadt. 1986 Degree from the Universität Kaiserslautern. Since 1989 Independent architect

**Hartmut Fuchs** (Prof. Dipl.–Ing.). 1952 Born in Berlin. 1971 High school diploma ("Abitur") in Bendorf in Ludwigsburg. 1971–78 Studied architecture in Stuttgart. Since 1981 Independent architect. Since 2000 Professor at the FH Nürnberg

**Office** 1995 German Architecture Prize, award and honorable mention. 1996 BDA Prize, Baden-Württemberg, two awards. 1997 German Architecture Prize, award. 1999 German Architecture Prize, award. 2001 German Architecture Prize, award

**Major Building Projects** 1990 Kunstakademie am Weissenhof, Stuttgart. 1994 Trade school, Karlsruhe-Durlach. 1996 Mörikegymnasium (upper secondary school), Ludwigsburg. – Senior citizens' housing complex in Neuenbürg. 1998 Park-

ing garage at the Bollwerksturm, Heilbronn. 1998 Elementary and middle school, Munich-Riem. 1999 Finance Office building, Schwarzenberg. 2001 Fachhochschule, Wiesbaden. 2004 German Embassy building, Tokyo

**Contact**
Mahler Günster Fuchs Architekten
Gutenbergstrasse 94a
70197 Stuttgart
Tel.: 0049-711-50530680
Fax: 0049-711-6159443
info@mgf-architekten.de

## Melchior Eckey Rommel Architekten AG

**Andrea Melchior** (Dipl.-Ing. Freier Architekt). 1961 Born in Heilbronn am Neckar. 1981–88 Studied architecture at the TU Berlin and TH Darmstadt. 1988 Degree from the TH Darmstadt. 1989/90 Employed in the architects' office of Lion, Paris. 1990–92 Employed in the architects' office of Heinle, Wischer und Partner, Stuttgart. Since 1992 Office partnership with Ulrich Eckey in Stuttgart
**Ulrich Eckey** (Dipl.-Ing. Freier Architekt). 1960 Born in Münster. 1981–88 Studied architecture at the TU Berlin and the TH Darmstadt. 1989 Degree from the TH Darmstadt. 1989/90 Worked in the office of Schürmann, Cologne. 1990–94 Worked in the office of Mahler Gumpp Schuster, Stuttgart. Since 1992 Office partnership with Andrea Melchior in Stuttgart. 1995–2000 Member of the academic staff of the Institut für Baukonstruktion und Entwerfen, Prof. Kramm, Universität TH Karlsruhe
**Marcus Rommel** (Dipl. Ing. Freier Architekt). 1965 Born in Trier. 1985–93 Studied architecture at the TU Kaiserslautern and the TH Darmstadt. 1994 Degree from the TH Darmstadt. – Course and workshop at the Internationale Solarbauschule Vorarlberg. 1992–95 Worked for various architects' offices in Darmstadt and Stuttgart. Since 1995 Independent architect in Stuttgart und Trier. 1997–2000 Project partnership with Melchior Eckey Rommel Architekten for realization of the Ochsenanger housing complex in Bamberg. 2000 BDA Prize for the region of Franconia for the Ochsenanger housing development in Bamberg, award. 2002 Special award, Clients' Prize for "High Quality – Reasonable Costs"
**Major Building Projects Melchior Eckey Architekten** 1992 Haus Vianden, apartment house with office, Odenwald. 1991/94 Presentation of EUROPAN 2 Halberstadt-Düsterngraben, project and development plan 1993/94, in collaboration with the offices of von Bassewitz und Partner, Hamburg, and Metrix, Rotterdam. 1994 Trade fair stand for Vianden Marketing Service, Frankfurt am Main. 1999 Housing complex at the Schopperplätzen in Neu-Ulm, 59 barrier-free apartments in the social housing sector

**Major Building Projects Marcus Rommel Architekten** 1996 Vertical extension of an apartment building, energy-efficient, minimum energy building, wood construction, Trier. 2003 Housing complex in Munich-Trudering. – Vacation home Pertzel, St. Gilgen am Wolfgangsee. 2005 Redesign of the Römerstrasse Leonberg, urban redesign of the center of the large county seat of Leonberg in multiple sections, competition 2001 (1st prize)
**Major Building Projects Melchior Eckey Rommel Architekten AG** 2000 Ochsenanger housing complex, Bamberg

**Contact**
Melchior & Eckey Architekten
Hinterer Holzweg 48
73733 Esslingen
Tel.: 0049-711-8179989
Fax: 0049-711-3277624
Melchior-Eckey@t-online.de

Marcus Rommel Architekten
Rotebühlstrasse 89/2
70178 Stuttgart
Tel.: 0049-711-2362808
Fax: 0049-711-2362810
mail@marcus-rommel-architekten.de
www.marcus-rommel-architekten.de

## Florian Nagler Architekten

**Florian Nagler** (Dipl.-Ing.). 1967 Born in Munich. 1986 High school diploma ("Abitur") in Bad Tölz. 1987 Studied art history and Bavarian history in Munich. 1987–89 Training as a carpenter in Egling. 1989–94 Studied architecture at the Universität Kaiserslautern, member of the academic staff, Chairs of Prof. Ermel and Prof. Eissler. 1991 Practical internship at the office of Auer + Weber. 1993 Practical internship at the office of Otto Steidle. 1994–97 Freelance work at the office of Mahler Gumpp Schuster (since 1996 Mahler Günster Fuchs), Stuttgart. 1996–99 Independent architect with offices in Stuttgart. Since 1999 Office in Munich
**Barbara Nagler** (Dipl.-Ing.). 1969 Born in Bayreuth. 1988 High school diploma ("Abitur") in Bayreuth. 1988/89 Studied mathematics and physics in Regensburg. 1989–95 Studied architecture at the Universität Kaiserslautern. 1993 Practical internship at the office of Utz-Peter Strehle. 1995/96 Freelance work at the office of Schlude Ströhle. 1996/97 Freelance work at the office of Knoche Gumpp. 1997–2000 Freelance work at the office of Florian Nagler. Since 2001 Partner in the office of Florian Nagler Architekten

**Office** 2000 Balthasar Neumann Prize. 2001 Mies van der Rohe Award, emerging architect special mention. – German Architecture Prize, honorable mention. – Ligna + Award
**Major Building Projects** 1997/98 German Pavilion, Expo 2000, Hanover, competition (1st prize), not realized. 1999 Distribution center, Bobingen. 2001 Lang-Kröll Residence and Studio, Gleissenberg. – Fiedler Residence, Penzberg. 2003 Data facility, Munich-Riem. 2004 FH Weihenstephan, Freising. – Urban design expansion, southwest Pfullingen. 2005 Church center, Munich-Riem
**Recent Publications** *Deutsche Bauzeitung*, special issue (Balthasar Neumann Prize), June 2000
**Contact**
Florian Nagler Architekten
Marsopstrasse 8
81245 Munich
Tel.: 0049-89-8200510
Fax: 0049-89-83928743
info@nagler-architekten.de

## Ortner & Ortner Baukunst

**Laurids Ortner** (Prof. Dipl.-Ing.). 1941 Born in Linz. 1959–65 Studied architecture at the TU Wien. 1967 Cofounder of the architects' and artists' group Haus-Rucker-Co in Vienna. 1970–87 Studio Haus-Rucker-Co in Düsseldorf with Günter Zamp Kelp and Manfred Ortner. 1976–87 Professor at the Hochschule für Künstlerische und Industrielle Gestaltung in Linz. Since 1987 Professor of Architecture at the Staatliche Kunstakademie Düsseldorf
**Manfred Ortner** (Prof. Mag. art.). 1943 Born in Linz. 1961–67 Studied painting and art education at the Akademie der bildenden Künste Wien and history at the Universität Wien, degree: M.A. 1966–71 Art eduction instructor. 1971–87 Studio Haus-Rucker-Co in Düsseldorf with Laurids Ortner and Günter Zamp Kelp. 1993 Member of the Architects' Chambers of North Rhein-Westphalia, Berlin and Brandenburg. Since 1994 Professor of Design, Faculty of Architecture, FH Potsdam
**Office** 1987 Founded the architects' partnership of Ortner Architekten in Düsseldorf. Since 1990 Ortner & Ortner Baukunst GmbH in Vienna and Linz. 1992 Berlin Art Prize for Architecture. 1993 *Haus-Rucker-Co*, Architekturmuseum Basel. 1993 *Ortner & Ortner Baukunst*, Museum Francisco-Carolinum, Linz. Since 1994 Architects' office "Ortner & Ortner Baukunst," Berlin. 1994 *Ortner & Ortner Baukunst*, Galerie Aedes, Berlin. 1995 *Europäische Architektur des 20. Jahrhunderts. Österreich*, Deutsches Architektur Museum, Frankfurt am Main. – *Light Construction*, Museum of Modern Art, New York. 1996 *Kunst aus Österreich 1896–1996*, Kunst- und Ausstellungshalle der Bundesrepublik Deutschland, Bonn. – *Light Construction*, MACBA, Barcelona. –

*Gifts to Philip Johnson*, Museum of Modern Art, New York. 1998 Culture Prize of the State of Upper Austria for Architecture. – BDA Berlin Architecture Prize, award. 1998/99 *3 Bauten für Europäische Kultur*, Europäisches Design Depot, Klagenfurt. 1999 *Das Wiener Museumsquartier und andere spannende Geschichten*, Architektur Zentrum Wien. 2000 *Living Bridges*, NRW-Forum Kultur und Wirtschaft, Düsseldorf. – *Radical Architecture*, Museum für Angewandte Kunst, Cologne. 2002 Architecture Prize from the city of Vienna
**Major Building Projects** 1999 ARD Capital Studio, Berlin. 2001 Vienna Museum district. – Schiffbau, Kultur- und Werkzentrum des Schauspielhauses Zürich. 2003 Sächsische Landesbibliothek – Staats- und Universitätsbibliothek Dresden. 2004 Liliencarré Wiesbaden (urban entertainment center). 2001–2010 Campus Jungfernsee, technology part at Nedlitzer Kaserne, Potsdam
**Recent Publications** Heinrich Klotz, ed., *Haus-Rucker-Co 1967–1983*, Frankfurt am Main 1983. Dieter Bogner, ed., *Haus-Rucker-Co: Denkräume – Stadträume 1967–1992*, Klagenfurt 1992. *Ortner & Ortner. Baukunst*, Linz and Cologne 1993. *Ortner & Ortner: 2 Baukunstwerke*, Berlin 1994. Walter Hösel, ed., *Ortner & Ortner: 3 Bauten für Europäische Kultur*, Klagenfurt and Cologne 1998. *Ortner & Ortner: Wörterbuch der Baukunst*, Basel et al. 2001
**Contact**
Ortner & Ortner Baukunst
Gesellschaft von Architekten mbH
Rückerstrasse 4
10119 Berlin
Tel.: 0049-30-2848860
Fax: 0049-30-28488660
mail@ortner-ortner.com
www.ortner-ortner.com

Ortner & Ortner Baukunst
Ziviltechniker Gesellschaft mbH
Döblergasse 4
A-1070 Vienna
Tel.: 0043-1-5232812
Fax: 0043-1-5232812-28
baukunst@ortner.at
www.ortner-ortner.com

## André Poitiers

**André Poitiers** (Architekt Stadtplaner BDA RIBA). 1959 Born in Hamburg. 1979–81 Training as a cabinetmaker, Asmus Yachtwerft, Glückstadt. 1981–83 Training as a bank clerk, Hamburger Sparkasse, Hamburg. 1983–90 Studied architecture at the TU Braunschweig.

1991/92 Worked at the office of Sir Norman Foster, London. 1993/94 Instructor of Design, TU Braunschweig. Since 1995 Freelance architect in Hamburg. 1996 Became member of the BDA. 2000 Became member of the Royal Institute of British Architects. – Registration as an urban planner – First European Architects Forum, Venice

**Works, Competitions, Studies** 1994 Halstenbek Sports Arena, commissioned expert appraisal, realization currently in progress. – Lüdemann Park, apartment building and sports arena, urban development realization competition (1st prize). 1997 Parish center for the Johanniskirche, Hamburg, realization competition (1st prize). 1998 Doughnut, party headquarters of Bündnis 90/Die Grünen, project study. 2001 Haus der Gegenwart, international architectural competition (1st prize). 2002 42 Homes, invitational workshop and realization project, Switzerland. – Main administration building for the Süddeutscher Verlag, Munich, restricted realization competition, purchase

**Recent Publications** Kaye Geipel, *André Poitiers: 4 Shops*, Munich 2001. Kristin Feireiss, *André Poitiers: Objects in the Territory*, Berlin 2001

**Contact**
André Poitiers Architekt BDA RIBA Stadtplaner
Grosser Burstah 36–38
Burstahhof
20457 Hamburg
Tel.: 0049-40-37519808
Fax: 0049-40-37519821
office@poitiers.de

Carsten Roth Architekt

**Carsten Roth Architekt** (Mag. arch, M. arch.). 1958 Born in Hamburg. 1977–80 Studied at the TU Braunschweig, predegree examination. 1980–85 Studied at the Akademie der bildenden Künste, Vienna. – Master Student of Architecture under Prof. Gustav Peichl, degree: Mag. arch. 1985/86 Fulbright Scholarship, Virginia Polytechnic Institute and State University, Blacksburg and Alexandria, Virginia, M. arch. Since 1987 Office of Carsten Roth Architekt. 1998/99 Guest professor at the Gesamthochschule Kassel, Department of Architecture, as interim C-4 Professor, Chair of Design and Architectural Engineering. 2002 Critics' Prize from the Verband der Deutschen Kritiker e. V.

**Major Building Projects** 1994 Revitalization of an automobile factory, Hamburg (BDA Hamburg Architecture Prize, 1996). 1996 Studio building, Hamburg (AIV Building of the Year 1996 and honorable mention for the German Architecture Prize, Concrete Construction, 1999). – Office and exhibition building, Siek (BDA Schleswig-Holstein Architecture Prize 2000). 1998 Office and laboratory building, Synopharm GmbH, Barsbüttel (BDA Hamburg Architecture Prize, 1999, Architecture Prize for Metal Roofs and Façades, 2000, honorable mention). – Printing facility and CD packaging center, Röbel (Architecture Prize from the West-Hyp-Stiftung for exemplary commercial buildings, 2000, honorable mention). 2000 Logistics and fulfillment center, Röbel. 2002 Conversion of commercial buildings into a media center, Hamburg

**Recent Publication** Klaus-Dieter Weiss, ed., *Junge Architekten in Deutschland*, Basel et al. 1998

**Contact**
Carsten Roth Architekt
Rentzelstrasse 10b
20146 Hamburg
Tel.: 0049-40-4117030
Fax: 0049-40-456815
info@carstenroth.com

sauerbruch hutton architekten

**Louisa Hutton** (BA [Hons], AA Dipl, RIBA, Architect). 1957 Born in Norwich, England. 1977–80 Studied architecture at Bristol University. 1980 First Class Honors Degree from Bristol University. 1985 Diploma from the Architectural Association, London. 1987–90 Instructor at Croydon College of Art and Unit Master at the Architectural Association, London. Guest lectures at numerous British and foreign universities

**Matthias Sauerbruch** (Prof. Dipl.-Ing. AA Dipl. ARB, Architect BDA). 1955 Born in Constance. 1977–84 Studied architecture at the Hochschule der Künste, Berlin, and the Architectural Association, London. 1985–90 Unit Master at the Architectural Association, London. 1995–2001 Professor at the TU Berlin. Since 2001 Professor at the Staatliche Akademie der Bildenden Künste Stuttgart. Guest lectures at numerous British and foreign universities

**Office** Since 1989 Architects' partnership of sauerbruch hutton architects in London. 1992 *Projekte 1989–1992*, Galerie Aedes, Berlin. 1992 *Stadtlandschaften: Berliner Arbeiten 1989–1992*, Architekturforum Zürich. Since 1993 Office of sauerbruch hutton architekten in Berlin. 1998 Erich Schelling Architecture Prize, Karlsruhe. – *Photonikzentrum Berlin Adlershof*, Architektur-Galerie am Weissenhof, Stuttgart. Since 1999 Partnership with Juan Lucas Young and Jens Ludloff. 1999–2001 *WYSIWYG*, Architectural Association, London; Galerie Aedes, Berlin; galeria ras, Barcelona; XXI Bienal Arquitectura, Santiago de Chile; La Galerie d'architecture, Paris. 2000 Architecture Prize, BDA Berlin. – *Auf dem Weg nach Dessau*, Federal Agency for the Environment – Expo 2000, Dessau. 2001 Mies van der Rohe Award, nomination

**Major Building Projects** 1999 GSW main administration building, Berlin-Kreuzberg. 1998 Photonikzentrum, Berlin-Adlershof. 2001 Experimental factory, Magdeburg. 2002 Biological research, Biberach. 2003 Fire station and police precinct 35 for the parliament and government district, Berlin-Tiergarten. – City Hall, Hennigsdorf. 2004 Federal Agency for the Environment, Dessau

**Recent Publications** *sauerbruch hutton architekten: Projekte 1989–1991*, Berlin 1992. *sauerbruch hutton: projekte 1990–1996*, Basel 1996. *Photonikzentrum Berlin*, Berlin 1998. *WYSIWYG*, London 1999. *Umweltbundesamt*, Dessau 2000. Matthias Sauerbruch and Louisa Hutton, *GSW Hauptverwaltung Berlin*, Baden 2000

**Contact**
sauerbruch hutton architekten
Lehrter Strasse 57
10557 Berlin
Tel.: 0049-30-3978210
Fax: 0049-30-39782130
office@sauerbruchhutton.de
www.sauerbruchhutton.de

Axel Schultes Architekten
Charlotte Frank, Axel Schultes,
Christoph Witt

**Axel Schultes** 1943 Born in Dresden. 1963–69 Studied in Berlin. 1972–91 Partnership with D. Bangert, B. Jansen, St. Scholz (BJSS). Since 1992 Partnership in own office with Charlotte Frank and Christoph Witt

**Charlotte Frank** 1959 Born in Kiel. 1979–84 Studied in Berlin. 1987–92 Collaboration with Axel Schultes (BJSS). Since 1992 Partnership with Axel Schultes and Christoph Witt

**Major Building Projects** 1985 Administration building for the Protestant Church, Hanover (BJSS). 1991 Ministry of Commerce and Technology, Wiesbaden (BJSS). 1992 Kunstmuseum Bonn (BJSS). 1998 Baumschulenweg Crematorium, Berlin. 2001 Haus Knauthe, office and apartment building, Leipziger Platz, Berlin. – Office of the Federal Chancellor, Berlin. Currently in progress: Subway station, Reichstag, Berlin. – SpreeSinus, office and commercial building with apartment tower, Holzmarktstrasse, Berlin

**Recent Publications** Charlotte Frank, ed., *Axel Schultes: Kunstmuseum Bonn*, Berlin 1994. *Axel Schultes, Charlotte Frank: Kanzleramt Berlin*, Stuttgart and London 2001

**Contact**
Axel Schultes Architekten
Lützowplatz 7
10785 Berlin
Tel.: 0049-30-2308880
Fax: 0049-30-23088888
asa@schultes-architekten.de
www.schultes-architekten.de

Werner Sobek

**Werner Sobek** (Prof. Dr.). 1953 Born in in Aalen, Württemberg. 1974–80 Studied architectural engineering and architecture at the Universität Stuttgart. 1980–86 Member of the academic staff in special research department SFB 64 "Broad-Spanned Surface Support Structures" at the Universität Stuttgart. 1983 Fazlur R. Khan Award from the Skidmore, Owings & Merrill Foundation, New York. 1984 Worked for Skidmore, Owings & Merrill, Chicago. 1987 Award of doctoral degree in engineering from Universität Stuttgart. 1987–91 Worked at the engineering office of Schlaich, Bergermann & Partner, Stuttgart. – Instructor of "Structural Framework Design," Department of Architectural Engineering, Universität Stuttgart. 1991–95 Professor at the Universität Hannover (successor to Bernd Tokarz) and Director of the Institut für Tragwerksentwurf und Bauweisenforschung. 1991 German Award for Architectural Engineering, honorable mention. 1992 Founded his own engineering office. Since 1995 Professor at the Universität Stuttgart (successor to Frei Otto). – Director of the Institut für Leichte Flächentragwerke and the Zentrallabor des Konstruktiven Ingenieurbaus. 1995 *Werner Sobek: Bauten und Projekte*, Galerie am Weissenhof, Stuttgart. 1998 DuPont Benedictus Award. – Design Award from the IFAI. 1999 Founded the design office 3e – Werner Sobek Exhibition & Entertainment Engineering. – *Werner Sobek. Bauten und Projekte*, Landtag Baden-Württemberg. – '*Archi-Neering.' Helmut Jahn und Werner Sobek*, Schloss Morsbroich. 2000 Appointed to a second professorship as successor to Prof. Dr. Jörg Schlaich. – Founded the Institut für Leichtbau, Entwerfen und Konstruieren (ILEK). – German Steel Construction Prize, award. 2000/01 Guest professor at the Universität Graz. 2001 DuPont Benedictus Award, Exceptional Merit. – CBC Merit Award Finalist

**Major Building Projects** 1994 Ecole Nationale d'Art Décoratif, Limoges, architects: LAB.F.AC., Paris. 1997 Center court roof of the Rothenbaum Stadium, Hamburg, architects: Schweger + Partner, Hamburg. 2000 Trade fair presentations of Audi AG, architects: Ingenhoven Overdiek und Partner, Düsseldorf. – Sony-Center Berlin, architects: Murphy/Jahn, Chicago. – Haus R 128, Stuttgart. 2001 Interbank Lima, architect: Hans Hollein, Vienna. 2002 Bangkok International Airport, architects: Murphy/Jahn, Chicago. – Generaldirektion Deutsche Post AG, Bonn, architects: Murphy/Jahn, Chicago. Since 2002 International Conference Center, Barcelona, architect: MAP Architects, Josep Lluis Matteo, Barcelona

**Recent Publications** Werner Sobek, *Auf pneumatisch gestützten Schalungen hergestellte Betonschalen*, dissertation, Universität Stuttgart, 1987. Werner Sobek, Walter Haase, and Jochen Köhnlein, *Smart*

*Materials*, research and documentation, Research Report 2/98 of the Institut für Leichte Flächentragwerke, Universität Stuttgart, Stuttgart 1998. Werner Blaser, *Art of Engineering: Werner Sobek – Ingenieurkunst*, Basel et al. 1999. Werner Blaser and Frank Heinlein, *R 128 by Werner Sobek: Bauen im 21. Jahrhundert/Architecture in the 21st Century*, Basel et al. 2001

**Contact**

Werner Sobek Ingenieure GmbH & Co. KG
Albstrasse 14
70597 Stuttgart
Tel.: 0049-711-767500
Fax: 0049-711-7675044
mail@wsi-stuttgart.com
www.wsi-stuttgart.com

## Walter Stamm-Teske

**Walter Stamm-Teske** (Prof. Mag. arch.). 1948 Born in Zurich. 1965–69 Training as a construction draftsman in the architects' office of Theo Hotz and M. P. Kollbrunner. Since 1970 Participation in some 20 architectural competitions, of which about 12 earned awards or resulted in purchases. 1970–76 Studied architecture and earned a degree from the Akademie der bildenden Künste Wien, Master School of Prof. E. A. Plischke and Prof. G. Peichl. Since 1976 Independent architect specialized in low-cost, interactive housing developments, monument renovation, planning and building as a general contractor. Since 1979 Numerous publications. Since 1981 Guest lectures and seminars throughout the world. 1981–83 Assistant at the ETH Zürich under Guest Professor Klaus Vogt (Fosco, Oppenheim). 1982 Adjunct Lecturer at the ETH Zürich. "Self-Designed Living – Self-Managed Building". 1984–1991 Initiator and cooperative member of the Amtshaus Kaiserstuhl, training center for children and youth. 1985–88 Senior assistant at the ETH Zürich under Prof. A. Henz, Chair of Architecture and Planning. 1986–89 Instructor at the Höhere Schule für Gestaltung Basel, Department of Architecture, Interior Architecture and Product Design. Since 1993 C4 Professor of Design and Housing Construction at the Bauhaus-Universität Weimar. 1995/96 Expert advisor to the Building Council of the city of Weimar. Since 1996 Member of the Design Council of Weimar. – Expo projekt "Neues Bauen am Horn," Weimar, designated representative of the Bauhaus-Universität Weimar. Since 2001 Dean of the Department of Architecture at the Bauhaus-Universität Weimar
**Recent Publications** *Preiswerter Wohnungsbau in Deutschland 1990–96*, Düsseldorf 1996. *Preiswerter Wohnungsbau in den Niederlanden*, Düsseldorf 1998. Walter

Stamm-Teske et al., eds., *Wohnhaus e. G. Weimar – Gründung und Neubau einer genossenschaftlichen Wohnsiedlung*, Weimar 1999. *Preiswerter Wohnungsbau in Österreich*, Düsseldorf 2001

**Contact**

Prof. Walter Stamm-Teske
Lessingstrasse 15
99425 Weimar
Tel.: 0049-3643-583175
Fax: 0049-3643-583174
walter.stamm-teske@archit.uni-weimar.com

## Wandel Hoefer Lorch + Hirsch

**Andrea Wandel** (Dipl.-Ing. Architektin BDA). 1963 Born in Saarbrücken. 1983–90 Studied architecture at the TU Kaiserslautern and the TH Darmstadt
**Hubertus Wandel** (Dipl.-Ing. Architekt BDA). 1926 Born in Meseritz. 1950–52 Studied at the Polytechnikum Friedberg. 1955–58 Studied architecture at the TH Aachen. 1961–86 Teaching appointments in the field of architectural design and construction materials at the FH des Saarlandes in Saarbrücken
**Rena Wandel Hoefer** (Dr. Dipl.-Ing. Architektin BDA). 1959 Born in Saarbrücken. 1978–85 Studied architecture at the TH Darmstadt. 1986 Research in Los Angeles. 1989 Doctoral dissertation on Richard Neutra under the supervision of Prof. Günter Behnisch, doctoral degree. Since 2001 Chairman of the City Building Council in Saarbrücken
**Andreas Hoefer** (Dipl.-Ing. Architekt BDA). 1955 Born in Hamburg. 1975–85 Studied architecture at the TU Berlin and the TH Darmstadt
**Wolfgang Lorch** (Prof. Dipl.-Ing. Architekt BDA). 1960 Born in Nürtingen am Neckar. 1983–90 Studied architecture at the TH Darmstadt and the ETSA Barcelona. Since 1999 State Chairman of the BDA Saar. Since 2001 Professor of Design and Architectural Design at the Hochschule für Technik, Stuttgart
**Nikolaus Hirsch** 1964 Born in Karlsruhe. 1984–90 Studied architecture at the TH Darmstadt. Since 2000 Unit Master at the Architectural Association, London
**Joint Awards/Exhibitions** 1998 BDA Prize Berlin. 2001 German Critics' Prize for Architecture. 2002 *Licht und Schatten*, Deutsches Architektur Museum, Frankfurt am Main
**Major Building Projects** 1982–94 Renovation and restoration of the Gothic Stiftskirche Saarbrücken-St. Arnual. 1996 Börneplatz, Frankfurt am Main (collaboration with Wandel Hoefer Lorch + Hirsch). 1998 Track 17 Berlin-Grunewald (collaboration with Wandel Hoefer Lorch + Hirsch). 1999 Landeszentralbank Saarbrücken. 2001 New Synagogue, Dresden. – Competition for St. Jakobsplatz Munich: Synagogue/Jewish Museum/Community Center (1st prize), realization currently in

progress. – Competition for the Spa Center on the Saarschleife (1st prize), realization currently in progress. – Vitrina administration building, Saarterrassen, Saarbrücken. – DB-Imm (Deutsche Bahn) administration building, Saarbrücken

**Contact**

Wandel Hoefer Lorch Architekten
Dolomitenweg 19
66119 Saarbrücken
Tel.: 0049-681-926550
Fax: 0049-681-9265595
info@wandel-hoefer-lorch.de

Nikolaus Hirsch
Kettenhofweg 113
60325 Frankfurt am Main
Tel.: 0049-69-749029
Fax: 0049-69-749028
nikolaushirsch@t-online.de

## Worschech Partner Architekten

**Claus D. Worschech** (Dr.-Ing. Architekt BDA). 1958 Born in Bad Lauchstädt. 1980–85 Studied architecture at the Hochschule für Architektur und Bauwesen Weimar. 1983–89 Participation in national and international design seminars and colloquia, author and co-author of learned articles on architecture. 1985 Degree. 1985–88 Research studies followed by award of a doctoral degree (Dr.-Ing.) in building finishing/design. 1988–90 Worked as an architect in the office of Thüringenplan, Erfurt (industrial building project planning). 1990 Founded the office of Dr. Ing. Worschech GmbH. 1991 Restructuring/establishment of the office of Worschech & Partner as Baukunst-Atelier, Erfurt. 1996–99 Instructor of Architectural History and Architectural Design at the FH Erfurt. – Membership on prize juries. Since 1999 Concentration on projects, competitions and artistic activity (painting, graphic arts, photography). 2001 "Talking Timbuktu," in collaboration with Susanne Worschech
**Laszlo Novotny** (Dipl.-Ing. Architekt). 1963 Born in Budapest, Hungary. 1982–87 Studied at the Hochschule für Architektur und Bauwesen Weimar. 1987 Degree. 1987/88 Worked at the project planning office of PTV, Pecs, Hungary. 1988–90 Worked at the architects' office of Franzmair, Salzburg, Austria. 1990–93 Worked at the architects' office of Büro Worschech & Partner, Erfurt. 1995–98 Instructor under Prof. Salzmann at the Hochschule für Architektur und Bauwesen in Weimar. 1993 Named a partner in the office of Worschech & Partner

**Volker Müller** (Dipl.-Ing. Stadtplaner). 1958 Born in Erfurt. 1980–85 Studied architectural engineering at the Hochschule für Architektur und Bauwesen. Weimar. 1985 Degree. 1985–90 Worked as a planning specialist in the Kombinat FLEIKO Erfurt, preparation and realization of investments. Since 1990 Worked at the office of Dr.-Ing. Worschech GmbH, Erfurt. 1993 Named partner in the office of Worschech & Partner. Since 1999 Concentration on city planning work and project management
**Ronald Holz** (Dipl.-Ing. FH). 1956 Born in Hohensaaten. 1987–90 Studied at the Ingenieurschule für Bauwesen Berlin. 1980 Degree. 1980–84 Worked as a construction supervisor in the Kombinat Wohnungs- und Gesellschaftsbau Frankfurt an der Oder. 1984–90 Director, Department of Value Preservation, city of Erfurt. Since 1990 Worked at the office of Dr.-Ing. Worschech GmbH. 1997 Named partner in the office of Worschech & Partner
**Major Building Projects** 1999 European Youth Meeting and Education Center, Weimar. – Office of the State of Thuringia, Berlin. 2001 City administration, Erfurt, new building and renovation. – Redesign of the railway station square, Nordhausen. 2002 Wohnscheibe Töpferstrasse, Nordhausen, modernization. 2003 Vocational Academy of Thuringia, Schloss Tinz, Gera. 2004 Thuringian State Office for Food Safety and Consumer Protection, Bad Langensalza. – Universitätsklinikum Jena, new building, 1st building phase, clinic and laboratory center. 2005 Angermuseum, Erfurt, renovation and new south wing

**Contact**

Worschech Partner Architekten
Fischersand 50
99084 Erfurt
Tel.: 0049-361-590820
Fax: 0049-361-5908212
info@atelier-worschech.de
www.atelier-worschech.de

## Zamp Kelp and Julius Krauss, Arno Brandlhuber

**Günter Zamp Kelp** (Univ. Prof., Architekt BDA, Dipl.-Ing., Stadtplaner). 1941 Born in Bistritz, Romania. 1959–67 Studied architecture at the TU Wien. 1967–69 Assistant to the Chair of Building Theory and Design 2, TU Wien, Prof. Dr. Karl Schwanzer. 1967 Founding member of the architects' and artists' group Haus-Rucker-Co in Vienna. 1970 Moved to Düsseldorf. – Joined the Architects' Chamber of North Rhein-Westphalia. 1971/72 Establishment of a Haus Rucker studio in New York. 1981 Guest professor at Cornell University, Ithaca, School of Architecture. – Guest professor at the Hochschule der Künste Berlin, Department of Design. 1987 Joined the Architects' Chamber of Berlin. – Opened his own studio in Düsseldorf. 1988 Guest professor at the Städelsche Kunstschule

Frankfurt, Department of Architecture. – University professor for building planning and spatial design at the Hochschule der Künste Berlin. 1993 Director, Department of Building Planning, Spatial Design, and Communication Engineering at the Hochschule der Künste Berlin. 1996 Guest professor at the TU Wien, Department of Architecture. 1997 German Architecture Prize, Concrete Construction. 1998 Member of the Institut für Metropole, Architektur, Design. – Architecture Prize, state of North Rhein-Westphalia. 2001 Member of the Design Council, Linz. 2002 Instructor of the architecture course, Internationale Sommerakademie, Salzburg

**Julius Krauss** (Dipl.-Ing. Architekt und Städtebauarchitekt). 1958 Born in Munich. 1979–89 Studied architecture at the TU Darmstadt. Since 1993 Architects' office in Darmstadt, concentration in architecture, architectural theory, and CAD systems. 1994/95 Project partnership with Zamp Kelp and Arno Brandlhuber

**Arno Brandlhuber** (Dipl.-Ing. Architekt, Stadtplaner). 1964 Born in Wasserlos. 1984–1992 Studied architecture/urban design at the TH Darmstadt, degree. 1988 Guest student at the Hochschule für Gestaltung, Darmstadt. 1989/90 Erasmus Scholarship, Università degli Studi di Firenze. Since 1993 Work as an independent architect. 1994–96 Project partnership with Zamp Kelp and Julius Krauss [1]. 1995/96 Brandlhuber architects' office [2]. 1996–2000 Instructor at the Bergische Universität Gesamthochschule Wuppertal. 1996–2001 Büro b & k+, Brandlhuber & Kniess + Partner [3]; b & k + b, m [4]; b & k + r [5]. Since 1999 + plattform, independent research platform. 1999 Instructor for the Semaine Internationale, Ecole d'architecture de Nancy. 2000 Interim professor of Elementary Architecture, Bergische Universität Gesamthochschule Wuppertal. Since 2001 b & k+ brandlhuber gmbh & co. kg (Managing Directors: Arno Brandlhuber and Martin Kraushaar; Björn Martenson, Markus Emde) [6]
Awards: 1997 German Architecture Prize, Concrete Construction. – BDA award for the Neanderthal Museum [1]. 1998 "Förderpreis" of the state of North Rhein-Westphalia [2]. – Architecture Prize for Exemplary Commercial Buildings for ≥2,56m [2]. – Architecture Prize, state of North Rhein-Westphalia for the Neanderthal Museum [2]. 2000 Cologne Architecture Prize for ≥2,56m, Kölner Brett [2] and Geisselstrasse [3]. – Wüstenrot Prize, award for Kölner Brett [2]. – Prix Rhenan, award for Geisselstrasse [3]. – Architecture Prize, Future Housing, for Kölner Brett [2]. – Architecture Prize, Future Housing, award for Geisselstrase [3]. 2001 German Architecture Prize, award for Geisselstrasse [3]. – Architecture Prize, state of North Rhein-Westphalia for Geisselstrasse [3]. – Clients' Prize 2002 (BDA, DST, GdW) for Stavenhof [2]. 2002 Coredesign, Architecture for ≥2,56m [2]

**Major Building Projects Günter Zamp Kelp** 1965 "Architekturtrainer," project for UIA, Paris 1965. 1972 "Oase Nr. 7," Documenta 5, Kassel, under the auspices of Haus-Rucker-Co. 1977 "Rahmenbau," Documenta 6, Kassel, under the auspices of Haus-Rucker-Co. 1996 Neanderthal Museum, Mettmann, with Julius Krauss and Arno Brandlhuber. 2000 "Jahrtausendblick/Steinzeichen Steinbergen," Rinteln
**Julius Krauss** 1996 Neanderthal Museum, Mettmann, with Günter Zamp Kelp and Arno Brandlhuber
**Arno Brandlhuber** 1996 Neanderthal Museum, Mettmann [1]. 1997 ≥2,56m, Eigelstein 1, Cologne [2, 3]. – Kölner Brett, Cologne [3]. 2000 Geisselstrasse, Cologne [4]. – Vaalser Quartier, Aachen [5]. – Stavenhof, Cologne [3]. Since 2000 Pasteurstrasse, Cologne [6]. Since 2001 Vulkan, Lichtstraße, Cologne [6]. Since 2002 DLR, Stuttgart [6]

**Recent Publications Günter Zamp Kelp**
Heinrich Klotz, ed., *Haus-Rucker-Co 1967–83* (publications of the Deutsches Architektur Museum Frankfurt), Braunschweig 1984. Diether Bogner, ed., *Haus-Rucker-Co: Denkräume – Stadträume*, Klagenfurt 1992. Heinrich Klotz, ed., *Architektur und Medialität: Bauten und Projekte*, 1990. Zamp Kelp, Julius Krauss, and Arno Brandlhuber, *Neanderthal Museum*, Berlin 1996. *Mediale Aureolen für die Stadt: Zamp Kelp Projekte 1987–96*, Berlin 1996. Torsten Schmiedekrecht, *Zamp Kelp: Expanding Space* (Architectural Monographs, 54), Wiley Academy, London 2000
**Julius Krauss** Zamp Kelp, Julius Krauss, and Arno Brandlhuber, *Neanderthal Museum*, Berlin 1996
**Arno Brandlhuber** Angelika Schnell, ed., *Junge Architekten in Deutschland*, Basel et al. 2000. *In Vitro Landscape*, Cologne 1999. *Political Landscape*, Cologne 2001. Actar, ed., *Verb 1*, Barcelona 2001. Bart Lootsma, ed., *Index-01: Werkbuch b & k+*, Cologne 2002

**Contact**
Zamp Kelp
Spanische Allee 70
14129 Berlin
Tel.: 0049-30-80499919
Fax: 0049-30-80499955
zamp-kelp@t-online.de
www.zampkelp.com

Julius Krauss
Karlstrasse 64
64285 Darmstadt
Tel.: 0049-6151-47357
Fax: 0049-6151-423738
feliz@hrzpub.tu-darmstadt.de

Arno Brandlhuber
b & k+ brandlhuber gmbh & co. kg
Tel.: 0049-221-546940
Fax: 0049-221-5469429
mail@brandlhuber.com
www.brandlhuber.com

## Günter Behnisch

**Günter Behnisch** (Prof. Dr. E. h., Dipl.-Ing. Architekt BDA). 1922 Born in Dresden, raised in Dresden and Chemnitz, married to Johanna Behnisch, née Fink, three children. 1928–34 Elementary school and Dürerschule in Dresden. 1936 His family moved to Chemnitz. 1936–39 Deutsche Oberschule in Chemnitz. From 1939 Sailor in the German Navy. 1945–47 Prisoner of war in England. 1947–51 Studies at the TH Stuttgart, degree of Dipl.-Ing. 1951/52 Work under Prof. Rolf Gutbrod. 1952 Founded his own firm. 1966 Founded Behnisch & Partners, partnership with Fritz Auer, Winfried Büxel, Erhard Tränkner, Karlheinz Weber, Manfred Sabatke (from 1970). 1979 Founded Behnisch & Partners, Behnisch, Büxel, Sabatke, Tränkner. 1967 Professor of Design, Industrial Architecture and Construction Design. – Director of the Institut für Baunormung at the TH Darmstadt. 1982 Appointment to the Akademie der Künste in Berlin. 1984 Dr. E. h. from the Universität Stuttgart. 1987 Emeritus. 1991 Professor at the International Academy of Architecture, Sofia. 1992 Honorary member of the Royal Incorporation of Architects in Scotland, Edinburgh. – Awarded Médaille d'or by the Académie d'Architecture, Paris. – Award of Merit from the International Olympic Committee for Special Achievements in the Field of Sports and Architecture. 1993 Hans Molfenter Prize from the State Capital of Stuttgart for special artistic achievement. 1994 Heinrich-Hertz professorship at the TU Karlsruhe. – Member of the International Academy of Architecture, Sofia. Award of Merit from the Lithuanian Architects' Federation, Vilnius. 1995 Honorary member of the Royal Institute of British Architects, London. 1996 Founding member of the Sächsische Akademie der Künste. 1997 Order of Merit from the Federal Republic of Germany. 1998 Fritz Schumacher Prize awarded by the Alfred Toepfer Stiftung F.V.S. 1999 Member of the Akademie der Künste Bayern. 2001 Wolfgang Hirsch Award from the Architektenkammer Rheinland-Pfalz. 2002 International Architectural Culture Festival Honorable Mention, Busan, Korea

**Recent Publications** Johann-Karl Schmitt and Ursula Zeller, eds., *Behnisch und Partner: Bauten 1952–1992*, Stuttgart 1992. Behnisch & Partner, eds., *Bauten und Projekte 1987–1997*, Stuttgart 1996. Dominique Gauzin-Müller, *Behnisch & Partner: 50 Jahre Architektur*, Berlin 1997. Günter Behnisch, *Der Pariser Platz: Die Akademie der Künste*, Berlin 1997. Peter Blundell Jones, *Günter Behnisch*, Basel et al. 2000

**Contact**
Behnisch & Partner
Architekten
Gorch-Fock-Strasse 30
70619 Stuttgart
Tel.: 0049-711-47 65 60
Fax: 0049-711-476 56 56
bp@behnisch.com
www.behnisch.com

Behnisch, Behnisch & Partner
Christophstrasse 6
70178 Stuttgart
Tel.: 0049-711-60 77 20
Fax: 0049-711-607 72 99
buero@behnisch.com

## Heinz Bienefeld

**Heinz Bienefeld** (Architekt BDA). 1926 Born in Krefeld. 1932–43 Schooling. 1943–48 Labor service, military service, confinement as a prisoner of war. 1948 Accepted into the course for Ecclesiastical and Secular Architecture at the Kölner Werkschule under the direction of Prof. Dominikus Böhm. 1952 Appointment as Master Student. 1952–54 Assistant to Dominikus Böhm. 1954 Travel in the United States, made possible by invitations from American architects. 1955–58 Employed by Gottfried Böhm. 1958–63 Employed by Emil Steffann. 1963–95 Self-employed as a freelance architect. 1975 Kölner Architekturpreis for the St. Andreas Youth Home, Wesseling. 1979 Award from the AK Rheinland-Pfalz for St. Willbrord Catholic parish church, Waldweiler. 1980 Kölner Architekturpreis for the Stupp Residence. 1984 Substitute for Prof. Georg Solms, Universität Gesamthochschule Wuppertal. 1985 Kölner Architekturpreis for the Schütte Residence. – BDA award from the State of North Rhine-Westphalia for urban renewal. 1986/87 Adjunct instructor at the FH Trier, winter/summer terms. 1995 Died in Wiesbaden. 1996 Posthumous award of the "Grosser Preis" of the BDA. 1997 BDA Architecture Prize from the State of Rhineland-Palatine

**Recent Publications** Manfred Speidel and Sebastian Legge, eds., *Heinz Bienefeld: Bauten und Projekte*, Cologne 1991. Ulrich Weisner, ed., *Neue Architektur im Detail: Heinz Bienefeld, Gottfried Böhm, Karljosef Schattner*, Bielefeld 1992. Wolfgang Voigt, ed., *Die Architektur von Heinz Bienefeld (1926–1995)*, Tübingen and Berlin 1999

**Contact**
Architekturbüro Bienefeld
Essiger Strasse 37
53913 Odendorf
Tel.: 0049-2255-83 78
Fax: 0049-2255-40 92
mail@architekturbuero-bienefeld.de
www.architekturbuero-bienefeld.de

## Gottfried Böhm

**Gottfried Böhm** (Prof. Dipl.-Ing. Architekt BDA). 1920 Born in Offenbach, the youngest of three sons of architect Dominikus Böhm and his wife Maria, née Scheiber. 1939 High school diploma ("Abitur") from the

Apostel-Gymnasium in Cologne. 1938–42 Military service. 1942–47 Studies in architecture and sculpture at the TH München under Adolf Abel, Hans Döllgast, Robert Vorhoelzer, and others; studies in sculpture at the Akademie der Bildenden Künste München under Josef Henselmann and others. 1948 Married to Elisabeth Böhm, née Haggenmüller, Dipl.-Ing., architect, four sons: Stephan, Markus, Peter, Paul. – Worked for his father Dominikus Böhm, projects in Cologne. 1950 Employed by Rudolf Schwarz, Wiederaufbaugesellschaft der Stadt Köln. 1951 Employed in the architects' firm Caetejan Baumann in New York. 1952 Collaboration with his father until his father's death in 1955. 1953 Period of work in Brazil. 1955 Assumes direction of his father's firm. 1963–85 Professor of Urban Planning and Industrial Architecture, RWTH Aachen. Since 1968 Member of the Akademie der Künste in Berlin. 1975 Awarded the "Grosser Preis" of the BDA, Bonn. Since 1976 Member of the Deutsche Akademie für Städtebau und Landesplanung, Berlin. 1982 Grande Médaille d'Or de l'Académie d'Architecture, Paris. – Honorary Fellow of AIA, USA. 1983 Member of the Académie d'Architecture, Paris. 1983/86 Adjunct instructor at the Massachusetts Institute of Technology, Cambridge. 1985 Adjunct instructor at the University of Pennsylvania, Philadelphia. – Dr. h. c. from the TU München. – Fritz Schumacher Prize, Hamburg. – Cret Chair Prize of the University of Pennsylvania. 1986 Member of the Academia Pontificia ad Pantheon, Roma. – Pritzker Architecture Prize. – Taught at Washington University, St. Louis

**Recent Publications** Ulrich Weisner, ed., *Neue Architektur im Detail: Heinz Bienefeld, Gottfried Böhm, Karljosef Schattner*, Bielefeld 1992. Wolfgang Pehnt, *Gottfried Böhm*, Basel et al. 1999. Gottfried Böhm, ed., *Gottfried Böhm: Bauten und Projekte – Auszug aus den Jahren 1985–2000*, Tübingen and Berlin 2000. Elisabeth Böhm, ed., *Gottfried Böhm*, Tübingen and Berlin 2001

**Contact**
Architekturbüro Böhm
Auf dem Römerberg 25
50968 Köln-Marienburg
Tel.: 0049-221-9 37 01 50
Fax: 0049-221-37 17 09
buero-boehm@netcologne.de

## von Gerkan, Marg and Partners

**Meinhard von Gerkan** (Prof. Dipl.-Ing. Architekt BDA). 1935 Born in Riga (now Latvia). 1939 Family moved to Poznan. 1942–53 Father killed on the eastern front; family fled, mother died; raised by foster parents; completed high school ("Abitur") at night school. 1954 Studies in physics and law at the Europa-Kolleg, Hamburg (three semesters). 1956 Studies in architecture in Berlin and Braunschweig. 1964 Degree in architecture. Since 1965 Free-

lance architect in partnership with Volkwin Marg. – Numerous prizes and successful competiton entries. – Major building contracts, jury member and expert assessor. Member of the BDA. Member of the Executive Board of the Hamburgische Architektenkammer. 1972 Appointment to the Freie Akademie der Künste in Hamburg. 1974 Appointment to the TU Braunschweig as Professor of Design (Section A) and Director of the Institut für Baugestaltung (Section A). 1982 Appointment to the Curatorial Committee of the Jürgen-Ponto-Stiftung, Frankfurt am Main. 1988 Guest professor at Nihon University, Tokyo. 1993 Guest professor at the University of Pretoria. 1995 American Institute of Architects, Honorary Fellow, USA. 1996 Award of merit from the Mexican Chamber of Architects. 2000 Fritz Schumacher Prize awarded by the Alfred Toepfer Stiftung F.V.S. 2002 Extraordinary member of the Berlin-Brandenburgische Akademie der Wissenschaften

**Volkwin Marg** (Prof. Dipl.-Ing. Architekt BDA). 1936 Born in Königsberg (now Kaliningrad), East Prussia (now Russia), raised in Gdansk, Poland. 1945 Fled to Thuringia, Germany. Since 1955 Residence in Berlin, high school diploma ("Abitur"). 1956 Studies in architecture in Berlin and Braunschweig, scholarship abroad for studies in urban development in Delft. 1964 Degree examination at the TU Braunschweig. Since 1965 Freelance architect in partnership with Meinhard von Gerkan. – Numerous successful competition entries, major building contracts, lectures and articles on aspects of architecture, urban development, and culture policy. – Member of the Vereinigung der Stadt-, Regional- and Landesplaner (SRL). – Member of the Hamburgische Architektenkammer. 1972 Appointment to the Freie Akademie der Künste in Hamburg. 1974 Appointment to the Deutsche Akademie für Städtebau und Landesplanung. 1975–79 Vice-President of the BDA. 1979–83 President of the BDA. 1986 Appointment to the RWTH Aachen as Professor of Urban Planning and Construction Design. 1996 Fritz Schumacher Prize from the Alfred Toepfer Stiftung F.V.S.

**Recent Publications** Meinhard von Gerkan, *Architektur im Dialog: Texte zur Architekturpraxis*, Berlin 1994. Meinhard von Gerkan, ed., *von Gerkan, Marg and Partner: Architecture 1966–1999*, Basel, et al. 2001. Meinhard von Gerkan, ed., *von Gerkan, Marg and Partner: Architecture 1999–2000*, Basel et al. 2002. Bernd Pastuschka, ed., *Meinhard von Gerkan und Volkwin Marg erzählen: Geschichten aus 40 Jahren einer gemeinsamen Profession*, Hamburg 2002

**Contact**
gmp – Architekten
von Gerkan, Marg und Partner
Elbchaussee 139
22763 Hamburg
Tel.: 0049-40-88 15 10
Fax: 0049-40-88 15 11 77
hamburg-e@gmp-architekten.de
www.gmp-architekten.de

Thomas Herzog

**Thomas Herzog** (Prof. Dr. Univ. Rom, Dipl.-Ing. Architekt BDA). 1941 Born in Munich. 1960 High school diploma ("Abitur") from the humanities-oriented Maximilians-Gymnasium. 1960–65 Studies in architecture and degree from the TH München. 1965–69 Assistant to Prof. Peter C. von Seidlein, Munich. 1969–72 Academic Assistant at the Universität Stuttgart. 1971/72 Fellowship at the Deutsche Akademie Villa Massimo in Rome. Since 1971 Independent architects' firm, collaboration with Verena Herzog-Loibl, Dipl.-Designerin. – Housing construction projects, commercial buildings, exhibition buildings, etc. 1972 Earned doctoral degree in Pneumatic Construction from the University of Rome. Since 1973 University professor at the Gesamthochschule Kassel for Design and Product Development. 1981 Mies van der Rohe Prize. 1982 First research and development work for the European Commission in Brussels. 1983–89 Partnership with Michael Volz. Since 1986 University professor at the TH Darmstadt, Chair of Design and Building Engineering. 1993 Gold Medal, "Grosser Preis" of the BDA. Since 1993 University professor at the TU München, Chair of Design and Architectural Construction II. – Guest professorships in Lausanne (EPFL). Since 1994 Partnership with Hanns Jörg Schrade. 1994 Balthasar Neumann Prize. – Culture Prize for Architecture from the regional government of Oberösterreich. 1996 Auguste-Perret Prize from the International Union of Architects (UIA) for applied technology in architecture. – Chairman of the "4th European Conference on Solar Energy in Architecture and Urban Planning." 1997 Mies van der Rohe Pavilion Award for European Architecture, Finalist. 1998 Leo von Klenze Medal. – EUROSOLAR Prize for Architecture and Urban Planning. – Grande Médaille d'Or from l'Académie d'Architecture. Since 2000 Chair of Building Engineering, several periods as guest professor at the Ecole Polytechnique Fédérale de Lausanne. 2000 Expert assessor for the Deutsche Forschungsgemeinschaft – General Commissioner of the Federal Republic of Germany for the International Biennial of Architecture in Venice

**Recent Publications** *Thomas Herzog: Bauten 1978–1992 – Ein Werkbericht*, Stuttgart 1993. *Thomas Herzog: Design Center Linz*, Stuttgart 1994. *Thomas Herzog: Die Halle 26 – für die Deutsche Messe AG Hannover*, Munich et al. 1996. *Thomas Herzog: Solar Energy in Architecture and Urban Planning*, Munich et al. 1995. *Thomas Herzog: Nachhaltige Höhe – Verwaltungsgebäude*

*Deutsche Messe AG Hannover*, Munich et al. 1999. *Thomas Herzog: Expodach – Symbolbauwerk zur Weltausstellung Hannover 2000*, Munich et al. 2000. Thomas Herzog, Ingeborg Flagge, Verena Herzog-Loibl, and Anna Meseur, eds., *Thomas Herzog, Architektur + Technologie*, Munich et al. 2001

**Contact**
Herzog + Partner
Imhofstrasse 3a
80805 Munich
Tel.: 0049-89-36 05 70
Fax: 0049-89-36 05 71 39
info@herzog-und-partner.de
www.herzog-und-partner.de

Josef P. Kleihues

**Josef Paul Kleihues** (Prof. Dipl.-Ing. Architekt, Hon. FAIA BDA). 1933 Born in Rheine. 1955–59 Studies in architecture at the TU Stuttgart (pre-degree) and the TU Berlin (degree). 1959/60 Study on scholarship at the Ecole Nationale Supérieure des Beaux-Arts, Paris. 1962 Founded his own firm and began working as a freelance architect. 1973–94 Professor at the Universität Dortmund, Chair of Design and Architectural Theory (since 1984 Chair of Design and Urban Development). 1979 Appointed Director of Planning for areas under new construction for the Internationale Bauausstellung (IBA) Berlin, 1984/87. 1984 Conceptual preparation and responsibility for two IBA-related exhibitions in Berlin: "IBA: Idee – Prozess – Ergebnis" (curator: Johannes Gachnang, Martin-Gropius-Bau) and "Das Abenteuer der Ideen" (curators: Vittorio Magnago Lampugnani and Claus Baldus, Neue Nationalgalerie). 1986–90 Irwin S. Chanin Distinguished International Professor at Cooper Union (Irwin S. Chanin School of Architecture), New York. 1987 Exhibition director for "750 Jahre Architektur und Städtebau in Berlin" (Neue Nationalgalerie Berlin). – Visiting Professor (Eero Saarinen Chair), Graduate School of Architecture, Yale University. 1988 Exhibition director for "Architektur und Städtebau des 20sten Jahrhunderts in Berlin und Internationale Bauausstellung Berlin 1987," Tokyo, Rome, Barcelona. – Commissioner for the contribution of the Federal Republic of Germany to the XVII Triennale Milan (Città del mondo e il futuro delle metropoli). 1989 Named an honorary member of the American Institute of Architects (HonFAIA). – "The Museum Projects," solo exhibition, Artur A. Houghton Jr. Gallery, Cooper Union, New York. 1991 "Architettura museali," solo exhibition, Palazzo delle Esposizione, Rome. 1994 Professor of Architecture at the Kunstakademie Düsseldorf. Since 1998 Emeritus

**Recent Publications** Josef P. Kleihues and Kim Shkapich, eds., *The Museum Projects*, New York 1989. Andrea Mesecke and

Thorsten Scheer, eds., *Das Kant Dreieck: Josef Paul Kleihues*, Berlin 1995. Thorsten Scheer, ed., *Hamburger Bahnhof: Museum für Gegenwart Berlin*, Cologne 1996. Andrea Mesecke, ed., *Josef Paul Kleihues: Themes and Projects*, Basel and Berlin 1996. Josef P. Kleihues, Claus Baldus, Ursula Frohne and Dankwart Guratzsch, eds., *Josef Paul Kleihues im Gespräch*, Tübingen 1996. Andrea Mesecke and Thorsten Scheer, eds., *Josef Paul Kleihues: Museum of Contemporary Art Chicago*, Berlin 1996

**Contact**
Prof. Josef P. Kleihues
Kleihues + Kleihues
Gesellschaft von Architekten mbH
Helmholtzstrasse 42
10587 Berlin
Tel.: 0049-30-3 99 77 90
Fax: 0049-30-39 97 79 77
berlin@kleihues.com
www.kleihues.com

Daniel Libeskind

**Daniel Libeskind** (B. arch. M. A. BDA). 1946 Born in Poland. 1965 U.S. citizenship. Studies in music in Israel (scholarship from the America-Israel Cultural Foundation) and New York. – Work as a professional musician before switching to architecture. 1970 Completion of architecture degree at the Cooper Union for the Advancement of Science and Art in New York City. 1972 Post-graduate degree in the theory and history of architecture, School of Comparative Studies in Essex. 1989 Winner of the competition for the extension to the Berlin Museum with Jewish Museum Department. Since 1990 Work as an architect in Berlin. 2001 Opening of the Jewish Museum in Berlin. 1998 Opening of the Felix-Nussbaum-Haus, museum in Osnabrück. Daniel Libeskind lives in Berlin and has worked on numerous architectural and landscape-planning projects all over the world. He is a member of the BDA. He is currently working on the following architectural projects and buildings: The Spiral, extension of the Victoria and Albert Museum, London; The Imperial War Museum – North, Manchester; The Jewish Museum San Francisco; Westside, amusement and shopping center in Brünnen, Switzerland; Maurice Wohl Convention Centre, Bar-Ilan-University, Tel Aviv; Atelier Weil, private studio/ gallery building on the island of Majorca; extension building for the Denver Art Museum, Denver, Colorado; Post-Graduate Centre at the University of North London. Libeskind has taught and lectured at many universities around the world. He is currently a professor at the Hochschule für Gestaltung in

Karlsruhe and holds the Cret Chair at the University of Pennsylvania. He has been a member of the Akademie der Künste and the European Academy of Arts and Letters since 1990. Daniel Libeskind has won numerous awards, including most recently the Hiroshima Art Prize, which is awarded to artists whose work serves the cause of peace. In 1996, he received the American Academy of Arts and Letters Award for Architecture and the Berliner Kulturpreis. He was awarded honorary doctorate degrees by the Humboldt-Universität in Berlin in 1997 and the College of Arts and Humanities of Essex University in 1999. He received the German Architecture Prize for the Jewish Museum in Berlin in 1999, and the Goethe-Medaille in 2000. His work has been exhibited in major museums and galleries all over the world and has been the subject of numerous articles in international publications in several different languages

**Recent Publications** *Daniel Libeskind: Radix, Matrix – Architekturen und Schriften*, Munich 1994. Daniel Libeskind: *Kein Ort an seiner Stelle – Visionen für Berlin*, Dresden 1995. *El Croquis: Daniel Libeskind*, Madrid 1996. *Daniel Libeskind: Fishing from the Pavement*, Rotterdam 1997. Daniel Libeskind and Cecil Balmond, *Unfolding*, Rotterdam 1997. Thorsten Rodiek, *Daniel Libeskind: Museum ohne Ausgang*, Tübingen 1998. Bernhard Schneider, *Daniel Libeskind: Jüdisches Museum Berlin*, Munich 1999. Thomas Lackmann, *Jewrassic Park – Wie baut man (k)ein Jüdisches Museum in Berlin*, Bodenheim 2000. Daniel Libeskind, *Process Unbound: Ein Werkstattbuch*, Munich 2001. Arnt Cobbers, *Daniel Libeskind*, Berlin 2001. Daniel Libeskind, *The Space of Encounter*, New York 2001

**Contact**
Studio Daniel Libeskind
Windscheidstrasse 18
10627 Berlin
Tel.: 0049-30-3 27 78 20
Fax: 0049-30-32 77 82 99
info@daniel-libeskind.com
www.daniel-libeskind.com

Karljosef Schattner

**Karljosef Schattner** (Prof. Dipl.-Ing. Architekt BDA). 1924 Born in Gommern. 1934–42 Attended upper secondary school in Magdeburg. 1942–45 Wartime military service; seriously wounded. 1946–48 Commercial training in Magdeburg, married Irmingard Ried. 1949 Moved to Eichstätt. 1949–53 Studies in architecture at the TH München under Hans Döllgast, Martin Elsässer, Franz Hart, Friedrich Krauss and Georg Werner. 1953/54 Work at the architects' firm of Franz Hart, Munich. 1955 Employed at a firm in Ingolstadt. 1956/57 Freelance architect in Eichstätt. 1957–91 Director of the Diocese Architecture Office in Eichstatt. 1985–94 Honorary professor at the TH Darmstadt. 1986 Heinrich Tessenow Medal from the Alfred Toepfer Stiftung F.V.S. 1989–91 Guest professor at the ETH Zürich. 1990 "Grosser Preis" of the BDA. 1994 Art and Culture Prize from the Association of German Catholics. 1996 Represented at the 6th Biennial of Architecture in Venice. 1996 Honorary Fellow of the Royal Incorporation of Architects of Scotland. 1997 German Legion of Merit. 1998 Honorary senator of the Katholische Universität Eichstätt

**Recent Publications** Ulrich Weisner, ed., *Neue Architektur im Detail: Heinz Bienefeld, Gottfried Böhm, Karljosef Schattner,* Bielefeld 1992. Wolfgang Pehnt, *Karljosef Schattner: Ein Architekt aus Eichstätt,* Stuttgart 1999. Klaus Kinold, *Karljosef Schattner: Architektur und Fotografie/Architecture and Photography,* Basel et al. 2002

**Contact**
Karljosef Schattner
Dipl.-Ing. Architekt
Spindeltal 32
85072 Eichstätt
Tel.: 0049-8421-90 12 63
Fax: 0049-8421-59 98

## Otto Steidle

**Otto Steidle** (Prof. Dipl.-Ing. Architekt BDA). 1943 Born to a farming family in Munich-Milbertshofen. 1949–56 Elementary school in Munich-Milbertshofen. 1956–59 School of Commercial Architecture in Munich. 1960–62 Practical internship at an architectural firm. 1962–65 Studies at the Staatsbauschule in Munich. 1965–69 Studies at the Kunstakademie in Munich. 1966 Founded the firm of Muhr and Steidle in Munich. 1969 Awarded degree and founded the firm of Steidle + Partner on Genter Strasse. 1974 Cofounder of the urban development group SEP – StadtEntwicklungPlanung. 1979/80 Professor of Design and Functional Planning at the Gesamthochschule Kassel. 1981–91 Professor of Planning and Architectural Design at the TU Berlin. 1986 Instructor of the architecture course at the Internationale Sommerakademie Salzburg. Since 1991 Professor of Architecture at the Akademie der Bildenden Künste in Munich. 1993 Director of the Akademie der Bildenden Künste in Munich. 1991/93 Guest professor at the Massachusetts Institute of Technology, Cambridge. 1991 Guest professor at the Berlage School in Amsterdam. 1991–94 Chairman of the Design Board, Salzburg. Since 1992 Member of the Board of Urban Design, Berlin. Since 1993 Direc-

tor of the Akademie der Bildenden Künste in Munich. Since 1994 Member of the Akademie der Künste Berlin-Brandenburg

**Recent Publications** Otto Steidle and Verena von Gagern, *Architectural,* Munich and Tucson 1993. Otto Steidle, *Bewohnbare Bauten,* Bern et al. 1994. Otto Steidle, *Fassaden,* Stuttgart 1995. Axel Menges, ed., *Steidle + Partner: Universität Ulm West,* Stuttgart 1996. Axel Menges, ed., *Steidle + Partner: Wacker-Haus, München,* Stuttgart and London 1998. *Michaelis-Quartier: Steidle und Partner,* Hamburg 2002

**Contact**
Steidle + Partner
Genterstrasse 13
80805 Munich
Tel.: 0049-89-3 60 90 70
Fax: 0049-89-3 61 79 06
architekten@steidle-partner.de
www.steidle-partner.de

## Oswald Mathias Ungers

**Oswald Mathias Ungers** (Prof. Dipl.-Ing. Architekt BDA). 1926 Born in Kaisersesch/Eifel. 1932–47 Elementary and secondary school in Mayen, high school diploma ("Abitur"). 1945/46 Military service, confinement as a prisoner of war. 1947–50 Studies in architecture at the TH Karlsruhe, degree examination under Prof. Egon Eiermann. 1950 Founding of an architects' office in Cologne and Berlin. 1956 Married to Liselotte Ungers, née Gabler (3 children). 1963 Appointment as a professor at the TU Berlin. 1965/67 Visiting Critic at Cornell University. 1965–67 Dean, Department of Architecture, TU Berlin. 1970 Licensed Architect in New York State. – Founding of an architects' firm in Ithaca, New York. 1971 Member of The American Institute of Architects AIA. 1969–75 Professor of Architecture at Cornell University, Ithaca. 1975–86 Professor of Architecture (Chairman) at Cornell University, Ithaca (emeritus). 1976 Founding of an architects' office in Frankfurt am Main. 1973/78 Professor of Architecture at Harvard University, Boston. 1974/75 Professor of Architecture at the University of California, Los Angeles. – Guest professor at the Hochschule für angewandte Kunst in Vienna. 1979/80 Professor of Architecture at the Hochschule für angewandte Kunst in Vienna. 1982 Accademia di San Luca, Rome. 1983 Founding of an architects' office in Karlsruhe. 1986–90 Professor of Architecture at the Kunstakademie Düsseldorf (emeritus). 1987 Member of the Akademie der Wissenschaften zu Berlin, "Grosser Preis" of the BDA. 1988 Honorary member of the BDA Berlin. 1989 Prix Rhenan, Strasbourg. 1992 Member of The Moscow Branch of the International Academy of Architects. 1997 Large Cross of the Order of Merit of the Federal Republic of Germany. 1999 International Marble

Architectural Award. – Dr. Ing. E. h. der TU Berlin. 2000 Akademie der Künste zu Berlin. – "Grosser Preis" of the DAI. 2002 Goethe Plaque from the city of Frankfurt am Main. – Honorary member of the Hochschule für bildende Künste Hamburg

**Recent Publications** Oswald Mathias Ungers, ed., *Architektur 1951–90,* Stuttgart 1991. Martin Kieren, *Oswald Mathias Ungers,* Basel et al. 1994. Oswald Mathias Ungers, ed., *Architektur, Bauten und Projekte 1991–98,* Stuttgart 1998. Oswald Mathias Ungers, *10 Kapitel über Architektur: Ein visueller Traktat,* Cologne 1999. Oswald Mathias Ungers, *Was ich immer schon sagen wollte über die Stadt, wie man sich seine eigenen Häuser baut, und was andere über mich denken,* Wiesbaden 1999. *Wallraf-Richartz-Museum Köln,* Cologne 2001

**Contact**
Prof. O. M. Ungers Architekt
Belvederestrasse 60
50933 Köln
Tel.: 0049-221-9 49 83 60
Fax: 0049-221-9 49 83 66
koeln@omungers.de
www.omungers.de

**Hubertus Adam** (∗1965) Studied art history, philosophy, and archeology at the Universität Heidelberg. Has worked since 1992 as an independent art and architecture historian and as an architecture critic for various learned journals and daily newspapers, most notably the *Neue Zürcher Zeitung*. 1996/97: Editor of *Bauwelt* in Berlin. Since 1998: Editor of the journal *Archithese*, published in Zurich. Numerous book articles, catalogue essays, and texts for periodicals on 20th-century architecture.

**Dr. Wolfgang Bachmann** (∗1951) Studied architecture at the RWTH Aachen, awarded degree in 1976. Dissertation on Anthroposophic architecture. Three years of practical experience in architecture and engineering firms. 1982: Editor of *Bauwelt* in Berlin. Since 1991: Editor-in-Chief of *Baumeister* in Munich. Has also written commentaries and short pieces on architecture and other subjects.

**Wilfried Dechau** (∗1944) Studied architecture at the TU Braunschweig. 1973–80: Academic assistant to the Chair for Architectural Engineering and Industrial Architecture under Prof. W. Henn at the TU Braunschweig. Since 1980: Editor of the *Deutsche Bauzeitung*, Editor-in-Chief since 1988. Since 1995: Instructor at the FH Biberach. Numerous publications and book projects.

**Christian Holl** (∗1968) Studied art, art education, and German in Stuttgart and Münster and later architecture in Aachen, Florence (Erasmus Scholarship), and Stuttgart. From 1995 to 1998: freelance contributor to the *Deutsche Bauzeitung*, editor since 1998. Instructor at the TU Darmstadt, winter semester 2001/02. His book *Soziale Stadt: Ein politisches Programm in der Diskussion* was published in February 2002. Articles for newspapers, books, and catalogues.

**Ernst Hubeli** (∗1947) 1968–73: Studied architecture, urban design, and media journalism at the ETH Zürich and at the TU and FU Berlin. Since 1982: Has operated his own architects' firm with Andreas Herczog in Zurich. Numerous building projects and competition honors. Scholarly publications on such subjects as urban renewal in Switzerland, conversion of derelict industrial areas, publicness and public space, image policy, high-rise buildings, individualization in housing construction. 1982–2000: Chief Editor of the journal *Werk, Bauen + Wohnen*. Numerous publications. Conferences on such themes as

"Planning the Uncertain," "Emotional Urban Design and the Architecture of Longing."

**Prof. Dr. Falk Jaeger** (∗1950) Studied architecture and art history in Braunschweig, Stuttgart and Tübingen. Architecture critic for popular and learned journals, radio, and television. 1983–88: Member of the academic staff of the Institut für Architektur- und Stadtgeschichte at the TU Berlin. 1993–2000: Professor of Architectural Theory at the TU Dresden. Since 2001: Editor-in-Chief of the *Bauzeitung*. Catalogue, book, and encyclopedia articles on aspects of contemporary architecture, architectural history, and monument preservation. Several book publications, including *Bauen in Deutschland: Ein Führer zur modernen Architektur* (1985), *Zurück zu den Stilen: Baukunst der achtziger Jahre in Berlin* (1991), *Baukunst für das neue Jahrtausend* (2001).

**apl. Prof. Dr. Gert Kähler** (∗1942) Studied architecture at the TU Berlin. Seven years of practical experience in architecture. University assistant at the Universität Hannover; awarded doctorate in 1981, postdoctoral dissertation in 1985. Since 1988: Work as a freelance journalist and scholar. Guest professorships in Braunschweig, Berlin, Aachen. Instructor at the Universität Hamburg, Hochschule für Angewandte Wissenschaften, Hamburg. Numerous publications on aspects of the city and architecture in the 20th century. Co-editor of *Geschichte des Wohnens* (1996–1999). Recent book publications: *Ein Jahrhundert Bauten in Deutschland* (2001), *HafenCity Hamburg: Spuren der Geschichte* (2001), Status Report on the Federal Government's "Architecture and Building Culture Initiative" (2001), *Wie gewohnt?* (textbook for secondary schools, level II, 2002), *SciFunCity: Planen und Bauen im Grossstadtdschungel* (children's book, 2002).

**Wolfgang Kil** (∗1948) 1967–72: Studied architecture in Weimar. Worked as an architect in East Berlin for several years thereafter. 1978–82: editor of an architectural journal, later freelance critic and journalist. 1992–94: editor of *Bauwelt*. Since 1994: freelance author in Berlin. 1993 and 2001: Journalism Award from the Bundesarchitektenkammer. 1997: BDA Critic's Prize. Numerous publications, most recently: *Gründerparadiese: Vom Bauen in Zeiten des Übergangs* (2000), *Neue Landschaft: Sachsen* (2001).

**Prof. Dr. Wolfgang Pehnt** (∗1931) 1950–56: Studied German, art history, and philosophy at the universities in Marburg, Munich, and Frankfurt am Main. Received doctorate in 1956. 1957–63: Copy editor at the Verlag Gerd Hatje, Stuttgart; appointed editor in 1963. 1974–95: Director, Depart-

ment of Literature and Art, (DeutschlandRadio), Cologne. 1992 and since 1996: Instructor at the Ruhr-Universität Bochum; appointed professor in 1995. Member of the Akademie der Künste, Berlin, and the Bayerische Akademie der Schönen Künste, Munich. Awards: Critic's Prize from the Verband Deutscher Architekten- und Ingenieurvereine (1984), Critic's Prize from the Bund Deutscher Architekten (1988), Erich Schelling Prize for Architectural History and Theory (1994), Fritz Schumacher Prize for Architecture (2001), and others. Numerous publications in learned journals, catalogues, reference works, multi-volume works. Has written for many years for the *Frankfurter Allgemeine Zeitung*. Numerous book publications on the history of architecture in the 19th and 20th centuries: *Rudolf Schwarz 1897–61: Bewohnte Bilder – Architekt einer anderen Moderne* (1997), *Die Architektur des Expressionismus* (revised edition, 1998), *Gottfried Böhm* (1999), and others.

**Dr. Hanno Rauterberg** (∗1967) Art historian; graduate of the Henri-Nannen-Journalisten-Schule. Editor for the culture pages of *Die Zeit*, writes for the newspaper on architecture, urban development, and contemporary art.

**Andreas Ruby** (∗1966) Architecture critic and theorist. Studied art theory and history and architectural theory in Cologne, Paris, and New York. 1999–2000: Executive Editor of the journal *Daidalos*. Since 2001: regular correspondent for *Werk, Bauen + Wohnen*. Consultant for architectural institutions in the development of concepts for symposia, exhibitions, and publications (Bauhaus Dessau, Archilab Orléans, Berlin-Beta Berlin, and others). Numerous articles on contemporary architecture in national and international publications. Book publications, including *Globalokal: Das Logistikzentrum von Ernsting's Family* (1999), *André Poitiers: Objects in the Territory* (2001).

**Amber Sayah** (∗1953) Editor at the *Stuttgarter Zeitung*. 1996: Critic's Prize from the Bundesarchitektenkammer. Numerous publications: *Neue Architektur in Vorarlberg: Bauten der neunziger Jahre* (1997), *Hermann und Valentiny* (1995), and others.

**Dr. Ullrich Schwarz** (∗1950) Studied German literature and sociology. Dissertation on the concept of aesthetic experience in the writing of Adorno, Benjamin, and Mukarovsky (1978, published in 1981). In the following years, instructor at the Universität Hamburg and work as a freelance

copy editor and translator for the Rowohlt Verlag, Reinbek. Since 1984: Managing Director of the Hamburgische Architektenkammer. 1992–1997: Guest professor of architectural theory at the Hochschule für bildende Künste Hamburg. Cofounder and director of organization of the Hamburger Architektur Sommer (since 1994). Co-editor with Hartmut Frank of the publication series issued by the Hamburgisches Architekturarchiv. Chief editor of annual *Architektur in Hamburg* (since 1989). Numerous book and journal publications, primarily in the field of architectural theory, including (as editor): *Peter Eisenmann: Zur Überwindung der Metaphysik der Architektur* (1995), *Risiko Stadt: Perspektiven der Urbanität* (1995), *C. F. Hansen und die Architektur um 1800* (2002). Regular contributor of articles to *Die Zeit*.

**Dr. Werner Sewing** (∗1951) 1969: Studied sociology, political science, and history at the Universität Bielefeld and the FU Berlin, degree. 1975/76: Instructor at the Institut für Soziologie of the FU Berlin. 1978–83: Academic assistant at the Institut für Soziologie of the TU Berlin. 1983–86: Instructor of urban and regional sociology at the TU Berlin. 1986–92: Instructor of architectural sociology at the TU Berlin. 1995: Awarded doctoral degree, dissertation: *Politik der Architektur: Eine handlungstheoretische Grundlegung der Architektursoziologie mit einer Fallstudie zur "Berlinischen Architektur."* 1995–2001: Academic assistant, Chair of Planning and Architectural Sociology at the TU Berlin. 1999: Visiting Professor, University of California, Berkeley. 2001: Visiting Lecturer and Visiting Critic at the Architectural Association in London. Numerous publications.

**Mag. arch. Dietmar M. Steiner** (∗1951) Studied architecture at the Akademie der bildenden Künste in Vienna; collaborated for many years with Friedrich Achleitner on *Architektur im 20. Jahrhundert: Österreich*. Until 1989: Instructor, Chair of History and Theory of Architecture at the Hochschule für angewandte Kunst in Vienna. Numerous articles on urban and architectural criticism and theory in international media; numerous exhibitions and publications. Since 1989: Independent architectural consulting firm in Vienna. 1995–99: Chief Editor for Architecture for the journal *Domus* in Milan. Since 1993: Director of the Architekturzentrum, Vienna. Member of the Executive Board of the International Confederation of Architecture Museums (ICAM) and des Advisory Committees for the "European Architecture Prize" and Commissioner for the Austrian Pavilion at the Architecture Biennial in Venice.

**Dr. Wolfgang Voigt** (∗1950) Lives and works as a historian of architecture in Frankfurt am Main. 1972–78: Studied architecture at the Universität Hannover. 1986: doctoral degree; 1998 post-doctoral dissertation. 1979–81: Member of the academic staff at the Hochschule Bremen; 1986–95 at the Hochschule für bildende Künste, Hamburg, where he also served as substitute professor of architectural history in 1993/94. Since June 1997: Deputy Director of the Deutsches Architektur Museum in Frankfurt am Main. His studies and publications have concentrated since the mid-eighties on the following themes: Homeland conservation and traditionalism in 20th-century architecture, Modernism in the "Third Reich," the history of the consequences of "racial cleansing" on the Garden City Movement, the early history of standardization in architecture, the early history of airport construction, the emigration of Jewish architects from Germany, Atlantropa and other modernist macro-projects.

**Klaus-Dieter Weiss** (∗1951) Author and publicist. 1979–87: Studied architecture at the TU München and the TH Aachen. Research and teaching at the Institut für Entwerfen und Architektur of the TU Hannover. Since 1987: freelance journalist. Regular critical contributions on architecture to media in Germany and abroad. Freelance contributor to the Berlin *Tagesspiegel*, *Architektur Aktuell*, and *Werk, Bauen + Wohnen*. Numerous book publications and monographs, including *Abschied von der Postmoderne* (1987), *Deutsche Architektur des 20. Jahrhunderts* (sound-and-image show, Venice, 1991), *Renaissance der Bahnhöfe* (1996), *Junge deutsche Architekten* (1998), *Nordische Botschaften Berlin* (2000), *Stadt und Kultur* (2001).

**Olaf Winkler** (∗1969) 1989–91: Studied ethnology and political science in Cologne. 1991–97: Studies in architecture in Aachen and Vienna, degree. 1997: "Förderpreis des Westfälischen Kunstvereins Münster" for Architecture. From 1997: freelance critic and journalist for architecture journals. From 2000: Editor-in-Chief of *Polis: Zeitschrift für Architektur und Stadtentwicklung*. From 2001: Editor of *Build: Das Architekten-Magazin*. Freelance work in the field of art, exhibitions in Münster, Berlin, and Cologne.

**Gerwin Zohlen** (∗1950) Publicist and critic in Berlin. After completion of his studies in literature, history, and philosophy in Heidelberg and Berlin, he taught at the Institut für Allgemeine und Vergleichende Literaturwissenschaft, FU Berlin.

Since the eighties, he has published articles on architecture and urban cultural issues, essays and critical articles in German newspapers and learned journals. Recent book publications: *Baumeister des neuen Berlin* (expanded edition, 2001), *Berlin: Offene Stadt* (1999), *Auf der Suche nach der verlorenen Stadt* (2002).

New German Architecture: 25 Projects

**Herz Jesu Kirche, Munich**
Florian Holzherr, Munich: pp. 43–45, 48 f.
Christian Richters, Münster: pp. 46 f.
**Biosphere and BUGA Flower Hall 2001, Potsdam**
Werner Huthmacher, Berlin/artur: pp. 51–57
**Nieuwe Luxor Theater, Rotterdam**
Christian Richters, Münster: pp. 61 top left, 62, 64 f.
Hisao Suzuki, Barcelona: pp. 59 f., 61 top and bottom, 63
**Berliner Bogen Office Building, Hamburg**
Christoph Gebler, Hamburg: p. 68
Jörg Hempel, Aachen/artur: pp. 67, 69 f., 72 f.
**Elementary and Comprehensive School Berlin-Hohenschönhausen**
Stefan Müller, Berlin: pp. 75–79
**Day-Care Center, Berlin-Karow**
Stefan Müller, Berlin: pp. 81–85
**RWE Tower, Essen**
Hans Georg Esch, Hennef: pp. 88, 90
Holger Knauf, Düsseldorf: pp. 87, 92 f.
**Engelhardt Hof, Berlin**
Stefan Müller, Berlin: pp. 95–99
**DaimlerChrysler Building, Potsdamer Platz 1, Berlin**
Roland Halbe, Stuttgart/artur: pp. 104 right, 105 left
Ivan Nemec, Frankfurt am Main/Berlin: pp. 101–103, 104 left, 105 right
**Haus der Stille—Temporary Monastery, Meschede**
Lukas Roth, Cologne: pp. 107–111
**School and Gymnasium in Scharnhauser Park, Ostfildern**
Roland Halbe, Stuttgart/artur: pp. 113–119
Arno Lederer, Stuttgart: p. 112
**Upper Vocational School for Social Insurance Education, Berlin-Köpenick**
Roland Halbe, Stuttgart/artur: p. 125 left
Christian Richters, Münster: pp. 121 f., 123 top, 123 bottom (except 2nd from left top), pp. 124, 125 center and right
Konrad Wohlhage, Berlin: pp. 123 bottom (only 2nd from left top)
**Senior Citizens' Housing Complex, Neuenbürg**
Christian Richters, Münster: pp. 127–131
**Ochsenanger Housing Development, Bamberg**
Gerhard Hagen, Bamberg/artur: pp. 133–135
Thomas Ott, Mühltal: pp. 136 f.
**Distribution Center, Bobingen**
Wolfram Janzer, Stuttgart/artur: pp. 139–143
**Saxon State Library—State and University Library, Dresden**
Stefan Müller, Berlin: pp. 145–151
**Halstenbek Sports Arena**
Klemens Ortmeyer, Brunswick: pp. 153–155
**Printing Plant and Logistics Center, Röbel**
Klaus Frahm, Börnsen/artur: pp. 159–165
**Federal Agency for the Environment, Dessau**
Bitter + Bredt Fotografie, Berlin: pp. 167–169
**Baumschulenweg Crematorium, Berlin**
Reinhard Görner, Berlin/artur: p. 175
Werner Huthmacher, Berlin/artur: pp. 176–179
Ulrich Schwarz, Berlin: pp. 180 f.
**Haus R 128, Stuttgart**
Roland Halbe, Stuttgart/artur: pp. 183–189
**Wohnhaus e. G. Weimar**
Claus Bach and Walter Stamm-Teske, Weimar: pp. 191–195
**New Synagogue, Dresden**
Roland Halbe, Stuttgart/artur: p. 197
Norbert Miguletz, Frankfurt am Main: pp. 198, 199 top right, 202
Lukas Roth, Cologne: pp. 199 top left, 200 f.
**European Youth Meeting and Education Center, Weimar**
Constantin Beyer, Weimar: pp. 205–209
**Neanderthal Museum of Human Evolution, Mettmann**
Peter Lippsmeier, Bochum/artur: p. 214 left
Michael Reisch, Düsseldorf: pp. 211 f., 214 center and right, 215

New German Architecture: 10 Signatures

**Behnisch & Partners**
Behnisch & Partners/Christian Kandzia, Stuttgart: pp. 218, 220, 221 bottom left and right
Klaus Frahm, Börnsen/artur: p. 219 top
Jörg Hempel, Aachen/artur: p. 221 top left
Dieter Leistner, Mainz/artur: p. 221 top center and top right
Gottfried Planck, Stuttgart: p. 219 bottom left and bottom right
**Heinz Bienefeld**
Sigrid Balke/Archiv Büro Bienefeld: p. 225 bottom left
Achim Bednorz, Cologne: p. 227 top
Klaus Kinold, Munich: p. 227 bottom left and bottom center
Dieter Leistner, Mainz/artur: p. 227 bottom right
Lukas Roth, Cologne: pp. 224, 225 top left and bottom center, 226
**Gottfried Böhm**
Hamburger Aero-Lloyd/Archiv Büro Böhm: p. 230 left
Manfred Hanisch, Essen-Rüttenscheid: p. 231 top left
Peter Kleinert, Cologne: p. 230 right
Dieter Leistner, Mainz/artur: pp. 231 bottom, 232 top left, 233
Inge + Arved von der Ropp/Archiv Büro Böhm: pp. 230 center, 231 top center
Hugo Schmölz/Archiv Büro Böhm: p. 232 top center
**von Gerkan Marg and Partners**
Busam/Richter: p. 239 center
Hans Georg Esch, Hennef: p. 239 left
Klaus Frahm, Börnsen/artur: pp. 236, 238
Heiner Leiska, Hamburg: p. 237 top
Klemens Ortmeyer, Brunswick: p. 237 bottom
**Herzog + Partners**
Peter Bonfig, Munich: p. 243 bottom right
Dieter Leistner, Mainz/artur: pp. 243 bottom left, 244 f.
Richard Schenkirz, Leonberg: pp. 242, 243 top
**Josef P. Kleihues**
Archiv Josef P. Kleihues: pp. 248, 250 top left, bottom left, and bottom center, 251 center
Hélène Binet, London: pp. 250 top center, 251 left
Steve Hall, Hedrich-Blessing, Chicago: p. 250 bottom right
Werner Huthmacher, Berlin/artur: p. 249 top
Peter Seidel, Frankfurt am Main: p. 249 bottom
**Daniel Libeskind**
Bitter + Bredt Fotografie, Berlin: p. 256 top (3rd from right) and bottom left
Steven Gerrard/Studio Daniel Libeskind: p. 255 bottom
Roland Halbe, Stuttgart/artur: p. 256 top (2nd from right) and top right
Miller Hare, London (visualization): p. 257
Florian Monheim, Meerbusch/artur: p. 256 bottom center and bottom right
picturesofmanchester.com/Len Grant, Manchester: p. 254 top
**Karljosef Schattner**
Klaus Kinold, Munich: pp. 260 top left, 261–263
Ingrid Voth-Amslinger, Munich: p. 260 top center
**Steidle + Partners**
Archiv Steidle + Partner: pp. 267, 268 top
Oliver Heissner, Hamburg/artur: p. 266 right
Karin Hessmann, Dortmund/artur: p. 266 left
Stefan Müller-Naumann, Munich/artur: p. 269
Michael Wesely: p. 268 bottom
**Oswald Mathias Ungers**
Eduard Hueber, New York: p. 274 top
Dieter Leistner, Mainz/artur: p. 273 top left, top center, bottom center
Stefan Müller, Berlin: pp. 273 top right, bottom left and bottom right, 274 bottom, 275

**Wolfgang Pehnt, pp. 280 ff.**
Behnisch & Partner/Christian Kandzia, Stuttgart: fig. 1
Dieter Leistner, Mainz/artur: figs. 2, 16
Karl Hugo Schmölz: fig. 3
Tomas Riehle, Cologne/artur: fig. 4
Dr. Ulm, Heidelberg: fig. 5
A. Pfau, Mannheim: fig. 6
Bayerische Staatsgemäldesammlung, Munich: fig. 7
Gerhard Kerff: fig. 8
Arno Wrubel, Düsseldorf: fig. 9
Neue Heimat, Bremen: fig. 10
Klaus Frahm, Börnsen/artur: figs. 11, 15, 20
Bauakademie, Berlin: fig. 12
Wolfgang Pehnt, Cologne: figs. 13, 17, 23
Jochen Helle, Dortmund/artur: figs. 14, 22
Robert Häusser, Mannheim: fig. 18
Reineke/Presse- und Informationsamt der Bundesregierung: fig. 19
Wilfried Dechau, Stuttgart: fig. 21
gmp Archiv, Hamburg: fig. 24
Uwe Rau: fig. 25
Schlaich, Bergermann & Partner: fig. 26

**Andreas Ruby, pp. 294 ff.**
O. M. Ungers, Cologne: fig. 1
Richard Rogers Partnership, London: fig. 2
Hilmer & Sattler, Munich: fig. 3
The City of Dresden: fig. 4
Hans Kollhoff, Berlin: figs. 5, 6
Josef P. Kleihues, Berlin: fig. 7
Uwe Rau: fig. 8
Udo Hesse, Berlin: fig. 9

**Werner Sewing, pp. 304 ff.**
Jörg Hempel, Aachen/artur: fig. 1
Stefan Schneider, Düsseldorf: fig. 2

**Hanno Rauterberg, pp. 312 ff.**
Landesarchiv Berlin: fig. 1
Peter Wels, Hamburg: fig. 2
Axel Schultes Architekten, Berlin: figs. 3–5
Werner Huthmacher, Berlin/artur: figs. 6–8
Kühler/Bundesbildstelle Bonn: fig. 9
Reinhard Görner, Berlin/artur: fig. 10
H.-Ch. Schink/Punctum: fig. 11
Ivan Nemec, Berlin: figs. 12, 13
Andrea Bienert/Bundesbildstelle Berlin: fig. 15
Walter Hahn/Sächsische Landesbibliothek: fig. 16
Jörg Schöner, Dresden/artur: fig. 17

**Wolfgang Kil, pp. 324 ff.**
Philipp Oswalt and Klaus Overmeyer: figs. 1, 11
Wolfgang Kil, Berlin: figs. 2, 3
Andreas Kottusch: fig. 4
Dieter Bankert: fig. 5
Photographiedepot, Frank-Heinrich Müller: fig. 6
Burkhard Przyborowski: fig. 7
Jens Rötzsch: figs. 8, 9
Zimmermann und Partner: fig. 10
KARO-architekten: fig. 12

**Wilfried Dechau and Christian Holl, pp. 334 ff.**
Thomas Herzog Archiv, Munich: figs. 1–3
Wilfried Dechau, Stuttgart: figs. 4–7
Boockhoff + Rentrup: fig. 8
Zooey Braun, Stuttgart/artur: fig. 9
Peter Lippsmeier, Bochum/artur: fig. 10
LOGID/Rainer Blunck: figs. 11, 12
Christian Gahl, Berlin: fig. 13
Constantin Meyer, Photographie: figs. 14, 15

This book is published in conjunction with the exhibition
entitled "New German Architecture: A Reflexive Modernism"
Martin-Gropius-Bau, Berlin
July 11 to September 16, 2002
To be followed by additional presentations in Germany and abroad

Catalogue

Editor: Ullrich Schwarz
Editorial Board: Ullrich Schwarz (Chairman), Stephan Feige, Claas Gefroi
Assistant for Image Acquisition: Stephan Heymann
Editing: Tas Skorupa
Translations: John S. Southard, Sandra Harper, Harry F. Mallgrave
Graphic Design: QART Büro für Gestaltung, Hamburg
Printed in Proforma, Helvetica
Design: Stefanie Langner and Söhlke-Produktion, Hamburg
Reproductions: Repromayer, Reutlingen
Production: Dr. Cantz'sche Druckerei, Ostfildern-Ruit

Cover illustration: New Synagogue Dresden (detail), Wandel Hoefer Lorch + Hirsch,
Saarbrücken/Frankfurt am Main, photo: Norbert Miguletz, Frankfurt am Main

Published by
Hatje Cantz Verlag
Senefelderstrasse 12
73760 Ostfildern-Ruit
Germany
Tel. 0711/4 40 50
Fax 0711/4 40 52 20
Internet: www.hatjecantz.de

ISBN 3-7757-1193-7 (German)
ISBN 2-7757-1194-5 (English)
Printed in Germany

Die Deutsche Bibliothek – Cataloguing-in-Publishing Data

New German architecture : a reflexive modernism ;
Martin-Gropius-Bau, Berlin 11 July to 16 September 2002 ... /
arrangement: NDA Neue Deutsche Architektur-GmbH.
Ed · Ullrich Schwarz. Hubertus Adam ... -
Ostfildern-Ruit : Hatje Cantz, 2002
Dt. Ausg. u.d.T.: Neue deutsche Architektur
ISBN 3-7757-1194-5

"Der Mensch ist das Tier,
das mit den Händen staunen kann."

Peter Sloterdijk für FSB

FSB Modell 1020,
Design Johannes Potente

FSB Modell 1035,
Design Heike Falkenberg

FSB Modell 1194,
Design Hartmut Weise

FSB Modell 1149,
Design rahe+rahe

FSB Modell 1069,
Design Nicholas Grimshaw

FSB Modell 1144,
Design Jasper Morrison

FSB Modell 1127,
Design Erik Magnussen

FSB Modell 1126,
Design Miguel Milá

FSB Modell 1163,
Design Hans Kollhoff

FSB Modell 1102,
Design Alessandro Mendini

FSB Modell 1179,
Design Ton Haas

FSB Modell 1103,
Design Hans Hollein

GROHEart®

**Life can be so simple.**

**When you reduce it
to essentials. Atrio.**

Atrio is modelled on the Bauhaus tradition of seeing things in their archetypal simplicity. Purist in approach, its reductive style creates an aura of peace and harmony. Check out Atrio's new, and essential simplicity now. Friedrich Grohe AG & Co. KG, P.O. Box 1361, D-58653 Hemer. www.grohe.com

GROHE

WATER TECHNOLOGY

Bei Klassikern weiß man, was man hat:
die VHV Berufshaftpflicht.

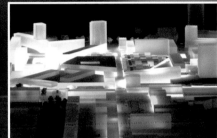
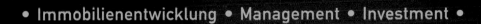

We would like to express our gratitude to our sponsors, and to the Institut für Auslandsbeziehungen, the Federal Government Commissioner for Cultural and Media Affairs, and the Kulturstiftung der Länder.
They all played a decisive role in realizing the exhibition *New German Architecture: A Reflexive Modernism*.

i f a  Institut für Auslandsbeziehungen e. V.

Sponsored from funds provided by the Federal Government
Commissioner for Cultural and Media Affairs by the
KulturStiftung der Länder

**Kultur**Stiftung
der Deutschen Bank

**Deutsche Grundbesitz**
**Management GmbH**

**Eurohypo**
Europäische Hypothekenbank der Deutschen Bank

FSB

**GROHE**
WATER TECHNOLOGY

M A B
*Defining the Art of Development*

SSS SIEDLE

**VHV///**
VERSICHERUNGEN

artur
architekturbilder agentur gmbh

DKV Deutsche Krankenversicherung AG
Die Nr.1 unter den Privaten
Ein Unternehmen der ERGO Versicherungsgruppe

**PPS**
Die Unternehmen der Medi@Bild Imaglog AG

sto

**TK**
Techniker
Krankenkasse
Gesund in die Zukunft

Birkle + Thomer,
Berlin

Ingenieurbüro Müller + Müller,
Ostfildern

Stadt Ostfildern

Wetzstein Ingenieurgesellschaft für
Haustechnik, Herrenburg